C000007704

ADVANCED GNVQ CORE SKILLS
COMMUNICATION

13.5.98.

ADVANCED GNVQ CORE SKILLS

COMMUNICATION

Desmond W Evans

LONGMAN

Longman
Longman Group Limited
Edinburgh Gate, Harlow
Essex CM20 2JE, England
and Associated Companies throughout the world

First published 1996

British Library Cataloguing in Publication Data
A catalogue entry for this title is available from the British Library.

ISBN 0–582–28872–X

Set by 30 in 10/12pt Palatino
Printed in Great Britain by
Short Run Press Ltd.

CONTENTS

TO THE STUDENT

Advanced GNVQ Core Skills: Communication is one of the three Core Skills (with Application of Number and Information Technology) which make up an essential part of your Advanced GNVQ study programme. It has been specifically written to help you prepare for and produce activities for your Advanced GNVQ portfolio in line with the NCVQ Core Skills specification revisions of 1995.

Right from the outset of your GNVQ studies, it is important that you appreciate the crucial part that the GNVQ Core Skill of communication will play as you prepare for a full-time job of work and unfolding career.

Over many years of specialist studies, management gurus and consultants have emphasised that the key ingredient in any work-related enterprise is not finance, not buildings, not plant or fixtures, but people. This conclusion is hardly surprising given the incredibly complex structure and activities of the human brain, which governs not only rational thought processes, but also moods, emotional responses and prejudices. The average human being comprises elements of both Captain Kirk and Mr Spock!

Therefore, effective communication at work requires the acquisition of a blend of knowledge and skills. For instance, successful telephone communication requires an understanding of modern electronic telecommunications features allied to skills in handling, say, demanding customers.

This text provides you with plenty of opportunities to acquire and develop communication know-how and the practical skills of working with and through other people. It follows closely the structure of the *Advanced GNVQ Core Skills: Communication* specification, and each chapter corresponds to Elements 3.1, 3.2, 3.3 and 3.4. To assist you, the element specification is printed at the start of each chapter. Each chapter supplies a mix of information and guidance on the communication knowledge you need to master, as well as practical guidance on developing the skills of communicating orally, in writing, through images and in reading and responding to various types of document.

To help you to become expert, a wide range of skills-building activities have been devised to give you plenty of practice. Also, each chapter includes opportunities for you to check your own progress and to share your views and experiences with your co-students. Lastly, at the end of each chapter there is a section of activities which may be used to build up your portfolio of evidence.

Before you begin your *Advanced GNVQ Core Skills: Communication* studies, I should like to emphasise how truly important they are (along with their two counterparts). No matter how expert you become in your chosen vocational GNVQ field, your career will not advance as you want it to, if your managers make the judgement that you're no good with people. Working conscientiously through this text will enable you to add communication expertise to your vocational prowess. Use them together, and you cannot fail!

I very much hope that my text will help to make your communication studies enjoyable and rewarding and wish you all success in your chosen career.

Desmond W Evans

ACKNOWLEDGEMENTS

The generous help and support of numerous organisations and individuals in providing approval for textual, image and diagrammatic material is gratefully acknowledged both here and in each individual instance in the text. Every effort has been made to trace the owners of copyright material. In a few cases this has proved impossible, and this opportunity is taken to apologise to any copyright holders whose rights may have been unwittingly infringed.

In addition, the conscientious and expert work of Bob Farmer, my copyeditor, and the publishing and production staff at Longman Higher Education is also acknowledged with my thanks.

D.W.E.

CHAPTER 1

TAKE PART IN DISCUSSIONS

Open your mouth, that I may know you.

Ancient Chinese Proverb

Element 3.1: Take part in discussions

PERFORMANCE CRITERIA

A student must:

1 make contributions which are relevant to the **subject** and **purpose**

2 make contributions in a way that is suited to the **audience** and **situation**

3 confirm that s/he has understood the contributions of others

4 make contributions which take forward the discussion

5 create opportunities for others to contribute

RANGE

Subject: straightforward, complex

Purpose: to offer information, to obtain information, to exchange ideas

Audience: people familiar with the subject who know the student, people familiar with the subject who do not know the student; people not familiar with the subject who know the student, people not familiar with the subject who do not know the student

Situation: one-to-one, group

DISCUSSIONS: THE WHAT, WHY, WHO, WHEN AND WHERE

The first element of Advanced GNVQ Core Skills: Communication has been devised to help you develop a key aspect of your oral communication skills, which deals with leading and taking part in a variety of discussions at work. During your study of Element 3.1 you will extend your knowledge and understanding of the various types of discussions which regularly occur in the workplace, the roles of their participants and the reasons why they take place.

You will also develop a range of practical skills to support you either as a leader or contributor in a range of discussions, which take place either one-to-one or in a group and in which you discuss a topic either with people you know or who are unfamiliar to you. In this way, you will learn to overcome any initial lack of self-confidence you may experience and develop the ability to handle yourself effectively in a range of discussion and presentation scenarios.

At the outset, it is important for you to remember that taking part effectively in discussions is based upon a number of oral communication skills *which can be acquired with patience and effort*, whether you are a 'life and soul of the party' extrovert, or a quiet and modest person who would rather let others take centre stage.

Why are discussions an important part of daily work?

Experts on organisations and behaviour at work are fond of stating: *An organisation's employees are its most precious resource!* In other words, it is not the plant, buildings, fixtures or stock which enable a business to thrive, but the people – directors, managers and operational staff who commit to it. They bring its 'dead' assets to life by setting targets for themselves to meet or exceed, and through a range of communications media by coordinating and directing its daily activities.

Of these media, the spoken word is often the most direct, the swiftest, the most persuasive and the simplest to employ. With the aid of modern telecommunications technology, discussions can nowadays take place, not only in a single office, face-to-face, but also by means of telephone and video conferencing which interlink business executives, customers and officials in high-rise office blocks and across cities nationally and globally. Voice mail systems also enable recorded messages to be routed to executives on the move, and mobile phones keep a roving sales force continually in touch with head office.

Nevertheless, such telecommunications media are only means to various communication ends. More important are the purposes for discussions in organisations.

The purposes of discussions at work

Discussions take place at work so that

- **Decisions can be made** either after a vote of the participants, or on the basis of a consensus (where a discussion leader sees that a majority has taken a particular view).
- **Information can be shared** either in a *one-way direction*, say from a board of directors to a group of middle managers, or in a two-way direction through a *two-way exchange of information* between a departmental management and its staff.
- **Staff can be consulted and their views expressed** perhaps about a change in the firm's pensions scheme or a proposed relocation of a factory; such consultations are vital when employees' goodwill and morale are concerned.
- **A workforce can be reassured and remotivated** say after a period of poor results, or after a take-over by another company.
- **Negotiations can be successfully held** as a normal part, say, of an annual review of pay and conditions, or as part of an effort to resolve an industrial dispute.
- **Innovative ideas can be developed** say during a brainstorming or 'buzz' group meeting called to solve a problem, devise a new product or identify an area of development.
- **Staff can be appraised** as a means of reviewing an employee's past performance and agreeing future objectives; a number of organisations operate staff appraisal schemes.

The above list is by no means exhaustive, and concentrates on discussions held by an organisation's personnel. However, important discussions also take place between a firm's staff and a range of *external associates:* bank managers, local government officers, suppliers, clients, customers and so on. Such discussions are characterised not only by their desired outcomes, but also by the need of an organisation to develop and maintain good public relations.

Within what frameworks do discussions take place?

Just as discussions take place within a wide spectrum of purposes, so they occur within a variety of frameworks, ranging from the highly formal meeting which is legally underpinned to a completely informal discussion which starts spontaneously. Figure 1.1. shows the degree of formality of some of the most common and popular frameworks:

Public sector organisations

- **Public meetings, convened by law:** say to review the proposed route of a new motorway and to hear objections from interested parties.
- **Committees of enquiry:** such meetings are often presided over by a judge and are called to look into a matter of regional or national importance, especially where a public service body such as the NHS or HM Prison Service is involved; where the matter has a legal basis, a *judicial enquiry* may be set up.
- **Regular meetings held by local councils:** councils (county, district, unitary, etc.) are either open to the public or held in closed session.
- **Open meetings:** often called by civic bodies such as conservation or environmental groups when a need is felt to air a contentious issue or publicise a local development.
- **Counselling sessions:** staff such as social careworkers and psychiatric nurses sometimes need one-to-one support to cope with the stresses of their jobs.

Private sector organisations

- **Board of directors meetings:** held on a regular basis to agree policy decisions, review progress and plan future strategies, etc.
- **Department meetings:** a manager and senior staff and/or entire departmental personnel meet to impart, obtain and exchange information, to secure feedback, to motivate or persuade to a viewpoint etc.
- **Cross-company meetings:** say of its health and safety committee, quality circles, staff association, etc.
- **Negotiating sessions:** held, say, by a firm's personnel managers and recognised trade union representatives.
- **Disciplinary or grievance interviews:** held as part of an organisation's statutory obligations under various employment acts.
- **Meetings of shareholders:** normally called on an annual basis to receive directors' reports, to reappoint directors or to vote on changes to a company's articles of association.
- **Meetings of creditors:** sometimes chaired by the official receiver, when people owed money by a bankrupt business learn about how much they may get back.

What kinds of rules regulate discussions at work?

At the formal end of the meetings continuum, where the proceedings are most formal, the rules governing them are written down to act as a reference source in case of disagreement, and so that participants can learn what procedural behaviour to adopt. For example, the inspector who chairs a statutory public meeting follows a set procedure which stipulates who may be called to give evidence and to speak. A local council's meetings are governed by its printed *standing orders* which set out the procedures for calling meetings, the powers of the chair, the procedures for introducing items for discussion and so on. In a similar way, a voluntary sector club or association relies upon a *constitution* or set of rules which members agree to abide by;

Figure 1.1 Different degrees of formality

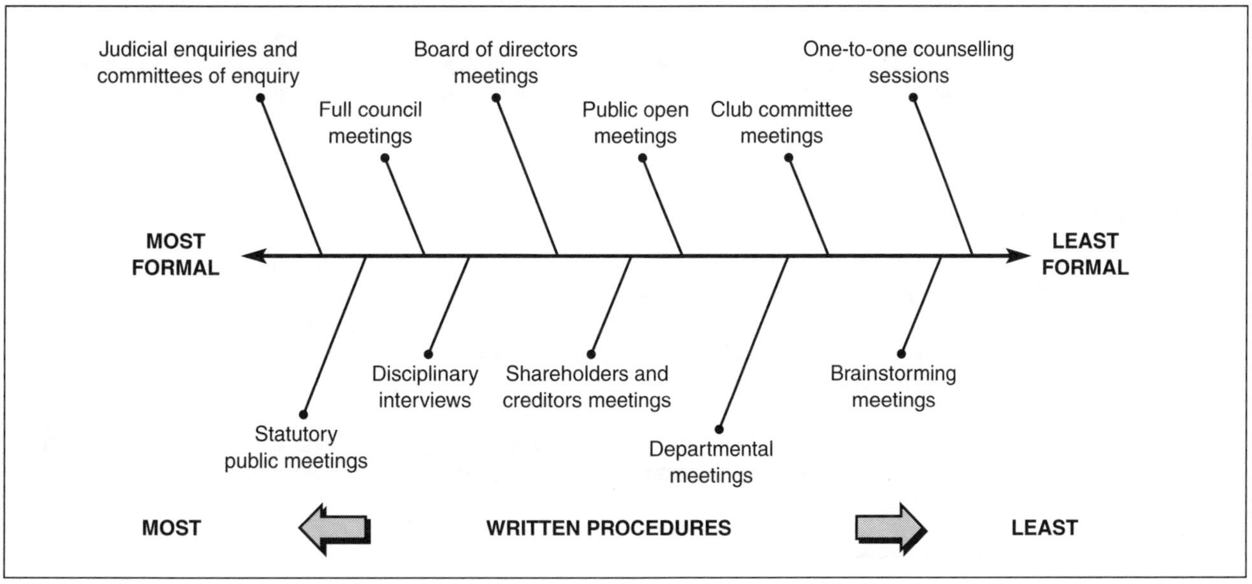

these include the conduct of meetings which both committee members and club members are obliged to follow. Figure 1.2 illustrates the kind of procedures to be followed at such formal meetings.

It pays to know the rules!

Whether acting as a chairperson or participant at a formal meeting, it pays to know the rules. For example, in some formal meetings, people taking part may only be permitted to interrupt a speaker on a point of order (because he or she is not following the rules) or on a point of information (say where a councillor has made a statement which is deemed false or erroneous. Again, in some types of meeting, items for inclusion in an agenda (a running order of the items to be discussed) have to be submitted to the secretary fourteen days in advance of the meeting. Also, in some formal types of meeting, such as a council meeting, a participant may declare during a lengthy debate:

> I move that the question be now put!

Such a manoeuvre obliges the chair to take a vote on what is now a *motion*. If it is carried, then discussion of the topic being debated is curtailed and a vote has to be taken directly. As these examples illustrate, unless you take the trouble to learn the rules of the game, you are likely to be at a disadvantage compared with wily and experienced players.

The above examples tend to occur in formal committee and public meetings. However, many important types of discussion take place in private

Figure 1.2 Meetings are governed by rules.

MEETINGS OF THE COUNCIL

Annual Meeting	2. (1) Each annual meeting of the Council shall be combined with an ordinary meeting and shall be held at the County Hall, Chichester, commencing at ten thirty o'clock in the forenoon, unless the Council or the Chairman shall otherwise direct.
Ordinary Meetings	(2) Ordinary meetings shall be held at the County Hall, Chichester, at ten thirty o'clock in the forenoon, unless the Council or the Chairman shall otherwise direct.
Chair for Election of Chairman of Council	(3) At the annual meeting of the Council, or at any other meeting of the Council at which the election of Chairman is before the Council, the Chair shall be taken by the Vice-Chairman of the Council, or, failing him or her, such member as the Council may elect.
Election of Chairman and Vice-Chairman	(4) The Chairman and Vice-Chairman shall be elected by secret ballot. Nominations are to be submitted in writing to the County Secretary by not later than 10.30 A.M. on the day before the meeting and must be signed by the proposer and also by the nominee to signify his or her consent to being nominated. If where there are more than two nominations for the office of Chairman or Vice-Chairman the first voting does not produce an absolute majority of votes in favour of any nominee, the nominee having the least number of votes shall be struck off the list and a fresh ballot shall take place, and so on, until an absolute majority of the members present and voting shall be obtained in favour of one nominee. Thereupon the appointment of such a candidate shall be proposed by resolution.
Leader of the Council	3. The leader of the majority group on the Council shall be designated Leader of the Council. If there is no group with an overall majority, then the Leader of the Council shall be elected by the full Council.
Extraordinary Meetings	4. (1) The Chairman of the County Council may call an extraordinary meeting at any time.
	(2) If the Chairman refuses to call an Extraordinary Meeting after a requisition for that purpose, signed by five members of the Council, has been presented to him or her, or if without so refusing, the Chairman does not call an Extrordinary Meeting within seven days, then any five members of the Council may forthwith call an Extraordinary Meeting of the Council.
	(3) Notice of the time, date and place of any extraordinary meetings of the Council shall be sent to every member not less than three clear days before the date of the meeting.

[Reproduced by kind permission of West Sussex County Council]

sector organisations, where the rules are not printed like standing orders and where it is much more difficult to learn them.

Written rules affecting meetings

- **Memorandum and articles of association:** required by company law, the memorandum and articles define aims, activities and procedure of a company and are lodged with a registrar of companies.
- **Acts of Parliament and standing orders:** Much council procedure is governed either by Act of Parliament, Local Government Act 1972, Public Bodies (Admission to Meetings) Act 1960, and approved rules in standing orders.
- **Written constitutions:** voluntary clubs, associations and societies adhere to rules and bye-laws set down in a *constitution* usually drawn up by founder-members; its rules also govern the composition of committees and meetings procedures.

Unwritten rules affecting meetings

- Take pains to learn the views and prejudices of the main players.
- Do your homework and prepare your ground before a meeting or discussion takes place.
- Watch and listen to learn the lie of the land before launching into personal views and positions.
- Stay calm and courteous at all times.
- Choose your words carefully and keep your statements short.
- Avoid at all costs causing hostility among other participants; learn to disagree pleasantly and without rancour.
- Heed the advice: Know when you've won, and shut up! Equally know when you've lost and live to fight another day!

Discussions and private sector cultures

Most private sector organisations are structured as hierarchies, where most power and authority are invested in the people at the top of a pyramid structure and least along its base (Fig. 1.3).

As a result of the hierarchic structure, employees in private sector (and many public sector) organisations occupy posts in which they report to a more senior person (overseer, supervisor, line manger, director, etc). Given this kind of layered or cascading authority, employees occupying the lower tiers of the pyramid tend to take the following approach when taking part in meetings with their more senior managers; in such circumstances, they learn:

- to prepare their ground carefully before meetings
- to speak neutrally and objectively
- to concentrate on facts rather than assertions

Figure 1.3 Most organisations are pyramidic.

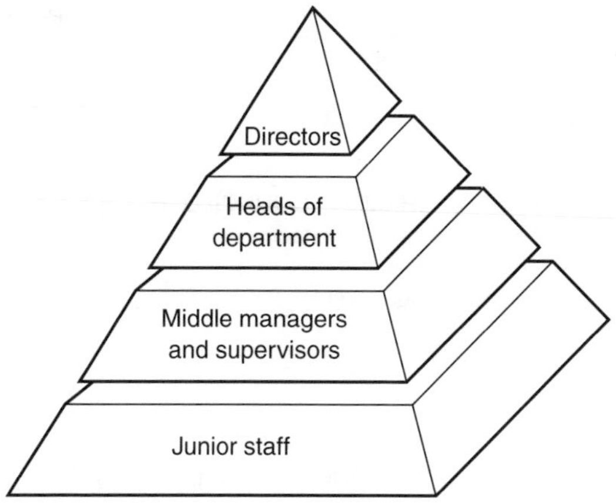

[Reproduced by kind permission of Pitman Publishing from D W Evans People, Communication & Organisations, 2nd edition, 1990]

- to maintain a calm and diplomatic approach
- to avoid confrontations and put-downs
- to explore beforehand who is for and who against discussion topics

As you can image, it is not always easy to express a strong disagreement with, say, your boss in a discussion which is underpinned by the culture of a hierarchic company, rather than, say, a public meeting in which a councillor's office enables him or her to speak much more freely. But later in this element you will learn the communication skills to use in just such a private sector situation.

What roles do people play in discussions at work?

Every working person experiences sooner or later the frustration of long-winded discussions which take place in meetings that seem to lead nowhere and where much hot air is expelled by gasbags. Nevertheless, such an outcome is never intended since all discussions at work – apart from those over coffee or lunch and those which maintain social links – *are intended to result in specific, work-related outcomes.*

Figure 1.4 illustrates some of the major roles which people take on at work and which directly affect the roles they play in discussions. Each employee acquires a set of objectives or a personal agenda which develops from the job they have been appointed to carry out, and which is detailed in a job description. Thus a company director must acquire the skills of absorbing high levels of information, of analysing complex situations objectively and rationally, and then of making sound decisions.

A middle manager needs to be able to interpret policies and communicate any parts relevant to the departmental staff clearly and positively, to monitor

Figure 1.4 A person's job affects his/her role in discussions.

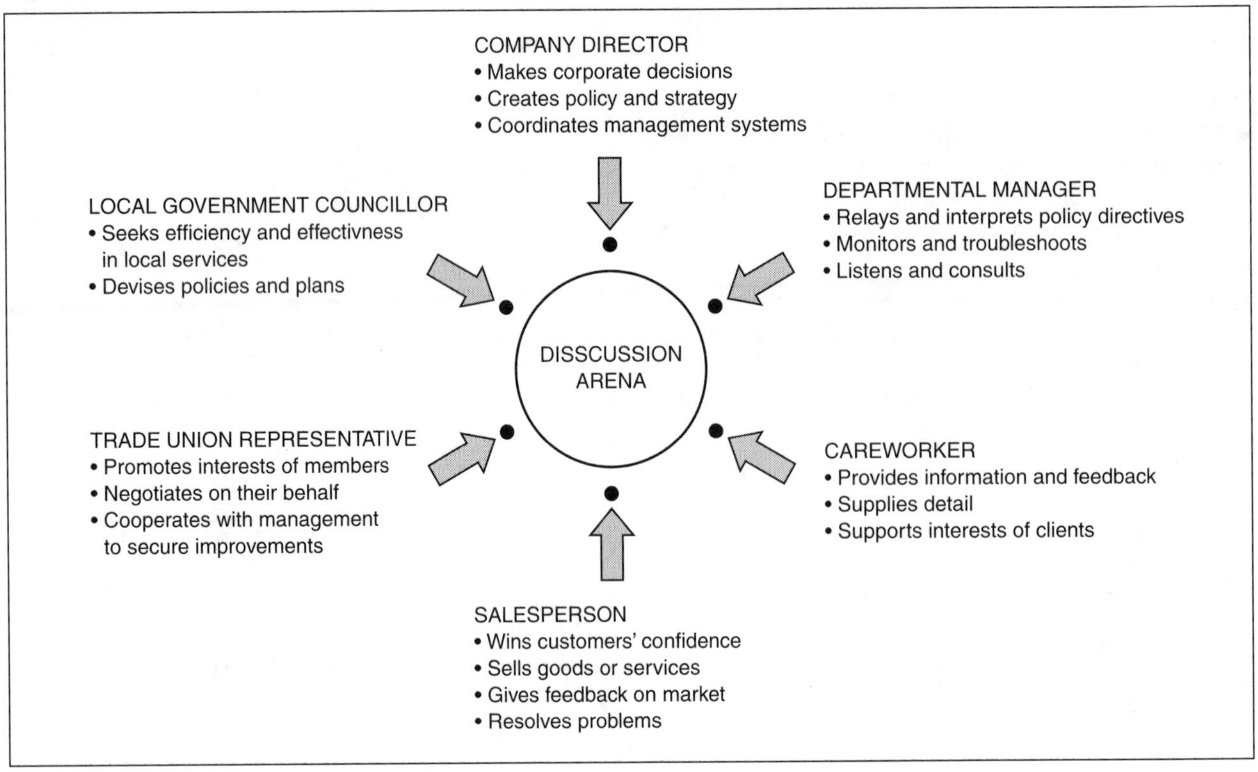

staff performance effectively and to promote motivation and morale.

A public sector careworker needs to gain the confidence of his or her clients and to communicate their needs convincingly to managers and administrators. A trade union shop steward needs to keep the confidence of his or her union's members by looking after their interests determinedly in negations and discussions with senior managers, which requires well-developed skills of debating and persuading.

What communication styles are used in workplace discussions?

As you are well aware, everyone has at his or her fingertips a wide range of communication styles, which are called into play depending upon the mix of people involved and the circumstances. For example, when among your friends at a disco or club you might well say:

> I think this music's really wicked! It really chills me out!

Using such colourful expressions helps individuals to bond on to a peer group and to feel that they belong because they share an up-to-date and highly personal language. That it is called colloquial or slang matters not a jot. However, in a job interview for a managerial post in a music shop, you might describe the same music in this way:

> I believe the band has developed a highly marketable sound which people will want to hear during their leisure time.

Gone is the slang. In its place is a more analytical choice of vocabulary which attempts to make the same idea more businesslike.

Just as people adjust their speech patterns and use of words to suit their company and the situation in their personal lives, so they do at work. A middle manager is likely to adopt one style to talk through a problem with a team of close assistants, and another when making an important presentation to the board of directors. Similarly, two nurses may review a patient's condition informally among themselves, but much more formally to the consultant doing the rounds. Figure 1.5 gives examples of different styles to express disagreement, and Figure 1.6 shows how people vary their communication style, or register, according to their situation.

There is therefore a mix of factors which affect the ways in which people communicate at work. This mix consists of the context or situation in which a message is to be delivered and discussed, which may be routine or crisis-driven; the nature of the recipient or audience at whom the message is directed, who may be laypeople or technical experts, customers, junior staff or directors; the nature of the message itself, which may be simple, technical, seeking to persuade or factual, and lastly, the medium or route in which the message is transmitted, which may be one-to-one across a desk, around a committee table, in an auditorium, over the phone or by means of a played-back audio- or videotape.

Figure 1.5 A register for expressing disagreement.

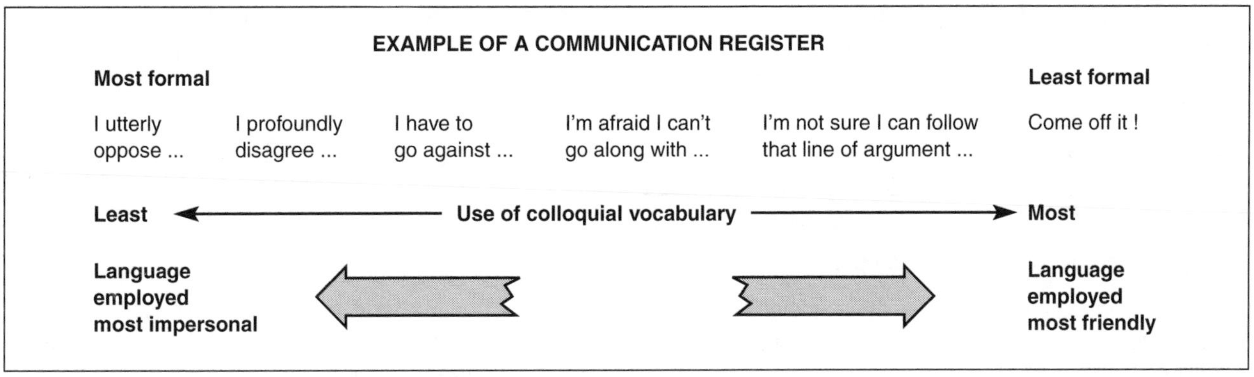

Figure 1.6 People vary their register to suit their audience.

Communicating with	Register characteristics
• High-status people • Strangers • People in authority	• Formal and careful choice of words • Selection of polite form or words • Least use of slang expressions
• Peep group colleagues • Friends and relatives • Low status people	• Informal and unguarded choice of words • Selection of familiar form of words • Most use of slang expressions

The ways in which people structure their spoken word ideas and select the vocabulary with which to express them tend to vary according to:

- **the nature of the relationship between sender and receiver**, e.g. between members of the same organisation, or employee/customer relations
- **the degree of closeness between them**, e.g. relatives, friends, peer group workers; closeness in age and/or identical gender
- **respective positions in an organisation (or social) hierarchy** e.g. departmental manager, apprentice or trainee
- **whether they are well known or unfamiliar to each other**, e.g. customer or coworker
- **the degree of formality or informality of the occasion**, e.g. boardroom presentation or annual office party

KEY POINTS

Four factors affect the way a message is transmitted, received and discussed:

1 The context or situation of the item being communicated

- Routine, daily matter
- Multimillion pound order
- High profile customer complaints

2 The nature and status of the audience or recipients of the message

- Junior staff
- Customers
- Visiting inspectors
- Senior executives
- Whole organisation

3 The nature of the message itself

- Factual
- Persuasive
- Technical
- Straightforward
- Sensitive
- Doom-laden
- Happy

4 The medium in which the message is conveyed

- Face-to-face
- One-to-one
- Small group
- Large group
- By telephone
- By audio or video

In order for communications to be effectively sent and received, so that their contents may be productively discussed, the message sender must take each of the above four factors into account. They must devise a suitable structure and style to meet

In both personal and working lives, people are able to click into and out of varying registers at the drop of the proverbial hat – often without realising it – such as the sergeant-major who can convert his blistering of a platoon of recruits to a modest gentility as soon as ladies arrive on the scene!

SUMMARY

This introductory section has covered the ground summarised by the following key points:

- Discussions occur frequently at work, since they are conducted through the fastest, most versatile and most flexible of all the available communications media.
- Their use is important since they enable policies to be devised and agreed, decisions to be reached, staff to be involved and consulted, problems to be resolved, fruitful negotiations to be effected, etc.
- Discussions take place across a wide range of frameworks in both public and private work sectors, perhaps a statutory public meeting, a full council meeting, an interdepartmental discussion or a one-to-one counselling session.
- Discussions may take place in situations of widely varying formality ranging from, say, a formal disciplinary enquiry to a casual shop-talking session of coworkers over lunch.
- Some discussions take place according to strict written rules of procedure; others against a backdrop of organisational cultures and long-standing custom and practice.
- People at work tend to bring into discussions the goals and objectives of their work roles, whether as director, manager, supervisor, operative or trade union representative.
- Oral communications in discussions are directly affected by a mix of context, profile of recipient or audience, the nature of the message and the medium it is relayed in.
- Oral communications are delivered in varying registers according to the mix of factors indicated above; different styles will suit different scenarios.

KEY POINT

Given the demanding organisational context in which work-based discussions take place, effective oral communicators rarely result from off-the-cuff utterances. On the contrary, they result from careful planning, practice and learning from mistakes.

What do you think?

1 A camel is a horse which was designed by a committee. What do *you* think is being criticised here?

2 Is the discussion process necessarily the best way of arriving at a decision or action to take? If so, why? If not, why not?

3 What do you see as the major advantages of the discussion as a communications medium at work? What do you consider its major disadvantages?

4 Why do you think written rules and procedures governing the conduct of certain types of meeting evolved? Are they still needed today, or are they a stuffy relic of the past?

5 What do you think are likely to be the effects upon discussions held by employees who occupy differing positions in an organisation's stepped hierarchy?

6 Is the concept of a communications register valid or is it artificial in reality?

7 In your view, can effective oral communications skills be learned, or is a person born with or without them?

Self-check review test

1 Supply three main reasons why discussions form a frequently used communications medium at work.

2 List three examples of written rules which govern the conduct of some types of meeting.

3 List four examples of people who are likely to chair discussions at work.

4 Explain why participants in discussions at work tend to pursue personal agendas related to their job roles.

5 Explain briefly why people at work adopt different oral communication registers for various situations.

When you have set down your own answers, compare them with those on page 197 and consult this section again if they differ.

Student pair skills-building activities

In student pairs, and with your teacher's guidance, carry out one of the following activities to extend and consolidate upon the above section.

1 Arrange to interview 3 or 4 members of your existing network of relatives, friends or neighbours who work in local private or public sector organisations. Your aim is to discover what kinds of discussions they take part in at work, for what purpose, how they are conducted and how this kind of oral communication aids decision making and action taking or contributes to building effective staff relations. Before you embark on your interviews, devise a short set of questions to help your interviews along. After each interview, make careful notes of what you discovered.

2 Research into *one* of the following:

- the articles and memoranda of association of a limited company
- the standing orders of a county council
- the constitution of a social/recreational club
- the Local Government Act of 1972 and the Public Bodies (Admission To Meetings Act) 1960

Produce a bullet-point summary of the key points you discover from your researches and share your findings with your class.

3 Find out what the following terms stand for in relation to the conduct and procedures of formal meetings:

executive committee quorum motion resolution
ultra vires *nem. con.* point of order
point of information casting vote chairman's agenda

Produce a clear, brief definition for each of the above terms.

4 Research into the roles of one of the following committee officers:

chair secretary treasurer

Produce a short fact-sheet on the responsibilities and duties of the officer you select in terms of the role they discharge at committee meetings and copy to your class members.

5 Make arrangements to watch 2 or 3 broadcasts of (a) *ITN News* (b) *Coronation Street* or *EastEnders* (c) *Top of the Pops* (d) The *Money Programme.* Compare and contrast the registers used in each of the three programmes you select and make notes of particularly interesting examples you find. Then brief your class orally.

In liaison with your teacher, deliver a 5–7 minute oral presentation to your class on your research topic. Your teacher may decide to use this opportunity as an assessment for Element 3.1, or as a practice go.

Skills-building group activity

First, read through the following work-based oral extracts:

1 I cannot emphasise too strongly the need for urgency over this matter, if the stiff penalty clauses in the contract are to be avoided and the vessel delivered on time.

2 Come on, Charlie, move yer 'arris, the afternoon shift bell's gone – as if you didn't know!

3 The MD's decided to attend, so I was wondering, Jack, if I could borrow your new computer projector for the presentation in London tomorrow. It would lend a bit of class to the show if you can spare it.

4 I realise your concern, Mr Khalil, it's just that the workflow isn't always steady and this leaves the girls with nothing to do sometimes. That's when they drift off outside. It's not entirely their fault and they're pretty good when there's work to be done.

5 This situation's tricky and needs a cool head. That's why I'd like you to tackle, it, Sara.

7 I very much regret the inconvenience you have experienced, Mr Wilkins. Yes, of course. I do assure you that the problem has been identified and rectified and that the printer will be reinstalled at your Birmingham premises tomorrow afternoon, if that is convenient to you. Right. Excellent. Thank you very much for your understanding.

8 Just thought I'd let you know he's on the warpath again, Gladys. Yeah, same thing. Yeah, he's just received last week's production figures. My pleasure!

9 Despite repeated warnings, Mr Davies, you have made no discernible attempt to improve your timekeeping, nor to modify your language on the shop-floor. I therefore have no alternative but to terminate your contract of employment directly, and shall confirm this to you in writing later today.

10 It's no good whingeing, Harry, the plate's stuck on there 'arder than ice on an Eskimo's backside in winter! If you don't give us an 'and soon we'll be 'ere all night, European Cup Final or not!

Now, decide the likely context of each extract and whether its register, style and use of words is appropriate and effective.

Also, discuss the varying choice of vocabulary in the extracts and consider why multisyllabic, latinate words work in some instances and short, monosyllabic Old English words in others.

To what extent does the delivery of a spoken message (intonation, speech rhythm, emphasis, pace, etc.) influence its effectiveness and impact upon its recipient(s)?

DEVELOPING PRACTICAL DISCUSSION SKILLS

'It ain't what yuh say, it's the way that yuh say it!'

Despite the old popular song, the content or 'what yuh say' certainly does matter! Nevertheless, the song is right in emphasising the importance of the way in which a spoken message is delivered, and this section will enable you to develop practical skills in leading and contributing to work-related discussions.

Just as any plumber, electrician or mason worth his salt accumulates a set of specialist tools which always accompany him, and which are kept carefully clean and maintained, so the effective spoken wordsmith takes care to develop and maintain his or her own verbal toolkit.

Pronunciation

In order for the spoken word to be received and understood, it has to be correctly pronounced. This involves learning where emphasised accents are placed:

indiscréet predóminantly áttitude

It also requires a knowledge of accepted usage, in which, for example, some letters may not be sounded:

psychology hors d'oeuvres heir scissors

And it also involves using foreign words and place names correctly:

panache (panash) weltschmerz (veltshmertz)

mañana (manyahna) Budapest (Boodapesht)

Lyons (Lee-on) Bremen (Breymen)

The British Empire has long since vanished, and foreign citizens are understandably irritated today by the British habit of anglicising foreign place names (Marseilles – Marsales, Frankfurt – Frankfort or Frankfert, Beijing – Pekin or Peking).

Correct pronunciation also involves the speaker in recognising those words in which *ph* at the beginning is pronounced 'fuh': *ph*obia, *ph*otogenic, *ph*armacy, etc. and those words which require vowels to be separately sounded: co-operate, re-entry, bi-ennial etc. It is important also to know when specific consonants change from hard to soft: category count (kay): cenotaph, century (see). Sometimes rules exist to help. For instance, an *e* immediately following a *c* always makes it soft, as it does also for *g*: garage (garaj).

Space does not permit an extended examination of pronunciation, but it does allow for a strong position to be taken: Correct, accepted pronunciation does matter. While nothing may be said at a meeting or gathering, a speaker does his or her image no good at all by using such (incorrect) pronunciations:

sorbet (sorbey, not sorbett) ogle (ohgel, not oggle)

quiche (keesh, not kweetch)

> ***KEY POINT***
>
> Whenever in doubt about the correct pronunciation of a word, take the time and trouble to look it up in a good dictionary, which will show upon which syllable the stress goes, and also provide a phonetic version of the word to assist its correct pronunciation.
>
> psycho (sī'kō) [note that the long dash over each vowel denotes that it is long s- eye' k- ow]
>
> aghast (agah'st) [which indicates the stress on the 'ah' which is also pronounced long]
>
> heinous (hān-) [hay-nuss: when a part of the word's pronunciation is omitted and shown by a final dash, it is because its pronunciation is straightforward: -nous = 'nuss']

Articulation and accent

Not to be confused with pronunciation, articulation refers to the ways in which words or phrases are uttered as a result of learned speech patterns, laziness or physical problems such as a lisp. It is also a known fact that every growing child adopts the speech patterns of those people with whom he or she closely associates. This is why people from different parts of the UK possess regional dialects and accents. Indeed, many such accents fall very happily on the ear. What does not sound as harmonious, however, is the slurred and run together articulation which is the mark of lazy speech.

Gissanuvverelpin! Entdunnuffink!

Wyinchajusshuddup! Sorlrigh ennit?

Reelygessupmenoas! Skay spoz!

Waddjawannadosevnin?

It is all too easy to slip into such lazy speech by leaving the *g* off the ends of words or articulating them as *k*: *nothing* becomes *nuffink*. And by running several words together, so that their individual sounds become blurred: *Why don't you* becomes *Wyincha*, and *I haven't done anything*! becomes *Entdunnuffink*!

However, poor articulation is not just the result of lazy speech, but also of a desire to sound posh or la-di-da:

Hello! becomes *Hellair!*

She's an awfully nice girl. becomes *She's an orfly naice gel.*

We're going down to Ascot tomorrow. becomes *Weah goin' dine to Arscot tumorrah.*

People from all walks of life tend to develop accents for various reasons: either because they believe their original speech modes are not acceptable in the circles in which they wish to move, or because they wish to suppress a strong regional accent, or because they move away from their home town and pick up another accent, thus blurring their original one.

KEY POINT

Hear yourself as others hear you!

In today's highly mobile society, it has come to matter not a jot whether someone has a Geordie, Black Country or Yorkshire accent. What does matter is when lazy or artificial articulation becomes so extreme that it prevents a listener from picking up and interpreting an oral message correctly, especially when the message is delivered by phone.

Because of the way our internal hearing works, resonating bones within our heads, what we hear as our own voices speaking can be very different from how others hear us. To test this out, record yourself (a) reading a passage from a book and (b) having a conversation with one or two friends.

All being well, you will be pleased with what you hear. On the other hand, this simple task may convince you more than any well-meant advice that your own articulation and accent would benefit from some attention and adjustment!

Eliminating irritating speech mannerisms

Just as an oral message may fail to get through because of slurring and the use of artificial accents, so may it fail because irritating speech mannerisms break the listener's concentration, as the following true story demonstrates.

Tripping over the five-bar gate

A long-serving lecturer was teaching English language on a warm summer's afternoon to a class of sixteen-year-old trainee secretaries. About halfway through the lesson, two students started to snigger and smirk. When tackled about their behaviour they began to giggle. The lecturer took them to task and demanded to know what was the cause of their mirth Whereupon, the whole class began to grin. On the culprits' desks were two sheets covered with five-bar gates: 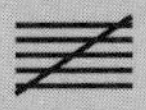

'What on earth are these gates?' enquired the lecturer. More sniggers and laughter. 'Come on, I mean to get to the bottom of this!'

'It's you, Mr Harris. We've been totting up every time you say "you know". You've said it ninety-six times in half an hour!'

'Ninety-seven,' corrected the friend.

Mr Harris was dumbstruck. He could not carry on. He'd had no idea, no idea at all. And every time he started to talk, a 'you know' seemed to hang poised on his lips, destined to become another bar on another gate. 'You'd better finish off exercise 3 on page 12. You know, I think I need time to sort myself out!'

Speech mannerisms, and body mannerisms, usually develop unconsciously. When speaking at length, especially if under some stress such as being interviewed, most people insert ums and ers into their utterances. Their role is to build time. Only a fraction of a second, but enough for the brain to conceive the next phrase or sentence. As an alternative, others employ stock expressions to act as buffers between one utterance and the next:

Know what I mean? If you take my point.
You see. As a matter of fact.

While such speech mannerisms form a natural part of thinking and speaking on the hoof, they can become extremely irritating if used too frequently, often without the speaker realising. The antidote is to learn to pause more often and a little longer between statements, and to let a short silence give you time to form your next utterance. At the same time, if you find yourself using such speech mannerisms, another helpful tip is to deliberately slow down the pace of your speech.

Again, it is extremely useful to record several conversational sessions between you and two or three friends to find out whether you are prone to the five-bar-gate syndrome! Moreover, if you can video such sessions, you will soon discover whether you have any unconscious, irritating body mannerisms, such as ring twisting, ear pulling or hair flicking.

Intonation and speech rhythms

Developing the skills of accurate pronunciation and clear articulation form a sound basis for effective speaking, but in themselves are by no means enough.

Every past school pupil has suffered in silence at a prize-giving when a guest speaker has droned on, seemingly for ever and eventually succumbed to either nodding off or day-dreaming. What usually causes such sleepiness is the speaker's flat, droning hum of delivery. He or she has not learned the importance of using a rise and fall in speech patterns to vary the impact of the words for the listener. Nor the need to employ emphasis upon specific words or phrases to point them up, just as emboldening printed words causes them to catch and hold the reader's eye.

Imagine how quickly a speaker becomes boring, and how soon his audience switches off if he delivers a talk thus:

> Gōod āft-ēr-nōon lād-īes ānd gēnt-lē-mēn. Ī ām plēased
>
> tō bē hēre tō-dāy tō tālk tō yōu ā-bōut lēaf mōuld.
>
> Lēaf-mōuld īs ān ūn-dēr-ēst-ī-māt-ēd bōon tō thē
>
> kēen gār-dēn-ēr. Īt īs fūll ōf nū-trī-ēnts whīch yōur
>
> ānn-ū-āls ānd pēr-ēnn-ī-āls nēed. Īt īs āl-sō fāsc-īn-ā-tīng
>
> tō prē-pāre.

If a gardening talk began with each syllable being given equal stress and length of delivery, and if the speaker's voice proceeded along a flat plateau, instead of rising and falling to emphasise key words and to indicate the ends of sentences, even the keenest gardener would soon be snoring!

Speaking development activities

1 In pairs decide how the above introduction to a talk on leaf mould should be delivered in terms of intonation, emphasis and pace. Decide which words deserve to be stressed, and when the speaker's voice should rise and fall.

2 Repeat activity 1 for the following concerned conversational piece:

> I was terribly sorry to hear the news of your son's car accident. How is Jim? I do hope it isn't anything serious. You must have been very worried. Is there anything I can do?

Consider where rises and falls, emphases and pauses should occur in order to communicate a sense of sincere concern and desire to help.

3 Try recording yourself speaking the following sentences, so as to check out how your vowels and consonants sound, and whether you are inadvertently clipping any word endings.

> Blue Sky Tours mean fine, warm days!
>
> Mining underground often requires working in confined spaces and in a hot environment.
>
> Tempered steel possesses both strength and elasticity as evidenced in the finest Toledo swords.
>
> Strict adherence to company regulations is essential
>
> Advertising is quickly becoming an integral part of people's everyday lives.
>
> Baking bricks is a back-breaking business!

Try asking some of your group to mark you out of 10 for clarity, and attention-getting delivery by playing back your best versions of the above sentences!

4 In a group of 3–5 students, take it in turns to record (out of earshot of the others) the following extract of a salesperson seeking to sell a hot beverage vending machine to a refectory manager:

> The beauty of this Multiserve model is that it's all built-in! Coffee, tea, chocolate, soup – the lot! See how easy the controls are, a fingertip's light touch, that's all. Moreover, the internal water volume measure's so accurate, not even the hardest finger-stabber can get a cup to run over. So, no chance of burned fingers! And, the cups we supply are all made of Styrofoam, which doesn't conduct the heat. Let me show you how easy it is to maintain. The entire back comes off when you flick this switch. Hey presto! The hot water reservoir's easy to check and to drain. Don't forget, we also supply an internal cleaner for the pipes and reservoir for use on a weekly basis. Cleaning the front's a piece of cake! No awkward nooks or crannies. Just remove this cup holder and a simple wipe's all you need. Incidentally, the Multiserve holds no less than 250 cups at a time. No risk of running out during your breaktime peaks!
>
> And wait till you try the drinks. Fabulous! Our R&D department scoured the land for them I don't mind telling you. Tea even beats Twinings! And this reconstituted soup's a winner – really tastes like minestrone. See those coloured lights at the back? Each one tells you when you've only got fifteen servings of the particular drink left, and for ease of reloading, our refill packs come in one hundred sizes, which fit exactly into their holders, see? Go on, have a play with it. I guarantee you'll like it. It's fast, it's guaranteed for three years and it's reliable. A gift at £ 899, and with your educational discount, a steal at £ 749!

When each recording has been made, replay them and decide which sounds the most effective and why. In a class cup final, play back what were selected as the two best small group tapes to decide upon an overall winner. Each class member should mark each recording out of 30 (3 × 10) on the basis of clarity, persuasiveness and appeal and effectiveness of delivery.

Developing active listening

One of the most valuable yet underappreciated skills which the oral communicator needs to develop is that of listening to what others say. Not just listening, but listening actively, which means *intently, with concentration, analytically and with empathy.*

Put into the above four short descriptors, active listening seems a simple skill to acquire. However, when set in the context of, say, a long and dreary meeting taking place in an airless, hot conference room, it becomes easier to appreciate the blocks to paying close attention to what is being said and to taking its content in alertly.

Blocks to active listening

- **Allowing oneself to become distracted** by say another person's jewellery, flash pen, tie, the gardener outside, or even an insect crawling up the wall!
- **Thinking only of what one wants to say next**: the self-centred syndrome!
- **Allowing day-dreaming or notepad doodling to take over** and thus to block out the incoming spoken-word message.
- **Starting a conversation** with the person sitting in the next seat (experienced chairs nip this in the bud by calling for only one meeting at a time).
- **Trying to do two jobs at once** perhaps by listening to the speaker while composing a shopping list for the evening meal.

Whatever the reasons for the occurrence, once your listening concentration has been broken, you immediately become vulnerable to the following outcomes:

- You miss a vital point and therefore become prone to making a mistake or misinforming someone after the meeting.
- You ask a silly question because you have not been paying attention.
- You are asked for a response which you can't give because you have lost your place in the proceedings.
- You appear disrespectful, even rude, in the eyes of the discussion leader and other participants.

As is readily appreciated, becoming the focus of such a clutch of outcomes is hardly likely to improve one's image or advancement prospects. It is important, therefore, to develop a set of techniques for overcoming the distractions or blocks to active listening. The following checklist includes aids to listening which have proved of practical use to countless people who take part in discussions, briefings and meetings:

Aids to active listening

- **Take the time to read all the documents relating to a discussion beforehand**. Mark key phrases with a highlighter. This will help you to become familiar with the likely subject-matter and better able to become involved and interested in it.
- **Take brief, bullet-point notes of the key points other participants make as they speak**. This not only helps you to take in and remember the main aspects of the discussion in hand, it also helps your brain to remain focused on the discussion, and so to avoid distractions.
- **Maintain an analytical, questioning inner approach to what is being said**. Ask yourself questions like

  Is this true? Do I agree with that? Is this fact or assertion?

  Such a technique also helps to keep one's mind attentive to the debate.
- **Study unobtrusively the non-verbal communication signs** a speaker sends while talking. For example, people being economical with the truth tend to avoid making direct eye contact; people unsure of their ground tend to stumble and um and er as they speak; people caught in an embarrassing position tend to bluster, etc.
- **Ask occasional questions to clarify anything you do not follow**, Would you mind explaining what you mean by ... Such an approach ensures that you do not lose interest and so allow your mind to wander.
- **Jot down short notes of the points you want to make when you can next speak**. This will not only help you speak more effectively, but will help you to remain focused on the way the discussion develops.

Interpreting non-verbal communication signals

Interpreting body language (as non-verbal communication is often termed) has become a central oral communication skill. Non-verbal communication (NVC) comprises several parts, which either separately or together transmit a wide range of signals (mostly visual, but occasionally aural) to others taking part in a face-to-face meeting.

- **Facial expression:** the face possesses dozens of muscles (which control frowning, eye blinking, lip pursing, smiling, etc., whereas those of the head control nodding, shaking, upward and downward tilting, etc.); as a result, human beings are able to transmit a host of expressions and head movements (Fig. 1.7) which act either to support what is being said, or sometimes to contradict it unconsciously.

Figure 1.7 A tilted head may reinforce a spoken message.

- **Gesture:** people from widely different cultures use their fingers, hands and arms to transmit signals which reinforce what is being said or respond to it (Fig. 1.8). For instance, finger stabbing while speaking is used to add emphasis. Holding the hands open and patting down on the air says, 'Let's calm things down here!' Folding the arms across the chest signals a disbelieving, defensive or disagreeing response to what is being said.

Figure 1.8 Some gestures need no words to accompany them.

- **Posture:** the ways in which people hold themselves as they stand or sit also signal a wide range of messages, from the relaxed customer propping up his local pub bar, to the assistant standing erectly just behind an important leader, to the nervous interviewee sitting hunched up, waiting to be called (Fig. 1.9), to the overconfident executive lying back in his or her seat, hands behind head.

Figure 1.9 Hunched shoulders may be a sign of nerves.

- **Proxemics:** anthropologists have researched all kinds of social groups in terms of the personal space individuals require; that is to say, how near they will allow people in various relationships with them to approach and remain (Fig. 1.10). In Western cultures, we tend to keep strangers some two to three feet away, only permitting relatives or lovers to make body contact; high-status people tend to want to be in front of subordinates, (say going through doors) and to keep them more distant than say a co-worker; if other people stray unwantedly into the personal space area, then individuals will move away to re-establish it.

Figure 1.10 People adjust proximity using status and intimacy.

- **Paralinguistics:** a classic cartoon of a patient undergoing surgery, but with only a local anaesthetic had the caption: I know what I mean when I say 'oops'! Thus paralinguistics is the term given to the multitude of sounds people make which are not exactly words, but act as if they were.

> *Phew*! says the interviewee emerging from a gruelling interview.
>
> *Tut tut*, says the disapproving listener to a speaker's confessions.
>
> *Hmm*! says the listener who is sceptical about what he or she has just heard.

Other forms of paralinguistics include sucking in air over the teeth, blowing air noisily out of the cheeks, blowing raspberries, sniffing audibly and clucking the tongue on the mouth's roof.

The main feature of body language is that, while we all transmit NVC signals consciously at times to reinforce what we say, *we also send them unconsciously*. Thus the attentive listener/observer may sometimes be able to 'read between the lines' when NVC transmitted signals say more than the words a person is using. For example, a manager who has an assistant in his office may be drumming the desk with his fingers while saying,'Yes, yes, of course!' In such a situation, the manager is probably signalling impatience for the meeting to end, while pretending to be taking an interest for the sake of courtesy. Similarly, the experienced sales assistant in a departmental store who correctly interprets the mood of a customer striding along an aisle towards him or her, head jutting forward, eyes slitted and face either bright red or drained white knows a very angry person is about to approach and erupt!

In such ways, we all transmit emotions or feelings of anger, disbelief, strong agreement, scepticism, fear, boredom, deep interest and so on, either consciously or unconsciously. Moreover, an ability in the workplace to pick up NVC signals and to interpret them correctly is a most valuable skill. It enables a subordinate to pick up the vibes that the boss is unlikely to grant a much sought-after request, and so to retreat and wait for a better moment; it enables the salesperson to see that the customer on the receiving end of a sales pitch is ready to buy, so that the sale can be closed; it helps the nurse or carer to see through the polite 'I'm all right, thank you' of an elderly patient and to probe for the cause of discomfort or pain revealed in the signals of the facial expression.

At a discussion or meeting, such body language signals help the alert participant to spot who is for and who is against a particular topic, who is speaking committedly and sincerely and who is being evasive.

KEY POINT

Although people at work do not always say what they mean, their body language almost always means what it says! In other words, the NVC signals transmitted tend to be more truthful and sincere. We all become practised at telling white lies, or pretending ignorance in conversations, but we find it much more difficult to send bogus NVC signals, especially when our brains are concentrating on speaking. For this reason, it pays to become an NVC people watcher, and to develop the ability to weigh what people say against the body language messages they simultaneously transmit.

How to ask effective questions in discussions

Asking effective questions in discussions is not just a simple matter of changing the structure of a verb from *You are* ... to *Are you* ... ? If you stop to consider *why* people ask questions in discussions and during meetings, the following considerations emerge:

- to prompt someone to enlarge on a matter (which he or she may wish to gloss over)
- to obtain clarification of a point not well communicated
- to probe more deeply into a given topic
- to query or express scepticism and disbelief about what someone has just said

Moreover, if the following examples of questions are analysed, other considerations emerge. Questions are asked not merely to obtain further information, but to wind people up, to cause embarrassment, to communicate sarcasm, etc.

> I'm sorry, I didn't quite follow your last point. Do you mean that the profit generated was before or after the deduction of expenses?
>
> What do you mean by your statement that you had no reason to suppose the night cleaner did not know where the key to the telephone was kept? You just said everyone in the office knew, so why not the night cleaner?
>
> Do you really expect us to believe that Miss Henderson's horrific injuries were caused by stumbling over a trailing computer cable she herself had installed?

As the above illustrations show, asking questions in discussions or meetings is not an entirely simple process, since the questioner often uses the question as a device, not to secure information, but to score points. On the other hand, a quite different set of questioning goals and techniques are used by discussion leaders and meetings chairpersons to encourage shy or unforthcoming participants to play a more active role. For example, an experienced chairperson may deliberately introduce a topic and then immediately ask a retiring committee member this sort of question:

> I know you take a keen interest in this area, Mr Williams. What do *you* think we should do about increasing members' annual subscriptions?

Such a technique immediately involves Mr Williams and makes sure that he has a chance to express his viewpoint before more dominating and extrovert members seek to hijack the discussion. Again, practised chairpersons develop techniques of curtailing the extroverts who love the sound of their own voices and bring others into a debate like this:

> Quite, Mr Bottomely. And I can see Miss Larkins wants to add her views on your most useful suggestions.

Again, discussion leaders may need to prompt reticent participants by asking questions like this:

> Well, has anyone any ideas to add to Mrs Batel's [the dominant participant] suggestion of the usual visit to a London pantomime?

Such a technique ensures that the same old decision for a Christmas outing is not made by default.

Sometimes, especially during sensitive or stressful discussions, leaders need to take especial care in choosing the words of the questions they ask, so as to tease answers gently from others:

> Can you remember more precisely what Mr Atkin said to you when he assumed your computer had erased the report he wanted in the evening post?

> When was it, exactly, that you first became aware that your workmates' remarks were not just meant as jokes but were veiled racial remarks?

> Tell me what happened immediately before you saw Mrs Watson open the safe. Did she go straight to it, or did she look around first?

On more routine occasions, discussion leaders may simply need to ask a series of sequenced questions in order to ensure a hesitant opposite number keeps talking:

> What happened then?

> So what did you reply?

> Absolutely. Was that when you decided to make the complaint?

> And do you still think that was the right action to take?

Such nudging questions act as subtle prompts, which show active listening and encourage a speaker to continue and to provide additional information.

Open and closed questions

As you will have noticed, the above questions are framed so as to require a detailed answer, not just a simple yes or no. Such questions are called open questions; those which can be answered by a monosyllabic yes or no are termed closed questions. Naturally, experienced interviewers tend to employ open questions when probing and encouraging others to talk at some length.

The British are notorious for going to great lengths so as not to cause embarrassment or offence to others. While such a national trait is often praiseworthy, in discussions it can lead to obscuring what ought to be a simple question:

> I wonder if you would mind telling us, ah, what, ah you were doing, in a ah jobwise sense, after April 1988, till, um, well June 1993 to be precise?

> There appears to be a long gap in your cv, from April 1988 to June 1993. Would you please fill it in for us?

The most difficult questioning technique to master is that of getting a respondent to provide information which he or she is reluctant to articulate, without causing offence. Some useful prefatory phrases are

> Forgive me for asking, but ...

> I realise this is difficult for you, but I need to know why ...

> Please remember these discussions are absolutely confidential when I ask you why ...

Experienced interviewers also employ these techniques to get a respondent to enlarge on matters only briefly mentioned.

> 'I'm sorry, I don't seem to have got the hang of your last point. What was it again?

> 'I wonder if you could bear to go over that again. I think I need to make a note of your main points.

At all events, discussion leaders and chairpersons who get people to make positive and helpful contributions follow these question-posing guidelines:

KEY POINTS

- Never put people down or embarrass them by asking rude, sarcastic or impertinent questions.
- Don't be afraid to use silence after posing a question, so as to encourage the other person to respond.
- Ask open rather than closed questions.
- Have a series of supplementary or follow-up questions ready to keep a person talking who is becoming interesting.
- Using techniques of NVC to signal sympathy, empathy, attentiveness, agreement, etc; may help the speaker as he or she answers your questions.
- Use questions to activate 'sleepers' or shy people if you are chairing a discussion, as well as to cut short domineering participants.

How to disagree constructively

Probably the most difficult oral communication skill to develop is that of expressing disagreement with a statement which has just been made. As all *Star Trek* fans know well, mere human beings do not possess Spock's utterly rational Vulcan mind. On the contrary, humans are prone to egotism, emotional outbursts and frequently pull rank. For such reasons, as well as natural aspirations to advance in an organisation, participants in meetings and discussions who occupy the lower tiers of the hierarchic pecking order find it particularly stressful to express disagreement, with something a superior has just said. So some just keep silent, and to all intents and purposes they might as well not be at the meeting. Others only speak to agree or express supportive remarks. Funnily enough, such yes-men (or women) often earn the dislike if not contempt of the very superiors they wish to impress. Staff who can stand their ground and express their own views are seen to have leadership qualities. But not by expressing their disagreement like this:

> Oh, come off it! Anyone who's ever worked in sales knows about the problems of getting their expenses paid on time. Who d'you think you're kidding?

While such a register and choice of words might do in a peer group discussion, the underlying anger, sarcasm and overfamiliar language edging into rudeness reveals someone who has lost control, and as a result, blown any chance of making what might be a very valid point to the firm's accounts director. Consider this alternative:

> It would be easier to accept what you say if it squared with the experience of the sales staff. I worked in sales until last month, and found that late payment of expenses was not only a personal inconvenience, but a regular cause of general concern.

This version of disagreement is much calmer. It avoids making any overfamiliar remarks and links first-hand experience with direct knowledge of general unhappiness about the late payment of expenses in a way that it is difficult to take exception to because it is politely framed and expressed.

A number of techniques have emerged in organisational meetings to enable participants to disagree without raising other people's hackles. Typical devices are

I'm rather worried about ...
: Being worried is less provocative than being angry or disgusted or shocked about.

I don't quite understand why ...
: Expressing a personal failure to understand something enables a point to be made but still allows others to provide a more satisfactory or clearer explanation.

While I agree wholeheartedly about X, there are aspects of Y which do still bother me ...
: Making an initial concession by showing support for point X enables a speaker to disagree with point Y while still appearing to be a reasonable, compromising person

I take a different view of X because ...
: This is a prelude to a more forthright and direct disagreement which will be based on several reasoned points.

Individual skills development activity

See how many more constructive disagreement techniques you can collect from your observations of discussions at your study centre during the coming week. Jot down the sentence structures and report back to a Communication Core Skills general feedback. You may also find it instructive to collect some examples which you think did not work and explain to your group what you think was ineffective about them.

KEY POINTS

- **Never lose control of your temper in a discussion.** A most helpful motto here is: If you lose your temper, you've already lost the argument!
- **Avoid making personalised references about the person with whom you are disagreeing.** Don't use: I think you're talking rubbish, Sharon! Use: There seems to be a lack of hard fact about X, such as .... In other words, disagree with the point made and not the person making it.
- **Before expressing your disagreement, jot down counter arguments which are rationally and factually based, rather than just counter assertions.** Disagreeing is made much more difficult to refute if it is based on facts instead of opinions. Not unexpectedly, constructive disagreement relies upon active listening, careful analysis of weak arguments and the spotting of assertion dressed up as fact.
- **Never succumb to the temptation to embarrass or put someone down when expressing disagreement in front of others.** You may score a cheap point, but you will also make a long-term and determined opponent.
- **Take pains to clothe your disagreement in polite and neutral language.** Use: My experience persuades me to see things differently. Don't use: I think you lot need your brains tested!
- **Know when you've made your point and stop.** Overkill in disagreement only leads to resentment.

And remember that no single person enjoys a monopoly of truth or what is right. Seek to agree with what you can before disagreeing with what you can't.

Providing helpful feedback

If participants in meetings all remained sitting bolt upright, expressionless and silent, like the proverbial stuffed dummy, even the most assertive and self-confident speaker would soon falter and dry up, faced with such a lack of feedback about what he or she was saying! We rarely realise it, but when taking part in oral communication, we all rely on receiving a continual stream of feedback

- that reassures us the recipients are still receiving and taking in the message
- that it is being accepted and agreed with
- that it is not being accepted and disagreements are forming
- that recipients are becoming bored and switching off, thus making an alternative approach necessary

Such feedback takes a variety of forms:

- NVC signals like nodding, yawning, frowning, smiling, etc.
- paralinguistic grunts or murmurs such as uh-huh, mmm or harrumf!
- short responses like Absolutely! Quite! Not really, Oh, come now.
- doodling, fidgeting, *sotto voce* conversations, etc.

While sometimes we are unaware of the feedback we supply, there are times in oral discussions when consciously providing feedback signals is a most useful strategy. For example, in a group debate about a given topic upon which a majority decision has to be taken, it helps for like-minded participants to support each other by nodding, murmuring agreement or by interjecting remarks like

> John's absolutely right there, and in addition...
>
> Asha's hit the nail on the head! Why don't we ...

In such ways, sides or groups begin to gel and to work together to influence their undecided colleagues and the chairperson. By the same token, negative feedback can be used to counter a point:

> I think Lisa's got the wrong end of the stick there, what should be done is ...

However, do remember also that there can be advantage in not supplying such pro or anti feedback until you have checked out the lie of the land and are ready to show your debating hand!

SUMMARY

This section can be summarised by the following points:

- It is well worth taking pains to learn the correct pronunciation of unfamiliar and foreign words, so as to maintain a positive personal image and credibility.
- Clear articulation is important; it enables messages to be received promptly, correctly and without the costs of misinterpretation.
- Changes and contrasts in emphasis and speech rhythms help a speaker to hold a group's attention and to get key points across more interestingly.
- Active listening skills are crucial for effective oral communication; they help a participant to absorb what is being said and therefore to make sharper and more effective contributions. Active listening also helps to avoid the embarrassment of having slept through a key phase.
- Developing the ability to interpret NVC signals correctly and to transmit them appropriately (e.g. as encouraging support) significantly enlarges the oral communicator's skills.
- Extending effective questioning skills enables an oral communicator to obtain much fuller information from the reticent, to make effective debating points and to tease out responses from the reluctant.
- Learning to express disagreements constructively prevents a discussion participant from causing others' hackles to rise, contributes to winning over the undecided and demonstrates an ability to move a discussion forward without rancour or ill-will.
- Providing feedback (either positive or negative) provides support and approval for like-minded co-debaters or counters the points made by debating opponents; it also encourages the unsure or uncertain to expand upon points being made shyly or hesitantly.

KEY POINT

The nineteenth-century American author and humourist, Mark Twain, spoke volumes about the importance of developing oral communication skills when he said: 'It usually takes me more than three weeks to prepare a good impromptu speech.'

What do you think?

1 Should strong regional accents travel with mobile workers, or should they be left at home? What would you do if you moved to another part of the country where the local inhabitants found it difficult to understand your accent and use of dialect words?

2 How would you advise a close workmate whose lazy and ugly articulation was being mimicked behind his or her back by other staff?

3 What advice can you think of for eliminating irritating speech or body mannerisms which people often unconsciously acquire? Or do you take the view that they don't get in the way of effective oral communication and therefore don't matter?

4 How should speakers 'bring back into the fold' discussion participants who have slipped away into day-dreaming or doodle land?

5 Non-verbal communication, a crucial part of the oral communication process or twaddle?

6 As a discussion leader, how would you (a) endeavour to control a domineering chatterbox and (b) encourage a self-conscious shrinking violet to speak out?

7 'Speak the truth and shame the devil!' Are there ever any justifications for being *economical with the truth* in discussions?

Self-check review test

1 How are the following pronounced: *ae* as in orthopaedic, *arche* as in archetype, *age* as in montage, *aux* as in bureaux, *ei* as in feign and sleight, *ue* as in guerilla, *quet* as in tourniquet and soubriquet?

2 Why are intonation and emphasis important in using the spoken word?

3 List four techniques which help to sustain active listening.

4 What does NVC stand for? List four main components of NVC.

5 Explain the difference between an open and closed question.

6 What is a supplementary question? What is its purpose?

7 What techniques as leader of a group discussion would you employ to control a dominant participator?

8 Describe briefly two ways of expressing disagreement constructively.

9 Briefly outline four examples of feedback, two positive and two negative.

10 Explain how as a discussion leader you would handle a participant who was engaged in an intensive discussion with an adjacent person while a discussion was in full flow.

When you have set down your own answers, compare them with those on page 197 and consult this section again if they differ.

Small group and pairs skills-building activities

1 In groups of 2 or 3 students, arrange to make a video recording of *one* of the following types of programme:

- an extract of a presenter reading either the BBC or ITN news
- an extract of an interview, say between Jeremy Paxman, Brian Walden or John Humphrys and a politician from a programme such as *Newsnight* or *On the Record*
- an extract of investigative reporting from a programme like *Panorama* or *Dispatches*

Make an in-depth study of the extract you record in terms of the oral communication skills of the presenters involved, such as their use of intonation, emphasis and speech rhythms, as well as their choice of vocabulary, non-verbal communications and self-presentation techniques. Having made your notes and agreed upon who will do what, first show the extract to your class, and then deliver a 5–7 minute commentary and analysis on what you discovered.

2 As a student pair, plan and execute a week's study (during and around your studies and social life) of how you and your friends listen to others. As part of this project, devise a ten-question survey which aims to analyse your co-students' listening habits and to find out whether they have any techniques or tips to pass on. Find out what most distracts listeners and why. Present your findings as a 5–7 minute oral presentation to your class.

3 As a student pair, make arrangements to interview a teacher at your centre (whom you do not know). Your aim is to find out what techniques or tricks of the trade he or she uses (a) to gain and hold students' attention, (b) to spot when students are 'switching off' and how they are 'reactivated' and (c) to encourage diffident students to open up. Take notes of the main points which emerge and – without revealing identities – brief your class in a 5–7 minute presentation on what you discovered as well as what points are useful in the context of taking part in or leading a group discussion.

4 As a student pair, make a study during your working week of non-verbal communication in action. For example, you may be able to make a video-recording of a class discussion in action, or otherwise to jot down notes of particularly interesting examples of NVC signals which you observe, etc. Once you have amassed enough material (say for about ten different examples), compose a joint oral presentation for your class which explains and analyses the role played by NVC in the oral communications process.

5 As a student pair, obtain permission to observe a meeting at your study centre (or at work). For example, the meeting could be of the student association, a departmental staff meeting, an academic board meeting or a meeting of the centre's quality or health and safety committee.

At a meeting with the chairperson, explain that your role is to make notes of (a) how participants ask questions and express disagreements during the meeting for your Communication Core Skill studies. Make it clear that in no way will anything noted be attributable to any individual. Then make your notes and, in a suitably anonymous way, brief your class in a 5–7 minute presentation on what you discovered.

Student pair and group activities

1 This activity is a series of one-to-one discussions, followed by a report-back session to the whole class. Class members should pair up and then arrange to discuss *one* of the following topics for no more than five minutes:

(a) What makes me feel self-conscious when I speak to a group.

(b) My pet hates of speech and body mannerisms.

(c) What I think makes an effective speaker.

(d) What makes an effective discussion leader.

(e) What makes me switch off during meetings.

(f) Is the ability to interpret NVC signals a useful oral communication skill, or a dangerous pastime because of the likelihood of misreading someone else's body language?

(g) Today's radio and television interviewers have become rude and boorish while believing they are penetrative and sharp in their questioning of people in public life.

Immediately after the discussion, each student of the pair should note down (a) which points made as *a speaker* were felt to be communicated well or badly and why, and (b) which points *as a listener* were received and absorbed well or badly and why. Then, each pair should compare notes and afterwards feed back briefly on points of interest which emerged to the general class group.

2 Take part in a group discussion (lasting 10–15 minutes) on one of the following topics:

(a) Compulsory community service should be introduced for both male and female adults for the duration of their nineteenth year.

(b) 'Tomorrow belongs to us!' Should this be the slogan for today's young women?

(c) Legalising both hard and soft drugs would be a recipe for social disaster on a massive scale.

(d) Greed for money on the part of directors, officials and players is ruining sport as a worthwhile spectator pastime.

In liaison with your teacher, make arrangements for the four discussions to take place within a short space of time, each having a discussion leader, a number of participants (say 6–8) and two passive observers (say from another group). After each discussion has taken place, the following students should report back in a general wash-up:

- Each discussion leader reports on the demands of leading a group discussion.
- Each participant reports on the problems associated in getting across one's point of view and having it accepted.
- Each pair of observers reports how the discussion was handled, how effective it proved, what positive and negative aspects were observed and whether any useful conclusions were drawn.
- All participants (at the end of the wash-up) report on any points which helped them to study Element 3.1

Before starting the activity, please check the summarising activities on page 182 as students may be able to produce portfolio oral summarising work as an additional outcome.

Skills-building simulation activites

In student pairs, study one of the following short scenarios and agree who will role-play whom. The player indicated should make prior notes on the structure in the discussion he/she will follow, while the receiver of the information must respond on the hoof.

In liaison with your teacher, arrange either to tape or to video your discussion, so that it may be played back to the general class for analysis. As a role-player of one of the twin roles, make notes after the role-play on what your aims were during the discussion, what oral communication techniques you sought to employ and the extent to which you felt you achieved your desired outcomes.

In a general class wash-up, explore the issues of each scenario, what an ideal outcome should be, and how this might best be achieved by one or both role-players. Also share experiences which arose from undertaking the role-play.

LUGGAGE SECTION IN LARGE DEPARTMENTAL STORE

- **Players:** customer and sales assistant; customer to make prior notes
- **Context:** damaged suitcase

The customer purchased a new, de luxe crush-proof suitcase, with towing handle and wheels from the luggage section just over two weeks ago to take on holiday to Málaga. When collecting it from the carousel at Málaga airport, immediately after the outward flight, the suitcase's wheels were found to have been ripped off. No one at the airport could throw any light on this. The damage caused a lot of inconvenience due to the bulk and weight of the suitcase and the fact that the customer suffers from a weak heart. Now, the customer has brought it back and is demanding a replacement under the guarantee.

However, the sales assistant is aware from a sales briefing by the representative that the guarantee does not cover 'negligent treatment on the part of the purchaser or carriers'. On examination, it appears that the wheels were torn off by a particularly strong force, such as being caught in a lift door or being trapped and held while on a moving luggage cart.

Role-play the discussion as you believe it should proceed.

WORKS MANAGER'S OFFICE

- **Players:** works manager and factory operative; factory operative to make prior notes
- **Context:** repeated lateness arriving for the 8:00 A.M. to 4:00 P.M. shift

The works manager is annoyed about the operative's recent bout of late arrivals for the day shift. Previously he/she has been a good timekeeper and worker but for the past month has been arriving once or twice a week up to 20 minutes late. Workmates covered for him/her initially but now believe he/she is swinging the lead.

The works manager believes the behaviour is bad for morale and that a first official disciplinary warning should be given.

The reason for the operative's late arrivals is that his/her spouse has fallen ill with chronic asthma. When unpredictable attacks occur, such as on days of poor air quality, he/she is totally incapacitated and unable to help in getting breakfast, or in driving the children to the school bus pick-up point (in the opposite direction to the factory). Hence the lateness. The manager's dilemma is that to make an exception for one is to make an exception for all.

Role-play the discussion as you believe it should proceed.

MANAGER'S OFFICE AT THE RESTEEZEE NURSING HOME

- **Players:** manager and supervisor of the south wing; both manager and supervisor to make prior notes
- **Context:** Complaint from son and daughter of Mrs Pearson, aged 87, a bedridden client

The manager has recently received a strongly worded complaint from Mrs Pearson's children who were shocked to discover serious bedsores on their mother's buttocks and thighs when visiting over the week-end. In their letter, they said they found it intolerable that such a situation should occur in an allegedly high-class nursing home which charged expensive fees. In their view the bedsores had undoubtedly arisen because Mrs Pearson had been left unmoved and bedlinen unchanged for periods that were too long. The manager telephoned them and promised an immediate investigation and follow-up. This scenario centres upon a discussion between the manager and the supervisor of the south wing. Ever since a dispute over pay, when the proprietors refused to move staff on to new, nationally approved pay rates, Resteezee has been boycotted by local nursing and ancillary employment bureaux, and staff turnover has increased. As a result, the south wing supervisor is running activities on a wing and a prayer. And last week, two new clients who are both infirm were admitted to the south wing. The supervisor knows of a local well-trained and experienced nurse keen to find work, but only willing to work at the nationally approved rates for nursing home nurses.

Role-play the discussion as you think it should proceed.

DISCUSSIONS AND MEETINGS: THEORY INTO PRACTICE

The preparation phase

Reading associated papers

Of course, it is not always possible to prepare for a discussion or meeting. Sometimes they arise spontaneously – on the shop-floor, in an office or even in a corridor – as people meet and one point leads to another. However, more formal discussions and meetings are often advertised in advance by the issue of a *notice of meeting* memo. Associated documents, agenda, written motions, minutes, tabled papers, etc. (see Element 3.2), are also distributed beforehand.

It is essential that you make the time to brief yourself by reading such papers carefully, making summary notes as you do so (see Element 3.4), particularly on the business items of the agenda. In this way you will go into the meeting or discussion fully prepared, not only knowing what each item of business is about, but also having formulated your approach or response to it. Such attention to detail not only builds personal confidence but also reduces the need for quick thinking on your feet.

Preparing personal position notes

Assume, for example, that you are a committee member of a sports club which is finding it hard to make ends meet financially. The honorary treasurer has therefore persuaded the chair to include the following item on the agenda for the next meeting (Fig. 1.11). You take the view that such a hefty increase in the annual subscription would be counterproductive, and so decide to put forward an opposing view. By preparing your position before the meeting, as shown in Figure 1.11, you will be able to make your points much more forcibly and confidently, since you will have a handy prompt at your elbow, and will not have to construct your points as you speak. Remember that to be effective, such notes have to be short and sharp, and that you may find it easier to read your handwritten capitals when speaking.

Figure 1.11 It helps to prepare your position.

Proposal To Increase Annual Membership Subscription From £25 to £40

- Second increase in five years
- Will impose hardship on many members - especially teenagers
- Membership has been in decline: this move will worsen situation – law of diminishing returns

Counter Proposals:

- Re-examine club running costs to see where added savings could be made
- Produce break-even chart to plot how many members subs would cover running costs
- Explore possibility of lowering subs to attract much larger membership

Figure 1.12 Make sure your notes can be read at a glance.

Refurbishing Of Training Suite

Essential, priority needs: Est £

- New OHP Projector and Screen 450
- New, more powerful loudspeakers for cine projector 250
- Repairs to Flipboard Stand 50

Desirable if budget allows:

- Computer Screen Projection Unit 1000
- Larger CCTV Monitor 450
- Purchase of more video training cassettes 500

Estimated purchase costs:

a) Essential items: £ 750

b) Desirable items: £ 1950

You should also adopt this approach to prepare any points you wish to make, whether stemming from an agenda, or simply from your knowledge of what are likely to form the main points for discussion at an informal gathering. Such a schematically set out notesheet (Fig. 1.12) provides a see-at-a-glance prompt for easy reference while speaking. It helps the speaker to avoid missing out an item because he/she didn't think of it soon enough. Also, whenever appropriate, the inclusion of researched, estimated costs provides immediate answers to queries and may well strengthen the speaker's position if opponents seek to use expensive costs as a blocking argument. As Figure 1.12 indicates, it pays to go into discussions prepared!

Sounding out other participants

Experienced committee members – politicians, local councillors, company directors and public service managers – make a practice of sounding out fellow participants before a meeting in order to find out how they are likely to respond to a given item on the agenda. In this way, they seek sometimes to avoid becoming a lone opposing voice, and to know on whom they can rely for support, etc. Advance knowledge of the stands that coparticipants are likely to take can be of significant help when attempting to secure a particular outcome during a meeting or discussion.

Reviewing the opinions of the chairperson, customer or boss

In a similar way, it is sometimes helpful to reflect upon the views (and prejudices) of the other person or people who will take part in the discussion. Recalling, say, the chair's long-term dislike of long-winded speakers may prompt you to keep your notes short and sweet; remembering that the customer you are scheduled to see likes to think the best deal has been saved up for him or her will aid you in framing the discount you are enabled to make, and so on.

Participating in meetings and discussions

Making an effective contribution in meetings and discussions certainly depends on conscientious preparation. It is also assisted by the use of a number of techniques, which though simple, participants often forget to adopt.

Effective participation at meetings

- **Make it a habit to arrive in good time:** this will enable you to obtain a favourable seat (see below); it will also enable you to pick up useful items of small talk as participants arrive.
- **Before leaving for the meeting, check you have all relevant papers and notes with you;** nothing is more irritating than to discover a key document has been left behind.
- **Ensure you have 'marked your agenda card';** do not miss an opportunity to speak on topics important to you.
- **Remember to listen and look alertly at participants as they speak:** interpret their covert as well as overt positions and reactions.
- **Remember also to take down brief notes of the main points which emerge;** this will enable you to refer accurately to what was said (dates, quantities, names, etc.) and will help you maintain concentration; also you may have to deliver subsequently an oral summary of the meeting (see Element 3.4).
- **Check out the lie of the land before diving in with a controversial point of view;** know who is likely to support you and play to them by encouraging them to offer their support.
- **Remember to use your prepared notes when you obtain your chance to speak;** also remember to maintain eye contact with other participants as you speak; burying your head in your papers will reduce the impact of what you say by more than 50%!
- **Keep your points short, sweet and relevant to the topic under discussion;** know when to stop and remember the value of saving your best point till last.

While it takes time and effort to acquire the skills of making a positive contribution in a meeting or discussion, such a contribution can be negated in the blink of an eye by falling into traps.

The main thrust of these guidelines may be summarised in the advice which Clem Attlee was supposed to have given the rumbustious Nye Bevan when confirming him in the post of minister of health just after the Second World War. Just as Nye was leaving the prime minister's office, Premier Attlee remarked, drily, "Oh, and try to remember, Nye, not to insult someone the day before you need to ask him a favour!"

KEY POINTS

Avoid the following pitfalls at all costs:

- arriving late without a copper-bottomed excuse
- talking over someone to prevent him or her from getting into the discussion, or otherwise attempting to dominate the discussion
- losing your temper
- being rude, sarcastic or dismissive of others; deliberately causing someone to lose face in front of others
- using crude or bad language
- displaying a lack of interest in the proceedings by yawning, sighing, talking to others outside of the debate, etc.
- day-dreaming, doodling or otherwise losing complete touch with what is being said
- making personal attacks on other participants

How to structure an effective contribution

About 2,500 years ago, Aristotle, a Greek philosopher and drama critic, wrote a treatise on how to write good plays. In his view, the plot was most important and needed to possess a clear beginning, middle and end. The same is true of an effective contribution in a discussion. Above all, it needs to embody a clear structure which listeners find logical and clear to follow. Of course, there are as many possible structures as discussion points; nevertheless, the following guidelines will help you to compose and deliver effective spoken contributions in a discussion:

Figure 1.13 shows how a discussion contribution can be planned as the discussion progresses. (1) Note that the speaker decides to provide a *beginning* and link to previous speakers by pointing out their failure to take account of local changes, both in employees' lifestyles and increased local traffic. (2) The middle of the contribution is then structured to comprise four points in favour of the proposal: the speaker knows that two-thirds of the female employees have children of school age; that the proposal will result in the same total monthly hours being worked; that both employer and employees will stand to benefit from the change because improved morale will lead to improved productivity; that high-volume rush-hour traffic, mornings and evenings, causes stress, and that some people prefer to start and finish work early and others later. (3) The *end* comprises the repetition of the key point that workforce morale could be improved at no cost to the firm.

How to structure an effective contribution

1 If possible, jot down brief notes of the key points made by earlier speakers, so as to recall quickly what was said.

2 Also, draw up a set of *brief* point prompts before speaking, similar to Figure 1.13.

3 While speaking, keep a watchful eye on the chairperson and other participants; look for signs of agreement or disagreement, and for attempts by others to contribute or by the chair to curtail your contribution. Try to make all your points before being countered or cut short. You may need to speed up, or to interject a holding phrase like 'If I may just conclude ...' This signals to others that you have picked up their NVC signals and you are likely to get another 30 seconds.

4 Employ a strategy similar to Figure 1.13, which shows clearly at the beginning the view you will take, which elaborates it simply and clearly as a series of middle development points and which rounds it off emphatically (perhaps by repeating what is felt to be the strongest point).

5 After concluding, be ready to be opposed by counter arguments and to have a further point or two up your own sleeve, just in case.

Figure 1.13 Select relevant points and keep them brief.

Discussion Topic: Suggestion To Introduce Flexible Working Hours

Responses noted from earlier speakers:

Agree!

John wrong: 2/3 female staff working mums with kids at school

Jean right: golden opp to give staff lift and increase productivity!

Points Jotted Down For Own Contribution While Others Speak:

Key Points:

1 Prev spkrs – not allowed for work/social changes

2 Must now respond to employee-mums = 2/3 with kids at schl

2 No losers! Parents gain & cmpny – boost morale / higher prod! Same total hours wkd by end of month

3 Stress of local rush hrs probs

4 Also – people diff biol clocks – larks/owls

5 Ideal opp improve wkfce morale at no cost!!

Making such notes for oneself within the short timescale of a discussion would actually enable their writer to express them more briefly, virtually as one-word prompts, such as 2/3 mums – kids/schl and, incr'd prod/morale → no cost ! In the text they have been extended to make them easier for you to follow.

KEY POINT

Some discussion leaders invite participants by name to make respective contributions. Others allow the hurly-burly of debate to unfold. In the latter case, you may sometimes have to make the most of a split second to prise your way into the argument. For this reason, listen for a speaker's voice to drop – at the end of a sentence, or to catch breath – and then interject with a confident, ultrabrief opening remark which the leader allows and which *captures the initiative*:

> Good point! Moreover, I believe ... Sorry, can't go along with that ... Precisely! That's why ... Hold on, Gary! ...

With any luck, such snappy openings will enable you to get your two penn'orth out and into the discussion arena!

How to lead discussions effectively

Everything so far dealt with in this section is grist to your mill as a discussion leader in that the role is very much like that of the soccer player turned referee, and sometimes the poacher turned gamekeeper! It is helpful, firstly, to review the duties and obligations of a discussion leader and of a meeting's chairperson.

Developing the skills needed to lead discussions and meetings

Both check-lists are quite short but encompass a demanding set of skills and flair to be developed. This skills set embraces three main areas:

- **Subject and procedural knowledge:** to be effective, a leader should be well briefed in both the subject-matter and detail of the topics for discussion, and also – where meetings are concerned – in the precise nature of any procedural regulations, so as to be an expert judge and arbiter should the need arise.

Main duties of a discussion leader or chairperson

An effective discussion leader's main duties are:

- to ensure that all who should be present are, and to delay the start for a short while if anyone is late arriving; some formal meetings may not take place unless there is a sufficient number of participants present
- before the start of the discussion, to define simply and clearly what the discussion topic is about; and sometimes to summarise very briefly its issues or major contentions
- to act in the following roles during the discussion:

  umpire/referee and decision-maker over any procedures which may apply

  controller of order and courtesy and anticipator/forestaller of any conflict

  encourager of participants who tend to be passive and mostly quiet, so that everyone has an opportunity to contribute

  restrainer of participants who are overtalkative and domineering, so that everyone has an opportunity to contribute

  interpreter of any queries or uncertainties which may arise

  summariser and recapper of the main points made during discussion

  interpreter of the feeling of the meeting, i.e. for what outcome the majority has opted (without a vote being taken)

  vote taker/counter if the discussion group appears to be deadlocked, and holder of a casting vote in case there is a tie
- to ensure (if it is the custom) that someone takes notes of the discussion and reproduces them as a summary record
- to ensure that, following the discussion, any agreed actions are carried out within a given deadline, and to brief any absent group members on what took place

The duties of a chairperson are the duties of a discussion leader plus a few extra:

- to ensure that procedural rules are kept to (e.g. council's standing orders)
- to sign the minutes of the previous meeting as a true record once the committee has confirmed this to be the case
- to coordinate a review of any matters arising from these minutes
- to regulate the amount of time allocated to each agenda item so that the meeting does not overrun and each item is given a fair airing
- to ensure that actions are implemented by designated members as appropriate
- to employ interpersonal and social skills to keep discussions moving, members amenable and to ensure that opportunities for wise decision-making are taken advantage of
- to be scrupulously fair and neutral (except for casting votes)

- **Interpersonal and social skills:** undoubtedly the most demanding area, given the complexity and cussedness of human behaviour; here a flexible mix of roles is needed: diplomat, coaxer, curtailer, tolerator, humorist, timekeeper, referee, judge, soother, pacifier etc.
- **Action initiator and delegator:** most agenda items are intended to lead to actions being taken, and so a key leader's role is to delegate, encourage or otherwise cajole participators to accept the personal responsibility for seeing that a particular something gets done.

Becoming skilled in subject and procedural knowledge is largely a matter of having the commitment to become thoroughly familiar with the discussion group's terms of reference and/or any appropriate written regulations. Developing interpersonal skills is much more difficult. Perhaps the best way is to adopt a people-watching approach. All around us at work or study, people are continually interacting. Mostly, we turn a blind eye and deaf ear to scenarios which do not directly affect us. However, by actively undertaking a people-watching approach, all kinds of occurrences suddenly come into focus and serve to provide ready examples of both good and bad interpersonal and social behaviour.

Use the following prompts to assist you in developing your powers of people watching:

- How does a person in authority handle someone who is (a) angry, (b) distressed or (c) shy and reserved?
- How does a discussion leader (e.g. a teacher) restrain interruptive and dominating students?
- How does a discussion leader curtail a speaker's flow without appearing discourteous and brusque?
- How does an experienced leader (a) anticipate and prevent conflict between two participants, or (b) if it erupts, restore order and calm?

In a similar way, you can make a regular practice of watching or listening to radio and television programmes in which discussions take place, such as *Today*, *The World at One*, *PM*, *The Moral Maze*, *Newsnight*, *Dispatches* and so on, so as to observe experts (on both sides of the table) at work. During such a people-watching process, make notes of useful phrases and verbal techniques which you could add to your own discussion-leading repertoire.

General group skills-building activity

DISCUSSION LEADING

In liaison with your teacher, form small groups of 2 or 3 students, and arrange to view/listen to and, if possible, tape a radio or television programme in which a leader coordinates a group discussion. During the programme, make notes on what techniques you spotted which appeared to work (plus any which didn't). Compare notes with your co-researchers, and then produce on one side of A4 a summary of your findings. Share this with your class, together with, if possible, edited examples taken from the programme you researched.

How to give an effective presentation

As with delivering effective contributions at meetings or in discussions, three key phases are needed to provide an effective presentation:

Preparation → Delivery → Follow-up

Preparation

All effective presentations rely on the following preparatory sequence being conscientiously carried out:

1 Careful research into the subject matter produces *relevant, accurate and up-to-date data.*

2 Classification of assembled information into essential, possibly useful and superfluous allows the *superfluous* to be discarded. The structure of the presentation can be designed first from the *essential* informational points and then the *useful*, if space and time permit.

3 Thoughtful and logical structuring of the data puts them into a suitable sequence of points, which not only have an *introduction, development and conclusion*, but which embrace a suitable structure, such as chronological, major-to-minor topics, pros and cons arguments, single, persuasive view and so on.

4 Sensitive thought should be given to the make-up of the presentation's *audience* along these lines: large or small group; young or old; experts or laypeople; happy with technical jargon or seeking a simplified approach; plus any likely outlooks, views and prejudices. It is essential to devise a profile of the recipients in order to be able to deliver the presentation in an appropriate register and style.

5 During the preparatory phase, attention should also be given to what parts of the presentational material should be developed into *audiovisual aids* (AVAs) in order to provide aural/visual appeal and to reinforce key points (see below).

6 A key part of the preparatory phase is to decide on the method to be employed to *store the main presentational points*. Many experienced presenters favour postcard-sized sets of cue cards which they make out similar to Figure 1.14.

7 If at all possible, visit *the location of the presentation* to check out in advance

- size of room and acoustics
- availability of AVA equipment such as overhead projector (especially size of screen)
- VHS video play-back equipment
- location of electricity sockets and health/safety considerations of trailing cables
- ability to dim lights and to obtain blackout/dim lighting for projection, etc.

Such a checking visit is worth its weight in gold if it indicates any problems or deficiencies well before the stressful period which naturally precedes a presentation.

8 Once the presentation's structure has been finalised, *design and make the AVAs*. Effective AVA media include printed handouts, overhead projection foils and slides, video film, projected computer displays, models, samples, etc. Remember that giving out a hand-out *during* a presentation distracts people, but that an audience appreciates being told that there is no need to take notes because a summary will be issued at its close.

9 Perhaps the most important part of the preparatory phase is *rehearsal*. Without rehearsals, it is impossible to check whether the planned presentation will badly overrun available time or prove too short. Also, illustrations for projection need to be checked. Moreover, if the presentation is to be given by more than one presenter, it is crucial to practise the hand-over phase, much like changing batons in a relay race.

Figure 1.14 clearly illustrates how cue cards should be boldly and simply set out using capital letters and emboldening and underscoring to make key points stand out. A numbered set of cue cards is an invaluable presentation aid because the short, bold and sequenced bullet points serve as instant prompts. They can be picked up at the flick of an eye, and do not cause the presenter to lose eye con-

Figure 1.14 Many speakers use a pile of numbered cue cards.

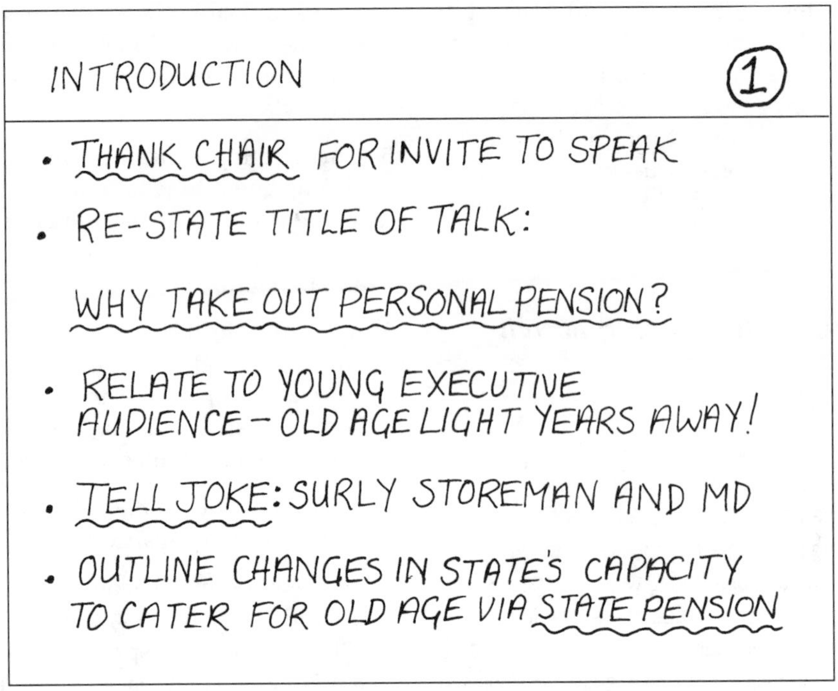
INTRODUCTION
1
• THANK CHAIR FOR INVITE TO SPEAK
• RE-STATE TITLE OF TALK:
WHY TAKE OUT PERSONAL PENSION?
• RELATE TO YOUNG EXECUTIVE AUDIENCE – OLD AGE LIGHT YEARS AWAY!
• TELL JOKE: SURLY STOREMAN AND MD
• OUTLINE CHANGES IN STATE'S CAPACITY TO CATER FOR OLD AGE VIA STATE PENSION

tact with the audience. Also, they may be scarcely needed once the speaker is in full flow and feeling confident. But each card *is there*, should the speaker dry or falter. Moreover, they can be used inconspicuously by the speaker, being passed smoothly from one hand to the other or simply turned over on a table or a lectern. Other prompt techniques include a sequence of OHP foils at which the speaker can glance, or an A4 set of sheets with text made out in coloured pens and keywords highlighted.

KEY POINTS

- Make sure your cue cards, OHP foils and other support material are readily to hand and in the correct sequence before starting, also that the OHP or slide projector is correctly focused.
- Seek to establish and maintain a positive rapport with the audience from the very outset.
- Take deep breaths if feeling nervous just before starting; this prevents your first sentences sounding like a series of jerky gasps.
- Keep your chin up as you speak, so that your voice projects to the back of the room.
- Take care neither to gabble, nor to mumble; take your time at the start; once into your stride, you will find your own natural speech rhythms as your confidence grows.
- Don't forget about eye contact; but don't fix a single person piercedly for a long time.
- Keep a careful eye on the audience for NVC response signals; eye contact with you, nodding and leaning forwards are all positive signs; yawning, fidgeting, looking away from you are negative and you should vary your pace, quickly more to your next AVA, pose a question, etc. in order to regain attention.
- Keep an eye on the clock; running out of time or over time signals a lack of courtesy and professionalism; plan your presentation in sections with timings included on your cue cards or notes.
- Don't panic if you lose your place or dry up; simply stop speaking and check your last, current or next cue card to re-establish your place; then start again.
- Remember (as appropriate) to leave enough time after you close your presentation for a question and answer session; if your presentation has done its job, your audience will want to take an active part after a period of sitting passively; and if you have done your preparation well, you should have anticipated the nature of any hot potatoes and prepared your answers.
- Lastly, remember to thank your chair and your audience for your invitation, for being so lively, etc; never omit the social graces on such occasions, they do matter.

Delivery

As the list on page 27 indicates, most of the work needed to ensure an effective presentation is done in the preparation phase. However, the proof of the pudding lies in the delivery. Here, the key need is to establish a good rapport with the audience. Indeed, many highly experienced speakers adopt a light-hearted approach, telling a joke at the start to break the ice. How an individual establishes rapport depends very much upon his or her personality. But common denominators include making eye contact with the group, smiling, appearing confident and being natural. Showing nervousness or anxiety tends to make an audience feel embarrassed and puts them off a speaker.

Some speakers like audience members to ask questions at any time during their presentations; others decide it puts them off and affects their overall timing. Decide which approach you feel comfortable with and advise your audience at the outset. Also at the outset, tell your group whether a summary will be issued.

In terms of the register and style you adopt, remember that it is easier to move from the more formal to the less formal than the other way around, and that, however well you know your audience, overfamiliarity or picking out and embarrassing individuals are two no-nos of presenting.

Post presentation delivery

What needs to be done post-delivery depends upon the nature of the presentation. At work there may be follow-up activities to perform, say if you won a decision to proceed with a new project. At all events, you should take care to clear the table or lectern of your paraphernalia before a following speaker arrives. You should similarly pack up and remove any equipment brought with you, so as to leave a conference room as you found it. It is also kindness to remove any hand-outs left on chairs, etc. Remember, too, that a pleased audience likes to mingle with a speaker after a presentation to ask follow-up questions, etc. This can be a most useful opportunity to obtain further feedback and reactions. Lastly, thank-you notes to those people who provided assistance and support mark a considerate person who is always welcome.

How to use the telephone effectively

Many of the early guidelines of this section apply to telephone use. However, a key point to keep in mind is that your call-taker cannot see you (short that is of you both using a videophone). This basic fact is easily forgotten, but should prompt all phone users to speak clearly and with slightly more intonation and emphasis than in face-to-face situations. Another key factor is the rapid development of telecommunications technology over the past ten years. Today's computerised telephone systems provide camp-on-line, follow me, group conferencing, call waiting, group hunting and a host of other services. It is therefore essential to develop a confident familiarity with the telephone system you use, not least to avoid the embarrassment of cutting someone off or misrouting their call.

Effective call-making checklist

Before calling

- Make sure you are *fully familiar* with the private automatic branch exchange (PABX) your organisation has installed, so as to avoid frustration and loss of face.
- Ensure you have checked that that the number you will call up is the correct one; BT reckon that organisations waste millions of pounds each year on wrong number connections.
- Prepare your list of points and action requirements on paper or monitor screen beforehand to avoid oversights and omissions and to emphasise deadlines.
- Likewise draw up a checklist of questions (with answer spaces) so you can jot down the answers to sought-after information quickly and easily.
- Bone-up on personal/company data about your call-taker by calling up your client/contact database; it definitely does help to be able to refer to partner/children by name, or to ask after the new branch in Bournemouth just launched, and so on.
- Have to hand any files, papers or screened data you may wish to refer to during your call. 'Hang on a minute while I just fetch the file', sounds unprofessional and wastes time and money.
- Anticipate any tricky points, objections or snags likely to arise during the call; practise in your mind how you will handle them; jot down any prompts, etc.
- Know who are the decision makers in the organisation you are calling; avoid wasting time by allowing a hierarchy of support staff to make you repeat your message before telling you that they don't deal with that aspect.
- Arrange to avoid interruptions and distractions during calls, else you may miss a vital word or point; ensure your confidential calls *are* confidential.
- Plan your calls to take advantage of cheaper times and tarriffs.

During your call

- Always make time for suitably polite greetings and pleasantries: 'How are you John, still surviving?' They help to break the ice and re-establish rapport.

- Remember always that your contact cannot see your face; so make sure you *sound* decisive, concerned, interested, confident. Smile with your voice!
- Don't forget to check your notes from time to time and to supply spellings or repeats of key names, addresses, numbers and the like.
- Always obtain clear feedback as to whether the heart of the message has been correctly received and noted.
- Make sure that your required deadlines and actions are understood and accepted as being realistic and feasible.
- Remember to note down on a message pad any information supplied to you during the call by your call-taker, especially names, dates, phone numbers or addresses.
- However sorely tried or upset, *always conduct your calls calmly* and never lose your temper over the phone. Upsets on the phone are difficult to smooth over because of the nature of the medium and the time until a face-to-face meeting.
- Remember to close your call courteously, thanking your contact; try to keep your calls brief; telephoning is not cheap and someone may be trying to get hold of you.

[Checklist reproduced by kind permission of Pitman Publishing from D. W. Evans, *People, Communication & Organisations*, 2nd edition, 1990]

After the call

- Make it a habit to transcribe all scribbled notes of the call *immediately* and to route messages directly to relevant staff; call any arising meetings

Figure 1.15 A clear message surpasses a quick scribble.

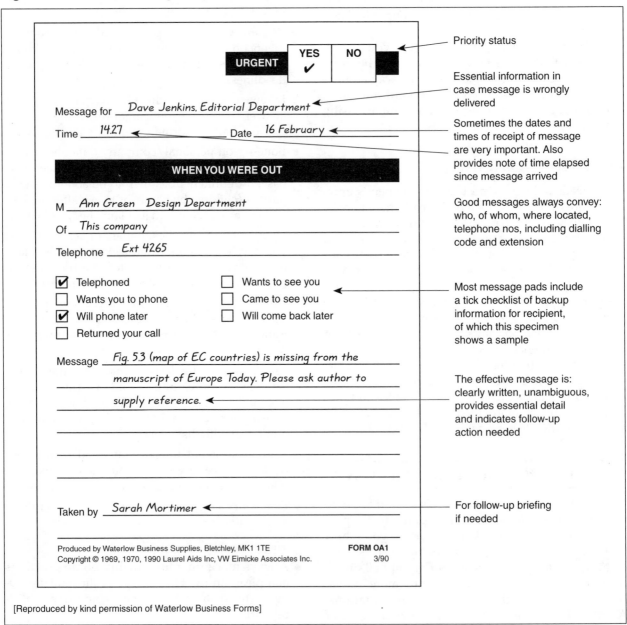

URGENT | YES ✔ | NO

Message for *Dave Jenkins, Editorial Department*

Time *14.27* Date *16 February*

WHEN YOU WERE OUT

M *Ann Green Design Department*

Of *This company*

Telephone *Ext 4265*

- [x] Telephoned
- [ ] Wants you to phone
- [x] Will phone later
- [ ] Returned your call
- [ ] Wants to see you
- [ ] Came to see you
- [ ] Will come back later

Message *Fig. 5.3 (map of EC countries) is missing from the manuscript of Europe Today. Please ask author to supply reference.*

Taken by *Sarah Mortimer*

Produced by Waterlow Business Supplies, Bletchley, MK1 1TE

FORM OA1 3/90

Priority status

Essential information in case message is wrongly delivered

Sometimes the dates and times of receipt of message are very important. Also provides note of time elapsed since message arrived

Good messages always convey: who, of whom, where located, telephone nos, including dialling code and extension

Most message pads include a tick checklist of backup information for recipient, of which this specimen shows a sample

The effective message is: clearly written, unambiguous, provides essential detail and indicates follow-up action needed

For follow-up briefing if needed

[Reproduced by kind permission of Waterlow Business Forms]

promptly on your local area network (LAN)/ messaging system, or you may forget.

- Make any entries on your electronic notepad or jobs list arising from the call.
- Clear your desk and refile all the papers you fetched out to do with the call; you will want them again one day.
- Make time to analyse the implications of the call and how it may affect you and your work before other tasks intervene and its impact dims.

Effective call-taking

Keep all the other points in mind, but above all, make sure you jot down the key points of the incoming message and secure essential names, dates, numbers, addresses, etc. Don't be afraid to ask two or three times for a tricky spelling or set of data. If you don't get them right, the whole point and cost of the call will be wasted.

Never be an anonymous call-taker; supply your name and job title from the outset. No one likes dealing with people who try to conceal their identify so as to avoid responsibility for any follow-up action the incoming call demands.

Call style

- Do sound cheerful, helpful, on the ball, competent, authoritative, in control.
- Don't sound casual, overfamiliar, sarcastic, icy, condescending, abrupt, impatient or intolerant.

Telephone support toolkit

Just as a wordsmith's toolkit includes dictionary, thesaurus, etc., so an effective telephone user needs to build up a handy kit of tools:

- a list of names, numbers, addresses and details of contacts, ideally kept in the form of a computer database so that the required information may be called up and displayed on a monitor
- a list of national IDD prefixes for long-distance calls, ideally in the form of a computer database.
- loaded abbreviated numbers for frequently used calls
- preprinted message pad and pens
- up-to-date directory of internal extension numbers
- access to national/international telephone directories and local/national *Yellow Pages*
- a list of local number prefixes
- access to local area (LAN) and wide area (WAN) communications modules
- PABX operating terminal

SUMMARY

The key points of this section are:

- Preparing for a meeting or discussion pays dividends; read associated papers, check agenda items and make prior notes on points you wish to make.
- Whenever possible sound out other participants, so as to gain a feeling of how the meeting is likely to proceed and on whom you might count for support.
- Good practice for taking part in discussions includes arriving in good time, taking a seat from which you can catch the chair's eye, watching speakers for NVC signals, making brief notes of speakers' key points, breaking in at the right moment, speaking shortly and sweetly, anticipating the objections of others.
- Avoid arriving late, talking over people, dominating the discussion, sleeping, being rude, sarcastic or dismissive, using bad language, losing your temper, engaging in personal attacks or putting people down.
- Structuring a discussion point with a clear beginning, middle and end using a logical sequence helps participants to stay alert and to grasp points more easily; it helps to jot down keyword prompt notes before speaking.
- It pays to listen and watch intently, so as to be able to get to speak when a speaker's voice drops or falters.
- Effective discussion leaders possess subject and procedural knowledge, diplomatic yet firm interpersonal skills, encouragement and restraint techniques, an ability to summarise ideas and an ability to monitor actions.
- Making an effective presentation relies upon (a) careful preparation: researching, classifying and structuring data, producing cue cards and AVA material, visiting the location and rehearsing; (b) a delivery which establishes rapport, keeps to time, allows for questions and maintains the social graces; (c) attention to post-delivery clearing up, thanking key support people and carrying out any arising tasks.
- Effective telephoning as a call-maker requires bringing out related documents and listing key points to make beforehand, establishing rapport with the call-taker, ensuring that the message's key points have been correctly understood and summarising key outcomes desired with their deadlines; as a call-taker it involves ensuring the taken message is correct, setting down a fair copy afterwards and attending directly to arising tasks.

What do you think?

1. How would you prepare to take part in, say, a discussion topic entitled: All school and college leavers not going on to higher education should be guaranteed a three-year training/apprenticeship scheme with a large employer on two-thirds of the salary of a postgraduate entrant. Outline your preparations either in support of or opposing the proposal.
2. What do *you* think the best way of preparing to speak in a discussion once it is under way?
3. Is there anything unethical or tacky about sounding out people's opinions before a meeting takes place?
4. Do you see any dangers in adopting a diplomatic, people-sensitive approach in discussions?
5. What irritates you most in the behaviour of others during discussions and meetings?
6. Place in an order of priority what you see as the most important skills of an effective discussion leader.
7. What features characterised one of the best presentations you can remember?
8. Only people who don't know what they're talking about need to establish rapport!
9. Is there such a thing as *telephonophobia*? If so why? Can anything be done about it?
10. What in your opinion are the five most important attributes of an effective oral communicator?

Self-check review test

1. List three typical documents you would be likely to receive prior to attending a formal meeting.
2. Outline briefly the features which would characterise a good set of notes drawn up beforehand to aid your speaking on a discussion topic.
3. What is meant by *lobbying*?
4. List five tips on effective participation in meetings and discussions.
5. Similarly, list five pitfalls to be avoided at all costs.
6. Describe briefly the main duties of a discussion leader.
7. What additional duties does the chairperson of a formal meeting discharge?
8. Explain in a set of about eight bullet points what to do in order to make an effective presentation.
9. What is a cue card? How is it used?
10. List briefly the main steps in making an effective telephone call.

When you have set down your own answers, compare them with those on page 197 and consult this section again if they differ.

Portfolio-building activities

ONE-TO-ONE DISCUSSIONS WITH FAMILIAR PEOPLE

Scenarios

Before undertaking the following one-to-one discussions, students should carry out preparatory research under their teacher's supervision and guidance.

1 Two students should take turns to role-play (a) a careers adviser and (b) him or herself. The topic to be discussed is What sort of career do you think would suit you best? The student playing him or herself *second* should do so with a different careers adviser role-player to avoid any advantage.

2 Two students should take turns as interviewer and interviewee for the following discussion topics:

(a) What do you see as the pros and cons of studying for a degree after your Advanced GNVQ studies?

(b) In which sector would you rather work, private or public? Give your reasons for your choice.

(c) What made you decide to choose your current Advanced GNVQ study programme?

(d) Looking back over your course so far, what do you see as the strengths and weaknesses of your Advanced GNVQ award?

(e) What particular communication skills do you consider to be most relevant to the career you propose to embark upon?

(f) With the benefit of hindsight, what would you change in your current course of study? Why?

(g) As an Advanced GNVQ student with significant experience behind you, what advice would you give a student successor about to join the course you pursue?

The duration of scenarios 1 and 2 is at your teacher's discretion, and is likely to amount to 7–10 minutes.

ONE-TO-ONE DISCUSSIONS WITH UNFAMILIAR PEOPLE

Scenarios

The interviewer role-plays a manager interviewing a job applicant, and the student the job seeker. The following discussion topics may be held with different job-seeking students:

(a) What aspects of your course of study do you think will be of most value in your career?

(b) Do you agree with the view that most people of your age will make three or four major career changes in their working lives? If so, what do you see as the best way to prepare for such an eventuality?

(c) What do you consider to the the most important qualities of an employee in a medium-to-large organisation?

(d) What qualities would you expect to find in the line manager you work for in your first full-time appointment?

(e) What sort of training and personal development do you think you will need during the coming five years in order to keep your personal career plan on track?

(f) What sort of IT developments do you expect to take place in your career/study sector during the next five years?

(g) What major trends and developments do you anticipate in your career/study sector during the next five years?

(h) Would you agree that the world of business has become too greedy and unethical over the past 5–10 years?

(i) How do you view the concept of profit? Can an organisation ever make too much profit? What should be done with the profit made?

(j) Given the extensive process of privatising public sector industries over the past fifteen years, do you see any virtue in returning utilities like water, electricity and gas to the public sector?

(k) What do you see yourself doing five years from now?

(l) Do you see any virtues in a school or college leaver taking the proverbial year off before starting a career or higher education? Are there any associated dangers?

Your teacher will establish the time limit for the above discussions.

ONE-TO-ONE DISCUSSIONS WITH UNFAMILIAR PEOPLE, UNFAMILIAR WITH THE SUBJECT

For the following discussion topics, the unfamiliar person poses the question:

1 What do you see as the major attractions for you of your favourite hobby?

2 What do you consider to be the most demanding challenge facing young people about to start full-time employment today?

3 Do you think that embarking upon adult life is harder for your generation that it was for your parents? If so why?

4 What major ambitions do you hope to achieve over the coming ten years?

5 What important things do you expect to get out of working full-time?

ONE-TO-ONE DISCUSSIONS WITH UNFAMILIAR PEOPLE, WHERE THE TOPIC IS UNFAMILIAR TO THE STUDENT

For the following discussion topics, the student is the question poser:

1 What made you take up your present career? Are you still glad you did?

2 What do you consider to be the most demanding aspects of your job?

3 What advice would you give to a young person about to enter your job field?

4 Looking back over your career, is there anything you would have changed? Why?

5 Have the widespread developments in IT proved a blessing or a curse in your job?

6 How much real progress do you think has been made in securing women's rights in the workplace over the past 10–20 years in your experience?

7 To what extent does a glass ceiling exist for women in your job sector?

8 What advice would you give to female entrants to your profession?

Your teacher will establish the time limit for the above discussions.

GROUP DISCUSSION TOPICS

1 Since the height of the 1988–93 UK recession, employers have moved increasingly to patterns of employment other than full time, including, part time, fixed-term contract, employing temps and freelance subcontractors. What do you think of this trend (a) from an employer's viewpoint and (b) from an employee's viewpoint?

2 The role and power of the trade unions have rightly diminished since 1979. Do you agree or disagree?

3 The introduction of some form of compulsory community service for the 18–23 age-group would benefit not only society, but the young adults themselves.

4 Alcohol abuse is far more dangerous than drug abuse among teenagers.

5 The trend away from marriage and the trend for those who do marry to divorce are rapidly destroying the fabric of a stable and worthwhile society.

6 Unless they can afford a live-in nanny, a couple with young children are kidding themselves if they think that both can work full time without causing adverse effects upon their offspring.

7 The government should introduce a national scheme of three/four-day working in order to make work available for all in the UK.

8 It's not the government's job to plan for its citizens' old age. If people choose to be reckless and short-sighted, that's their problem! Why should careful savers have to fork out for the feckless in the form of the taxes they pay?

9 In the UK, the ordinary people who make up the vast majority of the workforce have far too little to say in the running of the organisations to which they belong, even though they are its wealth creators. Changes in the law are needed.

10 Women still have a long way to go in securing equal rights and opportunities with men in the workplace, despite all the antidiscrimination legislation enacted, and commissions set up.

Discuss whether or not students should make notes to assist them in taking part. Before starting the activity, please check the summarising activities on page 182 as students may be able to produce portfolio oral summarising work as an additional outcome.

ONE-TO-ONE DISCUSSION SCENARIOS

The following one-to-one scenarios enable more complex issues to be discussed, and students should liaise with their teacher to obtain a fuller briefing on delivery arrangements before embarking upon them.

Clocking in and out

The director of social services at Midshire County Council is seriously considering the introduction of a clocking in and out system for staff located at both central and outpost locations in order to improve productivity, monitor claims for overtime, etc. He also maintains that it would improve safety and evacuation procedures. Accordingly, he has asked section managers to discuss the proposal with senior assistants in a recent confidential memorandum. Role-play the requested discussion, bearing in mind that many of the social services staff consider themselves to be – and indeed are – professionals.

Introducing a staff appraisal scheme

The managing director (MD) of your company chaired a recent board meeting at which there was a proposal to introduce a formal staff appraisal scheme. No clear-cut decision emerged, so the directors asked the MD to sound out departmental managers and their senior assistants for their views. The major issues the directors explored included whether the scheme would be confidential and 'closed' or 'open', with appraisees being made aware of the contents of the appraisal report; whether the scheme should be linked to pay and promotion; whether the scheme should be voluntary or compulsory; and how the scheme should be introduced, if it were felt to be useful. As a departmental manager and a senior assistant, carry out an appropriate discussion.

Responding to customer needs 1

The head of department in which you study wishes to conduct a review of the type and nature of delivery of the courses currently on offer. He has asked for volunteers to carry out a series of interviews with local employers who either send employees to the courses on offer, or who are likely to employ qualifying students. You volunteered. Your brief is therefore to arrange to interview just such a local employer (say a personnel manager) and to find out how the current range of study programmes is regarded and what changes might be constructively introduced, either in terms of new programmes or modified delivery.

Responding to customer needs 2

Another head of department (not your own) is keen to establish the effectiveness of the course marketing and informational material currently in use, as well as the interview and induction procedures employed for full-time joining students. You volunteered to act as a survey officer and have been briefed to interview a full-time student to obtain his or her views on the effectiveness of the recruitment material and interview/induction procedures. You are also tasked with finding out what, if any, improvements could be introduced.

TELEPHONE ROLE-PLAY SCENARIOS

Two students, after consultation with their teacher, prepare respective roles to simulate over the phone *one* of the following scenarios.

Scenario 1

Student A role-plays the personal assistant of a senior manager in a private or public sector organisation. The senior manager is engaged in an important meeting in his office with the managing director, and has instructed Student A that he wishes to take no telephone calls until further notice. Not long after, the phone rings and it is Student B on the other end, role-playing an important customer/client. Student B insists on speaking directly to the senior manager, emphasising that he/she has an urgent problem which must be sorted out immediately, etc. and that only the senior manager can help because (a) it is confidential and (b) he knows all about it, and Student B hasn't got the time to explain it all to someone else, etc.

Role-play the telephone discussion using and developing this basic scenario. If possible, arrange to tape the conversation for later evaluation and analysis.

Scenario 2

Student A role-plays the Midchester branch manager of Homelectronics, a national group of chain stores which sell a wide range of televisions, hi-fi stacks, mobile cassette and CD players, personal computers, radios, etc. for domestic and social use. Student B role-plays a very upset and irate customer who, three days ago, purchased a Tanyo 14 inch colour tv with remote control. Ever since Student B got the set home and tried to use it, the Tanyo has displayed a most irritating intermittent fault – the horizontal hold on the picture slips and the picture keeps jumping. Student B has tried adjusting the horizontal hold button, but to no avail. Yesterday Student B spoke to a Homelectronics assistant, but forgot to ask for his name. The assistant promised that a service engineer would come out, so Student B stayed in all day, but no one came. Student A knows that two of the three Homelectronics maintenance engineers are currently away on a three-day training course. The third is heavily booked today. Student B's grandchildren are coming to tea today in order to see the new tv in action.

Role-play the telephone discussion using and developing this basic scenario. If possible arrange to tape the conversation for later evaluation and analysis.

Scenario 3

The location is Vulcan Engineering Ltd, a medium-sized firm which makes engine parts for the motor industry. The time is 10:30 A.M. Student A role-plays the deputy works manager (the works manager is away on annual leave). Student A has just been informed by one of the shop-floor supervisors that an argument has broken out in the packaging department between Karen Walker, a long-service packing operative, and Tom Saunders, a recently promoted supervisor. Saunders apparently made a vulgar, sexist remark when instructing Walker to get a move on. Walker took offence, and with seven other female packing operatives, has downed tools and moved into the female rest room. Saunders thinks he is being made a scapegoat and that the real cause of the stoppage is the new pattern of shift working recently introduced. What he said was only meant in fun. Word of the upset is rapidly spreading through the factory and two sides are being taken. A danger of wider stoppage seems imminent. Student B is the personnel manager whom Student A thought should be informed of developments immediately and whose advice is now sought on what to do.

Role-play the telephone discussion using and developing this basic scenario. If possible, arrange to tape the conversation for later evaluation and analysis.

Scenario 4

Student A and Student B are close friends, pursuing the same Advanced GNVQ course at the Wessex community college. Student A is the social officer of the student association (SA). The time is 8:45 P.M. on a Friday evening, and the SA is holding its regular monthly disco. Gary Davies, a student in the same class as students A and B, is taking the entrance money on the door. Student A has just seen him look around furtively then stuff several fivers into his back pocket. Student A is shocked and goes into the SA office, where he/she rings. Student B and explains what he/she has just seen, asking for advice on what to do.

Role-play the telephone discussion using and developing this basic scenario. If possible, arrange to tape the conversation for later evaluation and analysis.

Scenario 5

Student A is the evening duty manager at Middleton leisure centre. Earlier this evening, a daily routine check after pool closure revealed a toxic substance in the swimming-pool. How it got there is a mystery, as is the extent of potential danger to the day's swimmers. However, the pool must be closed indefinitely and drained, while an investigation is carried out and the pool made safe for use. Also, the pool's users need to be contacted in order for health checks to be carried out. The centre's manager has left strict instructions that staff who are aware of the situation are to speak to no one about it, until he has had an opportunity to hold a meeting first thing tomorrow with Middleton council officers and health and safety specialists. Student B is a reporter on the local *Middleton Chronicle* who has got to know that something mysterious has happened at the centre, and that it concerns the swimming-pool. Student B is also a very keen investigator, who can smell a good story a mile off! So, Student B telephones Student A in order to pursue the matter.

Role-play the telephone discussion using and developing this basic scenario. If possible, arrange to tape the conversation for later evaluation and analysis.

ORAL PRESENTATION SCENARIOS

Individual students, in liaison with their teacher, should research and then present one of the following topics to a suitable group, who may be familiar with either the presenter or the topic, or both. Before starting the activity, please check the summarising activities on page 182 as students may be able to produce portfolio oral summarising work as an additional outcome.

1. Employment prospects during the coming three years for school and college leavers in the local district, supplying a rationale of which job sectors are likely to increase and which to decrease.
2. The impact of information technology (IT) upon the teaching/learning process in your study centre during the past ten years, together with likely future trends.
3. The likely effects of significant increases in the numbers of UK citizens who are aged 65+ in the coming decade upon the social services, welfare state, relatives, etc., and the likely burdens imposed on those of working age.
4. The impact currently being made upon the student's likely employment sector (e.g. business, health and social care, leisure and tourism, engineering, manufacturing) of *either* computer-based administration and telecommunications systems *or* manufacturing, construction or engineering technology, and the most likely trends which will occur during the next five years.
5. How *either* a selected private *or* public sector organisation is likely to develop and change in the student's locality during the coming 3–5 years and why.
6. How patterns of work have changed in a selected local employment sector over the past five years, and why. What likely future changes will occur over the coming five years, and why.
7. How the role of women, at work and at home, has changed over the past 15 years, and likely future trends, supplying a rationale for them.
8. How best should the 'great' be put back into Great Britain in terms of *either* commerce and industry *or* the public service.
9. Are the Greens winning or losing the environmental battle with industry and government?
10. If today's young adults are the UK's most important asset and resource, what needs to be done to enable them to achieve their full potential?

Your teacher will advise you on the duration of the presentation, the nature and extent of the audiovisual aids you should use, as well as the time, location and make-up of your audience, etc.

CASE STUDY: GETTING THE MESSAGE

It was Gary Hammond's first job. The memory was still bright of the day some three weeks ago when he'd rushed into the kitchen at home to tell his Mum he'd got the job at Goldsmiths, a company which distributed books and magazines nationwide from a large warehouse complex.

'I got it'! he'd yelled excitedly, 'Trainee manager in the despatch department – start Monday!' That evening there were celebrations in the Hammond household and Gary was bursting to start work after his recent success in his GNVQ Advanced Award in Distribution.

'Well done, lad,' his Dad had said, gruffly, 'They're a good firm and you'll have no trouble fitting in there, I'm sure. Have to mind you p's and q's though, I'll be bound, until you know the ropes.'

Gary waited until it was morning teabreak time. Then, quietly, he slipped out of the distribution department's open-plan office and knocked hesitantly at the office door of Mrs Grenfell, the despatch department manager.

'Come in', said Mrs Grenfell. 'Oh, it's you, Gary. Hope it's nothing too complicated, I've got to go out in a few minutes.'

'Oh, well. I could come back later.' Mrs Grenfell paused, picking up the crestfallen look on Gary's face and the twitching of a muscle in his right cheek.

'Just a moment, Gary.' She picked up the phone asked her secretary to reschedule her appointment for an hour later. 'Sit down, I've got the feeling that there's something on your mind that needs sorting out.'

'How did you know?' asked Gary, surprised and now feeling embarrassed, wishing he'd gone to the staff canteen for his teabreak.

'Intuition and experience!' replied Mrs Grenfell. 'I've seen your kind of look before and know that something's bothering you. Come on, out with it, while I pour you a cup of tea.' Gary's muscle began to twitch faster, and his jaw flexed as he ground his back teeth.

'Well, ah, I've decided to give in my notice!' Having managed to articulate what had been on his mind for the past week, he felt a little less nervous, although beads of perspiration began to form on his forehead.

'You what?' gasped Mrs Grenfell, whose intuition and experience had not prepared her for this bombshell. 'But you've only just arrived! I thought you were settling in nicely and Jack [Gary's immediate supervisor] has been saying how hard you've been working. What's brought all this on?'

A long and difficult pause ensued. Gary coloured and then, taking a deep breath, gave out a torrent of words. 'I just don't know where I am! I just don't know why I'm doing what I'm doing. Every time I allocate a pallet for a consignment of books, someone tells me it's the wrong pallet, or it's in the wrong place, and if I move it, someone else tells me that it was okay where I first put it! I don't know how to work the computer properly to check the delivery schedules, and every time I ask, people are always too busy. They just say, "Oh, don't worry, you'll soon pick it up," but I'm not!'

Mrs Grenfell's mouth edges had dropped at this unsuspected outburst. Quietly she interposed and asked, 'And how are you getting on with Jo, Alan and Bridget [Gary's co-workers] in the office?'

'Well, all right I suppose, but they keep geeing me up about my qualifications and taking the mickey. I don't think it exactly made their day when I arrived, though I'm sure I don't know why. I've done my best to fit in with them.'

'What makes you think you're not fitting in with them?'

'Oh, I dunno. I always have to start a conversation. They'll never volunteer anything. I have to ask constantly about the least thing – where does this go, what's this form for, where do I go to find out about that? Makes me feel really small! And they're always having a go at me for working too hard. Too hard! I hardly know yet what I'm doing.'

'What about Jack, how are you getting on with him?'

'Jack's okay. He's the only one I think who has accepted me. Trouble is, he just doesn't seem to have the time to answer my questions and so on. His desk seems like the battlements of a castle – with Jack's bowed head just visible in between!'

'Well, at least your sense of humour's not entirely disappeared,' said Mrs Grenfell, smiling encouragingly. 'Is that all of it off your chest, I mean?'

Gary looked own, feeling like a kid who'd rushed in to his mum to complain about being picked on by the street gang. 'I shouldn't have come. It just seemed to get on top of me. I'll let you get on, I'm sure it'll sort itself out.'

'Sit down please, Gary. You see, it won't sort itself out, just like that. And you needn't feel bad about coming to see me. In fact, you've done me a very good turn.'

'How d'you mean?' asked Gary, wondering what she was driving at.

'Well, your coming to see me has brought matters to a head. I've been meaning to look into the way in which Goldsmiths handles the appointment of people like you, and we certainly need prospective managers who've studied distribution. I want you to promise to say nothing about your resignation thoughts or this interview to anyone for the time being. And I'd like you to come and see me at 11:00 A.M. tomorrow. And please don't worry. You *will* fit in here at Goldsmiths, but I've got some earnest thinking and planning to do.'

Gary got up and left, as Mrs Grenfell turned to a filing cabinet to lift out a folder entitled Induction Procedures. Walking slowly back to the office, his mind raced as he wondered whether he'd done the right thing at all. Yet Mrs Grenfell had seemed to understand how he felt.

[Case study reproduced by kind permission of Pitman Publishing from D. W. Evans, *People, Communication & Organisations*, 2nd edition, 1990]

Case study questions

This case study shows how oral and non-verbal communications can be used constructively and destructively at work. In groups of 3 or 4, discuss the following questions and then supply your responses in a general class analysis.

1 What would you have done in Gary Hammond's situation? Do you think Gary took the most appropriate action in seeing Mrs Grenfell?

2 How good were (a) Mrs Grenfell's NVC and (b) Mrs Grenfell's oral communication skills in her discussion with Gary? Would you have handled it any differently?

3 In reality can the behaviour of employees like Jo, Alan and Bridget towards Gary be anticipated and avoided, or is it up to Gary to find a suitable communications way of handling the situation?

4 Should students who have not worked in a full- or part-time post be prepared for the negative and unkind ways some people communicate their feelings at work? Or is it up to them to create their own survival mechanisms?

5 Should Mrs Grenfell have gone further to adopt a 'walk the talk' or 'listening ear' approach where Gary and other new employees were concerned? How important is it for managers to seek opportunities to have informal chats and discussions with employees by regularly moving around their departments in an unstructured way?

CHAPTER 2

PRODUCE WRITTEN MATERIAL

What is written without effort is in general read without pleasure.
Samuel Johnson

True ease in writing comes from art, not chance.
Alexander Pope

Element 3.2: Produce written material

PERFORMANCE CRITERIA

A student must:

1 include information which is accurate and relevant to the **subject**

2 check the text is legible and the meaning is clear, correcting it if necessary

3 follow appropriate standard **conventions**

4 present information in a **format** that suits the **audience** and purpose

5 use structure and style to emphasise meaning

RANGE

Subject: straightforward, complex

Conventions: spelling, punctuation, grammar

Format: pre-set, outline, freely structured

Audience: people familiar with the subject who know the student, people familiar with the subject who do not know the student; people unfamiliar with the subject who know the student, people unfamiliar with the subject who do not know the student

WHAT *IS* GOOD WRITING?

Two of the eighteenth century's most polished and widely read writers, Samuel Johnson and Alexander Pope, were both fully aware of the effort needed to write well. They considered good writing to be a craft to be learned, an art to be mastered. And even in our much faster and technology-reliant lifestyle, at the end of the twentieth century, their advice holds true. Careless, slapdash writing reads just like that – careless and slapdash! Such an approach has the effect of significantly diminishing any importance or truth in what has been written, and equally lowers the estimation of the writer in the eyes of his or her readers.

The key features of good writing

What, then, distinguishes good writing from bad? The following check-list illustrates some of the particularly important features of good writing, whether in the form of a novel, laboratory report, drama or job application letter:

Relevance and accuracy

A good piece of writing *stays relevant to its chosen subject*, it does not wander off the point or introduce stray pieces of information with little or no relationship to the central theme; *it is also accurate* in terms of human nature, quoted statistics, summarised events or logical analyses.

Correct use of English and accepted formats

A good written piece, no matter whether an article, brochure, report or letter, is communicated, firstly through a use of English in which all spellings are correct, all punctuation marks used according to accepted convention and all ideas expressed through grammar and syntax uses which follow established usage conventions. Such a piece of writing also conforms to a currently accepted set of format or layout rules. A letter follows different rules from a memorandum or set of minutes. If a piece is expressed within a uniquely created format, then it must set out a clear sequence of points in such a way as to make them easily absorbed and understood.

Use of appropriate structures, tone and styles

A good piece of writing readily establishes a rapport with its readership by creating a structure, tone and overall style which is suited both to its intended audience and the context in which it is written, whether factual, subjective, persuasive or argumentative, and whether intended to inform, persuade or move to act.

The key features of bad writing

By contrast, an ineffective piece of writing fails to create and maintain communication with its intended recipients.

- **It rambles and is full of waffle** because no thought has been given beforehand to devising a suitable structure with a beginning, middle and end, which employs carefully researched data that is relevant, up to date and accurately set down.
- **It is littered with errors** of spelling, punctuation and grammar or accepted English usage.
- **It fails to keep to the currently accepted conventions of layout**, say of a fully blocked, openly punctuated letter (see page 71), or fails to establish its own coherent and readily understood structure and format.
- **It alienates its readership** by creating a patronising and condescending tone, through the composition of overlong sentences whose meaning becomes lost, or by using overfamiliar, colloquial language in a formal situation.
- **It is written without a clear idea of the main purpose**, say where a rude letter of complaint results in a delay in obtaining redress because the recipient (who can either help or hinder) takes offence, or where an admonishing internal memorandum is ignored because its overall tone results in the message and its writer appearing soft and ineffectual.

Samuel Johnson, quoted at the start of this chapter, once observed that, while not a master cabinet-maker, he fancied he knew a good table when he saw one! In other words, high quality is easily recognised. The same is true of recognising a good, effective piece of writing when we read it. This introductory section has concentrated on establishing two complementary sets of guidelines – what to strive for and what to avoid – in your own vocationally based writing. However, it is much easier to recognise what makes a piece of writing good, and therefore effective, than to develop expert skills in written composition and presentation.

How to become a good and effective writer is the subject of the following sections. As you work through them, keep firmly in mind that the ability to write effectively is one of the most important skills you will need to enable you to climb your personal career ladder. You will only be able to put into your writing what you put into acquiring good writing skills!

WRITING FOR A PURPOSE

In the world of creative writing, authors, dramatists and poets write to entertain, to uplift, to amuse, to cause people to think, to shock, to protest and so on. The reasons why people write in the world of work – directors, managers, clerks, customers, government officials, etc. – are just as varied. The table illustrates how written documents used in the workplace vary widely, in terms of their purpose, the type of language they employ and the way in which they are presented. The effective writer therefore needs to acquire an expert knowledge of how the purpose or intended outcome of a piece of writing impacts upon the structure, format and style in which it will be communicated.

The effective writing mix

The table indirectly shows that an effective piece of writing must employ three essential components in a triangular writing mix (Fig 2.1).

Figure 2.1 Effective writing has three components.

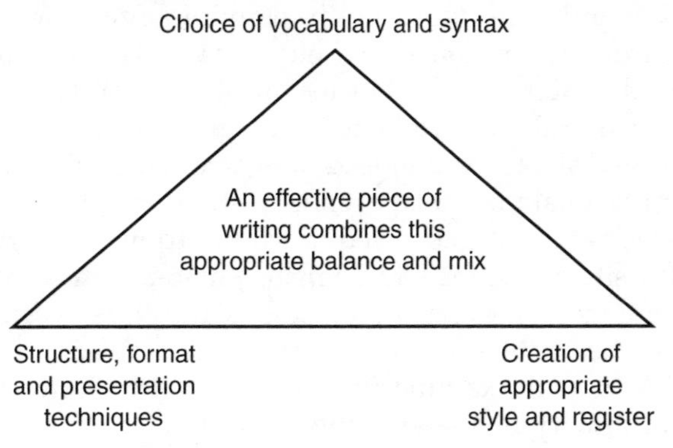

The choice of words

Consider, for example, the following set of alternative words for basically the same idea:

to kill	fire	wife	home	nice
to execute	blaze	lover	pad	pleasant
to murder	inferno	mistress	residence	great
to exterminate	conflagration	partner	domicile	wicked
to eradicate	holocaust	cohabitee	abode	congenial

The English language, deriving as it does from Latin, Anglo-Saxon, Norse, Norman French and a

Examples of different types of work-related writing

Reason for writing	*Type of document*	*Writing approach*
to inform or brief	report, notes of a meeting	objective, factual, disinterested; structured in logical sections
to instruct	memorandum, letter, operational manual	factual, clearly sequenced steps and points; avoidance of highly technical language
to propose	discussion paper, group memorandum	either loaded towards a favoured viewpoint or even-handed, outlining options; carefully structured with pros and cons
to record	minutes or notes of meeting, case notes, confidential résumés	essentially a factual, accurate record of the spoken word, summarising main points fairly
to persuade or motivate	advertisement, leaflet, brochure, motivational memorandum	careful choice of subjective words; selective use of points favourable to desired outcome; use of friendly, easy style
to discipline, or express grievance	letter, memorandum	formal, impersonal style; factual emphasis; careful use of words and expressions for accuracy and to avoid criticisms of bias
to present self positively	curriculum vitae, letter of application, job application form	mix of factual and promotional vocabulary; schematic format; careful choice of vocabulary; avoidance of colloquial, slang expressions

host of foreign words, is extremely rich in synonyms – alternative words which express the same or similar meanings. Moreover, such a choice can bring into play either a word with emotive overtones – murder, lover, home, nice, etc. – or words which are used in abstract, legal or technical ways and so are impersonal – exterminate, conflagration, cohabitee, congenial, etc. And indeed, it is no accident that the impersonal vocabulary tends to stem from Latin or Greek and not to be used much in ordinary, everyday situations; the Old English, Anglo-Saxon words were used in everyday situations and thus became enriched with emotional overtones.

You will examine the impact of the choice of vocabulary in a later section, but it is important to bear in mind at the outset that the use of different synonyms to express a given meaning will create different effects upon the reader.

Structure, format and presentational techniques

How a piece of writing is structured, formatted and presented has a similar significant impact upon its readers. For example, the endless pages of continuous prose paragraphs of a long novel make visual and concentration demands upon a reader who needs developed reading skills and extensive time in order to digest and absorb them. By contrast, the bold headings, use of colour and white space, together with snappy phrases and slogans of a display advertisement are instantly taken in and responded to, even by a tired commuter. Also, the practised use of desktop publishing word-processing techniques, such as larger type for headings and smaller type for footnotes, and emboldening, italics, contrasting fonts (e.g. Times New Roman, Candy and Modern), rules, boxes, tints and borders, can stimulate and excite a reader in ways unknown to many readers of pulp fiction.

In addition, the presentation of the written word within recognised formats (such as the internal business memorandum or letter) and the use of schematic and progressively indented layouts, with a referencing system such as a decimal point (see pages 73–75) can make all the difference between a reader's creased forehead, signalling difficulty of uptake, and a series of nods communicating prompt understanding of text as it is read.

Appropriate style and register

The third component of the mix is recognised perhaps most easily with the help of the following contrasting examples:

Impersonal, factual style: extract from an investigatory report

The essence of a flexible working hours system consists of establishing two distinct bands of working hours within a weekly or monthly cycle, and of ensuring that staff work to an agreed total of hours within that cycle, carefully logged and monitored.

Persuasive, subjective, selling style: extract from a magazine advertisement

Subtle yet sultry, expensive but irresistible, Seduction Parfum – only for the serious!

Easy, motivational, encouraging style: extract from an MD's memo to all sales reps

The economy's had a bad time, our industry's had a bad time, *we've* had a really bad time! But it's getting better – fast! Last month's sales figures showed an increase of 23% on the previous month. Yes, more than one-fifth additional sales. If we continue to grow like this over the coming 12 months, we'll have increased turnover by almost 300%, and I shan't be able to afford to pay your commissions!

Small group activity

In small groups of 2 or 3 students decide on what *exactly* it is about the style and register of each of the three above examples which makes them either factual, persuasive or motivational, then compare notes with the rest of your class.

SUMMARY

Each age creates its own written culture. Before the advent of radio and television in the mid nineteenth century, the educated public was used to reading page after page of minuscule print. Such works made no concessions where the reader was concerned, yet were most popular and widely read because there were no alternative communication technologies available to transmit stories (such as film, television or radio). Today, however, there is a plethora of communications media which communicate most effectively outside the written word – videocassette, audiotape, voice mail, videophones, broadcast TV and radio, graphic illustrations, etc. The written word has to compete for attention. And in order to compete, in terms of work-related writing, it has to be:

- **of use**: accurate, relevant and current
- **quick and easy to follow**: appealingly formatted and presented
- **easy to accept**: appropriately styled for both context and recipient(s)

KEY POINTS

Before committing pen to paper, or fingers to keyboard, make a habit of giving serious thought to these crucial questions:

- **What is my desired key outcome in producing and distributing a written document?** By marshalling your thoughts – and also by condensing them into a short title or theme – you will ensure that your writing stays relevant and faithful to your chosen outcome.
- **What format and text/graphics presentation techniques should I employ?** By giving careful thought to this aspect you will make an enormous difference to how promptly and effectively your written message is communicated and absorbed.
- **What will be an appropriate style for my written document?** Whether a piece of writing is formal and impersonal, friendly and persuasive or neutral and factual depends entirely upon the context in which it is composed, and for whom. Straying into an unsuitable style and tone can have disastrous consequences for getting your message across and accepted in the way you intend.

What do you think?

1. What do you think are the qualities of an effective piece of work-related writing?
2. How important is it for a piece of vocational writing to be correctly spelled, punctuated and grammatically expressed? Are such aspects unimportant if the main gist is communicated?
3. What irritates *you* in a piece of writing in terms of its approach, tone and style?
4. Do you think work-based writers consciously create a tone and style for a piece of writing as outlined in the above section, or do you think it simply happens unconsciously or spontaneously?
5. Is there something essentially tacky and below the belt about creating a style deliberately to persuade readers who may not be aware of the writer's intentions?

Self-check review test

1. Outline briefly four key features of good writing in a work environment.
2. List four main bad writing practices which undermine good writing.
3. Describe briefly four main reasons for using the written word in a work environment.
4. What are the three interlocking features of an effective writing mix?
5. Why is the English language so rich in synonyms?
6. Explain simply the difference between subjective and objective writing.
7. What is meant in a writing context by *register*?

When you have set down your own answers, compare them with those on pages 197 and 198 and consult this section again if they differ.

THE RESEARCHING, DATA-ORGANISING AND PLANNING PHASE

Effective writing relies upon ingrained, conscientious habits of

- researching information that is relevant and useful
- organising and classifying collected information
- planning a structure to transmit the information

Researching high-quality information

It seems strange to refer to information which is of high quality, yet on reflection, information can be of both high and low quality. For example, a section of a textbook produced in 1983, *Future Trends In Information Technology* is very likely to consist of predictions which are wide of the mark, simply because no one was able to predict the astonishing pace of the IT revolution, which in the ensuing thirteen years gave rise to videophones, laptop computers, colour copiers, the Internet or information superhighway, mobile phones and faxes, voice-input computing and so on. In other words, the information in a textbook published only a dozen or so years ago has been superseded.

Information may prove of low quality if it is based on inadequate research, fact finding and checking. Tabloid journalists are often guilty of inadequate research in their drive to have a scoop published within twenty-four hours. On the other hand, reputable scientists, academics, government departments and prestigious publications such as *The Economist*, *New Scientist*, *The Lancet* as well as journals published by professional institutions are rightly jealous of their international reputations, and employ rigorous policies of editing, reviewing and vetting of the articles and papers they print. For instance, before a major scientific advance is accepted, scientists and researchers across the world seek to repeat the experiment to see whether similar results can be obtained. If they cannot, they remain rightly sceptical, and the related scientific paper may remain unpublished.

In short, for researched data to have a potential usefulness in any projected piece of writing, it should be:

- **currently acceptable**: any facts and figures included must not have been superseded or become obsolete; views and analyses must still be valid, not old hat; this does not mean that sources older than 2–3 years need not be scrutinised, but it does mean that ageing or aged information should be very carefully assessed for present-day relevance and usefulness.
- **scrupulously accurate**: in certain instances numbers to three or four decimal points may be needed; a person's utterances may require exact quotation rather than hazy recollection; a set of facts or statistics may require to be extrapolated in a balanced rather than skewed way.
- **compared and cross-checked for validity**: even the most distinguished scientists this century have been known to falsify research data in order to obtain the results they wanted; it therefore pays, whenever time and available sources permit, to cross-check a single expert's views or findings in order to establish whether or not they are generally valid and widely accepted.
- **dutifully acknowledged**: a large number of university students come a cropper each academic year by reading out paragraphs in their essays, paragraphs purporting to be all their own work but actually lifted from a text or journal; the cropper comes when they look up to see their tutor reciting the same words from memory; thus all sources should be acknowledged, either in the body of the main text, as a footnote or in an appendix.

How and where to find out

When an irate motorist challenged a £50 bill for removing a saucer-shaped dent in the wing of his classic MG sports car, the panel-beater in charge of the paintshop explained it thus: 'To one leather hammer £5; to knowing how and where to use it £45!' The same is true of finding information – knowing how and where to locate it can be worth 90% of the job. And today, knowing how to call up the various sources of data stored on computer networks can enable a researcher to access highly specialised information in a matter of seconds, from his or her desktop PC. The following check-list is, in fact, only the tip of an enormous and growing iceberg of information. Indeed, social scientists not long ago coined the term *the information society* for the age we are living through, since they saw how information-reliant contemporary societies and nations have become.

Major sources of information

Public reference and study centre libraries

Public reference and study centre libraries contain informational directories of data about businesses, public sector organisations, and voluntary associations; they have government statistics , encyclopedias of general and specialist data, yearbooks of addresses and key data, e.g. *Writers' and Artists' Yearbook*, as well as records of parliamentary proceedings; other items include legal, financial and engineering guidelines or specifications; back numbers of trade and professional magazines and journals, daily national and weekly local newspapers, careers information, references on local history, details of local clubs and associations; the list goes on and on.

Libraries are increasingly acquiring databases on CDs which may be used interactively (like browsing) in areas such as general knowledge, careers information, biographies and history. Back numbers of some national newspapers may be accessed by means of microfiche readers, or computer software.

Local universities

Universities keep an enormous amount of information in various forms in their libraries. Some, like Manchester Business School, make available (at a fee) databases of information – say about limited companies – from an on-line computer, so that remotely located researchers or marketers may access it. Others may permit bona fide researchers to make use of their libraries, but not to take out books; however, limited photocopying is permissible for research purposes via library copiers.

Local weekly newspaper offices

All local newspapers maintain archives of their past editions which may be made available for public use.

Council archives

County councils include in their services archives departments which store all kinds of historical documents about the ownership and use of land, city charters, changes in roads and boundaries, etc; also, county council planning departments keep records of planning applications and changes of use of buildings.

Education and public relations departments of government agencies, professional institutions and multinational companies

Government departments, quangos and agencies, such as the Post Office, the Inland Revenue, and the Department of Trade and Industry (DTI) are a ready source of data; for example, the Inland Revenue provides free educational packs on taxation, and the DTI produced extremely helpful brochures and newspapers in the run-up to the 1992 Single Market; professional institutes such as the Institute of Management and the British Medical Association produce regular briefings and updates, and multinationals like British Telecom make freely available informational packs on, for instance, the history of the telephone and telecommunications.

Citizens' Advice Bureaux

Most towns possess a Citizens' Advice Bureau (CAB) in which experts work a rota in order to assist local residents (free of charge) to access an incredibly wide range of information; how to obtain unemployment benefit, how to receive entitlements for artificial limbs, how to recover a debt, how to apply for a council tax rebate, etc.

Local museums and art galleries

Larger towns and cities possess both museums and art galleries which store and display artefacts, historical articles and archaeological finds, as well as graphic and sculpted works; both mount regular exhibitions of local or national interest.

National information sources

Located in UK cities there are specialist centres of information, such as the Science Museum, the Victoria and Albert Museum, the British Library, and Her Majesty's Stationery Office (HMSO) in London; the Transport Museum and the Viking Museum at York; and the Naval Museum at Portsmouth. Specialist organisations, such as Croner, the Commission of the European Communities and Datastream, produce a range of updatable handbooks, booklets, brochures and on-line computerised databases in subject areas such as law, social care and health, building and planning regulations, business, etc. The UK government, through agencies such as the Central Office of Information, Department for Education and Employment and HMSO, also publishes at regular intervals a host of statistics, abstracts, reports and briefing papers in areas like health, education, employment, spending and saving, building starts, manufacturing outputs, social and demographic change.

Small group activity

In groups of 3 or 4 students, carry out the following research activity and then compare notes with the other groups in your class. Find out what sources of information are available in your locality which are relevant to your particular Advanced GNVQ study programme. Start in your own study centre library and then move on to your local public reference library, your local council information resources and then to any additional private sector or governmental organisations located where you live and study. Your research brief is to make a list of potentially useful information sources, using the following format. When you have completed your schedule, compare notes and sources with your other class groups and compile a best version of the schedule to be copied for all class students.

Title of info source	*Location*	*Frequency of publication*	*Catalogue or reference no.*
(include author, ISBN and publication year for texts)			(e.g. Dewey decimal)

The Dewey decimal system

The father of the modern library indexing system was an American, Melvil Dewey (1851–1931). He invented the Dewey decimal system while working at a training library in Albany in 1876. It is based on dividing all human knowledge into ten broad categories. Each category is identified by a three-digit code number coming before a decimal point:

000. general books	600. technology
100. philosophy	700. the arts
200. religion	800. literature
300. social sciences	900. geography, history
400. language	B biography, autobiography
500. science	

Within each section of one hundred points, the broad area of, say, languages is subdivided into a series of specialist areas. Thus books on the English language are to be found in the 420s. Alternatively, in the applied science section, books on business English applications are in the 651s. Further degrees of specialisation are indicated by the use of numbers behind the decimal point:

621.4021 Engineering: thermo dynamics
616.898 Family care

In this way, the Dewey decimal system is able to expand to include modern technologies like micro-electronics or new philosophical movements like post-modernism.

Libraries using the Dewey system display their books in consecutive order, starting with the 000s and ending with the 900s. In most libraries, reference books, which are not lent out, are kept in a separate area, but they are indexed in the same way.

The Dewey system is not international. The Americans have now replaced it with their Library of Congress system which uses a series of numbers and letters to break down knowledge in a similar way. In Great Britain, however, the Dewey decimal system is widely used, save in some universities.

Once you have mastered the logic behind Dewey's system, it will now take you only a minute or two to locate the section you need. The table on page 47 will show you how the ten categories are further broken down.

The ISBN

The initials ISBN stand for international standard book number. The ISBN book coding system was introduced into the UK in 1967, and every time a book is published in the UK (and many other countries) it is issued with its own unique ISBN by the Standard Book Numbering Agency. Bookshops may order any text from a publisher's distribution depot simply by stating this number (although if known, details of title, author, publisher, edition and date of publication help the order processors). ISBNs are often accompanied by a bar-code if the book is to be sold in shops using such price-reading equipment. A typical ISBN number looks like this:

0582 28872 X

> ***KEY POINT***
>
> When engaged in researching for a piece of writing, every time you find a useful source of information, make it a habit to record the following details in your notebook:
>
> Source title, author(s), publishing company, year of publication, edition number (e.g. 3rd) ISBN and Dewey decimal reference number.
>
> This may take a minute or two, but you will find it invaluable. Nothing is more irritating than to come across a really useful information source and then to lose it among hundreds or thousands of books because you took down no details to enable you to relocate it. Even when you may only wish to research or photocopy a couple of pages, you may wish to include details of the text or reference in a footnote, appendix or bibliography. Then you will have all the necessary data safely in your notebook.

Scanning informational texts and references

Just as it pays to develop a thorough knowledge of the whereabouts of relevant research information, so it helps to acquire a researcher's ability to skim potentially useful paper documents. The check-list on page 48 provides tips on how to save precious time and effort:

Dewey book classification outline

000	**General Works**	630	Agriculture
030	Encyclopedias	635	Gardening
070	Journalism	640	Household Management
		641.5	Cookery
100	**Philosophy**	650	Business Practices
150	Psychology	658	Management
		660	Chemical Technology
200	**Religion**	670–680	Manufacturing
220–280	Christianity	690	Building
290	Non-Christian Religions		
		700	**The Arts**
300	**Social Sciences**	710	The Landscape, Town Planning
310	Statistics	720	Architecture
320	Political Science	730	Sculpture, Metalwork
330	Economics	740	Drawing
340	Law	745	Decorative Arts
350	Public Administration	745.5	Handicrafts
355–359	Armed Forces	746.44	Embroidery
360	Social Services	750	Painting
370	Education	760	Graphic Arts
380	Commerce	770	Photography
385	Railways	780	Music
390	Customs, Folklore	790	Recreations
391	Costume	792	The Theatre
		793–799	Sports and Games
400	**Language**		
420	English Language	**800**	**Literature**
430	Germanic Language	810	American Literature
440	French	820	English Literature
450	Italian	830–890	Other Literatures
460	Spanish	See 400–490	Languages
470	Latin		
480	Greek	**900**	**Geography, History**
490	Other Languages	910	Geography, Travel
		913	Ancient World, Archaeology
500	**Science**	914	European Geography and Travel
510	Mathematics	915–919	Other Continents
520	Astronomy	See 930–990	History
530	Physics	929	Genealogy
540	Chemistry	930	Ancient History
550	Earth Sciences	940	History, Europe
551.5	Meteorology	950	Asia
560	Paleontology	960	Africa
570	Life Sciences	970	North America
580	Botanical Sciences	980	South America
590	Zoological Sciences	990	Australasia
		998	The Polar Regions
600	**Technology**		
610	Medicine	B	Biography and Autobiography
620	Engineering		

Figure 2.2 Check the contents lists for relevance.

CONTENTS

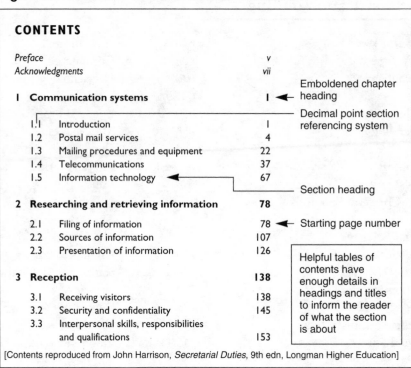

Emboldened chapter heading

Decimal point section referencing system

Section heading

Starting page number

Helpful tables of contents have enough details in headings and titles to inform the reader of what the section is about

[Contents reproduced from John Harrison, *Secretarial Duties*, 9th edn, Longman Higher Education]

- **On entering the library, make a beeline to either its computerised or paper-based catalogue**; check the range of publications by (a) subject and (b) author, if you are familiar with particular authors' work in your subject area. The catalogue will indicate the range of what the library holds; bear in mind that good texts are likely to be popular, so they may be missing from the shelves you browse through. Note down the appropriate details of likely data sources, and if they are not available, check the reservation procedures and reserve.
- **Check out the Dewey decimal number(s) associated with your area(s) of research**: make for the appropriate shelves and see what's in stock.
- Follow this process for assessing whether or not it is worth examining in greater detail the discovered information source:
  - **What is the date of the text's publication?** If over five years old, question the value of the information in the text, since it may have become out of date. Ignore reprint dates and go for the date of the latest edition, e.g. first published 1990, 2nd edition 1992, 3rd edition 1994. A useful tip on the value of the text is that if it has been frequently reissued as a new edition or frequently reprinted, this will be a direct result of its sales popularity, and probably of its worth as an information source.

Figure 2.3 An index is arranged alphabetically.

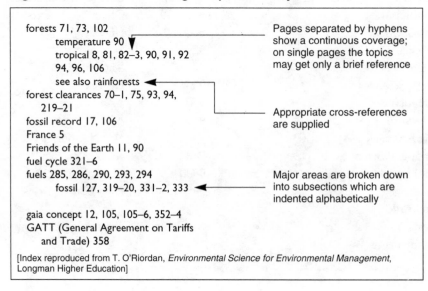

Pages separated by hyphens show a continuous coverage; on single pages the topics may get only a brief reference

Appropriate cross-references are supplied

Major areas are broken down into subsections which are indented alphabetically

[Index reproduced from T. O'Riordan, *Environmental Science for Environmental Management*, Longman Higher Education]

- **Who wrote the text?** What is its 'pitch'? Next, read the blurb on the back cover and any inside flysheets. This may tell you how expert the author is and what else he/she has written, which may prove a short cut to another useful data source. It may also tell you what the publishers see as its major selling points and hence its potential usefulness to you.
- **What is in the text's table of contents?** A quick skim through the contents table (Fig. 2.2) will promptly tell you whether the text's string of topics are relevant in whole or part to your research area. Note down chapter numbers and pages of likely material.
- **What is in the text's index?** Expert indexers extract from books key labels and references which are set out in alphabetical order at the back of the book (Fig. 2.3). Skim down each column and look for topics which are in your research area. Note down page numbers of likely topics. Remember that some indexers embolden the page numbers in which the topic is dealt with in most detail, and that 213-217 means that five pages are given over to the topic.
- **What is in a unit or chapter?** Before settling down to read in detail and to make notes of a selected chapter, skim through its title and section headings and check them for relevance (Fig. 2.4). Also, read the opening and closing paragraphs carefully, since they are likely to summarise (a) the chapter's contents and (b) its major points and conclusions.

Such initial checking techniques will save you valuable time. What is the use, for example, in devoting an hour to reading a text, only to discover it's an old edition? You should have been reading the latest edition. (Techniques of rapid and skim reading are examined in Element 3.4.)

KEY POINT

Remember that, if you are researching in an area in which change is frequent and extensive, you are much more likely to acquire up-to-date and useful information from journals, magazines, newspapers and bulletins than from published books. Even with the aid of modern printing technology, it is likely to take about six months to a year for a textbook to be written, and a similar time for it to be edited, printed and distributed. So, even if you find a just-hit-the-streets copy of a published text, its information may be up to eighteen months old. In contrast, a journalist may interview experts and have a newspaper article printed and published within days.

Also, because of the nature of the newspaper or journal medium, some writers and journalists tend to summarise their facts in short articles, which take less time to read and digest.

Organising and planning collected information

The information you collect from your researches is likely to take a variety of forms:

- summarised notes of texts, articles or reports
- notes of discussions and interviews with others (or audiotapes which will need to be summarised)
- photocopies of articles, papers or features from newspapers, journals or trade magazines
- copies of tables, charts, diagrams or graphics
- samples of brochures, advertisements or catalogues
- specimens and samples of products, trade demonstration samples or book inspection copies

Figure 2.4 Chapter outlines summarise chapter contents.

2 Descriptive statistics: tables and graphs

Objectives

When you have read this chapter you should be able to

- represent qualitative data using frequency distributions, relative frequency distributions, bar charts and pie charts
- represent continuous quantitative data using grouped frequency distributions, grouped relative frequency distributions and histograms
- represent discrete quantitative data

[Reproduced from M. Lawson *et al.*, *Maths & Statistics for Business*, Longman Higher Education]

As a result, the information you have assembled will come in a variety of shapes and sizes, which can look very daunting when it comes to making selections of key data, eliminating low-value, largely irrelevant data and reducing the overall information collected into a more manageable amount.

Organising information

Follow this sequence to prepare your collected data for your eventual writing structure:

1 Re-examine briefly all the information you have collected in order to refresh your memory.

2 Refresh your mind on the key points of the title or terms of reference of your research and writing project, for example:

Summarise the *changes* in *UK law* relating to the *care of the elderly* since *1980.*

Produce a *report*, including *recommendations*, on the *effects* upon *UK manufacturing* over the *past decade* of *information technology*, and how *small* UK engineering firms can cope with *increasing competition* from *multinational engineering giants.*

The italics indicate the key components of each set of instructions; they will direct and guide all relevant and accurate answers. So by checking back to your brief or terms of reference and highlighting its key elements right at the outset, you will ensure the material you select will be relevant and accurate.

3 Sift painstakingly through your collected data and organise it in three separate sets:

- essential data at the heart of my brief
- useful data of a secondary importance
- largely low-value and irrelevant data

4 Discard low-value and irrelevant data. Note you may decide to re-examine it as a final check before moving from skeletal structure to the full composition phase (see below).

5 Check the essential data to see which items are linked, as this example illustrates:

Report on IT in manufacturing

1 Article on introduction of CNC in toolmaking, written 1988

2 The empty factory: feature on robotics in the car industry, *Engineering Today*

3 Notes of discussion with works manager at Vulcan Engineering on computer aided design (CAD) systems and the CNC equipment used in both tool- and jigmaking

4 Information pack on CAD software marketed by Better by Design plc

5 Just in time – myth or achievable reality? main article in recent edition of *Production Manager*

6 Notes made on visit to Electroparts Limited, manufacturers of electric motors used in refrigerators, who employ JIT assembly practices

7 Notes made on Chapter 7 of J Grimshaw, *IT in Manufacturing*, 7th edition, Educational Press; class text gives general treatment of CNC, CADCAM, robotics, computerised stores and production systems, JIT, computerised MRP (manufacturing resource planning)

8 *Computerised quality assurance – the manufacturing experience*: notes made and graphs copied from a library text

A careful examination of these eight items of material is likely to reveal the following links:

CNC: 1, 3, 7 Robitics: 2, 7 CADCAM: 3, 4, 7
JIT: 5, 6, 7 Quality: 7,8

By establishing links between the assembled essential items of data, the beginnings of section or paragraph groupings will begin to emerge.

6 Having carried out the grouping exercise in item 5, consider in a similar way the material you classified as useful but of secondary importance. Most important, see what items you can add to your collection of essential points, for example:

CADCAM: printout of part of a typical set of programmed instructions (use part of as illustration?)

Thus CADCAM will now read

3, 4, 7 + p'tout illustration (Vulcan)

Having examined both your essential and secondary sets of data, you will have assembled a series of information sources which deal broadly with the same topic or closely related topics.

7 Your next task is to impose a coherent and logical structure on your cluster groups of data. What form the structure takes will depend entirely on the nature of your brief and the written-word medium you employ. For instance, you may choose to use a report structure: introduction, information, conclusions, recommendations; or the more formal: terms of reference, procedure, findings, conclusions, recommendations (see pages 76–78). Whatever format you use, your piece of writing will need to have a clear beginning, middle and end. Thus the most important composition decisions you make will occur at this stage. You have to decide what groupings of your assembled material are best suited to

- Background or Introduction or Overview
- Development or Detailed treatment or Findings ▶

- Conclusions (and recommendations if asked for) or Results or Outcomes or Summary of findings

There are various titles for each of the three sections. Thus a coherent and logically sequenced structure of the data for the IT in manufacturing report may well look like this:

1 **Brief**: clear summary of the task or instructions to be carried out (terms of reference in a formal report)

2 **Introduction**: reference to fast pace of change in past decade centring on CNC, robotics, CADCAM, MRP, JIT, computerised stores and production-line systems and quality assurance; implications of costs associated with IT-centred manufacturing on (a) multinationals and (b) small firms

3 **Information**:
   3.1 CADCAM in the manufacturing context
   3.2 CNC in toolmaking, jigmaking and production processes
   3.3 IT in production-line processes: robotics, JIT, computerised parts delivery – robot 'trains' from stores to production line
   3.4 Computerised quality assurance systems in manufacturing; random testing, statistical analysis, summary reports
   3.5 Computerised manufacturing resource planning – materials, parts, production and maintenance centrally controlled by computer

4 **Conclusions**: summary of major information points

5 **Recommendations**: as the information section will have emphasised the cost and human resource development implications of the topic, the recommendations section would concentrate on 3 or 4 approaches which small firms could adopt in order to stay current and competitive, such as:
   5.1 Know-how sharing with other small firms
   5.2 Shared purchase and access to expensive IT equipment

KEY POINT

Remember at the data-organising stage, effective sections or paragraphs deal with unified topic areas, for example, robotics, quality or JIT, but not a rambling mishmash of all three. By establishing early links and commonalities between each data item, you are effectively creating embryonic sections or paragraphs.

Using data cards to organise information

A very helpful technique for sifting and organising your raw data for a piece of writing is to make use of data cards (Fig. 2.5). In essence, these are the same kind of cards referred to on page 23 as a tool for storing spoken word key points. In the written-word context, the technique works as follows:

- For each researched item (brochure, notes, article, etc.) produce a data card (see example below) which contains the key information you abstract from it: title of work, author, publication year, etc. and a set of bullet points of key topics.
- As for the above procedure, prioritise your set of cards into essential, useful/secondary and largely irrelevant; bear in mind that you can save precious time in deciding whether a researched piece is or is not relevant before you make out its data card.
- When you have completed a data card for each research item, set them out in columns, rows or fans and look for the grouping similarities detailed in the above section, a process not unlike playing solo patience.
- When you have established your topic groupings, consider the best running order for each set of data cards, and (as also outlined above) how best

Figure 2.5 Data cards help to organise source data.

IMPLEMENTING TOTAL QUALITY MANAGEMENT ← Key data for references, footnotes, bibliography,
L&M Munro-Faure Pitman & Financial Times 1992

CHAP 9: SUCCESS STORIES - THE ICL EXPERIENCE pp 228-242 ← Quick references for consulting original text again.

- *Founded 1968; 26 000 employees - 70 countries*
- *TQM intro 1986; customer-driven, Director of Quality appt;*
- *£1m spent on TQM yearly* ← Easy to follow bullet points to act as memory-joggers for previous reading and note-taking of Chapter 9
- *TQM phases: Planning, Identifying Quality Costs, Training & Communication, Customer Opinion, Employee Opinion, Price of Non-Conformance, Prevention & Improvement, Benchmarking, Recognition*

NB Customer Service Graph p 240: Unnecessary Service Visits to structure the groups so as to provide a clear beginning, middle and end.

- During your writing phase, use each card as a memory-jogger, and tick or cross out each card's set of points as you use them. In this way, you will ensure that you do not overlook any important data.

Although the data-card system is rather more laborious than simply classifying the original researched items, it does have major advantages. It enables a very careful selection of points to be made, it avoids omissions and it becomes easy to compile footnotes, appendices and bibliographies from the clear display on each data card.

Effective structures for the written word at work

People working in both private and public sector organisations today have one key, common denominator – they are all busy. The post-recession creation of the 'flat' organisational pyramid was achieved by stripping out layers of middle management and operatives. Thus those employees left in work have been obliged to take on more responsibilities. This development has had a direct knock-on effect for written communications. In order to get read and acted upon, the written word at work today has to combine:

- brevity
- easy reading and visual appeal
- clear details of any actions required (by when)
- a positive, bridge-building approach and tone

A famous UK outplacement consultant (a specialist at securing posts for redundant managers) recently wrote that, in his view, a curriculum vitae had to make an impact within about ten seconds, or its reader would simply pick up another from the heap of job applications. Clearly, not all textual communications enjoy such a potentially short life; indeed, some complex reports may require two to three readings in order for their content to be absorbed and understood. Nevertheless, the creation of a structure for a piece of writing which makes it easier rather than more difficult for its structure to be taken up and accepted is a crucial factor in its overall effectiveness. The following section provides a set of helpful guidelines in devising effective structures for your written work.

Labelling and titling your written work

An essential habit is to label and title your written work correctly. Business letter subject headings could be:

Special offer on Arctura's five-year guaranteed vacuum double glazing!

Overdue January account £1243.95 customer account no. DC 539/6/93

Relocation of Solent Office Cleaners Limited from 1 July 1995

Report or memorandum titles could be:

Investigation into extending company activities into franchised, fast-food outlets

Trends and developments in geriatric care

Leisure centre development: the next decade

An investigation of current high labour turnover with recommendations for securing reductions to acceptable levels

KEY POINT

An effective title for a letter, memorandum or report is one which is short (ideally 12–15 words) but which simply and clearly acts as a summary for the document's main theme or content. As far as possible, effective titles communicate what, when where, why, who.

In addition to providing a clear title, a document heading also needs to detail who it is for, when it was produced, its status (such as whether it is confidential) and who has been sent a copy. The need to display such information was instrumental in the development of the currently accepted memorandum heading (Fig. 2.6). The following check-list summarises the key labelling and titling items you need to consider at the head of a written piece:

Key components of document headings

- the title of the work
- name(s) of its author(s) and job title(s)
- date of its production/distribution
- details of its recipient(s): names and job title(s)
- nature of the document's status (e.g private, confidential, for the personal attention of ...)
- indication as to whether a draft or final version (e.g. first draft, discussion draft)
- details of who has been sent a copy (e.g. circulation: copies to: informational copies to:
- any reference given to the work (e.g. computer file name dweitrpt.doc or DWE/sp/12/6/9X)

Figure 2.6 Most memorandums conform to this style.

MEMORANDUM

CONFIDENTIAL

To: Ann Thomas, Senior Care Officer **Date:** 3 June 199–

From: John Foster, Care Assistant

Copies to: Asha Khan, Headteacher
Kim Fox, Care Dept. Manager,

Subject: REQUESTED HOME LEAVE FOR JASON GOODMAN
10–14 JUNE 199–

I should like to draw your attention the recent request from Jason's guardians that he be allowed a week's . . .

Each of the above components has a job to do, from informing interested staff about who else has received a copy (essential when it is confidential) to a date of distribution. Inserting correct dates aids filing and indicates how up-to-date a document is likely to be. The insertion of a document status (such as confidential) encourages staff not to leave a letter or memo lying around for anyone to read. Note that some formal reports are given a front page which suitably displays details of status, title, authors, report commissioner(s) and publication date.

Setting the scene

This important first part of a document's structure carries out the following functions:

- to brief the reader on the document's context: the background, situation, brief or terms of reference against which it is being written
- to provide key references for the reader: who is involved, what the document is about, when and where did key activities take place, what is the desired outcome

Thus the function of an opening or introductory section is to supply a short, simple and clear summary of the purposes of the document so that its reader is fully equipped and prepared to take in the details which follow.

Detailing the message

The middle part of a document supplies the meat in the sandwich, such as factual details, arguments, persuasions or analyses, which communicate the key information involved. Unlike crime writing, no prizes are given to the authors of vocational documents for saving up the most important bit of information until the final paragraph. Effective middle sections tend to adopt the structure shown in Figure 2.7. Bear in mind, however that other common structures exist, such as the pros and cons structure and the argumentative structure.

Figure 2.7 Begin with the most important idea.

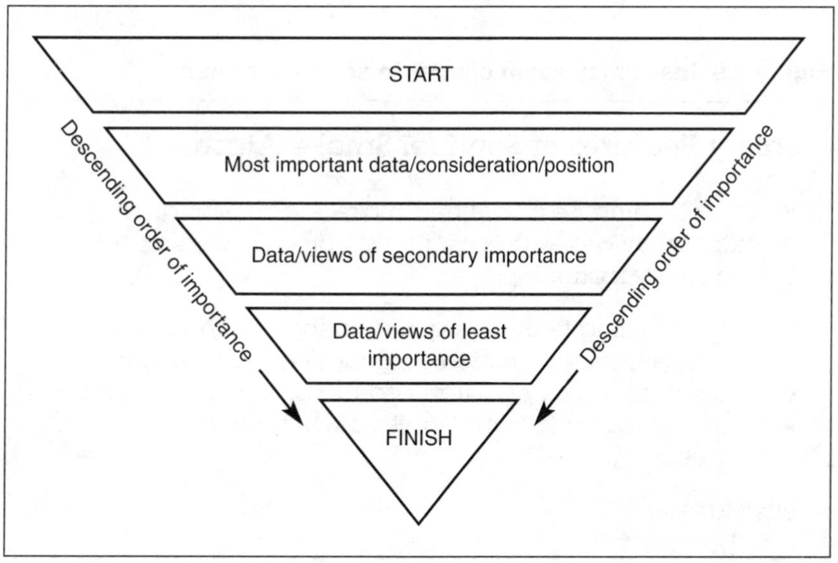

Figure 2.8 Business letters tend to use short paragraphs.

. . . My mother is aged 78 and suffers from chronic rheumatoid arthritis. As you will be aware, this inevitably results in some days being worse than others. She does need regular assistance with dressing and undressing and the use of toilet facilities; however, she does still enjoy clear mental faculties and would resent, I know, being treated as elderly and incapable. I should therefore need some reassurance about the qualification, caring and professional skills of your nursing staff.

Turning to financial matters, I should be grateful to receive full details of your tariff of costs for the range of services you offer. I have heard that you have self-contained apartments available at times for single residents, as well as shared twin accommodation for either married couples or residents of the same sex willing to share. I should therefore be pleased to receive details of both types of accommodation. Also, I understand your company offers insurance cover for increases in accommodation costs as a hedge against inflation in future years. Particulars of this scheme would likewise be welcome . . .

Recalling the important guideline about a document's need to be brief and impart a ready visual appeal, you should keep firmly in mind the need for a document's middle section to be divided into short, easily absorbed subsections. In terms of the business letter, this is achieved by the use of short paragraphs, sometimes preceded by paragraph headings (Fig. 2.8). Notice that each paragraph consists of no more than seven lines of text. As a result, its content is not too involved and is therefore readily understood. Each paragraph deals with a single, unified topic, the first with the mother's physical condition and the second with the costs of residing at the nursing home. Note, too, that each paragraph is made up of short, simple sentences which also help the reader to absorb their information promptly. Finally, each paragraph makes crystal clear what responses are requested of the recipient in terms of detailed information.

Although the conventions of letter layout rely essentially on strings of prose paragraphs, some letter writers use paragraph headings and bullet points with effect to combine a clear structure with quick and easy information take-up (Fig. 2.9). Note the use of an emboldened heading, the set of short bullet points and surrounding white space. All aid the reader in quickly absorbing the persuasive content of the sales message. The structure of a formal report (Fig. 2.10) follows a set of conventions which include setting out each findings section beneath a referenced and accentuated heading (in this case, emboldened initial capitals). Everything set out beneath this first subheading must refer explicitly to it. The next level of subheading refers only to the main pool inspection. Correspondingly, the points set out beneath it are concerned only with the main pool inspection. Other subsections are likely to be:

3.2 Diving pool
3.3 Children's pool area

together with ther related clutch of points. The highly schematised structure of the short formal report enables each point to be clearly alluded to in any subsequent document because of its unique reference, e.g. 3.1.1, 3.1.2, 3.1.3, and in further details, 3.1.1.1, 3.1.1.2. Another benefit of this schematised

Figure 2.9 Ideas may seem clearer in sections or lists.

Safety Features of Sentinel Smoke Alarms

When you purchase a Sentinel Smoke Alarm, you are buying an extensively developed and tested product with many built-in safety features:

- a simple testing feature, requiring only a torch to be shone at a special sensor – no tedious ladder erection needed!
- installed dry battery guaranteed to last at least 12 months
- automatic warning signal emitted when battery nearly exhausted

etc. etc.

Figure 2.10 Sections in a report may be numbered and indented.

3.0 FINDINGS

3.1 Inspection of the Swimming Pool Complex

The swimming pool at Midchester Leisure Centre is just short of international standard length. The pool complex comprises an eight lane pool, three metres in depth at the deep end, and adjacent diving pool and children's pool area with water-splash and toddlers' shallow bathing area.

3.1.1 Main pool inspection

An inspection of the main pool area revealed a generally satisfactory standard of safety and preventative precautions in place. However, the following items did not meet required safety standards:

3.1.1.1 ***Emergency flotation aids***

Two aids are elderly and disintegrating at the corners causing buoyancy material to break off

3.1.1.2 ***Raised floor tiles***

Three raised floor tiles were detected at the approach to the steps on the south side mid pool access point, exposing bare feet to cuts and bruising hazards

3.1.1.3 ***Handrail, north side, deep-end steps***

The handrail immediately next to the north side deep-end retaining wall has worn loose as a result of frequent use

structure is that the relationship of subsections to their respective section headings is immediately clear. Such clarity is also supported by the system of progressive indentation which moves data systematically towards the right-hand side of the page as it becomes more detailed and extending in meaning only its immediate subheading. Lastly, the use of double spacing and white space around the indentations causes the text to stand out and hit the reader's eye more strongly.

Figure 2.11 shows a bold heading for a general manager offering an overall employment package worth some £40,000. Beneath, it sets out its job offer and job expectations as a dual set of bullet points. The small print size is probably justified by the eye-catching annual pay package.

Figure 2.11 Catchy headlines persuade us to read small print.

General manager £40k

The Job

- To be responsible for the operation of two major refuse transfer stations and a civic amenity site located in Wandsworth.
- To provide strategic management, with particular emphasis on planning future waste disposal arrangements for the authority.
- To be responsible for the management of over 80 staff based at two stations and civic amenity site.
- Responsible for the efficient operation of budgetary and administrative systems as well as the negotiation of major contracts.
- To actively promote the running of the operations in a safety conscious and environmentally sensitive way.

The Person

The person we are seeking would ideally possess.

- An engineering background HNC/degree level.
- Significant managerial experience within the waste disposal industry or process engineering.
- Advanced negotiating skills.
- A flair for strategic thinking and priority setting in a dynamic environment.
- The ability to assume 'hands on' control when required.

Although experience in the waste industry would be an advantage, consideration will be given to candidates with other appropriate experience.

[Reproduced by kind permission of Western Riverside Waste Authority]

Closing the message

The closing part of a written message is, in many ways, the most important. Consider for a moment the time, trouble and cost of conceiving, processing, printing and distributing such a message. A two-page letter may take a manager and secretary between them some 30 – 40 minutes to dictate, transcribe, text process, print and deposit in a mail out-tray; add the costs of printed notepaper and envelope and internal and external collection and delivery. Believe it or not, the total cost in a London office block will be £20–30. It is highly likely, therefore, given the costs of such a letter, that it will impart important information, and will request its recipient to take some form of specific action, such as returning information, processing a sales order or confirming a hotel booking.

Figure 2.12 Requests for action should come in the conclusion.

> As our current fleet insurance policy expires in two months' time, I should be grateful to receive your firm quotation for the calender year commencing 1 July 199–. In order to carry out the necessary internal administration involved in changing the insurer for our company car fleet, I shall need to receive your written quotation no latter than Wednesday 12 May 199–. Please do not hesitate to contact me if you need any further information on the above telephone number, extension 2505.
>
> I look forward to hearing from you.

The request for action to be taken in a letter, memorandum or report is inserted at the close of the document, so that its reader will take it on board *after* having absorbed the related data of the middle section which precedes it. Figure 2.12 makes the following points, clearly and carefully:

1 The 'firm' quotation referred to stipulates a total, exact sum which will be payable, and not a vague ballpark figure on to which may be added several hundreds or thousands of pounds, thus wasting the writer's time.

2 There is a precise confirmation of the insurance period.

3 It is further stipulated that the quotation is wanted in writing, not over the telephone.

4 A very clear deadline is supplied for the delivery of the information, with a subtle hint that failure to meet it might result in the insurance company losing the business.

5 The closing stage ends with a polite offer of additional assistance if needed and a courteous closing statement.

The stock opening of Figure 2.13, 'It is recommended that ...', is both formal and impersonal. Note that a rational or logical reason is given for each recommendation. No deadlines are given, since the nature of recommendations is to advise. It will be for a future meeting of the council, probably of its leisure and amenities committee, to make any decisions arising from the recommendations given as a result of an in-depth investigation. Lastly, note the brevity of the recommendations, all the related detail will have been supplied under the findings.

Figure 2.13 Give reasons for your recommendations.

> **5.0 Recommendations**
>
> **5.1 Re-opening of Midchester Canal**
>
> It is recommended that the Council seek a National Heritage grant of £500,000 to be put towards the costs of re-opening the Midchester Canal; estimated annual income is put at £120,000, and the total estimated cost of renewal and re-opening of £1 million would be met with in some ten years.
>
> **5.2 Membership of the English Tourist Board, Southern Region**
>
> It is further recommended that the Council directly seeks membership of the Southern Region of the English Tourist Board; the Board offers extensive support and access to national marketing and informational facilities. Given the major policy shift of the county plan in terms of encouraging more employment opportunities in local leisure and tourism enterprises, membership of the Tourist Board would provide a valuable source of expertise and support.
>
> **5.3 Establishment of Central Tourist Information Office ....**

The three options in Figure 2.14 are given briefly and clearly. A rationale is supplied for each one, along with a brief summary of its main advantages and disadvantages. Finally, the working party comes off the fence by making clear its preference for Option 1.

Closing sections of a written document make absolutely clear what actions are desired of its recipient(s) and, if appropriate, by when. Sometimes they summarise the key points of middle sections and provide a final view or decision reached after a pros and cons discussion.

Figure 2.14 Sometimes you may be asked to choose an option.

CONCLUSIONS

Three viable alternatives are open to the Trust, which are set out below.

Option One

To allocate £750,000 from the Trust's financial reserves to pay for the repairs and refurbishements urgently needed for Mead House residential home. This option would have the advantage of minimising disruption to residents, since it could be effected in stages, but would seriously deplete financial reserves.

Option Two

To put Mead House – with its extensive grounds – on to the property market; this option might result in the Trust acquiring some £1.2–1.4 million to invest in obtaining an alternative residential home. However, the property market is currently very slow and such an option for re-housing residents might take many months, if not years.

Option Three

To relocate individual residents in other of the Trust's residential homes. This option would be financially least expensive, but the potential impact upon residents in terms of the stress and confusion resulting could prove severe. Also, fitter residents have established long-term networks of friends and social activities in the immediate vicinity of Mead House.

The advice of the Working Party is take up Option One, and to develop a number of fund-raising activities in order to make good the Trust's current level of financial reserves.

KEY POINTS

- Never attempt to compose a document without first having drawn up a set of points in a logical sequence to use as guidance and reference; writing from off the top of your head will almost certainly cause you to waffle and wander.
- Make sure that the main headings, and sub-headings you devise communicate simply and clearly what their section is about. Avoid single-word headings that convey very little information, e.g. Employment, Opportunities.
- Almost always start each new paragraph or section with your most important point and work downwards to your least important; your aim is to communicate directly and easily, so no prizes for the delayed surprise or sting in the tail.

Opening section

- Always check that you have fully set the scene or context of your written document, so that your reader grasps quickly the main reason for it, and its most significant parts; use the five Ws – who, what, when, where, why – to check that your opening section is complete.

Middle section

- Before starting to compose your middle section, go over your set of points once more to check that they are in a suitable order and that nothing has been omitted. Cross out each point on your planning sheet as you set it down; this will ensure that you do not overlook anything when you are concentrating on choosing the best words and sentence structures. Remember to divide your middle into clear subsections with suitable headings. Do not allow a subsection to go on for too long. Keep in mind that an individual subsection or paragraph should deal with just one unified topic or theme. Do not mix points which have no connection with each other in a single section.

Closing section

- Before commencing your closing section, make sure you have crystallised your desired outcome, usually what you want the recipient to do, or what final standpoint you wish to communicate. If appropriate, supply a suitable deadline, not one which is unrealistic or impossible to meet. Avoid using sentences like 'I look forward to hearing from you *as soon as possible*,' which comes across as vague and undemanding as the Spanish manana!
- If you are expected to convey a decision, do so; don't sit on the fence. If appropriate (as in a discussion paper) include a brief summary of the main points from your middle section which justify the final view you communicate. ▶

- Almost without exception, your written documents should be composed as a series of written sentences, whether as a series of prose paragraphs or schematically set out report sections. Therefore seek to construct grammatically correct sentences which are short rather than long. If you have access to a grammar-checking software application, use it on sections you are unsure about.
- Always carry out conscientious proof-reading and topping and tailing checks before distributing a written document; errors in spelling and punctuation will certainly detract from its impact. A name omitted from a circulation list or the failure to label a document confidential may have serious human relations consequences.

Different structures for various writing needs

The following examples illustrate various commonly occurring structures, all with clear beginnings, middles and ends, which are used by work-based writers for letters, reports, discussion papers, analytical writing, advertising brochures, etc.

Business letter

- **Introductory paragraph:** provides reason for writing and main context points, such as dates, references, people involved.
- **Development paragraphs:** supply details of letter's theme, e.g. details of new product, reasons for complaint, details of overdue account, features of nursing home.
- **Closing paragraph:** clear details of actions or outcomes requested or required; statement of any deadlines set or desired; summary of any actions requested of letter's recipient, etc. Courteous close, e.g. I look forward to hearing from you.

Discussion paper

- **Preamble or introduction:** a brief outline of the scope and nature of the matter for discussion with any major informational points.

  Arguments for/advantages/benefits: a series of paragraphs or sections which detail in a logical sequence the points in favour of a given viewpoint.

  Arguments against/disadvantages/costs: a parallel series of points against a given viewpoint or proposition.
- **Summary:** a closing section which briefly and objectively evaluates the strength of either position and comes down clearly either for or against.

Note: Sometimes the context is such that no choice is made in the paper, since it is a briefing document for, say, a board of directors or a management meeting.

Informal report

- **Introduction:** sets out the purposes of the report, who asked for it and deadline for submission; also provides a brief background or context for the report who, why, what, where, when.
- **Information:** a logically sequenced set of paragraphs or sections which detail the main findings of the report.
- **Conclusions:** a summary of the main points of the report, together with any recommendations, if they were asked for in the brief.

  Note: An informal report indicates at its head who it is for, who is its author, the date of its distribution, who has been sent a copy, as well as a clear title (usually a summary of the brief).

Advertisement brochure or leaflet

- **Eye-catching slogan and graphic:** the slogan's purpose is to gain the reader's attention, say by being funny, outrageous, hugely cost-cutting or cleverly unusual.
- **Development of main selling points:** a very succinct listing of the item's main selling features and benefits, usually ending with a main or unique selling benefit.
- **Action conclusion:** a statement aimed at persuading the reader to take prompt action to buy, e.g. Offer ends in seven days! Post your order now and enjoy a 25% saving!

Fact-sheet

- **Background:** this opening section details the background or context which the fact-sheet is responding to, perhaps to provide a briefing on an overseas state prior to an export sales visit or fact-finding mission.
- **Information:** the middle section provides the detailed, researched data under headings like climate, religion, centres of population, social customs.
- **Summary:** some fact-sheets summarise key informational points; others simply progress in informational terms from the most to the least important, ending there.

  Note: fact-sheets also include prominent titles, authorship, publication date and distribution list; they are also set out in a highly schematic format to aid uptake.

Short formal report

- **Terms of reference:** this opening section states (or quotes) the precise briefing for the report, say to undertake an investigation into a given situation and to provide recommendations for the resolution of any problems unearthed; it also details who asked for the report and when, as well as the deadline for its submission.
- **Procedure:** the section briefly details the research procedures which were followed in order to acquire the report's data, e.g. desk research, surveys, interviews, observation.
- **Findings:** the findings are set out logically to show the main features of the information uncovered; usually they proceed from most important the least important.
- **Conclusions:** the conclusions briefly summarise the main findings, *but they do not comment upon them* in terms of what might be done.
- **Recommendations:** this section is only included if specifically asked for in the report's terms of reference, and its points are listed from most urgent to least urgent.

  Note: The short formal report is characterised by a schematic layout and numbered referencing system; it is also written factually in the third person.

Scientific paper

- Title of paper
- Names of authors
- Places of work of authors/publishing location
- Date of publication of paper
- Abstract of findings and summary conclusions
- Introduction
- Methods
- Results and discussion
- References

What do you think?

1 What research methods and systems have worked for you?

2 What experience have you gained of short cuts to finding information in libraries which you can share with your class costudents?

3 What features of structure and layout and general information presentation do you expect to find in a good reference or study text?

4 What techniques have you tended to adopt so far in order to classify and organise your research data into a writing plan? What mistakes have you made which you can share in order to develop a pool of what to do and what to avoid doing?

5 Typical ways of structuring a written document include chronological, descending order of main points, pros and cons arguments and geographical survey. All of them comply with the beginning, middle and end guideline. What other possible structures can you add to your group's repertoire?

Student pair skills-building activity

First, choose *one* of the topics set out below:

1 **A letter:** you saw an advertisement recently for part-time work in a flexible-hours pattern as assistant to the production manager of a local factory which packages a range of cosmetics and perfumery products. The firm, Safepak Ltd, is looking for someone with business nous, an ability with numbers and good communication skills. Hours 18–21 weekly; pay £4.90 per hour plus productivity bonus.

2 **A discussion paper:** your study centre is considering timetabling some of its full-time programmes (including GNVQs) between 6:00 P.M. and 8:30 P.M. in the evenings, Mondays to Fridays in order to free up classrooms during the day, so as to cope with planned expansion. Your students' association has been invited to submit a discussion paper to your centre's next academic board meeting, which highlights the pros and cons of this proposal, as seen by the centre's student population.

3 **A short formal report:** your local district council is reviewing its sports and leisure amenity provision. As part of a wide survey, it has asked all interest groups to submit background material to inform its recreation and leisure committee. You both sit on a group committee of local youth clubs. Your committee has decided to respond with a report which details what is available and where deficiencies and shortcomings exist.

For the topic and document you select, compile a set of relevant points using an appropriate layout. Remember you are not composing the full document, but creating a working plan from which the complete document could be expanded and detailed.

How to structure paragraphs

As you will be aware, a range of written documents – letters, articles, discussion papers, memoranda, etc. – include extensive sections which are constructed and presented as prose paragraphs. You may be forgiven for assuming that their writers dive in at the beginning and surface some 200–300 words later, having composed and set down a string of sentences which emerged in some mysterious creative process. Nothing could be further from the truth. Effective writers of connected or continuous prose, as it is termed, decide beforehand how they will structure a paragraph, and where – in order to create varying effects – the main point or topic sentence of the paragraph will be inserted.

The loose paragraph

In a loose paragraph (Fig. 2.15) the sentence communicating its most important point comes first, so the rest of the paragraph tends to act as further explanation or to contain examples which flesh out the main point.

Figure 2.15 Loose paragraphs put the main point first.

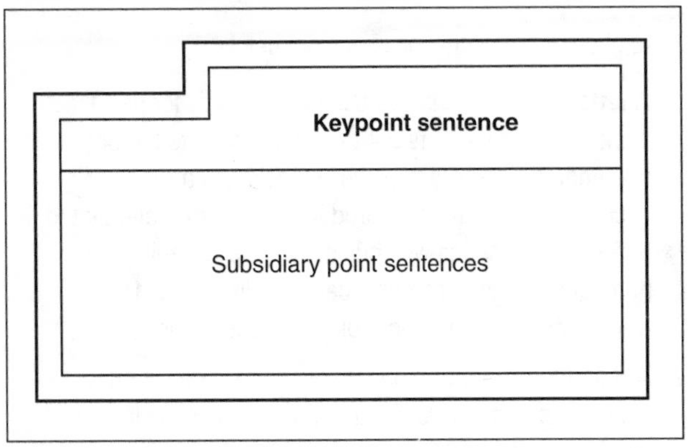

Example:

> *A good care worker is able to empathise with those people for whom he or she is responsible.* In other words, such a care worker must be able to imagine how it feels to be uncomfortable in bed, but unable to move without assistance. He or she must also be capable of imagining the awkward embarrassment a patient or resident experiences when wishing to bathe or to go to the toilet because they need help from another person. Such a care worker also needs a positive and outgoing temperament which can cheer up those being cared for – even on a drab winter's day or when depressed and down because of a chronic illness.

In the above extract, the three sentences which follow the main one all give examples of empathy, so they serve to enlarge the reader's appreciation of what the writer considers to be the key ability of a good careworker. Although loose paragraphs help the reader by stating the most important point first, they do have a downside. The reader unconsciously tends to skim over the rest of the paragraph in a search of the next main point. However, loose paragraphs are ideal for opening paragraphs of chapters, articles or papers because, by putting the main point in the first sentence, the writer can catch the reader's attention and hold it. Perhaps loose paragraphs are so called because they have a main sentence followed by a series of subsidiary sentences like a loose, flapping tail.

The mixed paragraph

In the mixed paragraph (Fig. 2.16) the main point is inserted in the middle; this enables a writer to work up to a peak of interest and then to descend from it.

Figure 2.16 Mixed paragraphs develop an idea then explore it.

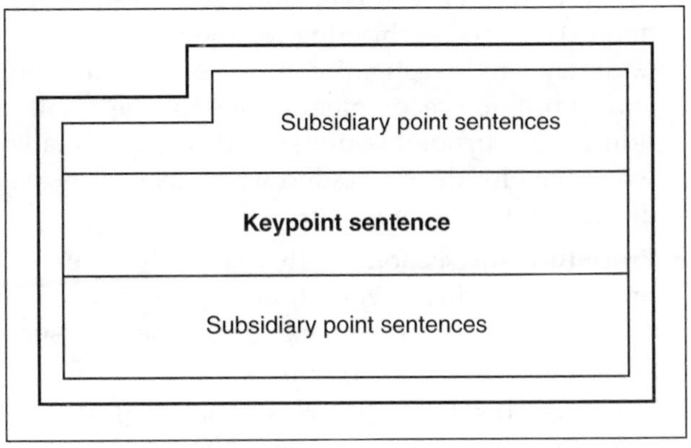

Example:

> The visitor's first sight of Barchester when arriving by train is of the Victorian gasworks, as the engine hauls its carriages around the final bend before coming to a stop in the main station. The entry into the station is not particularly remarkable, save for some enamelled hoardings advertising holiday-making at Barchester in the 1930s which amazingly have survived the ravages of improving and environmentally friendly redevelopment. Barchester's town centre is likewise unspoiled. It fairly bristles with cafes and restaurants – all with cheerful frontages: it boasts a fine art gallery and museum with a precious collection of early Anglo-Saxon jewellery as well as three cinemas, two discos and a bingo-hall. At the foot of the town centre's high street lies Barchester beach, all golden sand, green seaweed and pink candyfloss. *Barchester has everything for the traditional British holiday-maker!* Indeed, Barchester's bed-and-breakfast landladies are known to be the sternest in the land. Not a speck of sand nor a single seashell mars the orderliness and cleanliness of the sitting and breakfast rooms over which they preside. In fact the only cleaner thing about Barchester is its trams. Their spotless blue, yellow and white livery is a joy to behold, and a ticket to the pier and back costs only 35p!

The advantage of the mixed paragraph construction is that it allows its writer to build up the reader's interest quietly and steadily, to make a central point and then to embellish or add to it. Mixed paragraphs are useful to construct when wishing to create a variation between the rush to communicate an important point and the desire to save it up (thus tantalising the reader) until the very last moment.

The periodic paragraph

For conscious effect, the main point in the periodic paragraph (Fig. 2.17) is deliberately held back until its end, causing the reader's interest and expectation to grow during the build-up.

Example:

> I was driving along the motorway towards a seaside marina. It was a sunny Sunday morning and I was taking my sister out to look at the yachts and motor-

Figure 2.17 Periodic paragraphs pack their punch near the end.

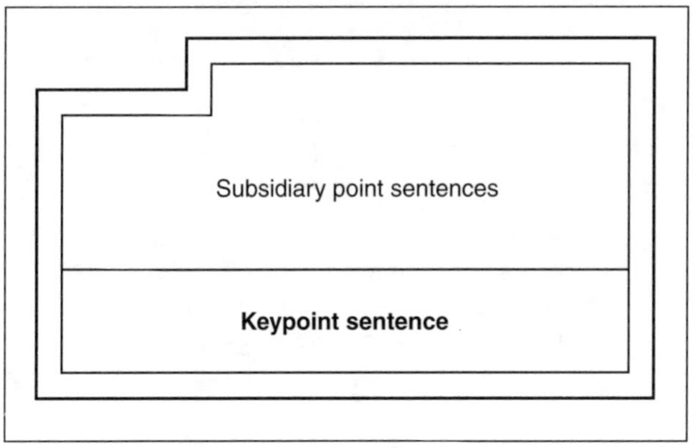

boats, so that my wife could get on quietly with preparing lunch. The traffic was busy, but not that busy. We came upon the accident suddenly after a gradual bend in the road. We were flagged down by several agitated people who had got out of their cars on the hard shoulder to go to the aid of a small car which had turned upside down, having rolled down a short embankment. Fortunately, any possible further motion had been halted by a stand of saplings. As we arrived, three teenagers were scrabbling out of the car's side windows. One had a gaping wound across her forehead; another seemed to have broken an arm. I opened the boot of my car, looking for something to use to help the victims of the accident and found only a dirty curtain, a half-empty de-icing canister and a map of Kent. Past me raced a young man and woman, each carrying first-aid kits. I felt bad and inadequate. *I recalled the campaign slogan: First aid saves lives! and purchased the largest one on offer at the service station two miles down the road once it was clear that the kids were basically all right.*

The main advantage of the periodic paragraph structure (so called because the main point is left until the end or final full stop) is that the reader's interest is maintained over an extended period. All the preceding sentences have to be absorbed *before* the impact of the main sentence is released. As a result, the final sentence of the paragraph acquires a dramatic or emphatic force. The whole thrust of the paragraph is towards its final sentence, and so the paragraph ends on a high note. Figure 2.18 compares the impact of the three paragraph structures from start to finish.

How to structure sentences

If paragraphs are the macrostructure, sentences are the microstructure. At least as important as paragraphs, sentences are the basic unit of developed written communication. Even sentences of only four words may have an enormous impact upon millions of people: *The war is over!* The following section provides a series of helpful tips on how to construct sentences which will have the desired effect on your reader.

Sentence length

The rule of thumb is to avoid constructing sentences of more than 30 words. In fact, of more than 25 words if a good deal of them are multisyllabic. English language experts have found that sentences of more than 30 words tend to cause their readers to have difficulty in comprehending them:

> While I would be prepared to give sympathetic consideration to what you are endeavouring to establish, and although the circumstances of the cloudburst you describe as having a direct bearing upon the accident are no doubt – at least in our own mind – relevant and true, I think you will have to agree that the arrival of the fire-engine around the corner you detail in your accident sketch was entirely coincidental, depending entirely upon the decision of the senior claims inspector.

Most of us get lost in the above sentence about halfway through. The writer creates so many ifs, buts and maybes that he loses control entirely of the sentence's construction. By seeking to roll up into a single sentence what ought to be two or three, the writer only manages to cause confusion and creased foreheads.

However, dangers also exist in composing a succession of short and simple sentences:

> The morning was dark and wet. The alarm failed to go off. I awoke late. So I missed breakfast. I also missed the bus. I arrived at work three-quarters of an hour late. Miss Parkinson gave me a right rollicking.

Unless we knew better, we might assume that the writer of the above piece was young and inexperienced, having difficulty in linking together more than one idea in a sentence. As a result, the writing appears immature and juvenile. This problem can be

Figure 2.18 Impact against time for three paragraph structures.

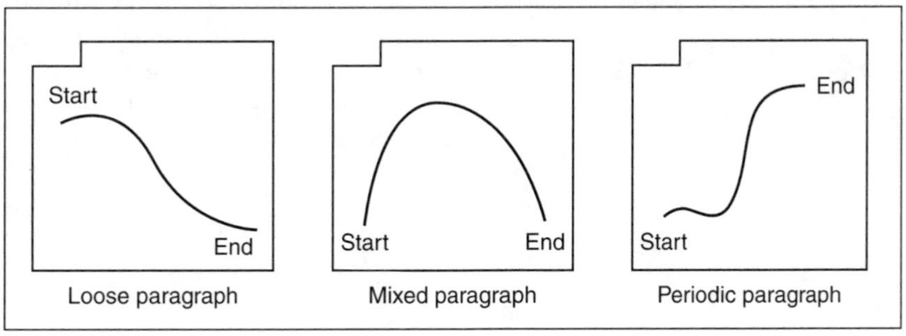

overcome by using conjunctions, words that link ideas together.

Despite the weaknesses of producing a succession of very short sentences it is possible to create effective emphasis by using just one or two. The finish to the following extract is short and sweet:

> The past sales year has been characterised by problems associated with a very slow emergence from recession. As a consequence, recovery of demand in the UK home market for our range of stainless steel kitchenware has been slow. Fortunately, export demand grew significantly during the past financial year, and has spearheaded our performance. We have far exceeded our sales target. Well done every one!

Quick question: Is the above paragraph loose, mixed or periodic?

Linking connected ideas within a single sentence

As we become more proficient in constructing sentences, we progress from composing successions of simple sentences like these:

subject	verb	extension
The morning	was	dark and wet
I	awoke	late

With experience, we become capable of both comprehending and composing connected ideas or messages, which we link into a single sentence:

> *As* the morning was dark and wet, I awoke late *and so* missed breakfast.

Connectors (grammatically termed conjunctions) like *as* and *and so* are used like railway couplings to link three ideas together within a single sentence. But note that each connected section must possess a subject (doer word) and a verb (action word) in order to sustain grammatical correctness. The following connectors or conjunctions are in general use for composing sentences:

Sentence connectors

The train was late *because* the guard fell sick.

Although the treatment was still being developed, she volunteered to try it.

If you promise to accompany me, I shall go to the meeting.

Either you accept our offer, *or* I call an official strike!

As you elected to plead guilty, I have decided to impose a moderate penalty, *which* I very much hope you will take heed of, *since* another appearance before this court will most certainly not find me as generous.

The main connecting conjunctions used to link ideas in a single sentence are

and, but, then, next, yet   either or, neither nor   as, because, since   if, whether, as if   where, when, what, which, why, how, until   though, although, even though   in order to, so as to

There are two ways of linking connected ideas; conjunctions may be used as the first word in the sentence, or they may come later on:

> *Although* the treatment was still being developed, she volunteered to try it.
>
> She volunteered to try it, *although* the treatment was still being developed.

These sentences contain two ideas: *she volunteered to try it* is the main idea, *although the treatment was still being developed* is the secondary or subordinate idea. By placing the subordinate idea first, a greater sense of expectation and impact is created in the reader, who has to wait for it.

Other sentence connectors

Separate sentences may also be linked together or contrasted by using the following types of connecting word:

Reinforcers: moreover, furthermore, indeed, in addition, certainly

> The personal stair-lift is absolutely safe! *Moreover,* we guarantee its construction for five years.

Contrasters: however, on the other hand, even so, nevertheless

> This type of polypropylene is extremely strong. *However,* it does become brittle over time.

Useful pairs: either ... or   neither ... nor   both ... and   not only ... but also   the more ... the more

> *The more* people live longer, *the more* money the state has to earmark to pay for their health services.

Using conjunctions and connectors like those illustrated above will help you to structure sentences which are interesting to read and which convey their meaning clearly because they run and flow together.

Individual skills-building activities

Select *one* of the following topics:

(a) The qualities which an effective communicator displays
(b) The effect upon current written communication practices of the IT revolution
(c) Breaking through the glass ceiling – how today's young female professionals can make it to the top

TASK 1

Devise a skeletal, bullet-point plan spanning three paragraphs of continuous prose relevant to your topic's title.

TASK 2

In the three paragraphs you are about to compose, use constructions which incorporate (once only) *each* of the following connecting words/ phrases:

moreover furthermore however nevertheless
not only... but also although because so as to
whether yet which as soon as after having

You may use each one either as the first word of a fresh sentence, or within a sentence.

TASK 3

Write out your three paragraphs in full, with the first having a loose, the second a mixed and the third a periodic construction.

TASK 4

Circulate your version among your co-students and decide which compositions are particularly effective and why.

SUMMARY

The key points of this section are:

• For research to prove useful and its data acceptable to your readers, it must provide information which is accurate, up-to-date and cross-checked for validity and which acknowledges its sources.

• Useful local sources of information include study centre and public reference libraries, local universities, newspaper offices, the Citizens' Advice Bureau, council archives, museums and art galleries.

• Library catalogue systems include the Dewey decimal system, the Library of Congress system (for USA material) and author/subject computerised databases which cross-reference.

• An ISBN gives a published document a unique reference and is to be found on the inside flysheet.

• Key items to check when scanning a reference document for potential usefulness include cover blurb, publication date, date of last edition, date of last reprint, the table of contents and subject index, chapter headings and section headings, first and last paragraphs of chapters.

• A systematic approach to organising collected data prior to devising a writing plan is (1) divide material into essential, useful and largely irrelevant; (2) focus on the essential data; (3) set out main points on data cards (or similar) (4) organise cards into a suitable beginning, middle and end (5) use sequenced cards as prompts while composing the written document.

• Commonly employed beginning, middle and end structures include introduction, information, conclusion; context, development, action required; background, pros, cons, conclusion; slogan, development, action, conclusion.

• Paragraphs can have different effects upon readers by positioning key sentences either at the start (loose), in the middle (mixed) or at the end (periodic).

• Interest can be given to a piece of continuous prose by providing a variety from short, simple sentences to sentences of two or three clauses linked by connectors (conjunctions).

• The choice of words used in writing has a significant impact upon how a piece of writing will be received, ranging from factually and impersonally to subjectively and emotively or from familiarly and easily to formally and ritually.

What do you think?

1 Is the time and effort put into constructing varied paragraphs and sentences worthwhile in terms of winning a reader's active interest and influencing his or her responses?

2 If your own response to question 1 was broadly no, why do advertising agencies employ copywriters?

3 What, in your view, constitutes effective sentence structure and vocabulary choice?

4 Should a would-be writer in a work context possess a knowledge of English grammar, or is this something that can safely be left to a secretary?

5 What are the plus and minus factors of software support facilities such as spellchecker, grammar checker and thesaurus?

Self-check review test

1 What key features does effective research data possess?

2 List five major local sources of information,

3 Explain briefly how the Dewey decimal classification system works.

4 What is an ISBN? What is its purpose?

5 Outline succinctly how you would scan and skim a potential research document in order to assess its usefulness.

6 Outline briefly a suitable system for organising collected research data, so as to provide a plan for composition.

7 Describe briefly how you would structure a document such as a letter or memorandum which requires action to be taken by its recipient.

8 What are the five main sections of a short formal report?

9 Describe briefly what the following terms stand for: schematic layout, progressive indentation, white space.

10 List four textual display techniques, available from a modern WP package and which enable a writer to display text appealingly and emphatically.

11 Explain the difference in effect of loose, mixed and periodic paragraph constructions upon a reader.

12 What is a conjunction? Explain how conjunctions can be used to transform several simple sentences into one complex sentence.

When you have set down your own answers, compare them with those on page 198 and consult this section again if they differ.

> ***KEY POINT***
>
> When you are writing a continuous piece of prose, remember to vary your sentence structure as the above examples illustrate. Make use of connecting conjunctions to compress two or three ideas into a single sentence and thus to make it more interesting. Use the short, simple sentence sparingly for effect, but watch the length of your sentences carefully, so as to avoid losing your readers through becoming long-winded and rambling.

Individual skills-building activities

1 Select one of the following research activities and then carry out the tasks indicated below.

(a) Find out how your study centre library catalogues and classifies its reading and study materials and how it presents information about these systems to its library users.

(b) Find out the scope and nature of the role played by your county council's social services department and how this role is discharged.

(c) Find out what support services are available to small manufacturing businesses in your locality and the extent of their uptake by business owners.

(d) Find out what services are available in your locality for tourist visitors and local residents seeking leisure activities.

(e) Find out what developments are taking place in your locality to protect the environment and what kinds of actions are currently being taken in this area.

Tasks

(i) First obtain suitable and sufficient research data to enable you to produce an outline plan for a short informal report.

(ii) Next, organise your collected material into a suitable skeleton or outline plan, using either the data-card approach or an alternative you find helpful.

(iii) Submit your outline plan to your teacher for guidance, feedback and assessment.

(iv) When your outline plan has been returned, compose a suitable short informal report (of about four sides of printed A4) and submit this to your teacher for assessment, together with your outline plan.

2 Compose a letter of complaint, using these details:

Subject of complaint: Melody personal CD player
manufacturer's ref no. BJ 349821 XZ

Purchased: Midchester Hi-Fi Store, 57 High Street
Midchester, Midshire MM1 2RD
Date of purchase: 24 June 199–
Cause of complaint: CD disks rub against casing; music sounds distorted
Cost of CD player: £99.95
Sales assistant: Sharon

3 Pass the letter of complaint you produced for activity 2 to a fellow student. This student assumes the role of Mr/ Ms Kim Davis, the manager of Midchester Hi-Fi Store. Mr/Ms Davis asked to see the Melody personal player, and it was sent to the firm's repairs department for inspection. The inspecting technician has traced the defect to a dent in the casing caused by accidental damage such as being dropped. Thus it is not covered by its guarantee, according to Midchester Hi-Fi. Cost of transferring the mechanism to a new case is £35.00. Write a suitable letter to the complaining customer aimed at resolving the matter.

4 First undertake suitable research and then devise a display advertisement (using the dimensions of an A4 sheet of paper in landscape alignment) for *one* of the following posts:

(a) a secretary for your headteacher or principal

(b) a school/college senior caretaker or college maintenance engineer

(c) a refectory manager

(d) a fixed-term contract summer vacation manager to organise leisure activities for summer-school overseas students learning English as a foreign language

(e) a school/college nurse

5 Having undertaken your research, compose a leaflet (two sides of A4) which provides suitable information about your Advanced GNVQ course of study to potential future students. Your leaflet will form part of an information set to be used by your study centre at a variety of evenings – marketing, career, parents', etc. – in the schools in your study centre's catchment area. Mature students may produce a similar leaflet for adult students which will be available from local public libraries, etc.

When all leaflets are completed, display them in your baseroom and decide in a class discussion which ones proved most effective and why, in terms of structure, content and visual appeal.

CURRENT CONVENTIONS OF FORMAT AND DISPLAY

Technology-led changes in document formats

Over the past hundred years or so, various ways of putting written documents together, called document layout or format, have been devised. Such conventions were often adopted by large organisations to save time and money. For example, typing a customer's name and address within a displayed frame at the foot of an A4 letter enabled it to be displayed easily in a manila window envelope, simply by folding the notepaper in a prescribed manner. In this way, the effort required to type the same address on an envelope was eradicated. Technology has also played an important part in defining how documents will be set out. For instance, the accepted fully blocked business letter format (see the example on page 71) came about as a result of the ability of electric/electronic typewriters to turn down to a new line and to move across to the left-hand margin automatically. Thus it was very easy for the typist to start every fresh entry – address details, salutations, subject-headings, paragraphs, complimentary closes, enclosure references, etc. – all to a new line at the left-hand margin. Moreover, when text-processing software was developed in the 1980s, word-processing (WP) operators could choose to avoid a succession of ragged text edges at the right margin, simple by selecting a justification icon from the toolbar of a Windows WP package. By the same token, it became just as easy to select text and to embolden it, underline it, set it in italics or in a contrasting font and print size.

As a result of rapid changes in technology, format conventions which had lasted for decades were changed or ignored in a matter of a few years. In the 1950s and 1960s, for example, it was customary for letter addresses to be punctuated by a series of commas at line ends and full stops at the ends of abbreviations:

Rev. John Simmons,
The Vicarage,
21, St. Jude's Cres.,
WINCHESTER,
Hants.

Such a system was called closed punctuation, and as you will see, involved the typists in making nine keyboard depressions for the full stops and commas. The drive for office productivity swept such a convention away, and today, virtually all business letters are composed using open punctuation – no punctuation – saving time and money without losing accuracy or clarity:

Rev John Simmons
The Vicarage
21 St Jude's Cres
WINCHESTER
Hants

Given the far-reaching impact of IT changes in document production, it is true to say there are far fewer formatting rules today than there were 20 years ago. However, some have survived, and these are detailed below, together with guidance and examples of currently accepted formats, together with explanations and tips on good practice.

The business letter

The term *business letter* refers to all letters which are produced by a wide variety of private, public and voluntary organisations. Usually, such letters will have a preprinted letterhead at the top of their portrait-aligned A4 notepaper (Fig 2.19). Such letterheads are carefully designed, using a mix of logos, fonts and print sizes to transmit a particular image: respectability, modernity, fun, reliability, etc.

Figure 2.19 Most organisations have a preprinted letterhead.

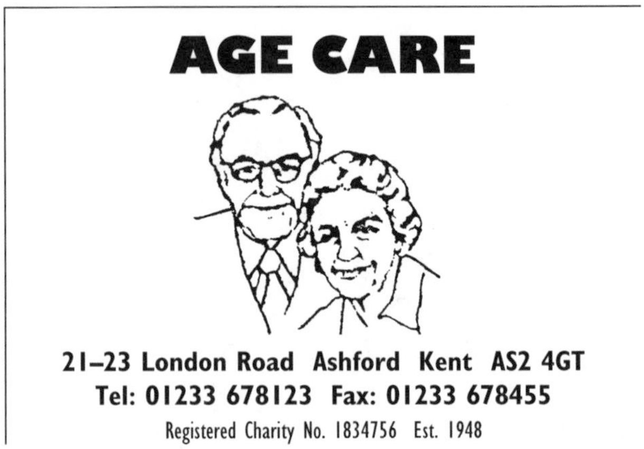
AGE CARE
21–23 London Road Ashford Kent AS2 4GT
Tel: 01233 678123 Fax: 01233 678455
Registered Charity No. 1834756 Est. 1948

Beneath the letterhead the text of a business letter is inserted within a frame (of white space) made up of top, bottom, right and left margins. These margins are either the ones preset in the WP software, or result from changes made by the WP operator using the page setup commands. In order to save time and assist non-expert writers, many software packages today provide a series of predesigned templates (for letters, memos, reports, bulletins, etc.) which can be picked off the shelf and which automatically place keyed-in text at set positions (Figs. 2.20 to 2.23).

Figure 2.20 This report template shows three levels of heading.

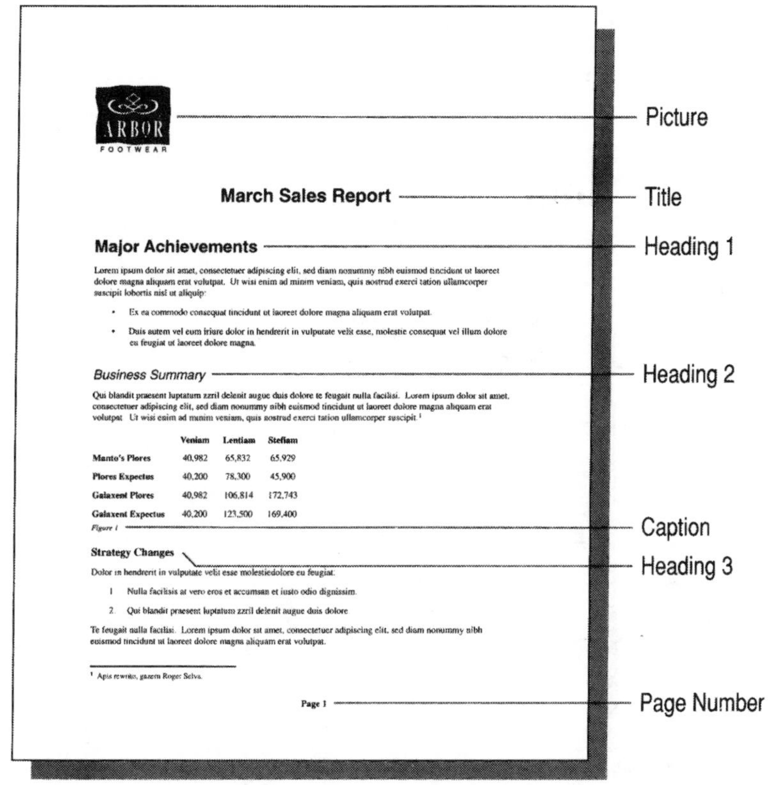

[This figure from the *Word User's Guide* is reproduced with permission from Microsoft Corporation]

Figure 2.21 A memo template with the usual message header.

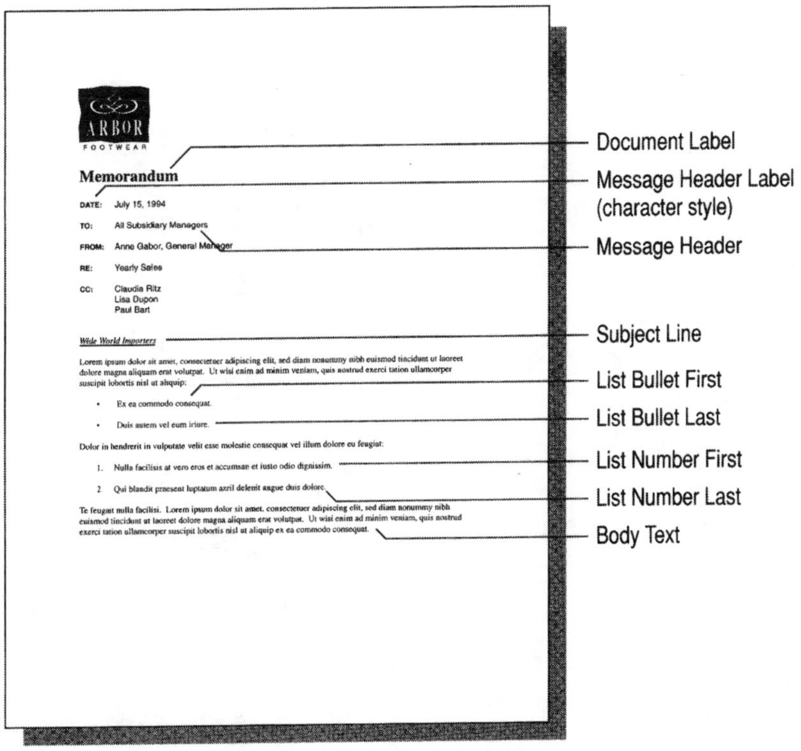

[This figure from the *Word User's Guide* is reproduced with permission from Microsoft Corporation]

Figure 2.22 A letter template using the fully blocked format.

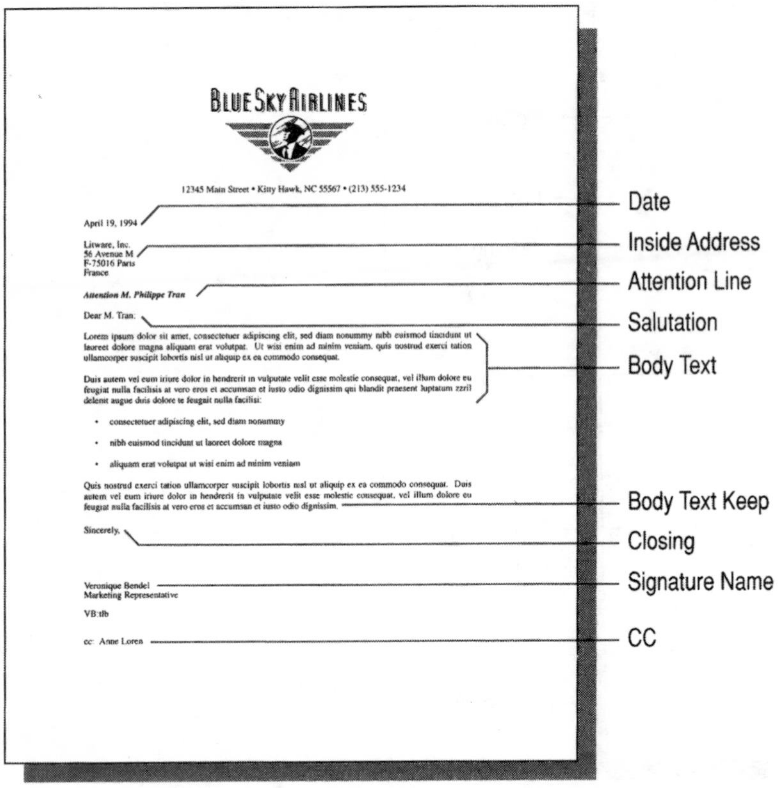

[This figure from the *Word User's Guide* is reproduced with permission from Microsoft Corporation]

Figure 2.23 This brochure template handles art and quotations.

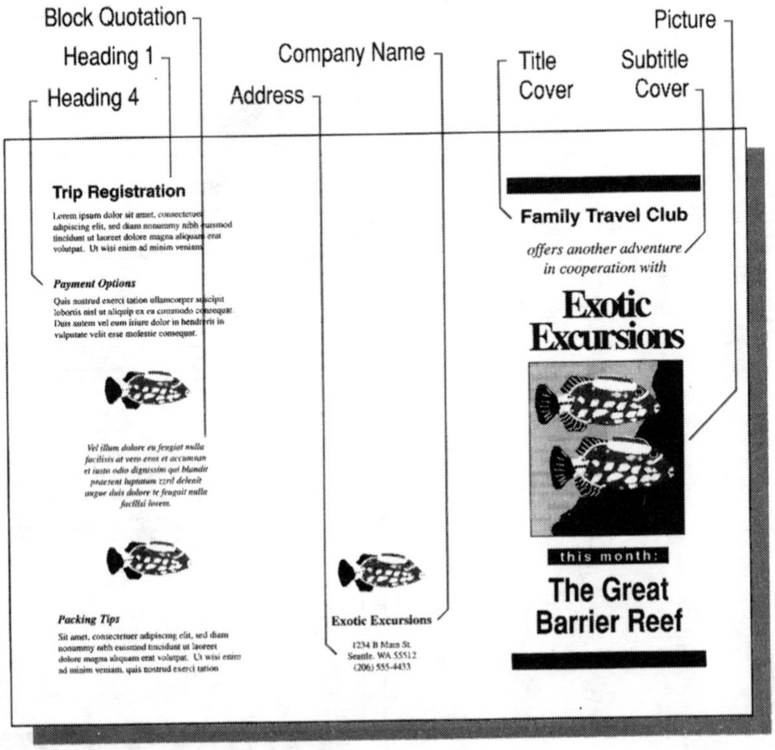

[This figure from the *Word User's Guide* is reproduced with permission from Microsoft Corporation]

Before considering a complete example of a standard format for a business letter, the following points should be carefully committed to memory:

1 **The letter's status:** if a letter is given a personal or restricted reader status, then

PERSONAL or **CONFIDENTIAL** or
PRIVATE & CONFIDENTIAL

is usually prominently displayed (in emboldened capitals) as the first typed or word-processed entry under the printed letterhead. The related conventions are that, if an envelope and letter are labelled personal, then only the denoted recipient should open and read the letter, since its contents are personal to him or her. Confidential means it may well be that a personal secretary or personal assistant has been given authority by his/her manager to open such mail. However, it must be kept away from prying eyes at all times.

2 **Our ref/your ref:** these invitations are often printed under the letterhead. If they are not, the writer inserts them. They invite the letter writer to inset a unique reference for the letter being produced under *Our ref* and to cite or quote that given on a letter which is being replied to under *Your ref*. Such references may be a mix of dates and numbers which identify the letter in a reference system: 6/95/24 indicates the twenty-fourth letter produced in June 1995; or they link the initials of the letter writer and text processor, DWE/gf. Letter references help to identify a specific letter in a busy office and make it easier to file correctly for quick retrieval.

3 **The letter's date:** the UK running order convention is day, month, year, and the month is always set out in full: 6 June 1995. The abbreviations st, nd, rd and th, are no longer used. Remember, too, that the year must be shown in full: 1995 not '95.

4 **The recipient's name and address:** a recipient is either referred to by name and title – Mr David Edwards, Ms Sarah Jones, Mrs Lata Patel – or simply by job title – The Sales Manager, The Senior Care Officer, The Accounts Director. Letter-writers tend to use this form when they do not know the name of the person to whom they are writing. When using a personal name, it is customary to add the person's job title:

Mr David Edwards Sales Manager	Ms Sarah Jones Senior Care Officer
Mrs Lata Patell Accounts Director	

Note that in this combined form of address, *the* is dropped from the job title. Remember, too, Sir *Gordon* Richards – the first name is set out in full, as are Lady Pamela Fanshawe-Smith, Dame Vera Lynn, etc. If a partnership is being written to, it will be referred to as Messrs – Messrs Smith and Wesson; only the surnames are employed.

5 **Letters after recipients' names:** in some instances it is appropriate to include the letters which recipients are entitled to display after their names. The running order is (1) decorations, medals and honours; (2) first degrees; (3) second degrees; (4) memberships of professional bodies. Note that the initial Mr, Ms or Mrs is dropped:

Joan/John Smith OBE BSc PhD FRCS FIM

The proud possessor of such letters is an Officer of the Order of the British Empire, a bachelor of science, a doctor of philosophy, a Fellow of the Royal College of Surgeons and a Fellow of the Institute of Management. Remember that all possessors of PhD degrees are entitled to be referred to as doctors; thus the letter may begin Dear Dr Smith or Dear Sir or Dear Madam.

6 **The postal address:** the recipient's postal address is added immediately after the job title; it includes the organisation's name, street, town, county and postcode. To aid clarity, letter writers often set the town or city in capitals: The Royal West Sussex Hospital, Chapel Hill, HORSHAM, West Sussex HO3 1HP. Note, too, that a number of large conurbations are also set in capitals without the need to cite the county in which they are located: LIVERPOOL, BIRMINGHAM, LONDON, LEEDS, etc. Such large cities usually have a numbered postal district after their names.

7 **The salutation and complimentary close:** UK business letters have salutations and closes which must be used correctly in pairs.

Dear Sir (or Dear Madam) ... Yours faithfully

This pairing is used when a formal letter is being sent to a person not known to the writer.

Dear Mr/Ms/Mrs Smith ... Yours sincerely

This pairing is used either when sender and recipient know each other, or when the writer wishes to transmit a more friendly approach. Note that the *f* and *s* of faithfully and sincerely are always set out in lower case (not as capitals); remember too that no commas are needed after the endings as long as the open punctuation format is being used. Partnerships are referred to as Dear Sirs. The close Yours truly has now fallen out of fashion. Sometimes regular correspondents who enjoy a close professional relationship may close: With best wishes, Sincerely or With kind regards. The use of these closures is a matter of personal judgement. Until fairly recently, some business letters simply printed the firm's name under the closure: Yours faithfully...Global Ball-bearings Limited. Again, this practice appears to be dying out.

8 **The author's name and job title:** a space of three lines is usually left under the closure to allow for the author's signature; there then follows the author's name and job title:

Yours sincerely

Sarah Jones
Senior Care Officer

Today, many female letter-writers do not indicate their marital status in such letter closures. The appropriate form of address when writing to them is Dear Ms Jones, or the more formal Dear Madam. Ms was invented in the United States as a blanket form of address which concealed whether its owner was a Miss or a Mrs. When a letter closes J P Singh, it is acceptable (in the absence of any further information) to write back to *Mr* J P Singh or Dear *Sir*.

9 **Letter enclosure and copy references:** in order to ensure that it is not overlooked by the recipient and left inside an opened envelope, an enclosure which is sent with a letter is referred to after a space, under the job title either as *enc* or *encs* (for two or more). If the writer wishes to inform the recipient and those copied of the letter's distribution, then the names of people sent a copy will be listed after *copy to* or *copies to*. The abbreviation *c.c.* (for carbon copy – a reference to the use of impregnated dry ink sheets) is now much more seldom used and is in reality obsolete.

Figure 2.24 is a typical business letter which employs both the open punctuation and fully blocked letter format, far and away the most commonly used today. Note that while no punctuation (other than for apostrophes in addresses) is used in the the text above and below the body of the letter, the message – set out as a sequence of paragraphs – is normally punctuated.

> ***KEY POINT***
>
> The niceties of how to address bishops, earls, archbishops, knights and other notables are clearly set out in *Blackwell's Styles and Forms of Address* – a useful book to include on your shelves.

Key to sample business letter

1 Logo of Strawberry Hill Health Centre – a caduceus.

2 The full postal address of the centre, including trading name, postcode, telephone and fax numbers, and a slogan embracing its mission statement.

3 Indication of the letter's status.

4 Our reference and your reference built around composition dates and initials of those involved.

5 The date of the letter's production.

6 The recipient's address; note that Worcester is capitalised and that the letter is openly punctuated.

7 The salutation; Dear Mrs and Yours sincerely have been chosen to make what is in effect a sales letter appear more friendly.

8 The letter's subject-heading, which summarises briefly but clearly what the letter is about.

9 The letter's message set out in the customary beginning, development and closing statement structure. Notice the double spacing between the paragraphs to make them stand out and to break down their content, and notice that all the letter's typescript entries commence from the same left-hand margin.

10 The letter's complimentary close is suitably spaced to allow for a signature.

11 The author's name and job title are clearly set out beneath the signature space.

12 The abbreviation denoting the sending of an enclosure with the letter is the final textual entry; note that some organisations – especially solicitors – add a symbol like --- or / in the left-hand margin level with the line of text in which reference is made to the enclosure, so as to catch the eye.

13 Further preprinted text (usually in small print) at the foot of the A4 sheet relates to the legal entity of the business. Strawberry Hill Health Centre is a limited company and the small print gives details of its registered office, company registration number and country of registration, all of them required under UK company law.

> ***KEY POINT***
>
> Figure 2.24 shows how open punctuation and a fully-blocked format save time in production as well as in sorting and routing mail by its emboldened and capitalised subject-heading. The letter's contents are more readily absorbed because the letter is broken down into four paragraphs, its author is clearly identified and the enclosure is clearly signalled.

Figure 2.24 A typical business letter with open punctuation.

(1) (2) **STRAWBERRY HILL HEALTH CENTRE**
250 Downs Road Strawberry Hill Worcester Worcs SH12 6AW
Tel: 01905 736726 Fax: 01905 736500
Caring about your future

CONFIDENTIAL (3)

Our ref: AK./dc./6/95/12 (4)
Your ref: FGT/3/9_

20 June 199– (5)

Mrs F G Thomas (6)
36 Chestnut Avenue
Strawberry Hill
WORCESTER
Worcs WS10 4AJ

Dear Mrs Thomas (7)

STRAWBERRY HILL HEALTHY WOMAN SCREENING PROGRAMME (8)

(9)
Thank you for your letter of 16 June 199– in which you enquire about the features and fees of our Healthy Woman Screening Programme.

The Strawberry Hill Health Centre has been offering this particular programme to women over the age of forty who wish to obtain valuable reassurance about their state of health and also the benefits of early diagnosis should any condition come to light. The programme is run by our highly experienced team of female doctors and nurses. All tests are conducted in complete privacy and confidentiality, and in case of need, immediate referral to our Strawberry Hill Independent Hospital is available, subject to status.

The Healthy Woman Screening Programme has been designed along modular lines. At its centre is the basic and essential screening, including tests of sight, hearing, blood-pressure, heart condition, cholesterol level, body weight and fitness. Additional modules of the programme include: mammary and cervical screening, tests for osteoporosis and hormonal balance. I have enclosed a full tariff of the associated costs of the modular programme and would advise you of our free-of-charge initial consultation which provides you with expert guidance on which particular modules would be appropriate for you.

The Healthy Woman Screening Programme is undertaken by appointment. Please ask for our Healthy Woman receptionist on the above telephone number. Meanwhile, I shall be pleased to assist with any further information requests you may have.

Your sincerely (10)

Asha Khan
Information Services Manager (11)

enc (12)

Strawberry Hill Health Centre Division of Albion Health Services Limited (13)
Registered Office 21–25 Old Moorgate London EC1 3GT Registered Number 948567 England

The report

Organisations use two distinct types of report:

- the preprinted report form used for routine tasks like accident and equipment servicing and maintenance
- the one-off investigatory report used for problem solving and decision making; the writer organises the material for such reports within a framework of format and presentation conventions

This section concentrates on the one-off investigatory report, but you will also have an opportunity to design a routine report.

The short informal report

The short informal report is extremely useful for setting out information in response to a number of requests:

> We need to find out first what a colour copier would cost to purchase or lease and what its operational and maintenance costs are.
>
> Why *have* our telephone costs increased so much?
>
> How would the introduction of personal bleepers support our residents? And how expensive and reliable are they ?

Senior managers in all kinds of organisation are constantly seeking to obtain information in a form which is

- short and also easy to take in
- broken down into easily managed chunks of information
- displayed via text-processing techniques which highlight key facts and/or views

As most short informal reports are restricted to an internal circulation in an organisation, many of their users employ a memorandum type of document (Fig. 2.25), which enables most of the necessary labelling information to be inserted, perhaps using a WP template. Such a memorandum heading serves very much like a business letterhead. The rest of the A4 sheet on which it is printed and filled out is also similar to a business letter, in that it too employs exactly the same conventions for setting margins – top, bottom, left and right. Attention should be paid to the amount of right- and left-hand margins needed if such reports are to be stored in ring-binders, etc., so as to ensure that part of the text is not obscured beneath binder clips and retainers.

The structure of a short, informal report tends to be divided into three parts, under section titles like

INTRODUCTION
INFORMATION
CONCLUSIONS

As this type of report does not usually exceed two or three sides of A4, it tends not to use numbers to reference its sections, and relies instead on a degree of schematic layout and use of word-processing techniques (emboldened capitals, bullet points and section headings, etc.) to make its content easy to absorb.

Skeletal format of a typical short informal report

Figure 2.26 illustrates a typical format for a short informal report, which adapts the memorandum head format. The report deals with a request to investigate waste in the use of stationery and reprographic services in a medium-to-large organisation. An effective format for a short informal report breaks its information down into manageable chunks, which follow a logical sequence and which are signposted by clear section headings. In this example, use is made of

CAPITALISATION	Initial Capitals
bold	***bold italics***

to make clear which subsections of the report relate to which major sections. In addition, the report's format makes use of *white space* (the double lines between entries) and *progressive indentation*:

Correspondence and Internal Mail
    Outgoing Mail Practices

in order to signal the reader a progression from major to minor sections. The outline has been completed in Figure 2.27.

Figure 2.25 Short informal reports use headings like a memorandum.

MEMORANDUM

Status:	CONFIDENTIAL			
To:	Sandra Wilkinson Senior Scientific Officer		**Date:**	22 July 199–
From:	Kevin Anderson Chief Laboratory Technician		**Copies:**	Centre Director
Subject:	STORAGE OF TOXIC SUBSTANCES AND NEW GOVERNMENT LEGISLATION . . .			

Figure 2.26 A typical skeleton for a short informal report.

CONFIDENTIAL

FOR: **FROM:**

REF: **DATE:**

REPORT TITLE: **REPORT ON THE PREVENTION OF WASTEFUL USE OF STATIONERY AND REPROGRAPHIC SERVICES**

INTRODUCTION

XXXXXXXXXXXXXXXXXXXXXXXXXXXXXXXXXXXXXXXXXXXXXXXXXXXXXXXXXXXXXXXX
XXXXXXXXXXXXXXXXXXXXXXXXXXXXXXXXXXXXXXXXXXXXXXXXXXXXXXXXXXXXXXXX
XXXXXXXXXXXXXXXXXXXXXXXXXXXXX

INFORMATION

Range of Stationery Investigated

XXXXXXXXXXXXXXXXXXXXXXXXXXXXXXXXXXXXXXXXXXXXXXXXXXXXXXXXXXXXXXXX
XXXXXXXXXXXXXXXXXXXXXXXXXXXXX

Correspondence and internal mail

Outgoing Mail Practices

XXXXXXXXXXXXXXXXXXXXXXXXXXXXXXXXXXXXXXXXXXXXXXXXXXXXXXXXXXXX
XXXXXXXXXXXXXXXXXXXXXXXXXXXXX

Wasteful Use of Associated Stationery

XXXXXXXXXXXXXXXXXXXXXXXXXXXXXXXXXXXXXXXXXXXXXXXXXXXXXXXXXXXX
XXXXXXXXXXXXXXXXXXXXXXXXXXXXX

Photocopying Practices

XXXXXXXXXXXXXXXXXXXXXXXXXXXXXXXXXXXXXXXXXXXXXXXXXXXXXXXXXXXXXXXX
XXXXXXXXXXXXXXXXXXXXXXXXXXXXXXXXXXXXXXXXXXXXXXXXXXXXXXXXXXXXXXXX
XXXXXXXXXXXXXXXXXXXXXXXXXXXXX

Increase in Stationery Costs

XXXXXXXXXXXXXXXXXXXXXXXXXXXXXXXXXXXXXXXXXXXXXXXXXXXXXXXXXXXXXXXX
XXXXXXXXXXXXXXXXXXXXXXXXXXXXXXXXXXXXXXXXXXXXXXXXXXXXXXXXXXXXXXXX
XXXXXXXXXXXXXXXXXXXXXXXXXXXXX

CONCLUSIONS

Major Areas of Concern

XXXXXXXXXXXXXXXXXXXXXXXXXXXXXXXXXXXXXXXXXXXXXXXXXXXXXXXXXXXXXXXX
XXXXXXXXXXXXXXXXXXXXXXXXXXXXX

Issue of Revised Guidelines on Stationery and Reprographic Use

XXXXXXXXXXXXXXXXXXXXXXXXXXXXXXXXXXXXXXXXXXXXXXXXXXXXXXXXXXXXXXXX
XXXXXXXXXXXXXXXXXXXXXXXXXXXXX

Review of Stationery Control Procedures

XXXXXXXXXXXXXXXXXXXXXXXXXXXXXXXXXXXXXXXXXXXXXXXXXXXXXXXXXXXXXXXX
XXXXXXXXXXXXXXXXXXXXXXXXXXXXX

Meeting of Section Heads to Discuss Staff Training and Development Needs

XXXXXXXXXXXXXXXXXXXXXXXXXXXXXXXXXXXXXXXXXXXXXXXXXXXXXXXXXXXXXXXX
XXXXXXXXXXXXXXXXXXXXXXXXXXXXX

COPIES TO:

XXXXXXXXXXXXXXX
XXXXXXXXXXXXXXX

Figure 2.27 The filled-in skeleton of Figure 2.26.

CONFIDENTIAL

FOR: MRS K LEE OFFICE MANAGER **FROM:** MS A SHAW PERSONAL ASSISTANT

REF: AS/17/JKX **DATE:** 15 NOVEMBER 199-

REPORT TITLE: REPORT ON THE PREVENTION OF WASTEFUL USE OF STATIONERY AND REPROGRAPHIC SERVICES

INTRODUCTION

On Tuesday 29 September 199– you asked me to investigate the current wasteful use of stationery and reprographic services in the department which had come to your attention. In the report upon my investigations you requested that a set of recommendations should be included identifying strategies for obtaining an immediate reduction in the costs incurred by such wasteful practices. The report was to be submitted to you by Friday 17 November 199–.

INFORMATION

Range of Stationery investigated

The range of departmental stationery investigated comprised: A4 and A5 headed notepaper, internal A4/A5 memoranda sheets, fanfold computer print-out paper, A3 and A4 80 grm bond and copy paper, fax rolls, and all sizes of both white and manila envelopes in use.

Correspondence and internal mail

Outgoing Mail Practices

Discussions with both section leaders and support staff, together with examinations of discarded correspondence stationery revealed a number of wasteful practices, including primarily excessive errors in both text production and printing, which leads to an excess of rejected note-paper sheets and envelopes. Some managers were also seen to be using headed note-paper as scrap-paper. Further, white bank envelopes are being used where manila ones would be quite acceptable.

Wasteful Use of Associated Stationery

The wasteful practices relating to associated departmental stationery of particular note were found to be: the use of fresh A4 envelopes for internal routing of both confidential and non-confidential papers, despite the official policy regarding the re-use of wallets and envelopes for this purpose; the widespread practice of distributing widely internal draft reports etc. and then re-distributing the final copies; the dumping of large quantities of bond A4 general copy paper which could be guillotined and re-cycled for jotting-pad use.

Photocopying Practices

Staff are generally lax about using section photocopying cards, thus making it difficult to apportion arising costs appropriately. Almost no instances were found of staff backing extended reports, memoranda or schedules etc., thus doubling copy paper costs. Further, a failure to report a fault in the departmental copier for over seven days resulted in an estimated number of 17 reams of paper being wasted because of an intermittent creasing fault.

Increase in Stationery Costs

My investigations revealed that, as a result of a significant increase in wasteful practices such as those indicated above, departmental stationery and reprographic costs have risen in the first three quarters of this financial year (as against the same period for the previous year) by some 47%, or £5,550. When allowance is made for increases in purchase costs etc. the increase still amounts to some £4950. A restricted investigation for the past six weeks indicated that these costs appear to be rising further.

Figure 2.27 The filled-in skeleton of Figure 2.26 *continued.*

CONCLUSIONS

Major Areas of Concern

The investigations undertaken fully justify the concerns you raised. In general staff do not display any sense of careful use or control of stationery and reprographic materials. Moreover, section heads do not take sufficient interest in the malpractices which have crept into the work practices of their staff. Given the significant rise established in departmental stationery costs, the following recommendations are made:

Issue of Revised Guidelines on Stationery and Reprographic Use

All staff should be issued with a memorandum which re-establishes clearly accepted departmental procedures for using stationery and reprographic services, together with a reminder of, say, a sanction whereby excessive costs in these areas will be set against other areas of section budgets, such as the work area refurbishment programme.

Review of Stationery Control Procedures

In view of the wide-spread growth in wasteful and costly practices, it is recommended that a specific section head (or other appropriate senior staff member) be given the job of monitoring stationery and reprographic costs and usage as an important, ongoing part of his or her job role.

Meeting of Section Heads to Discuss Staff Training and Development Needs

In order to address the longer term problems associated with the above findings, it is recommended that you call an early meeting of section heads in order to discuss and design a programme of staff training and development – to prevent, for example, the wasteful use of stationery arising from: spelling and syntax errors, inexpert use of the photocopier, cost-control and allied matters.

COPIES TO:

At your request, informational copies of this report have been sent to:

All section heads
Accounts manager
Purchasing manager

Notes on the featured short informal report

The main points to note about Figure 2.27 are

- The introduction makes clear the five Ws – who, what, when, where and why the report was commissioned – in a *brief* preamble.
- The information section breaks down the findings simply and clearly into four main headings and two subheadings, proceeding from what was investigated to summarising, again briefly, the major findings. Note that an information section rarely makes judgements about the findings; this is left for the conclusions/ recommendations section
- The recommendations are supplied succinctly – *with reasons for them.*

The short formal report

This type of report is best regarded as a more developed form of its informal counterpart. Although deemed to be short (in comparison with long reports, by say judicial enquiries, public meetings inspectors, etc.) the formal report's format has been designed for much more extensive findings, covering say between three and eight sides of printed A4. The formal report's format is characterised by a logical referencing system for its main points and its minor points and a more highly schematised layout.

Referencing a short formal report: mixed and decimal point systems

In essence there are two ways of supplying a referencing system for this type of report. A system may be adopted along these lines:

EXAMPLE OF MIXED REFERENCING SYSTEM

Main sections: I, II, III, IV, V

Major Subsections: A, B, C, D, E

Minor Subsections: 1, 2, 3, 4

Points of Minor Subsections: (i) (ii) (iii) (iv)

Using this type of referencing system will allow a point of a minor subsection to be referenced as III C 2 (iv) or IV B 3 (i). While it works, such a mix of roman and arabic numbers as well as brackets is generally considered ugly. By contrast, the decimal point system is much more elegant:

EXAMPLE OF DECIMAL POINT REFERENCING SYSTEM

Main sections: 1.0, 2.0, 3.0, 4.0, 5.0

Major subsections: 1.1, 1.2, 1.3, 1.4 (or 2.1, 2.2, 2.3, 2.4)

Minor subsections: 1.1.1, 1.1.2, 1.1.3, 1.1.4

Points of minor subsections: 1.1.1.1, 1.1.1.2, 1.1.1.3, 1.1.1.4

Thus a minor point in the third major section of a report using the decimal point system might be referenced as 3.4.1.2 or 3.2.4.3 As you can see, the use of the decimal point system is very straightforward and many believe it to be easier on the eye. Figure 2.28 is an example of a typical short formal report. However, because this text has limited space, the findings section is shorter than it would be in a real report.

Notes on the featured short formal report

There are distinct similarities in the format of the short formal report and the short informal report. However, the formal report has an extra section – procedures – to indicate to the reader the nature and extent of the investigatory researches undertaken. The data for thorough reports includes reading of documents, interviews with selected people, observation of activities and processes, canvassing and surveying, and making comparisons with other organisations, etc. The formal report is written

Figure 2.28 A short formal report (the findings are abridged).

LAKE DISTRICT LEISURE AND OUTDOOR ACTIVITIES CENTRE

CONFIDENTIAL

FOR: P J Kirkbride Centre Manager   **FROM:** A Hussain Chair, Working Party

REF: AH/dy/12   **DATE:** 14 February 199-

REPORT ON THE PROPOSAL TO INTRODUCE FLEXIBLE WORKING HOURS AT THE CENTRE AND RESIDENTIAL COMPLEX

1.0 TERMS OF REFERENCE

On 12 December 199– the Centre Manager instructed a specifically set-up working party to investigate the practicality of introducing a system of flexible working hours in all centre administrative, operational and residential departments, and to make appropriate recommendations. The report was to be submitted no later than 20 February for consideration at the next meeting of the Board of Trustees.

2.0 PROCEDURES

In order to obtain up-to-date, relevant information and responses the following procedures were adopted by the working party:

2.1 Current centre administration, operational and hospitality practices were reviewed with appropriate managers and the study of current procedures and standing orders.

2.2 A number of recreational and outdoor centres were visited which already operate a flexible hours system.

2.3 Current working practices and procedures were observed in each Centre department, together with work-loads and peak and trough activity times.

2.4 Soundings of likely staff responses to the introduction of a flexible working system were taken from their line and senior managers.

2.5 A feasibility study was undertaken regarding the likely costs of moving to the proposed system (see Appendix 1).

Figure 2.28 A short formal report (the findings are abridged) *continued.*

3.0 FINDINGS

3.1 Principles of the Flexible Working Hours System

The essence of a flexible working hours system consists of establishing two distinct bands of working hours within a weekly or monthly cycle and of ensuring that staff work in practice an agreed total of hours by the end of the cycle.

3.1.1 Core Time Band
During this period (say 1015 and 1545) all staff are present at work, allowing for normal lunch-time arrangements (Note: alternative Core Time Bands may be needed for the two-shift restaurant and cafeteria staff, as well as, on occasion, for Activity Team Leaders on extended activities etc.)

3.1.2 Flexi-time Band
Periods at the beginning and end of each day (say between 0745 to 1015 and 1545 to 1815) are worked at the discretion of individual staff members in whole or part, taking overall essential manning levels into account.

3.1.3 Credit/Debit Hour Banking
According to previously agreed limits and procedures, staff may take time off if a credit of hours has been established, or make time up if a deficit has been created. Some centres insist that a full total of hours must be worked by the end of each working week, while others allow credits or debits of hours to be carried forward, until the end of each month by which time each staff member must have worked neither more or nor less than his or her contracted monthly hours.

3.1.3.1 Logging of hours worked
Given the overall flexibility of some schemes, it is important in the area of credit/debit hour banking to keep in mind the administrative costs of logging hours daily on an individual basis – say by a clocking in and out machine, to which some staff may object.

3.1.3.2 Variations in existing patterns of work
Consideration of the existing differences in work patterns – say between the regular hours of office staff, the irregular hours of activity leaders, and the current two-shift system worked by hospitality staff must also be given. Evidence was freely forthcoming of a readiness to adopt new working patterns as long as they were seen to be fair by all staff.

3.2 Discussions with Departmental Managers

Most Centre departmental managers were in favour of introducing a flexible working hours system, anticipating an improvement in both productivity and staff morale. The Hospitality Manager saw advantages in establishing a 'handing over' overlap period between shifts which could be introduced as part of the system. Also, during summer months, the Activities Manager thought she would be able to extend the length of the working day for outside activities without having to pay for over-time. However, the Centre Office Manager expressed concerns about the costs of implementing such a system.

3.3 Soundings of Staff Views

Discreet soundings of staff views were made (through Centre Managers) at all employment grades.

3.3.1 Summary of favourable responses
Centre administration staff were particularly enthusiastic, especially since a number of staff have children of primary school age, and the system would aid their delivery and collection. Managers' secretaries also thought the scheme would enable them to work longer when their principals were in and to take more time off when they were out. Activities staff seemed less enthusiastic, since they were accustomed to working irregular hours in any case, and were concerned that the new system did not result in 'more work for the same pay'. Married staff were generally keen to have an opportunity to avoid rush hour peaks in terms of car travel and shopping.

Figure 2.28 A short formal report (the findings are abridged) *continued.*

3.3.2 Summary of unfavourable responses
Most of the unfavourable (or sceptical) responses came from senior staff tiers. Some managers were concerned about staff being absent when they were needed, and some supervisors felt that their work-load might increase as a result of the introduction of the proposed system. Uncertainties were also conveyed about annual leave and staff cover, as well as about sickness cover.

3.4 Costs of introducing and implementing a Flexible Working Hours System

After careful investigation, the Working Party's considerations regarding costs were that improvements in staff morale would improve productivity in quantifiable financial terms. Also, the introduction of the system would be likely to increase significantly the amount of bookings per week the Centre could manage effectively, thus increasing Centre income by an estimated £7,400 p.a. An initial pump-priming sum of some £850 (estimated) would be needed to acquire logging equipment and to amend certain administrative procedures.

4.0 CONCLUSIONS

The Working Party arrived at the following main conclusions after six weeks of intensive investigation:

4.1 The flexible working hours system is capable of being introduced into the Lake District Leisure and Outdoor Activities Centre with some minor modification, to take into account unique Centre operational needs.
4.2 The system of monthly, rather than weekly hour crediting and debiting is more suited to the Centre's patterns of work, and would be more widely supported by staff at all levels.
4.3 Introductory and routine implementation costs lie well within the scope of the Centre's budget, and within 3–6 months of operation, increased revenue is firmly expected to occur.
4.4 A clear majority of canvassed staff indicated that the scheme would be accepted, and even welcomed.

5.0 RECOMMENDATIONS

The Working Party makes the following recommendations:

5.1 That an ad hoc committee or working party be set up to manage the introduction of a flexible working hours system before Easter 199–, so as to have it in place before peak summer bookings.
5.2 That all Centre managers are requested to produce for the ad hoc committee a feasibility study (within three weeks of the acceptance of these proposals) detailing how they would plan the introduction of the system in their work sectors.
5.3 That selected staff in key working areas are provided with a development programme on the delivery and maintenance of an FWH scheme.
5.4 That a suitable set of procedures for staff guidance be drawn up and added to the Centre Staff Handbook.
5.5 That a suitable communications means be devised for informing all staff of any decision taken to implement the above recommendations.

entirely in the third person, avoiding all mention of I, you and we. This is to help make the report read impersonally and objectively. As a result, many of the report's sentences use the passive construction: *Uncertainties were also conveyed...*

The short formal report also makes particular use of progressive indentation to indicate a move from major to minor points (see 3.1.3 and 3.1.3.1/2). Notice that no recommendations are made in the conclusions, which are simply a factual summary of the main findings. Note, too, the structure of the recommendations: That... be...

The display advertisement

The key function of any advertisement is to persuade its readers to move towards the point of view the advertisement desires to promote and (usually) to take prompt action, such as purchasing the advertised product or service. Given this clear objective, all display advertisements employ a mix of communication techniques to capture the reader's attention then to persuade him or her to accept the displayed message, and act upon it:

- **Visual/graphic design:** for instance, a photograph, line drawing, symbol or cartoon. This component catches the eye most readily. Do you recall the photograph of a 'pregnant' City gent advertising contraception on the London Underground in the 1980s ?
- **Headline/slogan in bold capitals:** the headline or slogan is also intended to catch the eye and mind of the reader:

  Whoosh Washes Brightest, Fastest, Cleanest!

- **Advertising copy:** this is the term used to describe the detailed advertising message; it is generally composed in extremely short word groups, which may not act as grammatical sentences:

  Whoosh reassures! Its unique cleaning action revitalises your wash. Whoosh's biological enzymes remove even the stickiest stains and oiliest marks. Amazing ! Yes, and amazingly cheap to use. Move over to Whoosh and you'll see a brighter, radiant family within the week. Guaranteed! Because, Whoosh washes brightest, fastest, cleanest!

Figure 2.29 Text and graphics combine to advertise Whoosh.

- **The action statement:** most display advertisements end with a clear and urgently expressed action statement (often with a prompt such as a special introductory offer with an imminent deadline) to encourage the reader to act directly:

  CUT OUT THE COUPON BELOW TO SAVE 30p
  ON YOUR MOVE OVER TO UNBEATABLE
  WHOOSH AND UNBEATABLE VALUE!

Note that the language of hard-selling display advertisements seeks to influence the emotions rather than cold logic. The syntax used is short and snappy, and the words used are carefully chosen to convey (in the above example) a message to weekly washers of Whoosh's comforting effectiveness, cheapness and fast action especially in the context of the loved family (who deserve only the best). Putting the above mix of display advertisement components together might result in the design of Figure 2.29.

The fact-sheet

Fact-sheets are just what their name suggests, sheets (of A4) on which facts are set down in a logical sequence (Fig. 2.30). They are generally used to brief

Figure 2.30 Fact-sheet: like a report but more broken-down.

FACTSHEET NO. 24 EARLY DEVELOPMENTS OF THE TELEPHONE

1 Early Discoveries

1.1 The early discoveries which led to the development of the telephone were made by **an Englishman, M Faraday and a German, G Reis.** In **1831** Faraday discovered that metal vibrations could be converted into electrical impulses – the basis of telephonic communication.

1.2 In **1861** Reis put together the essential components needed for telephonic transmission and reception:

Transmitter: electric circuit, metallic point and membrane
Receiver: metallic needle, coil, resonance box

1.3 This basic equipment was able – in 1861 – **to transmit both speech and music.**

1.4 Reis coined the word **telephone** to describe his invention.

2 Consolidating Developments

2.1 In **1876** the Scottish-American **Alexander Graham Bell** successfully contested Reis's telephone patent on the grounds that the equipment did not perform as described.

2.2 With a **co-inventor, Elisha Gray,** Bell worked on a system aimed at transmitting several calls along a single line simultaneously. Bell concentrated on the acoustics involved, and Gray on the electrics.

2.3 The result was the invention of the **harmonic telephone** – a system able to transmit and receive different frequencies of sound.

2.4 In 1874, Bell constructed a **steel diaphragm receiver,** and at this time Gray developed a **mobile membrane transmitter** – both successful but not entirely functional prototypes.

2.5 By **1876,** Bell had **perfected his telephone intervention** which was demonstrated at the **centenary festival of Philadelphia.**

2.6 The **first commercial use of the telephone** took place in **1877** when the **first telephone exchange** was set up in **Hartford Connecticut.**

[Adapted from *Great Modern Inventions* by Gerard Messadie and reproduced by kind permission of Chambers Harrap]

people at work by communicating a set of data about a specific topic. For example, a fact-sheet might be used by a local council to detail how it has spent its annual income from tax-payers, or one might be employed to brief a group of export sales executives about a foreign country they are about to visit on business.

There is no predetermined format for a fact-sheet. However, all that you have learned in this section about the size and appearance of text and the use of schematic layout is entirely useful in designing an effective fact-sheet. Perhaps the closest cousin of the fact-sheet is the short formal report, in which each point is clearly referenced and displayed.

Fact-sheet guidelines

- Start with a suitable set of labels, such as those of a memo head.
- Use a set of progressive section headings, say, from 12 point capitals to 10 point initial capitals.
- Make sure before text processing that your sections are in a suitable, logical order: fact-sheets usually move from the most important topics to the least important topics.
- Use a suitable referencing system to number your points so that your fact-sheet users can refer easily to them in, say, meetings or memos.
- Use white space and indentation generously so as to make each point stand out clearly.
- Keep each point short and stick to a factual style.
- Make sure that all references are inserted: production date, distribution list, informational copies, etc.

Notes on the featured fact-sheet format

As you will have noticed, there are distinct similarities between the format of a fact-sheet and the format of a short formal report. Both employ number references, schematic layout and progressive indentation. Note, however, that the fact-sheet format tends to present its factual information in a much more broken-down manner, where a fresh section is given for almost every point made. This approach aids significantly the uptake of essential data. Also, the use of emboldening for key names, dates, laboratory equipment and places helps the reader to notice and to commit them to memory. In essence, an effective fact-sheet resembles a skeletal report or essay plan; the main difference is that its points are expressed through full grammatical sentences.

The documentation of meetings

The documentation used to service meetings has taken on particular structures and formats to meet two contrasting needs. Firstly, to enable participants to prepare for the impending meeting, and secondly, to receive a written record of what took place in it. The following section provides a set of helpful examples which may serve as models for your own meetings documents.

The notice of a meeting

All participants need to be advised in advance on a regular basis of the timing and location of forthcoming meetings. This may be effected by a postcard (Fig. 2.31), emailed message (Fig. 2.32) or letter, depending upon the degree of formality the meeting enjoys.

Figure 2.31 Some meetings are called by postcard.

Midshire Association Of Licensed Victuallers

NOTICE OF COMMITTEE MEETING

The next Committee Meeting will be held on:

Day: *Wednesday* Date: *23 April 199-*

Time: *7.00 p.m.* Venue: *The Half Moon, Silver End*

I hope you will be able to attend.

signed:

Tim Willis

Honorary Secretary

Figure 2.32 Some meetings are called by email.

Unclassified Page 1

TECHNICAL BRIEFING

To: All Principal Engineers
From: Comm Systems Manager

PURPOSE OF BRIEFING
Revised interface protocol

Date: 8 July 199–
Venue: G Lab
Start time: 1500
Finish: 1700

PLEASE BRING EXISTING SPECIFICATION

Meetings agendas

Essentially, there are two types of meetings agenda produced in advance of any meeting. The first is the agenda which is sent to all participants, usually some 7–14 days before the meeting. The second is a development of the first, called the chairperson's agenda. This provides enlarged spaces between each agenda item, which the secretary who services the meetings uses to provide helpful prompts, hints and other information – for the chairperson alone – to help him or her to run the meeting effectively.

In most meetings conventions, the general agenda tends to be like a sandwich. At its head are these regular items:

- **Apologies for absence:** here an opportunity is provided for the chair to advise the meeting of those participants unable to attend.
- **Minutes of the last meeting:** here the chair invites members to comment on the previously circulated minutes, but only to correct errors or omissions.
- **Matters arising from the minutes:** some meetings employ this item to enable a brief discussion to take place, say on some action which was requested at the previous meeting.

The middle items of the general agenda are for the fresh business of the meeting to be indicated, e.g.

- Proposed purchase of colour photocopier

Agendas may include anything from three to twelve or more such new business items, but able chairpersons limit items so as to avoid protracted meetings. The closing items of the agenda also follow a regular pattern; they are included to enable members briefly to raise any item they wish to air, and to agree the date of the next meeting. Time-wasting suggestions during any other business are usually thrown out by the chair.

- Any other business
- Date of the next meeting

The general agenda in Figure 2.33 and the chairperson's agenda in Figure 2.34 enable you to become familiar with their respective structures.

Minutes of meetings

There are two main types of minutes used to record the proceedings of meetings. The first are called resolution minutes and the second narrative minutes. Resolution minutes record simply and solely the actions agreed, and are usually taken at board of directors meetings. The following item gives an example:

6. Associated Ballbearings Limited

It was resolved to seek a purchaser for Associated Ballbearings with immediate effect.

Figure 2.33 A general agenda begins and ends in a standard way.

THE NATIONAL INSTITUTE OF COMPUTER SERVICES MANAGERS

NEWTOWN BRANCH

The next Committee Meeting of the Branch will take place on Wednesday 5th June 199– in the Shelley Room of the White Unicorn Hotel, 7.30 p.m. for 8.00 p.m.

Agenda

1. Apologies for absence
2. Minutes of the last meeting
3. Matters arising from the minutes
4. Publicity for new season's programme of events
5. Topic and speaker for meeting: Wednesday 4th March 199–
6. Visit to PC User Exhibition
7. Proposal to levy an admission charge at meetings:

   That an admission charge of £2.00 per head be levied by the Branch as an admission charge to meetings to cover the cost of coffee and biscuits and to contribute towards branch funds

   Proposer: Mr J Pearson
   Seconder: Mrs M Jenkins

8. Any other business
9. Date of next meeting

[Reproduced by kind permission of Pitman Publishing from D. W. Evans, *People, Communication & Organisations*, 2nd edition, 1990]

Figure 2.34 A chairperson's agenda is for the personal use of the chair.

THE NATIONAL INSTITUTE OF COMPUTER SERVICES MANAGERS

Newtown Branch

CHAIRMAN'S AGENDA

For the Branch Committee Meeting of Wednesday 5 June, to be held in the Shelley Room of the White Unicorn Hotel at 8.00 p.m.

CHAIRMAN'S NOTES

1. **Apologies For Absence:**
   Mr Booth will be visiting his wife in hospital.
   Mr Williams hopes to come but will be late – visit to London.

2 **Minutes Of the Last Meeting:**
   Mr Carpenter has intimated that he was not categorically against the change of venue for Branch Committee Meetings, and that his remarks as they appear in the Minutes of the Last Meeting have been misconstrued.

3 **Matters Arising:**
   Item 6. The manager of the Blue Boar has confirmed that the Committee Room of the Hotel will be available on the third Wednesday of each month from 1 August onwards.

   Excelsior Printing Ltd. have promised the New Season's programmes by Friday 26 June at the latest.

4 **Publicity For New Season's Programme Of Events:**
   There does not appear to be any likelihood of the Newtown Chronicle repeating last year's price for the display advertisement. I spoke to the advertising manager on the 'phone last Thursday.

5 **Topic And Speaker For Meeting: Wednesday 4 March 199–**
   Lord Grenville has written respectfully to decline our invitation to speak. Copy of letter attached.

6 **Visit To PC User Exhibition, Olympia:**
   The Olympia management have confirmed that they still have vacancies for parties on Saturday 25 September. 15% discount on admission charges for parties over 25.

7 **Proposal To Levy Admission Charge At Meetings:**
   As you will recall, John Pearson proposed a similar motion at last year's June meeting. His motion was defeated last year 6:2.

   I understood Harold Jones is concerned about the Branch's ability to fund its activities in the programme for the New Season.

[Reproduced by kind permission of Pitman Publishing from D.W. Evans, *People, Communication & Organisations*, 2nd edition, 1990]

Narrative minutes (Fig. 2.35) are much more frequently employed by clubs, committees and various in-house meetings personnel. As their name suggests, they tend to tell the story by supplying more detail about who said what. For this reason, some chairs prefer them, since they indicate, retrospectively, who proved to be correct in the event, etc. However, they are more lengthy and can become tedious if too much detail is supplied. Nevertheless, they occur commonly and require developed summarising skills (see Element 3.4).

Figure 2.35 Narrative minutes use the heading in the agenda.

THE NATIONAL INSTITUTE OF COMPUTER SERVICE MANAGERS

NEWTOWN BRANCH

MINUTES

Committee meeting of The National Institute of Computer Service Managers Newtown Branch, held on Wednesday 5th June 199– in the Shelley Room of the White Lion Hotel at 8.00 p.m.

PRESENT A.J. Lucas, Chairman; M.T. Wilkins, Hon. Secretary; H. Jones Hon. Treasurer; F.C. Carpenter; M. Jenkins; G.O.F. Nelson; J. Pearson; K.D. Williams.

1. APOLOGIES FOR ABSENCE

Apologies for absence were received from R.T. Nicholas, Vice-Chairman, and E.W. Booth.

2. MINUTES OF THE LAST MEETING

Mr. Carpenter drew attention to item 6 of the minutes of the last meeting, Branch Committee Meetings – Change of Venue. He affirmed that his remarks had been misinterpreted and that he was not categorically against the proposed change of venue. By general consent it was agreed to substitute 'had strong reservations about' for 'was categorically against' in Item 6.

3. MATTERS ARISING

The Secretary reported that in connection with Item 6, the manager of the Blue Boar was able to offer his hotel's committee room on the third Wednesday of each month from 1st August onwards. The chairman then requested the Secretary to confirm acceptance of the offer by letter.

According to the latest information, the Secretary informed the meeting that Excelsior Printing Ltd. had promised the new season's programmes by Friday 26th June. Mr. Nelson pointed out that it was essential for the programmes to be available by that date for distribution purposes. The Chairman asked Mr. Nelson to liaise with the Secretary to ensure that the promised delivery date was met.

4. PUBLICITY FOR THE NEW SEASON'S PROGRAMME OF EVENTS

The Chairman, in referring to the branch's advertisement placed with the Newtown Chronicle, confirmed that the cost of such advertising was certain to increase. The Treasurer expressed his concern at any prospective increase in advertising expenditure in view of the agreed increases for speakers' expenses and mail-shots to members. After a wide-ranging discussion of the branch's expenditure on publicity, it was decided to place an order for six advertisements with the Newtown Chronicle instead of the customary seven to offset the anticipated increase in charges.

5. TOPIC AND SPEAKER FOR MEETING: WEDNESDAY 4th MARCH 199–

The Chairman asked the Secretary to read to the meeting the letter received from Lord Grenville, who tendered his apologies for having to decline the invitation to speak on 4 March. Suggestions were then requested for possible alternative speakers. Mrs Jenkins proposed that the Rt. Hon. Charles Hawkins, M.P. for Newtown East be approached, but it was generally agreed that M.P.s were subject to last-minute, unavoidable commitments in Westminster. Mr. Williams suggested Mr. John Farnham, Computer Services Manager for Global Computers, an acknowledged expert in developments in computer language. In the absence of any further suggestions, the Chairman requested the Secretary to write to Mr. Farnham inviting him to speak at the 4 March Meeting.

6. VISIT TO PC USER EXHIBITION, OLYMPIA

The Secretary relayed to the meeting the confirmation from the Olympia management regarding existing vacancies for parties on 25 September 199–. A discount of 15% was offered on admission charges for parties over 25 in number. Strong interest was expressed by all present, and the Chairman asked the Secretary to order 30 tickets at the party rate. Mr. Williams offered to arrange the hiring of a motor-coach and was requested to report progress at the next meeting.

Figure 2.35 Narrative minutes use the headings in the agenda *continued.*

7. PROPOSAL TO LEVY AN ADMISSION CHARGE AT MEETINGS

The Chairman referred the meeting to Mr. Pearson's proposal on the agenda for the meetings. Before asking Mr. Pearson to speak on his motion, the Chairman reminded the meeting that the subject of admission charges to branch meetings had arisen during the previous season. It was a difficult matter and the financial status of the branch merited that it be re-examined. Mr. Pearson emphasised the rise in the cost of meetings and referred to the minutes of the meeting of Wednesday 17 October 199–, which recorded his prediction that events would prove him right about the need for an admission charge. He was advocating a levy of £2.00, which he did not think would prove financially embarrassing to members and would not, in his opinion, result in falling attendances. Opposing the motion, Mr. Nelson felt strongly that members already paid a sufficiently large sum in annual membership fees to the Institute and that branch meetings should be funded from the allocation made to Institute Branches from Computer House. Mrs. Jenkins reminded the meeting that she had opposed the introduction of the charge when it was last debated, but felt that such a levy was the only fair way of keeping the branch solvent during the coming season. The Treasurer echoed Mrs. Jenkins' concern and stated that he was in favour of the motion. In view of the expression of conflicting views, the Chairman asked for a vote on the motion before the meeting. The motion was carried by 5 votes to 3.

8. ANY OTHER BUSINESS

Mr. Carpenter raised the matter of branch reports submitted to the Institute Journal. He had noted that for the past two quarters, no mention had been made of Newtown branch activities. The Chairman promised to look into the matter and to report back.

Mrs. Jenkins drew the meeting's attention to the new magazine, 'Computer Monthly'. She was personally acquainted with the editor and was able to recommend it to members without reservation.

9. DATE OF NEXT MEETING

The next Committee Meeting was scheduled for Wednesday 3 July 199–.

[Reproduced by kind permission of Pitman Publishing from D.W. Evans, *People, Communication & Organisations*, 2nd edition, 1990]

Conventions of reported speech

In order to compose correct narrative minutes, it is necessary to acquire an understanding of the conventions of reported speech, the mode in which narrative minutes are written. Simply, these require everything to be expressed in the third person – he/she/it or they – and in a series of past tenses of the verb: *She said the Hon Treasurer had been incorrect when he suggested that...* The following section explains how reported speech should be composed.

Reported speech

Reported speech – the system of indirectly conveying what someone has previously said – is frequently used in business and public service organisations.

Many written documents, such as minutes, reports, articles and summaries, report for the benefit of the reader what someone has actually said at an earlier time.

Reported speech is easily recognised by the absence of quotation marks and the introductory leaders such as

Mr Smith replied that . . .
He said that . . .
She hoped it would not . . .

The system for converting direct speech into reported or indirect speech is generally straightforward, though there are some pitfalls to be avoided.

Person	Singular	Plural
1st	I	we
2nd	you	you
3rd	he, she	they

Remember that, as a general rule, the first or second persons in direct speech become third persons in repeated speech:

'I shall ring you when I reach Bristol.'

He said that he would ring him/her when he reached Bristol.

In addition, it is important to avoid any ambiguities which may result in the change from direct speech to reported speech:

He thought he ought to resign.

This reported statement could have been as follows in direct speech:

'I think I ought to resign.'
'I think you ought to resign.'
'I think he ought to resign.'

To avoid such ambiguities occurring, it is sometimes necessary to insert a name or an identifying description:

Mr Jones thought Mr Brown ought to resign.
He thought the sales representative ought to resign.
He thought that he, Brown, ought to resign.

Tenses

In reported speech, the tenses of the verbs change as follows:

Direct speech	**Reported speech**
I go	He said he ... went
I am going	He was going
I went	He had gone, he went
I was going	He had been going
I have gone	He had gone
I have been going	He had been going
I had gone	He had gone
I shall go	He would go
I shall be going	He would be going
I shall have gone	He would have gone

Note, however, that sometimes we use the present tense to indicate a customary practice:

'I go to my sports club every Monday.'

He said he was accustomed to going to his sports club every Monday.

The distancing effect

Because the reporting of direct speech takes place after a lapse of time, some words require to be changed.

Direct speech version:

'I think *this* proposal deserves the close attention of everyone *here today*. I shall be speaking to the staff *tomorrow* and shall convey to them *these* suggestions, which have my support.'

Indirect speech version:

He said he thought *that* proposal deserved the close attention of everyone *there* that day. He would be speaking to the staff *on the following day* and would convey to them *those* suggestions, which had his support.

Note also

now becomes *then*
yesterday becomes *the previous day*

Using verbs in reported speech

When a lengthy exchange of direct speech is to be converted into reported speech in, say, the minutes of a meeting, it is necessary to avoid the dull repetition of 'he said that' and 'she said that', then 'he said that'. More expressive verbs should be used, such as *urge, insist, ask,* to convey the tone of the direct speech.

What do you think?

1 Do conventions of document format still matter today, given the advent of electronic mail and the extensive use of oral communications?

2 Why do organisations devote so much time and money to designing and producing headed notepaper, which employs coloured inks, graphic logos, varied fonts and point sizes and watermarked, 100 gram paper ?

3 Would it really matter if someone wrote a letter with this salutation and complimentary close: *Dear Mrs Smith... Yours Faithfully*?

4 Some written communication experts believe that the task of researching, structuring and text processing a short formal report is the most demanding of all forms of written communication. Would you agree? If not, what type of document production do you find more demanding and why?

5 What techniques of document layout and presentation do you find help you most to pick up, take in and understand a two- or three-page written document?

6 What features of printed display advertisements do you find impact upon you most effectively ?

Student pair skills-building activities

1 Research into the provisions of an up-to-date version of a Windows word-processing software package in terms of the features it embodies which assist a document producer to format and display text effectively and appealingly. Produce a fact-sheet on what you find out and distribute it to your co-students.

2 Arrange to interview several word-processing operatives in your locality. Your brief is to find out what tips and advice they can supply for producing effective documents, say letters and reports. Provide a short illustrated summary of your findings for distribution around your class.

3 Arrange to collect a series of printed reports in the public domain, such as annual shareholders reports, educational reports held in your library, professional institute reports, and local government reports. Analyse them in terms of the techniques which have been employed in devising their formats and display techniques. Brief your class on your findings by means of an oral presentation, supported by example hand-outs. Focus on what you consider to be effective and ineffective examples of work.

4 Do precisely the same as activity 3 above for a range of display advertisements you collect from glossy magazines, local newspapers, junk mail, etc, and similarly provide an evaluative presentation supported by examples from your collection.

Display examples drawn from the above activities around your baseroom to illustrate examples of good practice.

SUMMARY

The key points of this section are:

- Information technology has had a significant impact on the formatting of printed documents, and as there are, ultimately, no right or wrong ways of setting out written documents, their authors have to abide by what the majority expects to receive, and what embodies effective display and sequencing techniques.
- The most commonly used letter format is fully blocked with open punctuation; widely accepted salutations and closes are Dear Sir (or Madam or Dear Sirs)...Yours faithfully; Dear Mr (Ms, Mrs, Dr) Smith...yours sincerely.
- An internal memorandum heading includes these key labels: To: From: Ref: Date: Subject: It may also include a status reference (Confidential) and a reference to those sent a copy (Copies to).
- Both informal and formal short reports make use of: CAPITALISATION Initial Capitalisation, **emboldening** and *italics*, as well as underscoring to give headings and key words visual appeal; they also employ

  progressive

  indentation

  and the use of white space surrounding major headings and subsection headings.
- Short formal reports tend to make more use of number referencing systems to organise each point within a hierarchy of importance; the decimal point system – 3.0 3.1 3.1.1 3.1.1.1 – is most widely employed for this purpose.
- It is important that all recipients of internal documents are made fully aware (by appropriate entries of dates and entries like first draft or agreed final version) that they are consulting and using the most up-to-date version of any widely circulated document.
- Advertisements combine a mix of graphical/ visual appeal with snappy textual messages; most comprise a strong appeal to encourage the reader to take immediate, positive action, e.g. Hurry while stocks last!
- Fact-sheets employ most of the format and display features of reports and seek to summarise key data through a logically sequenced set of points.

USING STRUCTURE AND STYLE TO EMPHASISE MEANING

Before writing, put brain in gear

The final part of Element 3.2 examines how a combination of an appropriate structure and style act to emphasise how a written document is read, interpreted and responded to. The written documents you have already examined – discussion paper, letter, memorandum, report, advertisement, fact-sheet, etc – have indicated how different structures are used to communicate different types of message in quite different ways. For instance, a short formal report's structure is used to convey a wealth of detailed information in a highly developed way, where major sections precede minor sections, and major subpoints their minor counterparts. By contrast, the structure of a display advertisement is much simpler, since the message it seeks to impart is, by definition, short and immediate.

Thus, where effective structures are concerned, the motto must be 'horses for courses'. Indeed, the key to selecting an effective structure and style with which to deliver a specific message is to follow the simple yet important sequence of steps set out below.

Factors influencing the choice of written communications medium

First of all, consider the nature of your message you wish to transmit in terms of:

1 **Complexity:** do you have a large amount of data to communicate, or just a one-point message?

2 **Urgency:** must your message be delivered immediately or is speed of delivery not essential?

3 **Reception:** is it important that your message is received by a group or team simultaneously, say details of a programme of compulsory redundancy?

4 **Confidentiality:** is it important for your message to be delivered in individual sealed envelopes, or can it be displayed on a notice-board ?

Answers to key questions like those above will steer your choice towards a particular type of written document (or electronic text transmission system such as fax or email) which will be most suited to your desired aims, whether letter, notice, advertisement, fax, group email memo, etc. Such answers will also steer you towards an appropriate choice of document in terms of its structure and format.

Factors influencing the choice of document in terms of structure and format

The next key step is to consider the intrinsic nature of your message in terms of:

Desired aim: is your message aimed to inform or brief factually, to persuade or motivate subjectively, or to analyse critically and objectively?

Decisions in this area will directly affect the structure and format you employ. For example, the highly schematised layouts of short informal and formal reports and fact-sheets are ideal for conveying factual data, but not well suited for developing analyses or critical arguments, which benefit from the structure of a series of headed, continuous prose paragraphs. Similarly, messages with a strong but simple aim of communicating a highly persuasive message may require very little text but extensive, visually appealing graphics.

Factors influencing the choice of document in terms of its intended readership

The third key step is to consider the profile of the intended readership or recipients of your written message:

1 **By age:** is your readership young or elderly? Variations in age directly affect the ways in which people pick up and accept messages, thus requiring the writer to adopt varying styles to suit various age-groups. Compare, for example, the written styles of the magazines *Seventeen* and *The Lady*.

2 **By education:** are you writing for a highly articulate and educated readership who will be untroubled by multisyllabic, Latinate vocabulary, or will you need to select a format and vocabulary suited to readers with modest reading skills?

3 **By experience:** will you be communicating with experts who are comfortable with technical jargon, or will you need to simplify complex ideas to suit a non-expert, lay audience?

4 **By predjudice and outlook:** will your intended readers share your own views and outlooks, or will your message need to be slanted in such a way as to overcome the resistance of a readership with different outlooks and prejudices? In such instances, writers need to provide more extended rationales and justifications for ideas posed.

> ***KEY POINT***
>
> By considering carefully the constraints made upon your message and its transmission – in terms of its urgency, confidentiality and complexity – its basic purpose – in terms of informing or persuading – and the profile of your readership – in terms of age, education, experience and outlook – *before* you rush to write, you will already have progressed a long way towards constructing and delivering an effective message.

Style and context

Having examined carefully the prewriting phase, when considerations are given to the desired aim of the message and its impact on its intended readership, the next key steps concern the creation of an effective style, effective because it is appropriate to the situation or context in which it occurs. Consider the range or continuum of formality in Figure 2.36.

Letters seeking payment of an overdue account

Figure 2.37 shows a final letter to secure overdue payment before taking legal action. Notice here that, though not becoming rude or aggressive, the tone of the letter is deliberately terse and formal. The accounts manager has given up hope of securing payment of the debt while keeping the customer's goodwill, and has settled for recovering the money and cancelling the customer's credit arrangement.

Notice the following constructions which help to create the tone:

> In spite of . . . still remains outstanding; . . . the period of credit extended to your company . . . Unless the overdue account is settled in full within seven days . . . compelled to instruct . . . to undertake the necessary legal action to recover the debt.

Figure 2.37 A final demand is terse but not aggressive.

> Dear Sir,
>
> OVERDUE ACCOUNT: £1492.43
>
> In spite of the copy statement and reminders sent to you on 3 April 199–, 21 April 199– and 7 May 199–, your account for February 199– still remains outstanding; enclosed please find a final statement.
>
> As previously stated, the period of credit extended to your company was agreed as one calender month from receipt of statement.
>
> Unless the above overdue account is settled in full within seven days, I shall be compelled to instruct my company's solicitors to undertake the necessary legal action to recover the debt.
>
> Yours faithfully,

The writer deliberately distances himself from the reader in such formal language and the terse 'either . . . or' construction of the final paragraph.

Compare the tone of this letter with Figure 2.38, the sort of letter the accounts manager is likely to send when the account first becomes overdue and only a polite reminder is felt appropriate.

Contrastingly, the writer takes pains not to cause offence – the account may have been paid and an error occurred on the accounts computer, or payment may be being withheld because of a query which has not been communicated to the accounts department. Thus the tone and language employed are much more tentative. The accounts manager does not want to lose a good customer by upsetting him – certainly not at this stage:

> I should like to draw your attention to . . .

Figure 2.36 Formality in writing depends on its context.

Decreasing formality →

report to board of directors	official letters to customers, clients or patients	internal memoranda and notices	display advertisements
chief officers' reports to county councils	internal reports	faxed messages	email messages
scientific papers	in-house discussion papers	house newspapers and bulletins	telephone messages and hand-written notes

Figure 2.38 A polite reminder is concerned but courteous.

Dear Sir,

OVERDUE ACCOUNT: £1492.43

I should like to draw to your attention that the statement of account rendered to you at the end of March 199– for goods purchased in February 199– does not appear to have been paid according to our accounts records.

I should therefore be grateful if you would kindly confirm that the goods delivered (delivery notes XB45367, XC65434 and XG54786) proved satisfactory and that there is no reason why you should be deferring payment.

Please advise me as soon as possible if you are experiencing any problem in this regard, otherwise I shall look forward to receiving your cheque for £1492.43, which is now overdue according to the credit arrangements between us.

Yours faithfully,

Notice that the constructions are much less terse and more polite, and that words like *kindly* and *please* emphasize the writer's feeling of reluctantly having to remind the customer of the overdue account.

Figure 2.39 A direct mailshot is friendly and inviting.

Dear Householder,

A SURE WAY YOU CAN SAVE MONEY THIS WINTER!

Will your bank-balance get blown away by an 'overdraught' of cold air again this winter?

Our research has proved that up to 30 per cent of all money spent on home heating virtually goes up in smoke each year!

The guilty culprits are ill-fitting, single-glazed windows and doors, poor insulation in lofts and attics and exposed cavity walls.

Can you afford to let yet another year go by with your heating bills far larger than they need be? . . .

An example of a style of writing in quite a different context is found in Figure 2.39, a direct mail sales letter to house-owners seeking to sell them a full insulation service to double glaze and insulate their homes.

In this introductory part of the letter, the tone is much more easy and friendly – the firm of insulators is trying to establish a rapport or bond with the prospective customer, who is thus addressed not as Dear Sir or Dear Madam, but as Dear Householder, which appears less formal. Notice the attention-getting subject-heading of the letter. Who of us doesn't wish to save money? Also, the opening sentence poses a direct question which reinforces this subject-heading in a cheery, cheeky way by the studied use of the pun of 'draught of cold air' and bank 'overdraught'.

This friendly approach continues in the second paragraph with the deliberate use of the colloquialism 'goes up in smoke'. The use of persuasive language is also evident in the third paragraph, where single-glazed doors and windows become 'ill-fitting', implying that only double-glazed doors and windows will fit snugly! Lastly, the letter's author introduces a rhetorical question from his repertoire of stylistic devices in the fourth paragraph which invites the reader's response:

> No, I can't go on for another year letting my heating bills be far larger than they need be!

From this brief survey of three letters written in different contexts, it becomes clear that the circumstances in which a piece of writing is produced will have a significant impact upon the creation of a particular style.

Guidelines for devising a writing style appropriate to a given context

- **Consider the relationship between you and your readers:** is it based upon the organisational hierarchy – manager to subordinate or upon an equal, peer group standing – co-worker to co-worker?
- **Consider the context of the message:** is it high-level, formal and serious or intradepartmental and routine? Are external customers or clients involved, or internal, closely working colleagues?
- **Consider the purpose of the message:** is it to persuade in a friendly way (like an invitation to join the works hockey team) or to inform in an impersonal way (like an announcement of sales performance or statistics relating to the time taken to treat patients)?
- **Consider the extent of the message's readership:** Is it destined to be read confidentially by a single recipient, or will it be scanned by most of the organisation's workforce?

Small group skills-building activity

Jack Fairclough is a very able works manager who runs a successful factory which manufactures motor-car replacement parts. His factory is one of fifteen spread across the UK, which form UK Parts & Accessories plc. Jack's problem is that he hates paperwork, and is generally late in delivering to the manufacturing director his weekly report on production output, related costs and wastage rates. At a national works managers' meeting held on 21 January 199–, the manufacturing director emphasised the importance of receiving the weekly reports by 11:00 A.M. on Mondays at the latest, in order to enable him to produce a composite report for the company's board of directors. But Jack is still behindhand, and so the manufacturing director decides to send him a memo to resolve the matter.

In groups of 2 or 3 consider the following four versions of the memo, A–D, and decide in your group which one is likely to achieve the desired effect and why. Or provide your reasons for deciding that none is appropriate.

A Further to the National Works Manager Meeting of 21 January 199–, you are reminded of my reference to punctuality in the despatch of weekly production reports. This reference was occasioned by the need for the efficient compilation of national production figures which the Board requires in order to determine that requisite levels of productivity and cost controls are achieved.

I note, however, that your report is still failing to materialise by the designated 11:00 A.M. on Mondays. Unless your performance improves directly in this respect, I shall be compelled to take the matter further.

B At our last National Works Managers' Meeting of 21 January 199–, I stressed the need for all Works Managers to send in their weekly production reports to reach me no later than 11:00 A.M. on Mondays at the latest.

You will recall that I emphasised the importance of timeliness in this matter, so as to allow me time to absorb all the UK production data and to produce an effective summary report for the Board's weekly Tuesday meetings.

I should therefore be grateful if you would ensure that you give this matter priority, so that I am not regularly held up until your report is made available to me.

C At our last National Works Managers' Meeting of 21 January 199–, I mentioned how important it was for your weekly production report to reach me by 11:00 A.M. on Mondays. My own production picture, costs analysis and quality assurance evaluations all rely on my receiving works managers' reports in good time.

Your own factory is playing an important part at the moment in our national development programme, and for this reason, I am relying on you to get me your figures on time, so I can get my own report to the Board in good time.

I know you won't want to hold up this vital process, and set great store by your commitment as a team player!

D I'm concerned about not receiving your weekly production report on time. You remember I raised the problem at our last National Managers' Meeting of 21 January 199–, and told everyone how important it was to send in their reports to me by 11:00 A.M. Mondays.

Well, I don't seem to be receiving yours until Tuesdays or Wednesdays, and so I'm really held up in getting a full report to the Board in time for their Tuesday meetings, and giving them a complete picture of weekly output – where your own factory is doing so well.

It would certainly help me on Monday, if I had your figures along with everyone else's. I know I can rely on you.

[Adapted by kind permission of Pitman Publishing from D. W. Evans, *People, Communication & Organisations*, 2nd edition, 1990]

Syntax and style

The term *syntax* is simply a convenient label for the various ways that writers build ideas by creating word groups that convey meaning as either single words, phrases, clauses or sentences. Consider some definitions.

- **phrase:** a group of words with no verb included:

round the bend   with a bent axle
of all shapes and sizes   down and out

Phrases are used to add meaning to either nouns or verbs:

The white Porche careered wildly *round the bend.*
(adds meaning to the verb *careered*)
The caller at the door appeared to be a *down and out* tramp.
(adds meaning to the noun *tramp*)

- **clause:** a group of words with both a subject and verb which forms a part of a sentence:

although it was clearly in need of repairs
Alice fell immediately in love with the cottage
even if it took all she had
that she must have it

Clauses are, in effect, sentences in their own right which are linked together by conjunctions or linking words to form complex sentences capable of communicating several ideas within a single sentence:

Alice fell immediately in love with the cottage, *although* it was clearly in need of repairs.

Even if it took all she had, she decided *that* she must have it.

Using syntax effectively

In all writing, there are two key parts of speech around which meaning clusters, *nouns and verbs.* Nouns, or naming words, are the technical terms for the subjects of sentences (the doers) and the objects of sentences (which receive the actions of the doers).

Nouns

Johnny broke the *window.*
The *chemical* blistered his *skin.*

In order to extend the meaning of any given idea, we can add meaning to nouns in a variety of ways:

Little, seven-year-old Johnny broke the *upstairs* window with a *sharp* stone.

The *highly dangerous* chemical blistered his *unprotected* skin.

Such additional describing words are called *adjectives.*

Verbs

The care assistant *bathed* the elderly resident.

The swimming-pool lifeguard *was watching* the group of young swimmers.

Without reinforcements the battle *would* have been *lost.*

In a similar way, the meaning conveyed by simple verbs can be extended by adding a variety of descriptors in these kinds of ways:

The care assistant bathed the elderly resident *very gently.*

The swimming-pool lifeguard was watching *fixedly* the group of young swimmers.

Without reinforcements the battle *would have* been *utterly* lost long *before.*

Additional descriptors which describe verbs are called *adverbs.*

Personal and impersonal constructions

Most of the writing which people at work produce is written in an active, personal mode:

I should be grateful if *you* would kindly arrange for *me* to receive...

We have decided to implement the working party's recommendations.

However, sometimes the context of a piece of writing requires its author to adopt an impersonal tone, where I and you are kept out, and where only the third person – he, she, it, they – is employed. This can be effected in two straightforward ways.

Impersonal 'it' constructions

It was decided that the working party's recommendations be adopted.

The 'it' construction can be used with either an active or passive verb:

- **Active verb:** It *transpired* that the wound never healed properly.
- **Passive verb:** It *has been demonstrated* that the laws of physics still apply when...

Use of the passive voice of the verb

An alternative to 'it' constructions which readily conveys an impersonal tone is the passive voice of the verb. The active

I poured 250 cc of the liquid into the calorimeter.

becomes the passive.

250 cc of the liquid *were poured* into the calorimeter [by me].

The 'by me' can be left out, since it is understood, and thus the real doer of the action is concealed, hence the sentence's impersonal tone:

The sentence's tone *was made impersonal* through the passive use of the verb.

KEY POINT

- **Make sure that what you have written is a completed sentence.** Test your 'potential sentence' by identifying its subject = the doer of the action; then check that it has a verb which is communicating the 'action' of the sentence. Such verbs have to possess: a number – singular or plural; a person: first *I*, *we*, second, *you* or third, *he*, *she*, *they*: and a tense – *present, past, future* etc. If your sentence possesses a subject which 'controls' a verb meeting the above conditions, then it is a bona fide, actual, real and copper-bottomed grammatical sentence!

The down and out tramp *subject*	was asking *finite verb* *third person* *singular* *past tense*	for a drink of water

  Avoid the temptation to use single words or short phrases other than in advertisements or picture captions.

- **Select highly expressive nouns and verbs to communicate your meaning.** Avoid the ▶

need to load them up with piled-on descriptors such as adjectives or adverbs.

The hovel squatted at the end of the gorge.

is better than

The small, decaying house looked low and sunken at the end of the steeply sided, deep valley.

The shorter your sentences and the more expressive your choice of nouns and verbs, the more emphatically and memorably will you communicate your meaning. Lazy writers obscure their meaning by overuse of descriptors, just as ivy and mistletoe conceal the shape and structure of a strong tree.

- **Vary the length and structure of your sentences.** Important ideas are often best expressed in deliberately short sentences and are given increased impact if they occur after a build-up of points:

  Jackie fretted and paced up and down in the hallway, waiting for the postman's step. The clock indicated that it was, without doubt, 10:45 and that the postman was definitely late. Then, a rattle of the door-knocker preceded a rasping thud as a pile of letters and circulars fell through the letter-box. Jackie's eye immediately spotted the Midchester College logo on its white envelope. She snatched it up noiselessly and ripped it open. Her eyes raced down past the preliminary paragraphs, to the box at the bottom of her GNVQ Advanced Results Schedule. She had been awarded a distinction!

  Deliberately, the writer of the above piece builds up the sense of excitement and tension by moving from longer to shorter sentences and saves, up the keyword *distinction* until the dramatic final sentence. While work-based writing rarely calls for such drama, people at work do appreciate variety and emphasis in what they have to read.

- **Avoid composing sentences which become too long and complicated.** As has already been pointed out, sentences which contain more than 30 words (25 if multisyllabic) tend to baffle the average reader. Moreover, their authors tend to lose control of the meaning they are seeking to impart.

Style and choosing the right words

As you will already have determined, individual words are the building-blocks of both language and syntax. Inevitably, therefore, the way in which our written ideas affect our readers, for good or bad, is ultimately down to the vocabulary we decide to use as we go along the path of written composition.

Now the English language is remarkably rich in words (or synonyms to use the technical term) which convey a variety of shades of meaning around a central idea. As you can see from Figure 2.40, choice is extensive (and the list shown is by no means exhaustive). Moreover, some of the synonyms are complimentary – mature, venerable, well-preserved, etc – and others derogatory – crumbly, dusty, gaga, etc. Yet others are more impersonal and used medically – senile, geriatric.

The synonym for *old* we may decide to use in a given piece of writing will depend upon:

- **context:** formal at work, social at leisure, etc.
- **recipient:** line or senior manager, friend, relative, etc.
- **purpose:** to amuse, to discipline, to persuade, to inform, etc.

Although someone might get away with referring to an old person as a *gaga geezer* in privacy and among friends, using such a term might well prove ill-judged at work, when *elderly gentleman* would be more appropriate to describe a customer.

Connotative and denotative vocabulary

Do not be put off by the heading; *connotative* simply means possessing many layers of meaning, and *denotative* means conveying a single meaning.

Connotative words tend to be selected when writers seek to convince, move or persuade their readers, and denotative ones when seeking to inform, brief, argue logically or impart facts. Connotative vocabulary has its roots in the Anglo-Saxon, Norse, Danish and Middle German origins of English, whereas denotative vocabulary tends to stem from Latin, Greek and Norman French. One was the simple language of peasants and small farmers, the other was the administrative language of generals, kings, lords and barons. Here are some connotative words with their denotative counterparts:

Connotative words	Denotative counterparts
on the dole	unemployed
revenge	retaliation
home	residence
choke, stifle	asphyxiate
live with	cohabit
land	acreage
a rip-off	excessively priced
attacker, mugger	assailant
underwear	lingerie
helpmate	ancillary worker
wrong	erroneous
lying	mendacious
bastard	illegitimate

Figure 2.40 The word old has many synonyms and entailments.

mature grizzled

ancient aged elderly senile past it venerable

advanced in years senior citizen – **OLD** – antiquated geriatic crumbly dusty

hoary wizened decrepit gaga doddering patriarchal

superannuated well-preserved

Now compare the following two extracts, which have quite distinct aims. The first aims to rally a lone nation against impending Nazi invasion in 1940, and the other explains how to give first aid in the event of broken bones:

> We shall go on to the end, we shall fight in France, we shall fight on the seas and oceans, we shall fight with growing confidence and growing strength in the air, we shall defend our island, whatever the cost may be, we shall fight on the beaches, we shall fight on the landing-grounds, we shall fight in the fields and in the streets, we shall fight in the hills; we shall never surrender. (Sir Winston Churchill, 4 June 1940)

In this magnificent rallying cry to a people nervously expecting to be overwhelmed, Churchill displays his mastery of expressing his message in what is virtually poetic language masquerading as prose. Consider, for example, his key words:

> we shall fight seas oceans growing confidence strength air defend island cost beaches landing-grounds fields streets hills never surrender

Almost all the words originate from Saxon/Norse and are predominantly monosyllabic. The repetition of the refrain 'we shall fight' serves to give the passage a solemn rhythm, and the effect of the punctuation is to slow down the pace, which reflects the grave situation facing the British people. In effect, Churchill in his most careful use of the English language chose those words which were calculated to pluck at the nation's heartstrings and to encourage the blood to rise in the act of summoning up the resolve to fight it out with the Nazis to the death so as to save the homeland.

> ***Broken bones***
> Keep the patient warm and immobile and treat for shock if necessary. Apply a cold compress to the painful area and support it as comfortably as possible. If a broken bone protrudes through the skin and there is severe bleeding, stop the bleeding, but do not attempt to push the bone back in place. Make no attempt to clean the wound. Call an ambulance, or get the patient to a doctor.
> If it is essential to move the victim to prevent further injury, immobilize the affected limb with splints to prevent further damage. For emergency splints, use anything that will keep the broken bones from moving – newspapers or magazines or broomsticks or boards for arms or legs. Make sure the splints are long enough to reach beyond the joint both above and below the break. Apply them over the clothing, pad them with cotton wool or clean rags and tie them snugly, not too tightly, in place.
> *Reader's Digest Handbook of First Aid.*

By contrast, this passage is much more down to earth. It employs Latinate, multisyllabic words for accuracy – immobile, protrudes, etc. – and its general style is impersonal.

What do you think?

1 Consider the kinds of writing you have undertaken during the past 3–5 years. Did you ever pause to consider the kind of style you wanted to create before writing ? If your answer is an honest no, was this, in your opinion, because people create the styles they want unconsciously, or because this element of writing had not really occurred to you until now as creatable? Given your responses to these questions, how do you feel now about your ability to create a specific style to achieve a specific aim? Can it be done ? Is the attempt worthwhile ?

2 What in your view are the key aspects of a recipient's profile that the writer should take into account when producing a document?

3 Do you agree that documents can end up being either very formal or very informal? If so, what makes the difference in your view?

4 What aspects of employees' relationships in the workplace do you think influence the ways in which they write to each other? Should an employee take them into account or simply ignore them?

5 As you near the end of your study of Element 3.2, what do you think are the components which make up the tone or style of a written document?

Student pair skills-building activity

TASK 1

Over a period of about a week, collect 2 or 3 examples of what you consider to be good examples of the following aspects of style in written documents:

(a) formal, serious, high-status

(b) analytical and objective in a scientific way

(c) factual and impersonal

(d) persuasive and emotive

(e) friendly, appealing and influencing

TASK 2

In a general class session, exhibit your examples and explain why you consider them to be effective. Select the best two examples in each of the above categories, (a) to (e), and display them in your baseroom.

Choosing the right words

- Never be lazy and settle for vague or meaningless words or phrases such as nice, great, fairly, kind of, all right, more and less.
- Avoid tired and overworked words (termed clichés) such as *in this day and age, to be perfectly frank, a good deal, taking everything into account*. Clichés convey nothing; they merely pad out your writing and obscure its meaning.
- Select expressive verbs and nouns rather than surrounding drab versions with lots of adjectives and adverbs.
- Consider whether the words you choose will convey the meaning you intend or whether they tend to be interpreted in an unintended way. *Jack's colourful language was not always appreciated by female staff.* Was it interestingly expressive or just vulgar?
- Avoid multisyllabic, Latinate vocabulary if your message is intended to be simple and direct; but choose it if you wish to convey precise meanings in complex and abstract areas.
- Review your choice of words carefully before publishing them; consider their position on these registers: formal–informal, impersonal–friendly, factual–persuasive. Try not to confuse, irritate, patronise or lose your audience without realising it.
- Check your selected words in terms of your audience; check they match your audience in technical expertise, developed reading and comprehension skills, strongly held views, age, experience, etc.
- At work, save in the most informal writing, avoid words and expressions which are slang or colloquialisms, overfamiliar, sarcastic, aggressive or hostile; and similarly, avoid choosing words and expressions which end up making your writing long-winded, dull or vague.

SUMMARY

The key points of this section are:

- The structure and style communicated by a document depend upon its complexity, its urgency, its anticipated reception and its confidentiality.
- Paramount is the specific aim the document seeks to meet.
- It is important when creating a particular style and tone for a document to take into account the profile of its audience: age, gender, education, experience, views, prejudices and outlooks.
- All written documents embody a degree of formality or informality depending upon their context and for whom they are written.
- The context of a piece of writing is important and involves the document's purpose; the relationship between writer and reader; as well as the way in which it will be read, perhaps privately by a single recipient, or from a noticeboard by many people.
- The impact of a given written message relies heavily on its choice of (a) syntax, the ways in which its clusters of words are joined together, and (b) its vocabulary, the choice of words made to communicate meaning. Variations in these two areas will have a great bearing on whether a piece of writing is considered formal, factual and impersonal, or subjective, friendly and persuasive.

Student pair skills-building activity

As a working pair, select *one* of the following sets of words which are representative of vocabulary in common use within a particular job sector. Compose a paragraph of prose (of about 220–250 words) which would characterise the sector chosen and employ in it as many of the words listed as possible (without losing touch with realism) You may employ any word in any of its associated parts of speech (e.g allege, allegation). Seek to construct a tone and style suited to the vocabulary listed. When you have completed this activity, compare and evaluate your version with those produced by other class student pairs. Select the best on the basis of using the selected words most effectively.

THE WORLD OF ADVERTISING

new instant whiter fresh improved simply mild soft gently tangy fizzy sparkle gleam mature strong sharp fast-acting bigger better more extra real totally great prefer love lovely silky dreamy fast comfort security take-home family economy

THE WORLD OF MANUFACTURING

output line run batch shift gear prototype test-bed tool-room specification bench-mark quality assurance wastage piece-work modification CADCAM dimensions gauge operator supervisor parts maintenance swarf tolerance extrude bin measurement

THE WORLD OF HEALTH AND CARE

infirm chronic disabled paraplegic dosage medication mobility impaired physiotherapy regime post-operative massage contagious infectious dosage ingest incontinent psychosomatic placebo prognosis diagnosis geriatric juvenile sibling care order psychiatric abuse statutory socialize committal community stigma rejection

THE WORLD OF LEISURE AND TOURISM

amenity physical conditioning circuit musculature energy work-rate cross-trainer multi-purpose gymnastic aerobic soft/hard impact dorsal prone pectoral saturation accompanied local time package courier baggage carousel real-time booking conditions open ticket double booking half-board en suite bidet self-contained gourmet à la carte table d'hôte crêche inclusive insurance cover liability exceptions

THE WORLD OF SCIENCE

mass volume evaporate dilute agitate verifying experiment indeterminate results invalid tendency conversion catalyst toxicity suffused stress pressure spectrum microscopic granular evaporation viscosity extrapolate posit exchange demonstrate

THE WORLD OF FINANCE

asset capital profit expenses calculate balance debit liability depreciate gross compound net expenses creditworthiness fiscal speculate gilt-edged market-maker discount loss reserves check-digit audit trail creditor official receiver bankruptcy liquidation

Small group skills-building activity

TASK 1

In groups of 2 or 3 students, consider carefully each of the following extracts from a range of work-based written documents. Discuss for each extract why, where and how the style and tone have gone wrong, and which specific words or phrases are the culprits. Decide for each extract how it should be better expressed, and write down your preferred version.

1 I have to inform you that your enquiry will be dealt with in due course.

2 I must apologise for the delay in your receiving your vehicle after service.

As you will readily appreciate, motor-vehicle wheels need to be balanced dynamically as well as statically to avoid the transmission of vibration through the steering linkage.

Moreover, the diagnosis of misalignment in the nearside front wheel revealed that feathering and premature wear had been caused to the tyre, which as you realise, being asymmetrical in tread design is incompatible with tyres of another make.

I trust this explanation will satisfactorily account for the delay.

3 The reason I am writing to you on a plain piece of note-paper is because of the incompetence of your firm in supplying my order for company stationery, which you may just recall you received last December.

4 Mr Johnson said to tell you we seem to have dropped a bit of a clanger over the grinding machine. The drive belt's come adrift and we're up the creek for a spare. He says we're due for a drop next Monday and he'll give you a tinkle, OK?

5 It has come to my attention that departmental staff are in breach of their conditions of service as a result of unpunctuality.

Unless a substantial improvement is discerned in the immediate future, disciplinary measures will be taken.

6 Thank you for your enquiry, but my company only deals in genuine antiques.

7 Our current inability to meet the requirements of your recently remitted order is occasioned by an unanticipated shortage of the spare parts specified.

8 Due to circumstances beyond our control, there has been a temporary delay in effecting repairs to your lawnmower, which we hope to rectify as soon as the situation eases.

Assuring you of our best attention at all times.

9 Further to your memorandum of 14 June 199–.

Of course, in normal circumstances my department would be only too pleased to be of assistance with the provision of advertising material for your display on 21st August.

Regretfully, however, only reference copies of such material are kept centrally. You may care to try Sales.

Do let me know if I may be of any assistance in any other sphere.

10 Recommendations

Any future improvement in company turnover is entirely dependent upon either lowering or raising the price or the quality of our current product range.

If the latter option is adopted, the prospect of increased competition or a reduction in gross profits must be faced.

In such a clear-cut situation, the action needed to resolve the problem is self-explanatory

TASK 2

When you have completed analysis of the extracts, compare your notes and versions with the other groups in your class in a general discussion. When you have made your comparisons, seek to agree on what it is about – context, circumstances, people's feelings, etc – which directly influences the choice of words used in written documents.

Portfolio-building activities

PRODUCTION OF STRAIGHTFORWARD, WRITTEN DOCUMENTS

For people who know the student

1 Imagine that you are about to complete your Advanced GNVQ programme of study. Write a letter to your personal tutor and teachers to thank them for their help and support during your studies. This letter may be handwritten, and should cover about 1.5 sides of A4.

2 Produce, for your GNVQ communication teacher to vet and authorise, a set of instructions for *one* of the following:

(a) How to use your departmental photocopier cost-effectively

(b) What steps to take if a student suddenly requires immediate first aid

(c) What procedure to follow for submitting a GNVQ portfolio assignment

The set of instructions should be word processed and not exceed one side of A4

3 Design and produce an informational leaflet for your co-students which explains simply and clearly where in your study centre and locality useful sources of information are to be found which relate to your GNVQ course of study.

This leaflet should extend over not more than two sides of A4, which may be folded, etc., and may include some form of clip-art or similar graphic illustration. The use of cut-and-paste, photocopied graphics is also permitted.

4 Produce a short report on current trends and developments in your vocational study area in both the UK and EU. Your report is intended to brief your co-students, and should thus take into account their background and subject-experience to date. The report should be two or three sides of A4 in length and incorporate a suitable format.

5 Produce a curriculum vitae (for use in either obtaining part-time work as a student or for your forthcoming job applications) which your teacher will scrutinise and advise you upon. Present your CV in an appropriate printed (or handwritten) format and aim not to exceed three sides of A4. Give your CV a visual appeal through an attractive use of layout techniques.

6 Design a display advertisement which encourages your class of students (and any other parallel classes to take part in a trip to a London or regional museum or art gallery (such as the Natural History Museum, the Victoria & Albert Museum, the Transport Museum or the National Gallery). The display advertisement may include some form of graphic content and should be produced on one side of A3 paper.

For people who do not know the student

1 Compose a letter applying for an actual or simulated part-time employment post (say, as a sales assistant, factory operative, Christmas postal worker, summer-holiday delivery person or tourist guide, etc.) Your letter may be handwritten or printed and should not exceed two sides of A4.

2 Design a suitable fact-sheet for students who will succeed you in your Advanced GNVQ course of studies outlining what resources and facilities will be available to them at your study centre (a) for their studies and (b) in a social, sports and recreational context. Your fact-sheet should be printed on between two and three sides of A4.

3 Design a suitable brochure (not exceeding two sides of A4) which outlines what career opportunities are available in your locality for students embarking upon full-time careers in your GNVQ vocational sector. Your brochure may incorporate either clip-art or cut-and-paste, photocopied graphics.

4 Design a set of instructions to guide part-time students who wish to enroll at your study centre. Bear in mind that many of them will have no prior knowledge of your centre's geography, enrolment system or what sources of information and guidance are available. Your instructions should not exceed two sides of A4.

5 Compose a suitable fact-sheet which is intended to brief local employers about the nature and scope of your GNVQ programme of study, and what knowledge and skills completing students will emerge with, skills that local employers should be aware of. Your fact-sheet should be about two sides of A4 in length

6 Devise a suitable poster aimed at encouraging students at your study centre to take part in a series of evening meetings of an association which has been recently set up to promote interest in your area of study (such as the British Association of Young Scientists BAYS, or Young Engineers, Young Business Managers, Young Leisure and Tourism Officers, Young Health and Social Care Professionals). The poster should communicate appropriately the benefits and enjoyment which attendance at the series of evening meetings will provide. The poster may include some form of graphic content and should be produced on one side of A3 paper.

PRODUCTION OF COMPLEX WRITTEN DOCUMENTS

For people who know the student

1 Your personal tutor has given you a great deal of help and support during your Advanced GNVQ programme of study, and was instrumental in persuading you to put in a UCAS form for a degree course. Thanks to this support, you now have a guaranteed place to start your degree this coming autumn at the Heart of England University, nationally the most prestigious for your subject, and for which there is fierce competition. As a result, the university has an admissions policy that will not hold over places given from one year to the next. For the past four months, you have become seriously involved with another student on your study course. You have both decided to take a year out and to take a trip around the world – before life and the career crowd in on you. You see this as a once-only opportunity. Write a suitable letter to your personal tutor, explaining your decision. Your letter should be handwritten and should not exceed two sides of A4.

2 Recently, the government has decided to load both the grants and awards it makes to students of both FE/ secondary schools and HE in favour of students pursuing engineering, manufacturing, construction and science NVQ, GNVQ and degree courses. In order to finance this decision, the government has decided to cut by 10% the grants and awards made to students pursuing business, health and social care, leisure and tourism, art and design and hospitality courses. The rationale for this decision is that the former courses are undersubscribed and the latter are oversubscribed, but the UK economy is more in need of qualified young adults in the former subject areas.

This decision has either pleased or infuriated actual and intending students of various subjects. You decide to write a letter to the editor of a national broadsheet newspaper either supporting or opposing this educational policy. Your letter should aim to stir public opinion and increase awareness about this decision, but should also supply a rationale for the position you take. Your letter may be handwritten or printed and its length should be between 1.5 and 2 sides of A4.

3 You work for an enlightened employer, whose workforce includes a number of activists in the women's movement. As a result of an extended programme of lobbying by your staff association, your board of directors/ trustees has decided to give consideration to the introduction of a work-sharing policy. Such a policy enables two employees (say partners, a married couple or two friends) to discharge a single job between them; one works mornings, the other afternoons, or each works alternate days, alternate weeks, etc. Each receives 50% of the pay for the post. Under current EU law both would become entitled to employment rights and to take part in superannuation/pension schemes, etc.

The board has invited interested staff (who have briefed themselves on the subject) to submit discussion papers to inform any decision taken. You decide to produce a discussion paper which considers the proposal objectively and on its merits and demerits, and which comes to either a 'for' or 'against' conclusion. Your discussion paper to your board should concentrate on the implications for the department or section in which you work and should be sent to your head of department in the first instance. Produce a suitable discussion paper between three and four sides of printed A4 in length.

4 Having recently completed your Advanced GNVQ programme of study successfully, you are now three months into your first full-time post in your chosen field. For several months now, the government has been allocating funds to commerce, industry and to the public and voluntary sectors in order to improve and extend the use of IT-based equipment, software and telecommunications systems. In particular, the government is seeking to improve the access of young adults – technicians, managers and officers – to such IT provisions. Accordingly, it allocates £10 million annually to young employees in organisations (about £10,000 each) who submit reports, which a panel evaluates, on how additional IT equipment, services and systems could help them do their jobs better. The successful entrants receive a lump sum of £10,000 to spend (with their organisation's approval) on upgrading their personal workstations and/or office and/or motor vehicle, etc.

The actual title of the current report for which awards are being made is

> What additional IT-based provisions would enable me to do my job better, and how I would use them

The rules of the award require each report to outline the type of organisation and work the applicant does, what IT-based resources are currently available to him or her, what additional provisions would prove helpful (within the £10,000 ceiling), and what recommendations the applicant would make to spend the available funding most cost-effectively. The report should be addressed to your immediate line manager, and copied to Prof. J C Varkas, Department of Employment, and also to your managing director, chief officer or most senior manager. Produce a suitably formatted, printed report between three and four sides of A4 in length.

5 You work in the development department of one of the professional institutions which provide support in your vocational work area (e.g. The Institute of Management, The Institute of Leisure and Amenity Management, The Chartered Institute of Engineers). Over the past 10–15 years many books and articles have been written about the discrimination experienced by women in work organisations, but few in-depth studies have been undertaken. Your manager, Harry Lancaster, has therefore asked you to

undertake a small but detailed research project. This is how you were briefed:

> I'd like you to target about four female employees working in different posts within one or several organisations in our vocational sector, with varying job roles and authority, for example, a hospital administrative assistant, a nurse, a ward sister and a doctor. I'd like you to interview each one and to establish their views on whether being female affects their promotion, career advancement, etc., as compared with their male counterparts. Also I'd like you to canvas their views on whether such aspects are getting better or worse for women. Of course, you will need to assure them that any views given will be non-attributable.
>
> When you have gathered your evidence – plus any relevant national statistics you can discover – I want you to produce four anonymous case histories in a suitable format, topped and tailed by a suitable introduction and conclusion. The best versions produced by our team will be published in the institute's magazine in a three-part series to be entitled *Glass Ceiling, Fact or Myth*?

Produce a suitable printed response in not more than five sides of A4.

6 You work as an assistant manager in the personnel department of a large organisation in your vocational sector (e.g. business, manufacturing, science, leisure and tourism, health and social care). Recently there has been a lot of backbiting and hysteria among some staff as a result of some ill-informed publicity regarding one of your employees, alleged to have contracted AIDS. As a result of being harassed and shunned, the employee is currently on sick-leave. In order to help in restoring calm and to provide fully-informed reassurance to all employees, your personnel director, Kim Davies, has decided to distribute an informational brochure to all staff which provides clear information on how AIDS can, and more particularly *cannot*, be transmitted from one person to another.

The personnel director's brief emphasised the following:

> The brochure must not preach at staff, nor appear to single out any specific sexual orientation. Above all, it should combine a factual approach with an overall tone which stresses the unlikelihood of anyone acquiring AIDS while carrying out any of the work done by our organisation. Of course, there's no harm in emphasising the normal precautions to be taken in case of accident, mouth-to-mouth resuscitation, treating an open wound, etc. As you know, all of our first-aid cases are suitably equipped.
>
> I want *you* to design the brochure, because you know most of our staff well, and this being the case, you will be best able to pitch the brochure at a suitable level.

First carry out your researches and then design and produce a suitable brochure, not exceeding the equivalent of three printed sides of A4. Your brochure may include appropriate illustrations.

For people who do not know the student

1 You are an assistant manager in the information department of a professional institution in your vocational sector such as The Society of Business Managers, The Institute of Manufacturing, The Institute of Health & Social Care, The Association of Leisure & Tourism Managers, The Institute of Art & Design. Your line manager has passed you Figure 2.41 to deal with suitably.

Your enquiries at head office reveal that Mr Dawson had every intention of keeping his speaking engagement, until 2:30 P.M. on the day of the Conference, when he went down with a bad migraine attack, to which he is sometimes prone. He accordingly left a fax with the text-processing pool supervisor to be sent to Mrs Haiqa Khan, chair of the Warwick branch, expressing his apologies at not being able to give the talk, and suggesting she contact a Mr Bayliss in Leicester, who could probably substitute. You also discovered that the fax was given to a new temp to process. He thought it had been sent, but there was a transmission problem, as the supervisor discovered first thing this morning (22 February) when checking the fax transmission reports. As a result, the fax was not transmitted. You telephoned Mr Dawson to advise him of the situation. He is highly embarrassed, and is going to contact Mrs Khan and Ms Bishop. Your task is to compose a letter to Ms Bishop which you consider responds suitably, given the facts you have unearthed. Your letter should be printed and not exceed 1.5 sides of A4.

2 Compose a suitable letter (not exceeding two sides of A4) to your local careers service which explains the career path you wish to pursue, and which requests information on the following areas: (a) details of universities which specialise (and have good track records) in your field of study; (b) any helpful literature – you will need to be specific here on the sort of data you seek; (c) what other support services the careers service can provide. This letter may be printed or handwritten.

3 Simulating the role of a local careers officer, first research the areas detailed in (a), (b) and (c) of activity 2 *for your own study and career field* and then compose a suitable responding letter, which should similarly not exceed two sides of A4.

4 First carry out suitable research, then compose a discussion paper of between three and four sides of A4 on *one* of the following topics:

(a) The only element of morality and ethics left in the world of business today is: *It's only wrong if you get found out!* Therefore, to embark on a career in business as a Christian, Moslem, Buddhist or Hindu is to start with a severe handicap.

(b) The NHS seems so strapped for cash today that certain operations – for heart disease, transplants with a history of success or expensive drug therapy – are being denied

Appletrees
24 Southwold Avenue
Warwick
Warks WA2 3ET
Tel: 01962 345621

22 February 199–

The Information Officer
The Institute of Xwzabc
212–216 Bayswater Road
London W2 4FT

Dear Ms Fairfax

FAILURE OF INSTITUTE SPEAKER TO HONOUR SPEAKING ENGAGEMENT: MIDLAND REGION ANNUAL CONFERENCE, WARWICK CASTLE, THURSDAY 21 FEBRUARY 199–

I am writing to you on behalf of the Midland Region Committee of the Institute to register our extreme annoyance and disappointment about the failure of your Head Office Development Manager, Mr Pat Dawson, to keep the speaking appointment at our Annual Conference, held yesterday at Warwick Castle – he was to speak after dinner at 8.30 pm.

The arrangements were made some four months ago (3 November 199–). Mr Dawson agreed to deliver a 40 minute talk and to take questions on how the Institute was responding to NVQ and GNVQ awards in our sector up to Level 5, and how the planned flexistudy approach would support our members. I hold confirmatory correspondence in this regard.

Our Conference Secretary, Ms Penny Taylor sent all the necessary directions etc. and also arranged for a taxi to be waiting for Mr Dawson at Warwick station. However, Mr Dawson failed to materialise, and a substitute speaker (a member of our Committee) had to stand in at extremely short notice, much to her and our embarrassment.

I can understand that such eventualities may at times occur – due to ill-health or trains failure etc. But what I fail to understand entirely is the Institute's – and Mr Dawson's – failure to make any contact with us yesterday, nor to offer any explanations or apologies.

I should therefore be grateful if you look into this matter directly and advise me as to what happened. As you will appreciate, the credibility of Head Office has much diminished as a result of this unfortunate occurrence, and I wish to be in a position to explain matters fully at the Committee's next monthly meeting on 28 February 199–.

Your sincerely

Kim Bishop (Ms)
Branch Secretary
Institute of Xyzabc
Warwick Branch

some patients, simply because they are over 68 years old! Yet these very patients have paid in a working lifetime's health insurance contributions. Where's the fairness in that?

(c) The British Isles need more tourists like a hole in the head! We can't cope properly with the ones we get. They're usually just ripped off and herded around like cattle to spoil the peace and tranquillity of local residents unlucky enough to live in York, Bath, Stratford-upon-Avon or Stirling!

(d) The good thing about current art and design is that *anyone* can now do it! Gone are the days of drawing classes and life studies. All you need are a few big daubing brushes and the bottle to turn out something abstract and gaudy on a big enough canvas!

(e) The trouble with good design is that it always comes out so expensive that only the seriously rich can afford it!

(f) Manufacturing today has become the servant of mass-market advertising, dedicated to turning out poorly designed and cheaply specified goods that people don't really need and can't really afford to buy.

(g) Pure scientific research is a waste of time and effort.

5 First carry out appropriate research and then compose a

5 First carry out appropriate research and then compose a short informal report on what IT- based learning materials are currently available to support your advanced GNVQ programme of study, such as software packages, computer simulations, multimedia and interactive applications. Details of costs and availability should be included. The intended recipients of your report are your study centre's teaching and library staff.

6 You work in the planning department of Midshire County Council, which is based in Castle Approach, Midchester. Every five years, the council reviews and updates its county plan. This plan details how the council will support trends and developments in its economic and cultural infrastructures, such as the construction of a business and science park or leisure centre or arts complex, the development of small business clubs or nursing/ rest homes or manufacturing workshops. In order to create a revised county plan, the council's planning department has to research into county demographic economic and lifestyle trends, and to re-examine the scope and extent of current provisions. In order to provide data to inform the overall plan, you received earlier today this brief from your boss, the senior planning officer, Frances Charlton:

> I want you to dig out the main statistics available in your area [use your GNVQ field] which provide useful information on local trends and the ways in which employers or residents are using existing facilities. Then I want you to see what you can find out about what local people see as deficiencies in our provision or the support we give. Then you can write a short, formal report for me – with recommendations – to circulate at the next planning committee meeting which will be discussing the county plan's progress to date. Oh, and your report should be entitled something like. 'The Current Provision and Future County Needs in the Field of . . .'

7 Your study centre principal/headteacher is shortly to address an open evening of parents and prospective students about the courses, resources, amenities and opportunities for progression which your centre currently offers. S/he has asked your head of department for some assistance from your class. What is wanted is a fact-sheet which summarises the following information:

- the assessment results for your Advanced GNVQ study programme over the past three years
- the percentages (over the same period) of students who proceeded to higher education, who proceeded to another FE/school course, who proceeded to full-time employment and who belong to the 'other' category
- the number of university places available nationally in your subject-area, and an indication of average admission grade requirements
- indications of what careers/ appointments past students of your centre embarked upon, or typical national UK career patterns and opportunities
- details of the structure of your study programme, as well as an indication of programme content and assessment system.

The fact-sheet may incorporate suitable charts or other graphics, and should not exceed three printed sides of A4, suitably set out. The order of points in your fact-sheet is unlikely to match the above sequence of bullet points.

8 Following its past pattern of success and expansion, your study centre has decided to advertise in a national UK broadsheet in late August, when special supplements are published advertising what programmes of study are available at what study centres. Accordingly, since you know more about it than anyone, your head of department has asked each member of your class to devise a suitable display advertisement to meet the brief set out below. The best version(s) will be vetted by your academic board and may be used as the actual advertisement. Follow this design brief:

- The existing logo, centre name and address style should be incorporated.
- The advertisement should promote the attractions of your centre and the Advanced GNVQ programme you are pursuing.
- It should also be designed to appeal to the 16–19 age-group.
- Clear indications should be provided on what follow-up actions should be taken by the reader.

You may either design your advertisement on one side of A3 or one side of A4 for photoreduction.

9 Having designed a suitable display advertisement, you are now charged with designing and producing an information pack about your study programme and your centre, which would provide suitable information, as a follow-up for prospective students who respond to your activity 8 display advertisement. Your pack should include

- suitable details about your programme of study
- an outline of the study and recreational facilities available
- an indication of the attractions of your locality
- an indication of the type and cost of residential accommodation available locally
- details of any costs to be met
- a blank application form
- details of how an application will be followed up

At your teacher's discretion, you undertake the above activity individually, or in small student groups. Your target audience will be prospective students, but keep in mind the role played by parents or guardians in such decision making. Aim to produce a pack not exceeding the equivalent of five printed sides of A4. Before beginning this activity, have a look at the activity on page 107.

CHAPTER 3

USE IMAGES

A picture is worth ten thousand words

Ancient Chinese Proverb

There are three kinds of lies – lies, damned lies and statistics.

Mark Twain

Element 3.3: Use images

PERFORMANCE CRITERIA

A student must:

1 select **images** which clearly illustrate the **points** being made

2 use **images** which are suited to the **audience, situation** and purpose

3 use **images** at appropriate times and places

RANGE

Images: taken from others' material, produced by the student

Points: on straightforward subjects, on complex subjects

Audience: people familiar with the subject who know the student, people familiar with the subject who do not know the student; people not familiar with the subject who know the student, people not familiar with the subject who do not know the student

Situation: in written material; in one-to-one discussions, in group discussions

IMAGES AS COMMUNICATION

From pictures to words – and back!

Images in the form of pictures are much older than the written or printed word. Throughout Europe, Asia and Australasia, caves are increasingly being discovered which hold amazing drawings and outlines of prehistoric animals and Stone Age man, drawings perhaps 750,000 years old! Indeed, the 5,000 years preceding the birth of Christ saw alphabets emerge from streamlined versions of drawings. For instance, the letter *a* in our alphabet derives from the outline of an ox, which in turn grew out of ancient Middle Eastern hieroglyphics. The ancient Egyptians and Chinese devised early written documents using such hieroglyphics – picture outlines – to stand for ideas such as *house* or *warmth*.

Today, at the end of the second millennium, images enjoy a wider use and appreciation than ever before. We use them almost unconsciously – as icons – to navigate through our computer software, to maintain order on our roads, and as guidance and warning labels on items as different as radioactive waste and correction fluid. Moreover, the twentieth century has been characterised by moving pictures in the form of cinema and television films. This visual medium more than any other has increased our awareness of the world as 'spaceship earth' and enabled its peoples to see for themselves how the other half lives.

This century has also seen the widespread use of visual images to popularise and stand for whole ideologies, like the swastika and hammer and sickle. Likewise, myriad trade marks, logos and symbols – for soft drinks, trainers, jeans, etc. – have been published billions of times to promote countless products and services. In contrast to our Victorian ancestors, who were conditioned to devour acres of tiny print eagerly (since books and papers virtually made up their mass communications media), we are programmed from toddlers upwards to respond to graphic or visual images in order to be able to react favourably to hi-tech marketing messages, whether political, commercial or environmental.

In the 1960s, a communications specialist, Marshal Macluhan, coined the phrase: *The medium is the message*. What a person wishes to communicate is very much influenced by the medium employed. For example, the textual medium of the novel is ideal for conveying complex thoughts, moods and interactions among people. But it lacks the visual impact of film, with its immediacy and ability to capture of the senses of sight and sound. *Gone with the Wind* achieves one kind of communication, but documentary footage of the Vietnam War quite another.

The multimedia mix

The trend since the 1950s away from a reliance upon the single medium of the written word and towards a more varied mix of words, pictures and symbols

Images most frequently used in the workplace

Moving pictures	*Still pictures*	*Diagrams and charts*	*Textual embellishments*
films camcorder/ video films closed-circuit TV live transmissions film/TV transmissions used with multimedia PCs Video phones	photographs cartoons line-drawings clip-art sketches exploded drawings	maps pie chart line graph bar chart Gantt chart Z chart histogram pictograph scatter diagram flowchart number tables models icons and symbols	text and icon mix, e.g. presentation slides borders and decorations specialised fonts, e.g. poster fonts, script desktop publishing fonts, shaded boxes, shadows, etc.

has been marked. This trend has led to radical changes in people's working and social environments. Both schoolchildren and employees at work spend a significant number of hours each week concentrating upon VDU and television screens during their work and leisure hours.

Adding to the immense impact upon society of television over the past forty years is the emerging influence of CD-ROM communications media and materials, such as the *Encarta* multimedia encyclopaedia, computer games and computerised databases of works of art. While children's books have included for many decades pictures and illustrations, today's electronic multimedia 'books' combine a mix of moving film, still photograph, voice-over commentary, charts, diagrams, models and text – all capable of interactive access by the 1990s student.

Undoubtedly this trend to a multimedia communications mix will both accelerate and enlarge tremendously over the coming decade. And playing a central part in this change in communications media is the image. Therefore, Element 3.3 examines in depth the ways in which a wide range of images are used in a work context to transmit information to various kinds of recipient or audience. This element also provides guidelines and know-how which will enable you to employ images confidently and expertly in your own work-related communications. The table shows how people at work employ images in many different ways.

What do you think?

1 How do you think the use of images will develop in the workplace during the next twenty years?

2 To what extent is an increasing reliance on visual images likely to generate a new age of illiteracy and innumeracy?

IMAGES: CHOOSING THE BEST ALTERNATIVE

Given that there is a wide variety of image-making equipment available in the workplace, and that an abundance of image sources exist – commercial photographic libraries, clip-art, CDs, presentation templates in graphics packages, etc. – it is important to spend some time at the outset to consider what type of image is best suited to what type of vocational use. Consider for instance the following list of contexts in which images might be employed at work:

IMAGES AT WORK

Purpose	Image media
to bring distant executives into a CCTV meeting	CCTV conferencing
to train and develop staff	videocassette training films, multimedia CDs, interactive TV materials, etc.
to illustrate and to provide visual interest in an oral presentation	still slide pictures, computer-screened images, charts, diagrams, etc.
to communicate data most effectively	models, charts, diagram, drawings, maps, etc.
to store data most efficiently	tables, graphs, databases, spreadsheet structures, plans, drawings, etc.
to provide visual contrast, relief, emphasis, attractiveness, etc.	logos, trade marks, symbols, decorative borders, boxes shading, cartoons, clip-art images, etc.
to persuade and influence	photographs, cartoons, sketches, symbols, use of specialist fonts, etc.

As well as considering what type of image is best suited to a specific purpose, there are other factors which significantly influence the choice of image. These certainly include cost, potential effectiveness and availability. The list overleaf indicates some of the major factors to be kept in mind when selecting images or planning a presentation:

Choosing an image: key factors

- **type of recipient:** single, small group; large audience
- **type of information to be communicated:** simple or complex; active process or static illustration
- **availability and type of image-making equipment:** colour photocopier, computer-generated images for slide projection, CCTV/camcorder/video equipment for filming
- **time available:** 30 minutes or 14 days?
- **cost:** £3,000 for an in-house training video or £5 for a set of photocopied leaflets.
- **access to existing resources:** nearby photo-library, organisation's archives, materials for hire or purchase
- **specific purpose:** high-status meeting of board of directors or trustees; national or international advertising campaign
- **medium in which image is to be inserted:** brochure, video, slide, OHP transparency, report, bulletin
- **overall purpose of the message and the image:** to persuade, to brief, to shock, to amuse, to inform

Given the number of factors which actively influence image selection and effectiveness, it is not surprising that even professionals can get it wrong. We have all come across arty leaflets and posters in which the choice of colour and background image render the overlaid text – to be read quickly – quite illegible.

See the design as an overall, unified piece

In many communications media, images are included as part of an overall mix of white space, text, colour and paper type. In order to design an effective communication in this situation, it is important to keep in mind a number of design guidelines.

Successful design using a mix of communications media requires the designer to see them as a single entity. This means that each part or component should blend in with another and that no single part should exceed its intended role. In this way a photograph may dominate visually yet remain in perfect balance with its caption. In straightforward terms, such a unity would be evident in, say, a threefold leaflet because:

- its visual illustration and/or slogan immediately catches the eye
- its use of typography (mix of fonts and points) enables its message to be readily absorbed and remembered
- its visual images communicate effectively – to reinforce, provide visual relief, to emphasise, etc.
- its use of white space effectively breaks the message up into components which are readily understood
- its overall message prompts its reader to undertake the action intended or to modify his or her view as desired by the brochure's designer – all because of an effective harmony and balance of the components, which together create a unity of design.

Using colour effectively

Although monochrome images can prove very effective – as demonstrated by filmed documentaries and photo collections of inner-city life – there is no doubting the visual appeal and impact of colour. We are generally blessed with sight in full colour, and as a result, certain colour combinations have a deep effect upon us, since we have associated them with certain experiences over many years in our culture:

- **red:** aggression, blood, war, accident, anger, danger, prohibition, life threat, emergency, hot
- **green:** countryside, environment, tranquillity, safe to go, calm, nature, freshness, open air, sporting
- **gold:** luxurious, royal, precious, expensive, superior quality, exclusivity, long-lasting, warmth, sun and sand
- **black:** death, mourning, plague, fear, danger, horrid
- **white:** pure, virginal, clean, safe, holy, fresh, unused, empty, antiseptic
- **blue:** fresh, cold, clean, sea water, cleansing, heavenly, pure
- **yellow:** sunny, happy, outgoing, warm, nature, bright
- **black and yellow:** the most eye-catching combination; used by insects and animals to warn of danger, e.g. wasps, hornets
- **blue, green and white:** implies a sense of cleanliness and purity; used a great deal to promote toothpastes, washing-powders and water-associated products
- **blue and yellow:** sky, sand and sea colour; used to promote holidays, outdoor sport and leisurewear
- **gold/silver with black/red:** gold and silver imply costly, high-class and top-of-the range and, if used with red or black, suggest power and status

- **brown and pale yellow:** certain shades of brown and yellow can communicate sadness and depression; perhaps we see the colour of autumn preceding a grey winter

Student pair activity

Over a seven-day period, collect samples of coloured communications – advertisements, brochures, magazine illustrations, organisational public relations publications, etc. – which you consider illustrate uses of colour similar or identical to those indicated above. Set up an exhibition of the best examples on your baseroom noticeboards for all to see.

Keeping design clear and simple

The best designs have an elegance and clarity which derives from their simplicity. Consider for instance how nature has 'designed' dolphins and porpoises to move fast through water, and how smooth, polished, balanced and symmetrical they appear as a result. Yet they possess no unnecessary part or extremity; head, fins, tail and body all combine in a smooth yet powerful whole. Clear and simple design results from these component parts:

- **pleasing balance** of the parts which make up the whole
- **suitable use of colours** in harmony
- **absence of clutter** which obscures the message, be it words, colours or images
- **sufficient frame of white space** to surround and subdivide the message
- **appropriate use of size and proportion** to match, say, the size of a photographic image and the point size of an accompanying caption, or the area of printed text placed next to a drawing or piece of clip-art
- **pleasing combination** of textual and graphic information

Individual skills-building activities

Practise your ability to create an effective design by undertaking the following activity:

- **Design task:** *Either* produce an effective leaflet aimed at promoting your advanced GNVQ course to prospective students. *Or* produce an effective leaflet aimed at communicating the range of resources of your study centre library to existing centre students.
- **Materials:** Your leaflet must be of a threefold design. You may use whichever colour of A4 paper you think best suited and which you can access. You must decide what image material to employ (e.g. cut-and paste photos, clip-art, line-drawings, etc.) and you must also decide what type of printed text to use, and whether you can include any other use of colour in your brochure.
- **Equipment:** What type of equipment you use is up to you and depends on what you can access, but bear in mind that you should produce a leaflet suited for its intended purpose and readership.
- **Accompanying rationale:** On about one side of A4, write a commentary which explains why you designed your leaflet the way you did. Arrange to circulate the leaflets produced and to arrive at a class decision on which ones proved most effective as designs and why.

Example of a well-designed advertisement.

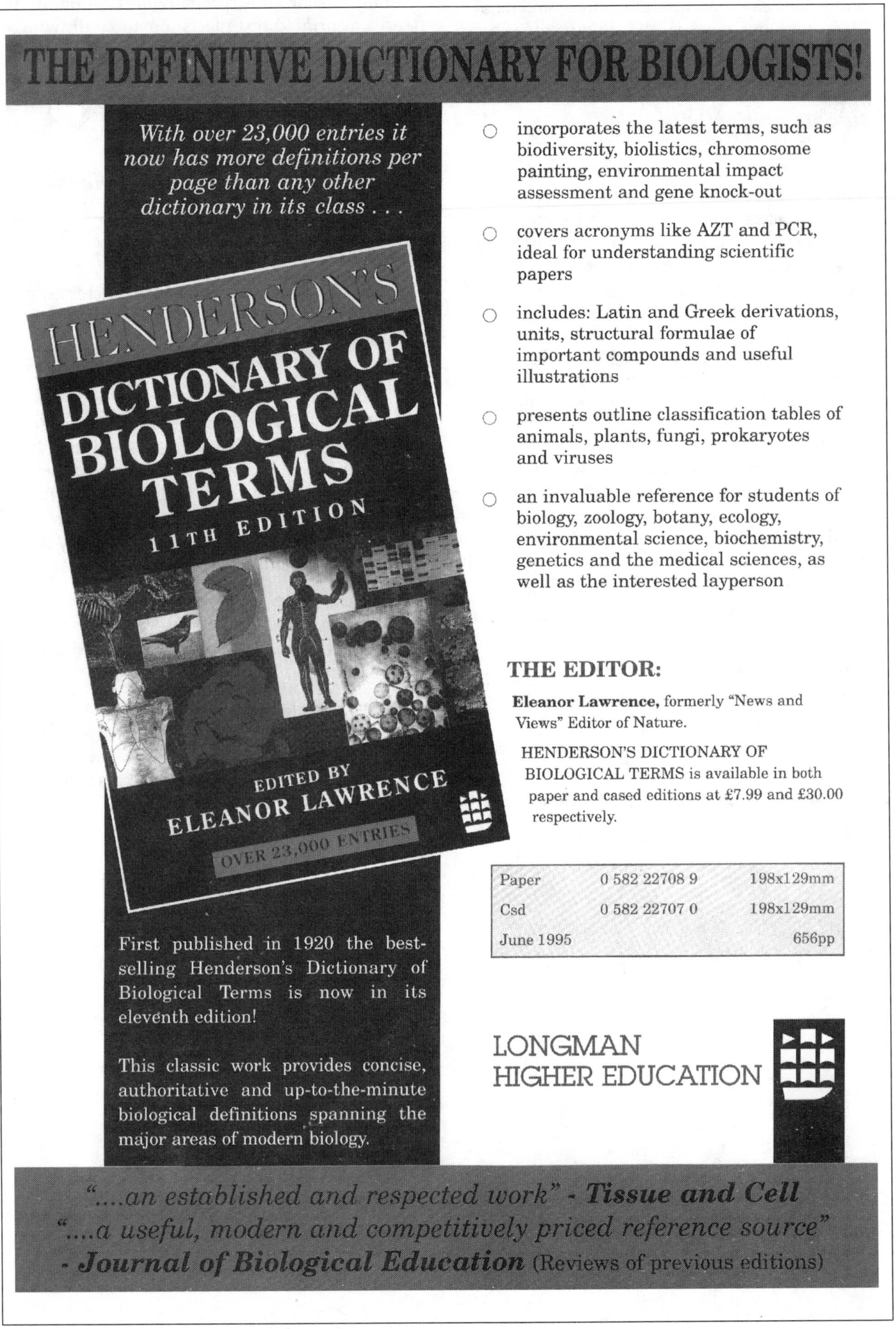
THE DEFINITIVE DICTIONARY FOR BIOLOGISTS!
With over 23,000 entries it now has more definitions per page than any other dictionary in its class . . .
HENDERSON'S
DICTIONARY OF BIOLOGICAL TERMS
11TH EDITION
EDITED BY
ELEANOR LAWRENCE
OVER 23,000 ENTRIES
First published in 1920 the best-selling Henderson's Dictionary of Biological Terms is now in its eleventh edition!
This classic work provides concise, authoritative and up-to-the-minute biological definitions spanning the major areas of modern biology.
incorporates the latest terms, such as biodiversity, biolistics, chromosome painting, environmental impact assessment and gene knock-out
covers acronyms like AZT and PCR, ideal for understanding scientific papers
includes: Latin and Greek derivations, units, structural formulae of important compounds and useful illustrations
presents outline classification tables of animals, plants, fungi, prokaryotes and viruses
an invaluable reference for students of biology, zoology, botany, ecology, environmental science, biochemistry, genetics and the medical sciences, as well as the interested layperson
THE EDITOR:
Eleanor Lawrence, formerly "News and Views" Editor of Nature.
HENDERSON'S DICTIONARY OF BIOLOGICAL TERMS is available in both paper and cased editions at £7.99 and £30.00 respectively.
Paper 0 582 22708 9 198x129mm
Csd 0 582 22707 0 198x129mm
June 1995 656pp
LONGMAN HIGHER EDUCATION
"....an established and respected work" - Tissue and Cell
"....a useful, modern and competitively priced reference source" - Journal of Biological Education (Reviews of previous editions)

What do you think?

1 Why do *you* think that images have become such a popular medium of communication at the end of the twentieth century?

2 Can you envisage a time when the written word will have become virtually extinct? If so, by when and why? If not, why not?

3 Do images supply information to the human brain differently than words? If so, in what kinds of different ways?

4 The camera never lies! True or false?

5 To what extent do you think we live in times when our ability to create powerful and emotive visual images is leading to the oversimplification and trivialisation of complex ideas? Can images cause knee-jerk responses?

6 To what extent do you think human beings are influenced by the use of colour in communications?

7 What do *you* think goes to make an effective design?

Self-check review test

1 Explain briefly why images have become a popular medium of communication since the 1940s.

2 What is meant by the term multimedia?

3 List five main reasons for employing images in a work context.

4 List five main factors which affect the choice of image used in a work context.

5 Explain briefly what is meant by the term unity in design.

6 What responses are generally associated with these colours in a communications context: red, green blue, white, gold?

7 What particular effects does the colour combination black and yellow possess?

8 What are the following: an icon, a logo, a trade mark?

9 Explain what is meant by the specialist terms: font, point.

When you have set down your own answers, compare them with those on page 198 and consult this section again if they differ.

HOW TO CREATE THE RIGHT IMAGE

Moving pictures

Everyone has, hidden away somewhere, old spools of film or videocassettes which contain well-meant attempts to capture *Our Family at Home, Our Holiday on the Costa del Sol, or No. 1 Son's First Christmas.* Of course, they are hidden away because they 'never came out right'. Either heads of a whole group were chopped off, viewers become airsick as shots spin crazily from one scene to another, or become confused as a result of editing of colossal proportions!

How then can the conscientious amateur produce and direct films which other people will want to see and enjoy rather than endure? As for all creative communication projects, making a film spans four major phases:

- creating the story
- constructing the set
- shooting the film
- adding captions and credits

Creating the story

Creating the story of a film is usually effected through the use of a storyboard (Fig. 3.1). A storyboard looks very much like a strip cartoon and has the same purpose, namely to summarise the main points and locations of the story to be conveyed. Storyboards are often used by advertising workers or television writers in order to explain to interested parties (particularly those putting up the money for the project) how the eventual film will be structured and shaped. Beneath each frame of the storyboard, concise notes provide information and interpretation.

As shown in Figure 3.1, it is perfectly possible to communicate both the visual location of each scene of a film, together with a summary of how the structure or story of the film will unfold. Storyboards tend to be presented in square or rectangular blocks of numbered key stages, from opening to closing shot. In this way, initial, 'go for it' decisions can be made without incurring extensive costs.

Once the producers have decided to make the film, its director and team will need to develop the following essential ingredients:

1 a *script* for any dialogue, presenter monologue or voice-over commentaries; a set of *director's notes* which give instructions and guidance for each scene

2 internal and/or external *locations* for filming

3 *sets:* fabricated simulations of, say, an office, a laboratory or a hospital ward

4 *props:* real or simulated items such as holiday brochures, paper wallets and products to be advertised

5 *costumes:* the dress shirts, frocks, overalls, tunics or labcoats which actors or participants will wear; make-up is also important where actors appear under intensive lighting

6 *actors and/or presenters:* people who can perform realistically under pressure

7 *film crew;* people who create and recreate sets exactly, lighting experts, camera operators, etc.

Figure 3.1 A storyboard summarises the main points of a story.

1 Opening shot
Presenter explains why garden flowers and shrubs do not always get the food and nutrients they need

2 Cut to R&D lab
Voice over details what the main ingredients of New Sprinklit are and what they do

3 Cut to garden scene
Sprinklit dispenser in foreground; voice over enthuses at difference made to flowers and shrubs thanks to New Sprinklit

Clearly also, any film-maker worth his salt must seek to use the best equipment available. However, not every film-maker needs to film an Exodus-type parting of the Red Sea, and a great deal can be achieved with a camcorder, tripod and effective lighting. In this regard, many effective, low-budget training films have been made with close-ups of presenters sitting in front of simple panel sets with stylised props and costumes (such as paper hats and masks) employed as alternatives to expensive costumes and locations.

KEY POINTS

The following key tips will enable you to make a worthwhile start in using the image of moving pictures in a workplace context:

- **Preparation is everything:** storyboard, script, sets, equipment, etc., all need to be prepared before uttering the proverbial 'Action!'
- **Ensure your actors rehearse beforehand:** do not rehearse in front of the camera, which is an expensive waste of time.
- **Do not attempt to shoot too much in one go:** structure your film in short rather than long scenes, which are thus easier to retake if need be.
- **Avoid as far as possible hand-held shots:** they can appear wavy and trembly; prefer where possible a solid base for your camera or camcorder, such as a tripod.
- **Avoid the temptation to play with the zoom:** nothing is more irritating than constantly moving, say, from a full-figure shot to someone's front teeth, and then back again. ▶
- **If you must pan, pan slowly and evenly:** avoid the fast-panning scenario, in which people, trees, cars and ground seem to have been launched into space.
- **Film people speaking using various angles:** try to avoid full-face shots; try diagonal or past one speaker's shoulders.
- **Take painstaking care with continuity:** if you have to return to a set and scene, you can be sure that someone in your audience will spot a change of tie, blouse, hairdo or prop.
- **Film 2 or 3 takes of a scene if possible:** it gives you an element of choice when it comes to editing.
- **Edit your story into an intelligible narrative:** avoid giant steps which ask your audience to take too much for granted and leave them confused.
- **Keep it simple, stupid:** the Americans call it KISS; memorable film messages are those which are clear, simple and direct, so avoid the clutter of babbling voices, busy sets and over-ambitious camera shots.

Photographs

Although moving pictures win the laurels for overall visual impact and generating interest, they are expensive and time-consuming to produce, and for the most part, require professionals to make them. It is therefore much more likely that your involvement with images at work will focus instead on the use of photographs, cartoons, line-drawings, sketches and clip-art within a paper-based mix of the printed word, symbols and white space. This section therefore examines each type in turn.

Student pair skills-building activities

In order to check out the above guidelines on effective film-making, carry out *one* of the following tasks.

TASK 1

Arrange to videotape several commercial television advertisements for contrasting products and services. Play back each one several times, and make notes on the main features of the advertisement's composition in terms of use of actors, effectiveness of sets and/or locations, suitability of spoken-word messages, the impact of dominant colours employed, techniques of photography, use of lighting, etc. Then select the advertisement which you think to be most effective. Compose short notes and give an oral presentation to your class on your chosen advertisement, stating what you think makes it effective and why.

TASK 2

Arrange to videotape a televised interview, perhaps presenters and politicians, a chat show or a news interview. As for task 1, seek to analyse the filming techniques which make it effective and interesting for the viewer. Likewise, provide a class feedback oral presentation.

Virtually everything mentioned about making moving pictures is relevant to the taking of photographs. However, the following check-list provides additional guidelines:

Taking effective photographs

- **Consider carefully the type of film best suited to your needs:** colour or monochrome; for prints or for slides; for processing or for instant development (such as Polaroid); with a speed of 100, 200 or 400. Film speeds are usually chosen to suit lighting conditions. Generally speaking, slower films are better for enlargement, and faster films are better in poor light conditions.
- **Become intimately acquainted with the camera you will use:** today the single lens reflex (SLR) 35 mm camera is very popular as are 'point and shoot' cameras with many automatic features, such as focusing and aperture setting; an excellent tip is to take two or three spools of shots, recording for each shot: focal length setting, depth of field setting, shutter speed, film type and general light and subject conditions. Over- or underexposure or any other problem can then be tracked back to your settings; quick progress can be made from trial and error. Generally speaking, the smaller the aperture, the sharper the photograph.
- **Avoid camera shake:** taking a sharp picture requires assuming a careful position if the camera is hand-held: arms locking onto the body or elbows resting on a static surface. Whenever practicable, use a tripod. A good rule of thumb is to avoid taking pictures with a shutter speed of less than 1/125s, unless the camera is firmly supported.
- **Over- and underexposure:** it takes practice and camera familiarity to arrive at a correct exposure for a given shot; many current cameras embody automatic features which advise the user on what shutter speed to employ in given light conditions when using a given aperture stop (e.g. *f* 5.6 – *f* 22), otherwise it is necessary to use a light meter.
- **Satisfying composition:** the key to effective photography is the selection of an appropriate composition of the proposed subject through the camera's viewfinder. Composition is made up of a set of relationships: the position of the principal subject relative to the background, the proximity of objects of a secondary value, the direction and intensity of the natural or artificial light, the impact of reflections, shadows or sun surfaces, the effect of strong and subtle colours, the relative visual impact of textures – say of sand, a deck-chair's fabric and sea water. Effective compositions draw the eye to the main subject and create a harmony in the overall structure of the components making up the photograph, the effect of its colours or tones, the appearance of textures and the effects of light and shade. Also of central importance is focus and the use of filters; focus can direct attention to the main subject while blurring out the background; filters can dramatise an otherwise flat subject.
- **Using flashlights for internal shots:** great care needs to be taken in matching aperture speeds, to flash-gun speeds, to *f* stops; many cameras now do this automatically, but tables are provided with most flash equipment to simplify this process. Whenever possible, use a flash attachment with a movable bulb-holder which can be pointed up to the ceiling, rather than at a human subject; this avoids the dreaded red-eye, when the flash turns people's brown or blue eyes red.
- **Seek to use lighting creatively:** avoid taking shots in bright, unbroken light; make use of shade and light from the side; use shadow to contrast with bright highlights; avoid shooting directly into sun-glare; use reflections to add interest, and unusual perspectives.
- **Set up your camera before asking subjects to pose:** adjust focal length, shutter speed, *f* stop, etc., otherwise you will end up with people's eyes squinting in bright sunlight, cracked and forced smiles or noses being scratched. Try to take pictures that look spontaneous, not stiff.

Figure 3.2 Lots of high-speed fun on a Laser sailing dinghy, well captured and composed.

[Reproduced by kind permission of Performance Sailcraft Europe Limited]

Figure 3.3 Notice the NVC direct eye contact and positive feedback expressed by the panellists, signalling interest in and acceptance of what is being said.

[Reproduced by kind permission of Labour Party News and Phil Maxwell]

Individual student skills-building activities

You are a photographer working for your local weekly newspaper. Shortly, your editor will be putting together a two-page spread about the range of work which goes on in your locality. The thrust of the article is to rebuild confidence in the local economy and its public sector services after the recession and to help in rebuilding demand. You have therefore been tasked with taking a series of pictures which relate to your actual study and will be used to illustrate the feature, a wide-ranging overview. Your editor gave you these encouraging instructions:

> Try to find some pics which really communicate! Use your discretion – the funny, unusual, the unexpected all help to sell our illustrious paper, oh, and don't forget to write some helpful captions for each shot, and what organisation they depict. Lastly, and mindful of the MOD affair, make sure you have permission before photographing in private premises or on private land !

You may use either colour or monochrome film, and submit photos of any size. But remember that professionals use enlargers to vet contact prints, since they are so small. Produce a suitable set of some 5–8 photographs and arrange their display in your baseroom. With your teacher's help, appoint a committee to decide which set has best met the editor's brief and why. As a part of portfolio work for Element 3.2, your teacher may ask you to compose the feature's textual content to accompany your photographs.

Figure 3.4 Notice the hand gesture of touching index finger and thumb with other fingers crooked, a typical NVC signal communicating precision and accuracy.

[Reproduced by kind permission of Labour Party News and Phil Maxwell]

Cartoons

The drawing of cartoons is virtually as old as primitive man's cave-painting, since one of the earliest signs of civilisation lies in the ability to see the funny side of things and to use humour to cut the pompous and egocentric down to size.

Cartoons are created to meet a variety of responses, including the simple intention to get a smile, making a political comment, making a serious point beneath the guise of humour or satire and driving home a moral about the workings of human nature. Like sketches, cartoons concentrate solely on simple, key features. For example, political cartoonists so exaggerate a particular feature of, say, a cabinet minister's wavy hair, jutting jaw or beetling eyebrows that he or she becomes instantly recognisable. Needless to say, such cartoon features are rarely flattering.

Some cartoons make timeless points such as pride coming before a fall, when a swaggering smarty-pants fails to see the missing floorboard around the corner. Others rely on interpreting topical events humorously, as for instance, in a cartoon of the election contest for the leadership of the Conservative Party in July 1995 which depicted a lack of party unity in terms of dozens of jockeys (contesting MPs) all vying with John Major to get out of a set of starting stalls first, so as to win.

Many editors, authors and publishers use cartoons to provide a sort of visual relief and to break up large chunks of text. Such cartoons may also be used to make a humorous (but telling) point related to the surrounding text.

For example, the cartoon below might be used to illustrate an article on the induction of new employees, or to make the point that in building relationships at work, as Professor Schumacher put it: Small is beautiful!

What makes a cartoon funny and successful?

William Wordsworth, the poet, once wrote that 'We murder to dissect.' In seeking to understand how things work, we kill them off. And this is the prob-

That's your bench, Hoskins. You'll soon get to know everyone.

lem with humour. We instinctively know when something we see or encounter is funny, but often fail entirely when we try to explain our experience.

What makes a cartoon funny? Certainly cartoons occupy the focal point of much humour, since what they express has to be instantly recognisable and communicate its point immediately. So, humour has to do with instant communication. It also has to do with routine, everyday life and the ways in which ordinary people live it. For example, one memorable cartoon displayed a baron on the battlements of his castle, which was under siege – arrows flying upwards and boiling oil hurtling downwards in a kind of furious stalemate. The baron is talking to a salesman dressed in early medieval clothes, but carrying a sample of his wares under his arm. In this case, a machine-gun. Clearly he is seeking a sales interview, but the baron responds, 'Come back later – can't you see I'm in the middle of a battle?'

And so cartoon humour has also to do with incongruity – the turning upside down of the expected. It has also to do with carrying the events and concerns of real life just that bit further, so that a valid, real scenario is depicted in an exaggerated way.

I've called you in because I'm not happy about the way things are going here in accounts . . .

In the cartoon below, the scene is entirely normal, if not banal. The head of accounts has called his section leaders into his office because he has something on his mind. What that something is has been incongruously and humorously pointed up through the use of Indian attire, and in particular, the public indication of high status by many large feathers in the head-dress. The humour stems from an apparent inversion of status. The departmental lieutenants seem to have pinched the boss's feathers, or authority, and he is by no means happy about it. This visual humour is further heightened by the low-key caption, in which the boss appears to be taking matters seriously in a normal way, despite the absurdity of everyone's clothes.

Have we murdered to dissect? Probably, but we have discovered some of the essential ingredients of cartoon humour; immediate and direct communication linked to the exaggeration, incongruity and inversion of ordinary events. Also, good cartoons communicate a sense of permanent truth, where the reader silently observes, 'Yes, that does happen.'

Cartoons, using the medium of humour are included in articles, features, news items and so on to

- provide visual relief
- to further emphasise a point made in the text
- to make a point that would be difficult to make in a serious vein
- to lighten the reader's burden during a heavy section of prose

Individual skills-building activities

You work in the copywriting department of Berghaus, Sinclair and Garcia, an EU advertising agency. Your team is currently working on a brochure for the Confederation of Employers. Assume that the Confederation of Employers covers the sector you are likely to enter, such as business, manufacturing, science, hospitality, leisure and tourism, health and social care. The brochure aims to increase the numbers of school and college leavers entering the confederation's vocational employment sector. The general thrust of the text of the brochure is to explain what working in the employment sector is like, what the prospects are for advancement, and what sort of qualifications are needed at various points of entry. The confederation is trying to avoid the brochure becoming dreary and thus not read, and so has asked for several cartoons to be interspersed in the run of the brochure which make a light-hearted comment about the sort of work employees in the sector undertake.

First carry out your researches into working in the sector, and then design one or two cartoons which would meet the design purpose outlined above. When you have finished, compare your versions with those produced by your co-students and decide which are most appropriate and why.

Clip-art

Today, approximately half of everything we read is produced by authors, designers and printers using some kind of desktop publishing system. As a result, we have become completely accustomed to even the humblest in-house bulletin or leaflet containing graphics, bold arrows, frames, borders, etc. In order to enhance their desktop publishing (DTP) packages, organisations like Pagemaker and Lotus include files of what they call *clip-art*; the term stemmed from the provision of ready-made artwork which could be accessed off the peg and clipped electronically on to pages of text.

Such images are capable of being imported, from resident files, into any document being created. They can also be cropped, enlarged or foreshortened, according to the size required. Today, as many as 10,000 different clip-art images can be stored on a single CD-ROM for instant use in PCs and DTP. Files of associated clip-art are usually stored together in a system which groups together images relating to sport, leisure, manufacturing, construction, office-work, restaurants, etc. Additional files are also supplied which make available a wide range of images – curved arrows, boxes, backgrounds, etc – to enable authors to design professional-looking diagrams and charts. Figure 3.5 shows typical clip-art.

The advantages of making use of clip-art images in brochures, bulletins, leaflets or notices are

- they are instantly available
- they are professionaly drawn and designed
- they are easily adjusted to a required size and location on a DTP page
- they normally come with copyright authorisations for any use
- they provide a simple way of illustrating text and of providing visual interest and appeal

Figure 3.5 Clip-art is scanned into a computer document file.

[Reproduced by kind permission of Lexis International Ltd]

But the disadvantages are:

- they sometimes embody a gaudy, brash design which instantly identifies them as clip-art; this can have an effect of devaluing the printed document in the eyes of its reader, since clip-art is so indiscriminately used these days
- it is not always easy to employ a clip-art image which is directly relevant and suited to its context and location; in this case it can become irritating and distracting
- unpractised users tend to overuse clip-art and incorporate images which are too dominant or intrusive

Line-drawings and sketches

Everyone who has sought to use a computerised drawing software package – with mouse and screen arrows and points – knows how difficult it is to produce line-drawings which look professional. Indeed, using such software to produce freehand drawings is even more demanding. However, as all mouse users know, practice does make perfect. It may be that you decide, and rightly, that as you are neither a DTP graphic artist, nor a contemporary Albrecht Dürer, you will limit your talents to rough sketches for internal use. But graphics software is constantly improving and making life easier for the non-professional, so it is worth trying out demonstration copies of upgraded software packages.

Whenever you are able to access suitable line-drawings or sketches, remember that the same composition guidelines apply as for photographs, cartoons or clip-art in terms of creating harmony, balance and symmetry on the page.

Importing images via scanners

Provided there are no accompanying problems with copyright permissions, a particularly useful new technology is the importation of existing images – from photos to diagrams – by means of a scanner. This is a piece of equipment which operates rather like a fax machine. Monochrome or colour originals are placed on a flat bed and scanned optically. The process converts the scanned image into an electronic file which a personal computer can accept and store. This file can then be imported – just like a clip-art image – into any work in progress, and can be cropped (reduced or enlarged) at will. This technology is particularly useful in organisations which create and distribute images on an extensive scale, such as advertising agencies, architects, designers, magazine publishers and research establishments. Scanners are also just as happy to import printed text documents, and many large organisations with established email networks use this facility to distribute electronic files of scanned-in correspondence, reports or other textual material without having to increase the paper burden on staff.

What do you think?

1 What do *you* think are the qualities of an effective training/personal development video?

2 For what sort of work-based communication activities would a still photograph be ideally suited?

3 What do *you* think makes for a successful cartoon?

4 Have we all arrived at the stage where we cannot cope with an A4 page of continuous prose unless it is peppered with images to break it down for us?

5 Clip-art: boon or turn-off?

Self-check review test

1 List the four main stages in the making of a video.

2 Explain briefly what a storyboard is and what it is used for.

3 Explain what the following specialist terms stand for in film-making: location, set, props, continuity.

4 List five tips which support the making of a successful video.

5 List five key steps in taking an effective photograph.

6 Explain the meaning of the following photographic terms: film speed, shutter speed, exposure, camera-shake, focal length, red-eye.

7 List three major uses of cartoons in printed, work-based documents.

8 What is meant by the term clip-art? Explain how and why it is used.

9 What is a scanner? What is it used for?

10 Explain briefly how desktop publishing has revolutionised in-house publishing.

When you have set down your own answers, compare them with those on pages 198–199 and consult this section again if they differ.

Maps

Maps, charts, tables, diagrams and models are probably used most often by executives in organisations. Such images are employed to store detailed information (usually a predominance of number communication) and to present it in an appealing and memorable way (usually by mixing number, word and 3D effects).

Maps (Fig. 3.6) are needed in most organisations to meet a variety of needs, from the modest location map which is sent to intending visitors of an organisation, to more detailed site maps for housing estate builders and the sophisticated maps with progressive overlays produced by county council planners. They have several key components:

- **clear title headings:** subject, location, date produced, designer and intended use; if a map is to be designed through progressive versions, it is essential to label them carefully.
- **customary orientation:** the vast majority of maps produced today are oriented with north at their top. Some maps indicate north (true or magnetic) by means of an arrow.
- **scale:** maps which display distances between various points or locations need to indicate the scale employed, for example, 1 centimetre to 3 kilometres; without a scale, they are useless.
- **suitable labels:** label major sites, towns, organisations, campuses, annexes, etc. Mapmakers often use a range of fonts or boldface to indicate relative importance:

  BIRMINGHAM Nether Wallop *Newcastle-Under-Lyme*
- **symbols and icons:** symbols and icons are used as shorthand and are explained in a key at the side or foot of the map.

Tables

In essence, tables are sets of numbers grouped together in columns, rows or other formats which store and convey information. Characteristically, tables comprise

- **a clear title** of the table's function and purpose
- **clearly labelled headings** for columns or rows
- **individual entries** may be whole numbers or fractions to several decimal places
- **subtotals** which form the sum of previous, individual entries
- **amounts to be deducted** from subtotals
- **overall totals** which communicate the sum of all entries

The individual entries of a table are equivalent to a single cell in a spreadsheet. Sometimes amounts in tables are expressed as percentages or fractions of a whole, and minus figures are either shown after a minus (–) sign or in brackets (£341,000).

Tables in spreadsheets

In spreadsheets, tables are made up of columns of figures (vertical) and rows (horizontal). Each individual entry is made within a cell, and the basis of the spreadsheet's attraction lies in its ability to link cells in formulas. For example, to obtain a total of a set of eight individual entries in, say, column D of a spreadsheet, an entry would be made in the cell D9, SUM(D1:D8). The brackets enclose the cells to be added together, and the colon indicates 'from 1 through to 8'. The result appears as an entry in cell D9. Moreover, if a single cell, say D6, is altered, the resultant change in the addition or sum total will

Figure 3.6 This map has a clear title, scale and key.

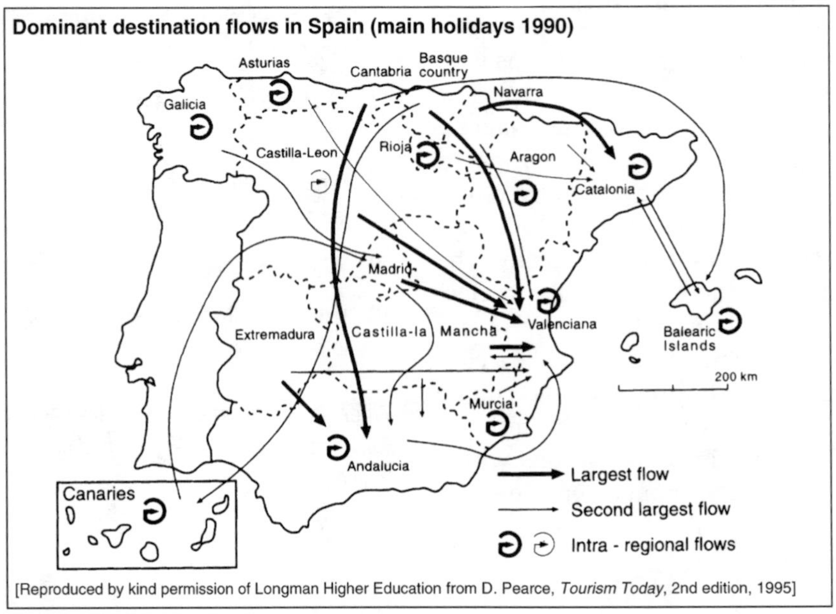

Figure 3.7 This table is clear but not visually appealing.

Clear title → **Discount Hardware Limited**
Sales analysis for year ended 199–

Individual headings for each column

Subtotals title, including values of £000 by row → Sales vaue in

Products	Jan	Feb	Mar	Apr	May	Jun	July	Aug	Sept	Oct	Nov	Dec	
Garden furniture	0.5	0.7	1.2	2.4	3.5	4.6	4.2	2.1	0.6	0.4	0.3	0.1	20.6
Paints	0.8	1.6	2.4	3.5	3.4	2.6	1.7	1.8	1.4	2.1	2.3	0.2	23.8
Tools	0.7	0.5	0.7	0.6	0.5	0.4	0.3	0.3	0.4	0.5	0.7	1.0	6.6
Washing machines	2.0	1.5	2.1	1.7	1.9	2.4	0.8	0.7	0.8	0.6	0.5	0.4	15.4
Refrigerators	2.1	1.4	1.5	1.4	1.8	1.7	1.5	1.7	1.6	1.5	1.4	1.2	18.8
Freezers	1.7	0.6	0.7	0.4	0.4	0.3	0.5	0.9	1.0	0.5	0.6	0.8	8.4
Kitchenware	0.7	0.5	0.3	0.4	0.7	0.5	1.2	0.4	0.5	0.4	0.5	0.8	6.9
Wallpaper	1.1	1.6	1.8	2.2	2.1	1.8	0.6	0.4	0.8	1.2	1.4	0.8	15.8
Total:	9.6	8.4	10.7	12.6	14.3	14.3	10.8	8.3	7.1	7.2	7.7	5.3	116.3

Subtotal by column

Individual headings for each row of associated figures

Inset combined total

[Reproduced by kind permission of Pitman Publishing from D.W. Evans, *People, Communication & Organisations*, 2nd edition, 1990]

also be automatically amended in D9. Such use of formulas enables spreadsheets not only to display complex calculations clearly, but also to effect rapid changes, say a 10% increase in some 15 of 198 entered products in a price-list, and to amend all totals accordingly.

Figure 3.7 contains a great deal of data in a comparatively small space, since analyses have been made in terms of sales (a) by product and (b) by month. Subtotals are supplied for each analysis producing the overall sales total of £116,300 for the 199– calender year. But tables set out like Figure 3.7 possess little visual appeal. They have to be studied in detail for their information to be taken in.

Individual skills-building activities

First study Figure 3.8 on page 120 and then answer the following questions:

1. Why are some projections and actual turnouts the same and some different?
2. What is a net cash flow?
3. How well did the business perform?
4. How easy/ difficult did you find the table to analyse?
5. Can you think of any other ways in which such information could be communicated which might be more effective?

SUMMARY

- Use tables to store detailed information, often recording volumes or totals against time-scales.
- Ensure the table is fully labelled: title, headings, scales, subtotals, totals, etc.
- Set subtotals and totals in, say, capitals and emboldened text and figures to make them stand out.
- Double-check the accuracy of additions, subtractions, percentage totals, etc.

Remember that tables are usually difficult and time-consuming to interpret. Prefer graphs and bar charts for more immediate visual appeal and uptake.

Figure 3.8 Table for skills-building activity.

Line	Receipts	3 months to June Projected £	3 months to June Actual £	6 months to September Projected £	6 months to September Actual £
2	Sales Debtors (including VAT)	20,700	20,700	51,750	46,000
5	Capital introduced	5,000	5,000	5,000	5,000
A	Total receipts	25,700	25,700	56,750	51,000
	Payments				
8	Cash purchases	16,100	20,125	29,900	29,425
11	Wages or Salaries (Net)	6,500	6,500	13,000	13,000
12	PAYE and NI	1,250	1,250	2,750	2,750
13	Capital items (for example equipment or vehicles)	2,500	2,500	2,500	2,500
15	Rent	1,125	750	1,875	1,875
15	Rates	120	120	240	240
16	Lighting and heating	225	240	450	500
16	Telephone and post	105	95	220	210
19	Interest	340	375	470	740
20	Bank and finance charges	100	150	200	250
21	Book-keeper	500	500	1,000	1,000
21	Professional fees	200	200	475	475
23	Insurance	200	200	200	200
24	General expenses	200	250	400	500
26	VAT	500	400	2,750	2,190
B	Total payments	29,965	33,655	56,430	55,855
C	Net cashflow (A, B)	(4,265)	(7,955)	320	(4,855)
29	Opening Bank Balance	Nil	Nil	Nil	Nil
D	Closing Bank Balance (Net cashflow – your opening balance)	(4,265)	(7,955)	320	(4,855)
		Overdrawn	Overdrawn	In Credit	Overdrawn

Trading Periods

[Reproduced by kind permission of National Westminster Bank from *The Business Start-up Guide*]

Individual skills-building activities

1 Research and then devise a table containing the following information about your class, setting out the data (a) for each individual and (b) as a set of totals: (1) age in years and months (2) sex; (3) height; (4) weight; (5) average age height and weight for male, female and both sexes; (6) male/female student ratio; (7) smoker and non-smoker totals and ratios by sex and by total group; (8) consumers of alcoholic beverages under headings: never, occasionally, regularly and frequently, with ratios by sex and total group. Provide a commentary of about 200 words to accompany your table.

2 Devise a spreadsheet table to record *one* of the following:

(a) the sales cost of snack foods and drinks in your study centre's refectory

(b) the sales cost of stationery items in your study centre's bookshop

(c) the cost of regular purchases made by your study centre department

(d) the possible and actual classroom occupancy totals and ratios for the study rooms in your department on a given day at a given hour

Ensure your spreadsheet is capable of providing useful totalled information and formulas which accommodate changes in base data. Also, provide a written commentary on the nature and scope of the spreadsheet you design in about 250 words. Display the class spreadsheets then decide which is most effective or best designed, and why.

Line graphs

Line graphs (Fig. 3.9) are produced by plotting data on a grid which has a vertical axis and a horizontal axis. By convention, the elapse of *time* is shown along the horizontal axis and *other quantities* along the vertical axis.

Figure 3.9 Line graphs are used for comparing two variables.

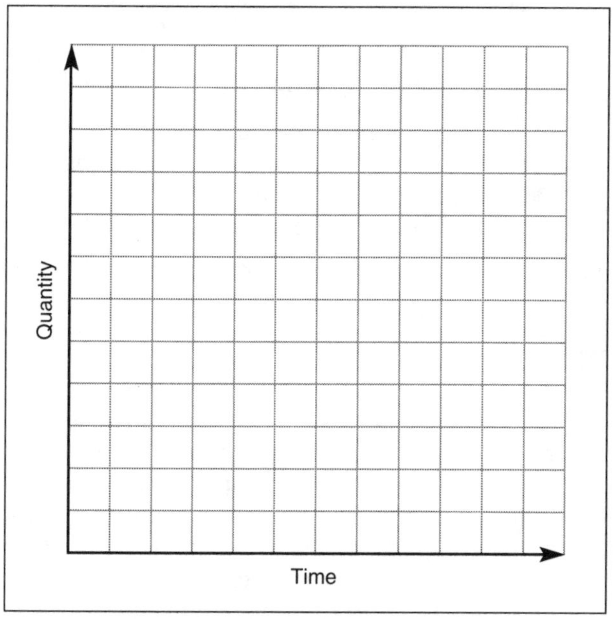

Line graphs are particularly useful when two or more items are to be compared, say the speed at which various liquids cool, or the demand for different types of domestic fuel. They are also extremely helpful for examining current trends and forecasting future trends. For example, the scales of certain types of share on the London Stock Exchange may fluctuate sharply day-on-day over a period of, say three months, but still show an overall upward trend as in Figure 3.10.

Line graphs are also useful for comparing the respective performances of different items, say a product range, a small group of patients, sales regions or districts. Or they can compare the same quantity measured over different periods, as shown in Figure 3.11.

Figure 3.11 Sales fall to a minimum in July of all three years.

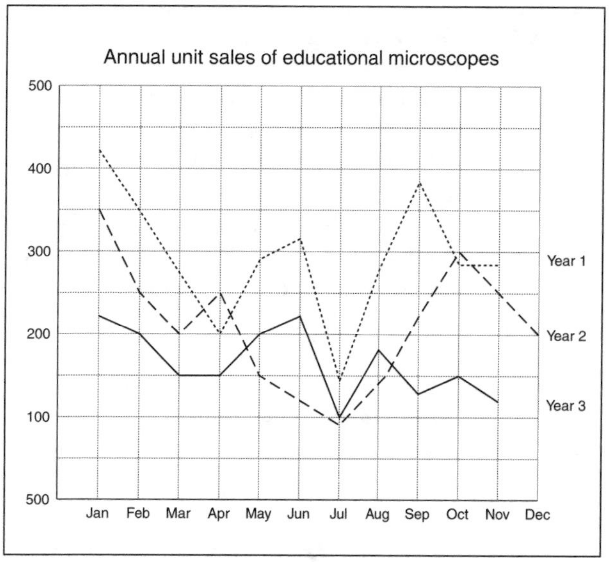

Of course, when several items are to be plotted on a line graph, it is important to make each one as clearly distinguishable from its neighbours as possible, usually through the use of bold contrasting colours, or if limited to black ink or toner, through the use of contrasting line patterns:

———— —•—•—•— —•••—•••— ••••••

Figure 3.10 Monthly fluctuations superposed on an annual trend.

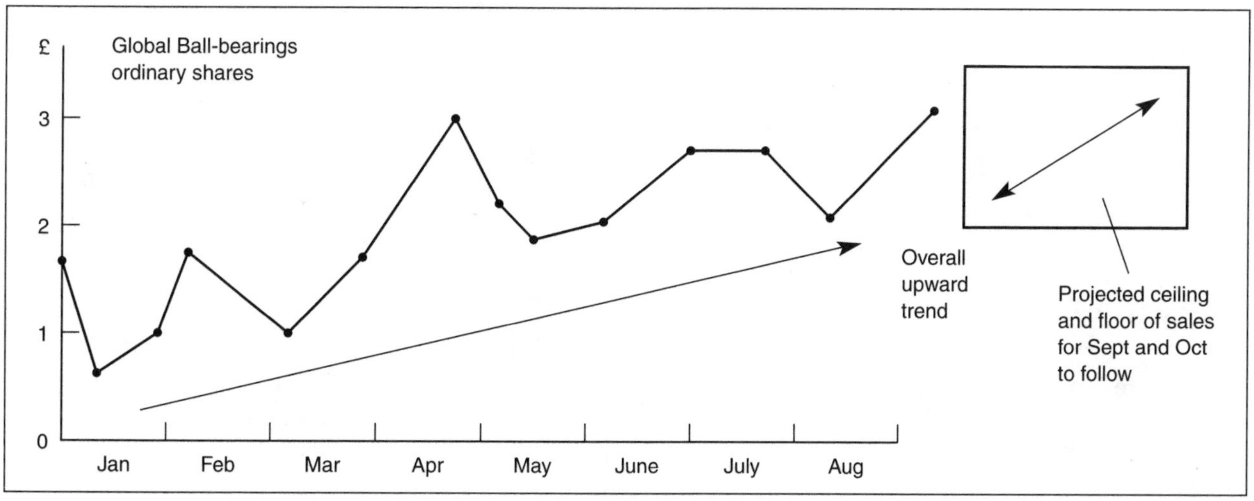

Many organisations use line graphs to communicate more vividly and emphatically information which is also stored on a table. To prove this point, here is an activity.

Individual skills-building activity

Convert the data for washing-machines, refrigerators and freezers contained in the table on page 119 into a line graph. Discuss how the use of the line graph changes the ways in which the data is communicated.

Breaking the vertical axis

Sometimes items are plotted on a line graph which embody large differences in their amounts or quantities such that one or more may go off the edge of the page. To avoid the need to use a large sheet of paper, a convention has for many years been adopted by scientists and engineers to break the line of the vertical axis in order to take out an appropriate wedge, as shown in Figure 3.12.

Figure 3.12 The wavy line convention to indicate an axis break.

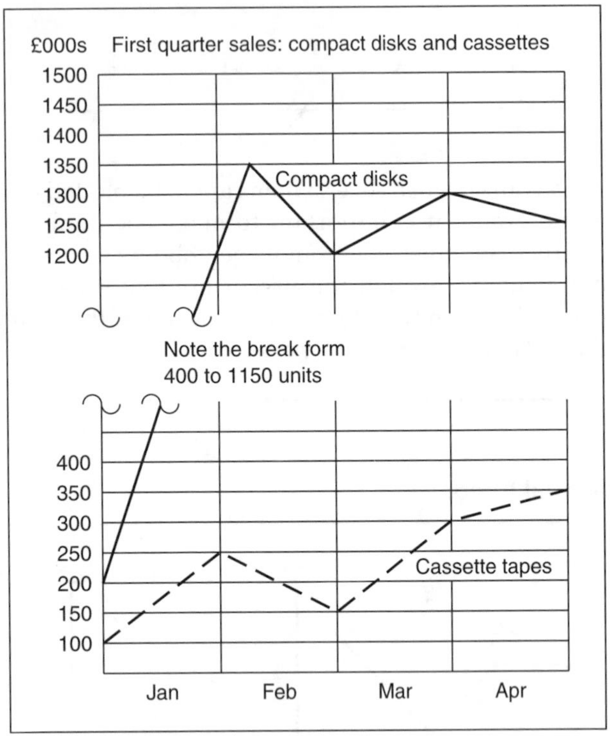

SUMMARY

- Ensure that your line graph is carefully titled, both axes are clearly labelled and the author and date are correctly shown. ▶
- Ensure also that your grid or matrix is equally graduated to ensure accuracy of plotting; this also goes for the frequency of the plotted points – say by month or week against value or quantity – so that like is always being compared with like.
- Choose vertical and horizontal scales which are sufficiently large to show differences in amounts of data and time spans, but which do not result in some items being of such a small size that it is difficult to differentiate between them; if needs be, use the axis-breaking technique to avoid this problem.
- Make sure each plotted line shows up clearly against its neighbour, if possible, using colour.
- Avoid trying to plot too many items together, especially if they are closely related in terms of amount or quantity. The human eye finds it difficult to unravel more than five or six plotted lines.

Pie charts

Another visually effective way of communicating and presenting number information is through the use of charts. Pie and bar charts use geometric areas – slices of a pie or rectangular bars – to provide a means of comparing one quantity with another. Moreover, the advent of computerised graphics packages has enabled chart designers to include visually interesting features such as three-dimensional bars and various forms of exploded segments.

Pie charts (Figs. 3.13 and 3.14) take on the circular form of a pie, so one can imagine the components which make them up as slices of the pie. In order to

Figure 3.13 Pie charts show percentages as sectors of a circle.

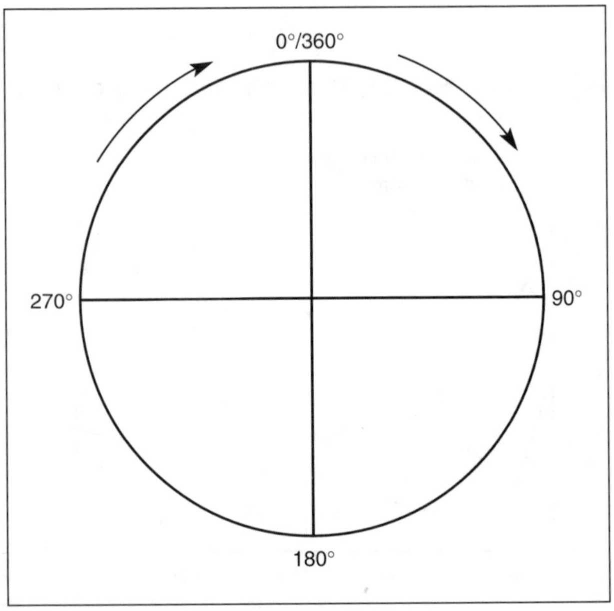

calculate the correct size of each sector of the circle (or slice of the pie), it is important to remember that a circle has 360°, and therefore each of its quadrants will have 90°. When seeking to allocate an appropriate size to a given sector, its proportion of a known whole must be transferred from a percentage into a total of degrees (where 1% is shown as 360°/100 = 3.6°):

$50\% \Rightarrow 180°, 25\% \Rightarrow 90°, 12.5\% \Rightarrow 45°,$
$7.42\% \Rightarrow 3.6° \times 7.42 = 26.71°$

Notice that Figure 3.14 includes a clear title and labels of the three components, or slices of the pie, Comfort Shoes, Melia Shoes and Other (probably the total of many small market shares); details of the share of the market of each sector, expressed both as a percentage (12.5, 23, 64.5) and as sales totals in pounds sterling; and to complete the picture, the total value of the UK shoe market, £500 million.

Figure 3.15 provides a detailed breakdown of Comfort Shoes' sales of ladies boots and shoes, which form 43.75% of its total sales. Not only does it supply this information in a visually appealing way, it also combines it with numerical details of percentages and sterling totals.

Figure 3.14 Exploded pie chart: a gap is left between sectors.

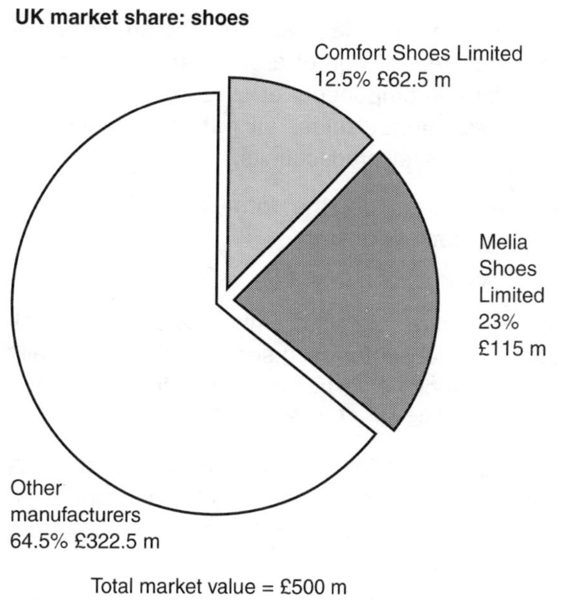

[Reproduced by kind permission of Pitman Publishing from D.W. Evans, *Effective Business Administration and Communication*, 1992]

Figure 3.15 Pie charts give visual appeal to numerical data.

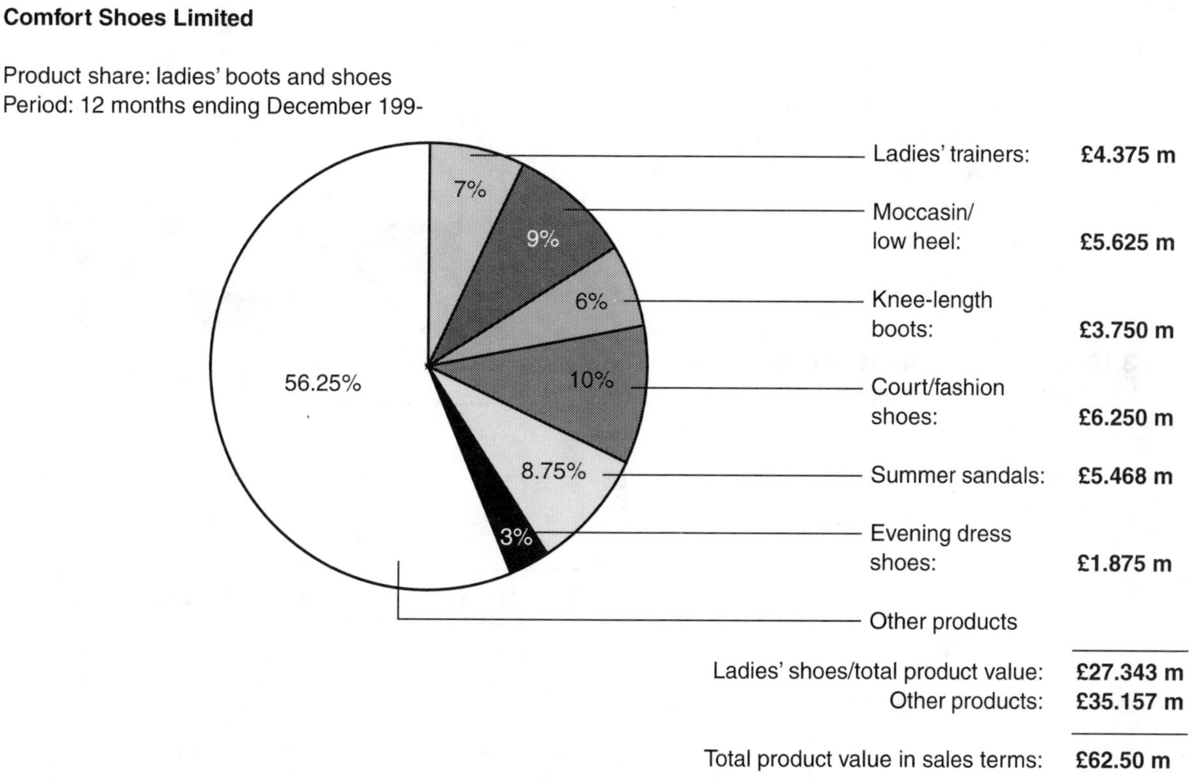

[Reproduced by kind permission of Pitman Publishing from D.W. Evans, *People, Communication & Organisations*, 2nd edition, 1990]

SUMMARY

- Remember that two types of data are essential to the correct design of a pie chart: (a) a known total for all components or slices of the pie, e.g. total UK market sales, all patients, all leisure centre users, all product units.
- Remember, too, the formula for finding the angle of each sector:

  sector angle = percentage × 3.6°
- An effective pie chart embodies a clear overall title, clear labels for each sector of the pie, details for each sector of its percentage (of the whole) and quantity totals (see Fig. 3.15).
- Keep in mind that pie charts effectively communicate up to five or six sectors of contrasting size, but they are ineffective for lots of sectors showing 3–7% of the whole.
- As with line graphs, pie charts benefit from the use of contrasting colours for each segment, or shading effects in monochrome.

Bar charts

As their name suggests, bar charts (Fig. 3.16) are constructed by juxtaposing a series of bars. Essentially, they form another way of displaying the same sort of information as is shown on a line graph when several items are compared. Bar charts employ exactly the same type of vertical and horizontal axes as line graphs, vertical for quantities and horizontal for time or different types of item.

Figure 3.16 Simple bar charts use the same axes as line graphs.

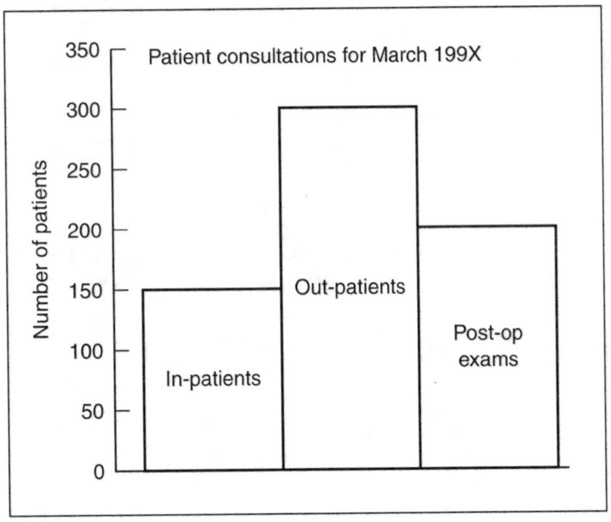

Stacked bar charts

Sometimes the data to be displayed in a bar chart is more complicated than that shown in Figure 3.16. It may be that, within each bar, there is not a single quantity to be compared, but three or four components. In this case, each bar is shown to have a total (of its components) and separately identifiable components. Figure 3.17 shows three regions of a house-building company (North, Midlands and South); each construct three different types of residence: houses, flats and bungalows. Thus it is possible to compare the number of residences built in each region by stacking them within each bar. However, for such a technique to work, the components of each bar must be exactly the same; (it would not work say, if South did not build bungalows, but did build one-room studios, since they would not be comparable.

Figure 3.17 Stacked bar charts: all bars use the same components.

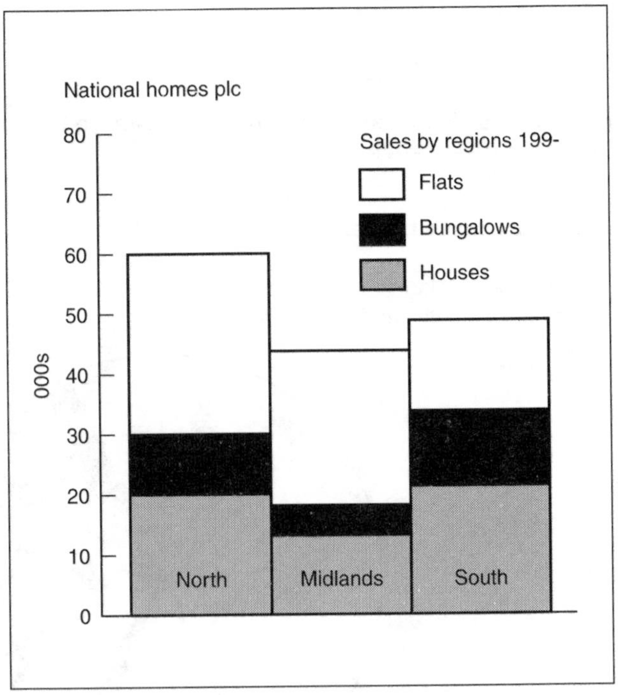

Three-dimensional bar charts

The three-dimensional bar chart (Fig. 3.18) is, in reality, no different in structure from its two-dimensional counterpart. But the third dimension does provide extra visual interest, as the following example illustrates. Three-dimensional bar charts are popular with chart designers who work with graphics software packages as they lend a greater sophistication to high-status presentations while being no more difficult to produce.

Figure 3.18 Three-dimensional bar chart: compare with Figure 3.11.

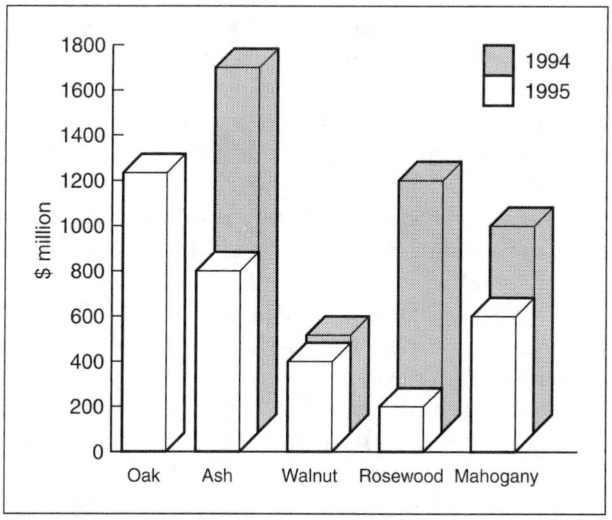

Histograms and frequency polygons

Histograms, frequency polygons and distribution curves are three ways of presenting identical information. Each displays a spread or distribution of data across a known spectrum or continuum. This aspect of charting is perhaps best explained through examples. For many years now, statisticians have been interested in the characteristics of populations or cohorts: the age range of citizens of a state, the results of students taking examinations, the concentrations of animal populations across a country or the purchasing habits of consumers. In a nutshell these charts plot quantities (how many, how much, etc.) against given extents (of time, of age, of 0–100, etc).

Figure 3.19 Histogram: each age-group covers 20 years.

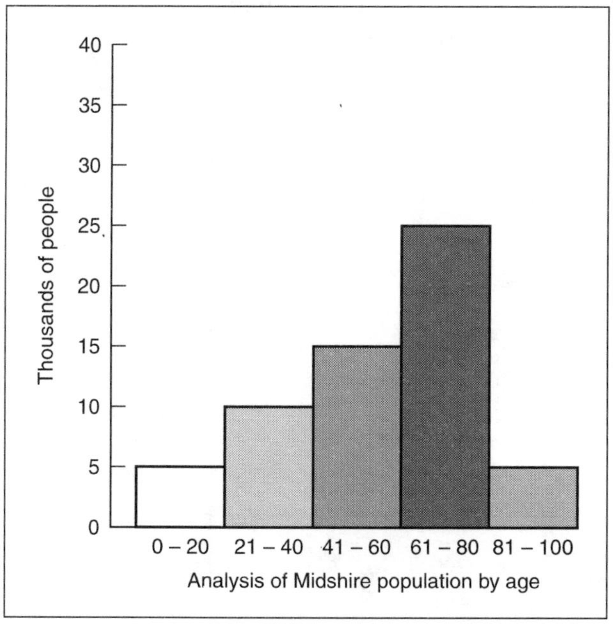

A histogram (Fig. 3.19) is very much like a bar chart in that it displays the relative amounts of a given total across specified components of a known range. What this means, quite simply, is best shown by the following example, which illustrates the distribution of the population of a county by age. Note that each age range is expressed in identical totals of 20 years, otherwise the respective areas of each bar in the histogram would not be based on the same parameters or features, thus invalidating the statistics.

A frequency polygon (Fig. 3.20) is produced simply by interconnecting the midpoints of each bartop in the histogram. It is a combination of histogram and line graph.

Figure 3.20 Frequency polygon: connect midpoints of each bartop.

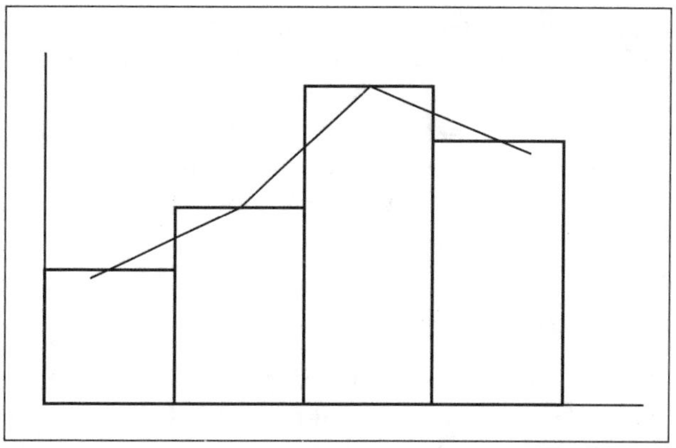

Distribution curves

A distribution curve (Fig. 3.21) is, in essence, a type of line graph which uses particular data – the spread of quantities across a given scale. Distribution curves take on many different kinds of shapes, depending on the nature of the data they express. For example, the distribution curve of the current

Figure 3.21 The shape of a distribution curve depends on the data.

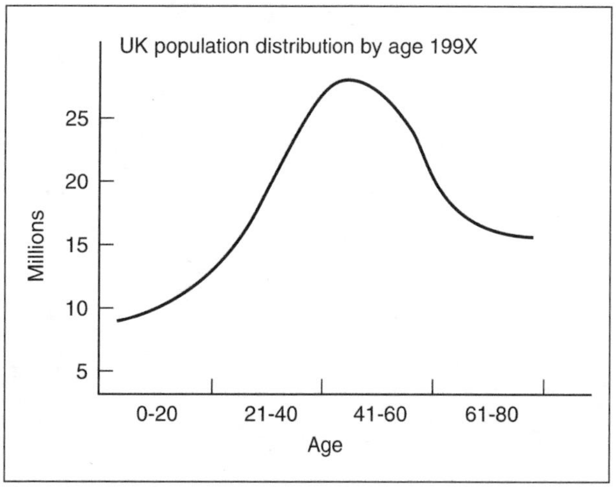

population of the UK is likely to show a preponderance of old rather than young people, simply because of falls in the post 1945 birth rate and the increased longevity of old people, thanks to advances in modern medicine. A *normal distribution* looks like Figure 3.22; it is a symmetrical distribution. A normal curve, statistically speaking, tends to possess a vast majority – nearly 70% of the total population – equally distributed within two narrow sectors either side of its mean, the middle of the distribution where the highest quantity is to be found. Beyond the first two sectors lie two further sectors, each containing about 12–14% of the total. And at the extreme edges of the normal curve lie two equal sectors of about 3–5% of the total. Consider an example. Take the intelligence range (called a quotient) of a randomly selected, statistically significant sample of people. The vast majority (nearly 70%) will prove to possess an intelligence straddling the mean, neither highly intelligent nor with severe learning disabilities. A further 28–30% may be expected to possess intelligence ratings either well above or well below the average. While at either end of the sample will lie the 3–4% approaching the level of genius or severe learning disability.

Skews in distribution

When a distribution curve departs from the above statistically normal curve, it is usually because some factor has caused what is termed *a skew*. In Figure 3.21 the skew is caused by significant numbers of people living longer and fewer couples having children. Skews may be caused by other factors, such as a defect in the sampling techniques employed, which may result in samples not being truly random; or skews may be caused by taking samples that are too small.

Standard deviations from the mean

In order to save time and to reduce sampling quantities, statisticians make use of the concept of *standard deviation from the mean*. Simply, this term describes the difference of individual items plotted from their mean or average. For instance, a company producing boxes of matches may decide to label them with the advice: average contents 50 matches. However, variations in packing accuracy may result in some boxes containing 53 or 54 matches and others 47 or 48. In order to satisfy their own internal quality control standards as well as trading standards officers, such a manufacturer may need to keep within a standard deviation from the mean of say ±2.

Similarly, in distribution curves, the statistician may state on the chart that the curve is accurate within so many points of deviation from the mean. In this way, smaller samples may be deemed accurate to within say 98%. Thus statistical analyses are often said to be accurate within ±2% or ±3%.

Scatter diagrams

Scatter diagrams (Fig. 3.23) are used to indicate trends when the relating data is spread over a relatively wide area, but within certain upper and lower limits. As an example, consider how many people are likely to book a Caribbean holiday in terms of their net income. Clearly the results are not likely to be uniform; a couple on a low income may have saved for years for such a holiday, whereas a successful executive may take his/her family to the Caribbean for a holiday twice a year. Nevertheless, despite the likelihood of a number of such variables, scatter diagrams enable trends to be plotted and spotted. Figure 3.23 shows the sale of ice lollies

Figure 3.22 Normal distribution: nearly 70% of the population lies within the two sectors adjacent to the mean.

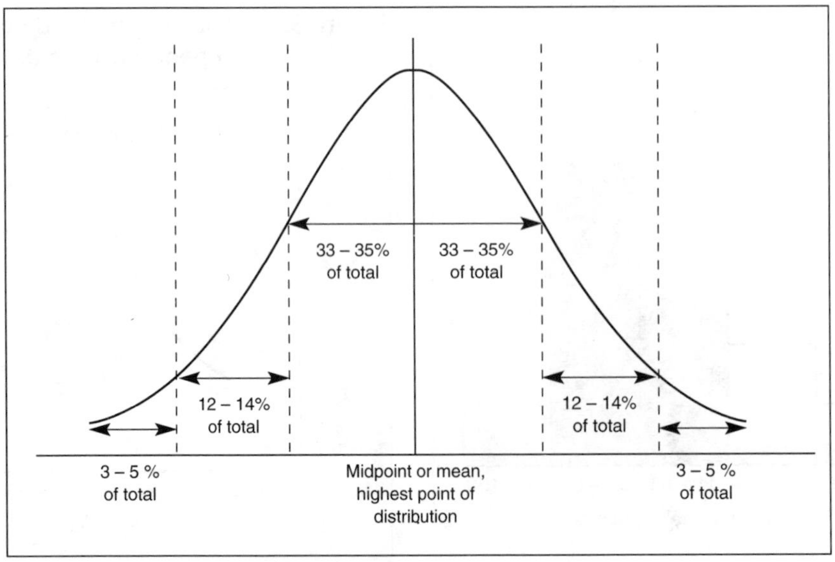

Figure 3.23 Scatter diagram: ice-cream sales against temperature.

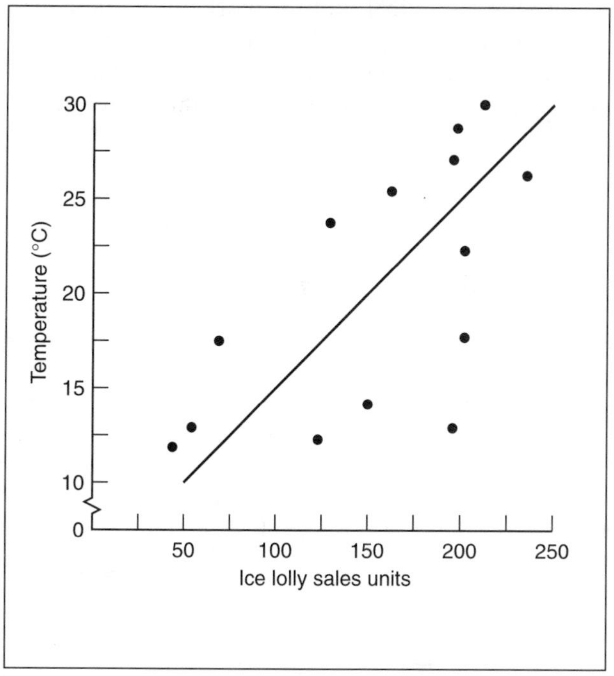

during varying degrees of temperature, say on a seaside esplanade or at an open-air pop concert.

By plotting the levels of ice lollies purchased against temperature, it is possible to determine varying levels of demand and to assist, say, an ice lolly manufacturer in planning production either for a coming week of low troughs, cool weather and sluggish demand, or for a heatwave.

Flow charts

Flow charts (Fig. 3.24) (overleaf) are so called because they represent a type of circuit or plumbing (with on and off taps), along which a decision process flows. They often used to enable people to make decisions. Sunday broadsheet newspapers, for example, often use them to help their readers to decide which type of pension, mortgage or motor car is best suited to their needs, financial circumstances, etc.

In the workplace, flow charts are perhaps most often to be found in the realms of workstudy and organisation and methods. For instance, in a production context, a works manager may wish to review in detail the processes which a machine operator follows in order to make a particular product. Flow charts are also employed as a means of supplying instructions to people when a variety of outcomes may occur. Figure 3.24 is taken from a set of instructions on how to design flow charts and indicates what to do in order to make a successful phone call.

Figure 3.25 Manufacturing and management use flow process charts.

Flow process chart – basic use of symbols
scrap note procedure – valuation

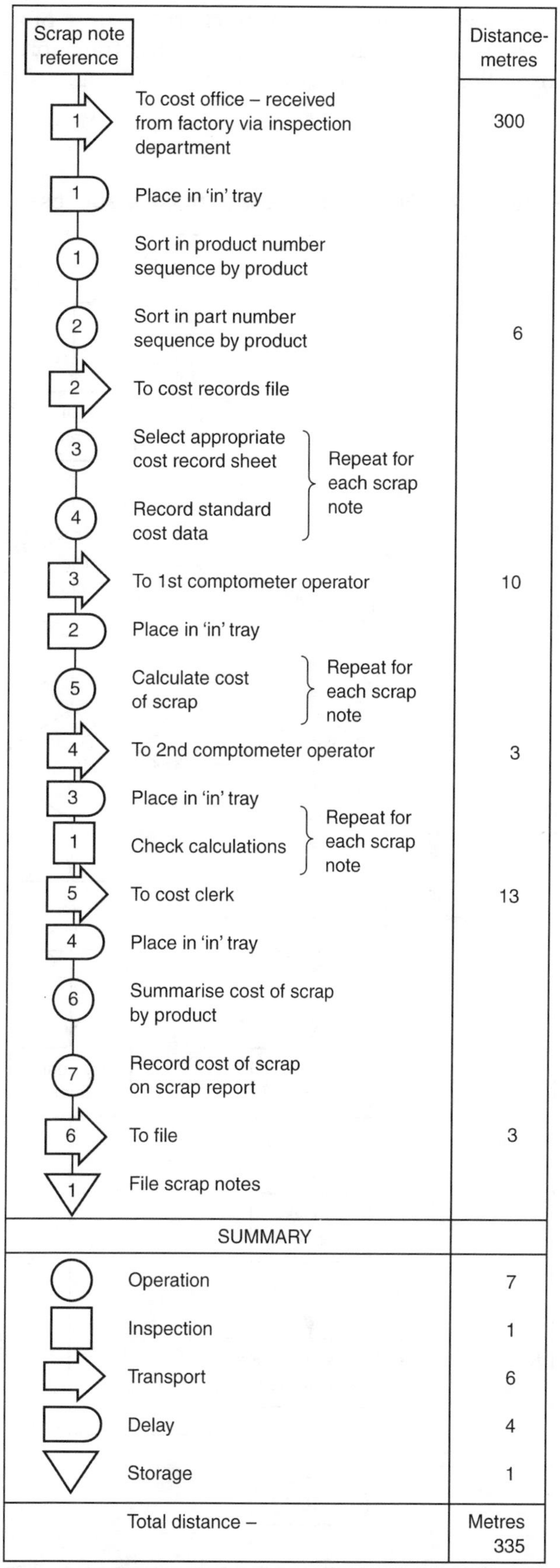

[Reproduced by kind permission of Pitman Publishing from D. W. Evans *People, Communication and Organisations*, 2nd edition, 1990]

Flow process charts

The flow process chart (Fig. 3.25) illustrated on page 127 is used in a manufacturing and management services environment to chart the flow of a work process in terms of operations, transport, inspection, delay, storage and distance. It employs a generally accepted set of symbols shown in the key at the foot of the figure. Flow process charts provide a valuable analytical tool for workstudy managers, since the data they provide is both factual and objective, comprising a series of measurements allied to observed and noted actions which staff undertake.

Figure 3.24 Flow chart: how to make a successful telephone call.

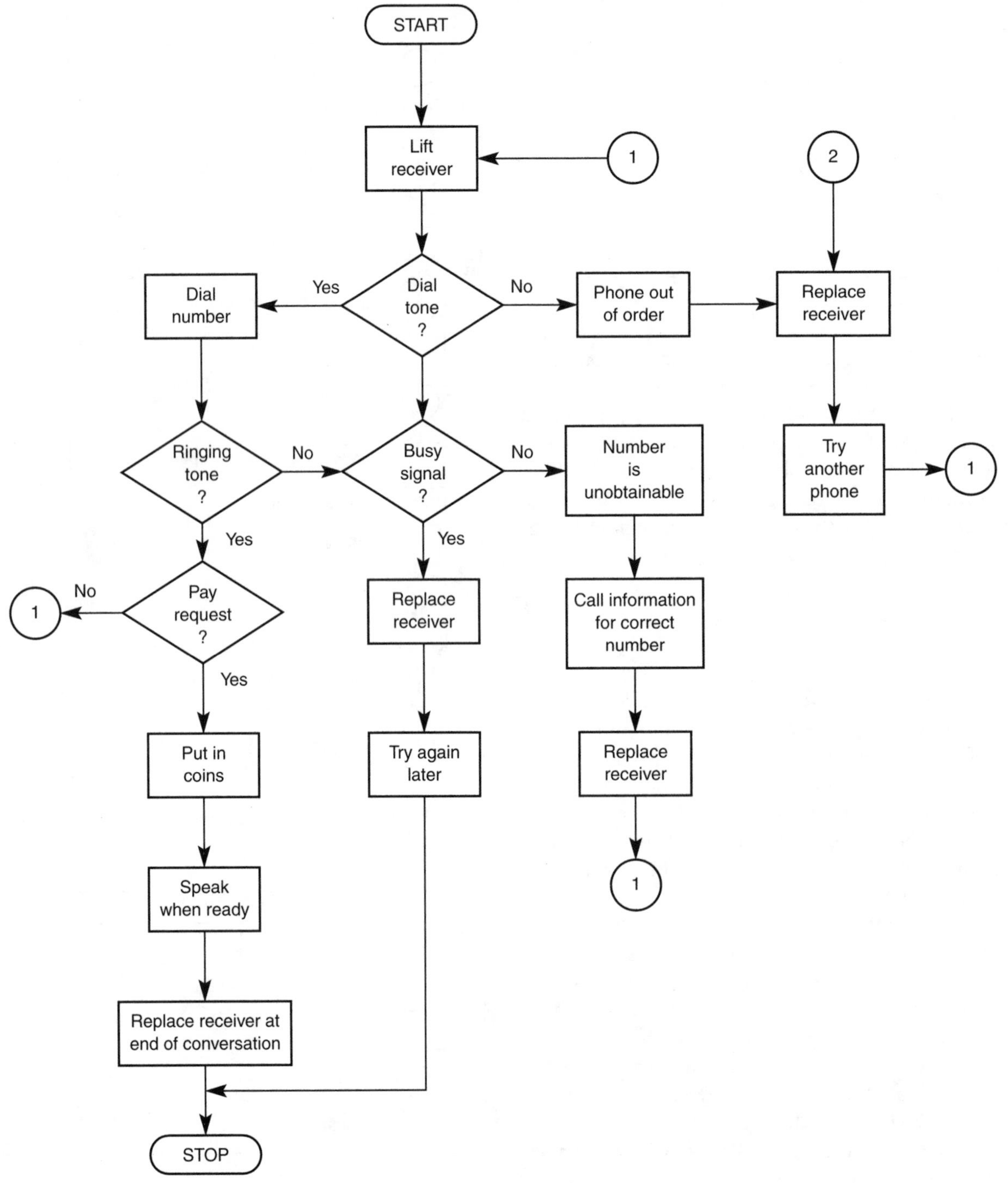

[Reproduced by kind permission of M & E Business Handbook, Pitman Publishing from J. Shaw, *Administration in Business*, 2nd edn.

Gantt charts

Gantt charts (Fig. 3.26) are named after their inventor, and are primarily used to assist the effective operation of a project or series of tasks which take place over time and within a given deadline. The illustration below shows how a Gantt chart may be used to plan the construction of a garage, say by a jobbing builder. The chart clearly shows how some tasks may be undertaken at the same time, but others are dependent on the completion of certain work. For example, footings may be dug and roof A frames assembled at the same time; but the laying of bricks cannot begin until footings have been both dug and cement foundations laid and hardened. In this way, a Gantt chart helps project planners to sequence and prioritise their work as a series of related tasks. The chart may also be used as a means of checking that progress is being made at the required rate.

Z charts

Z charts (Fig. 3.27) (overleaf) are so called because the plotted data resemble a letter Z. The Z chart, like graphs and bar charts, employs the customary vertical and horizontal axes to plot quantities against elapsed time. For the Z chart, these quantities are a current year and a rolling-forward year. Take, for example, the management of a leisure centre. They will naturally need to keep informed of their performance in terms of total income. The Z chart allows them to plot three types of data:

- quantities during a current calendar year
- cumulative quantities, e.g. income as it grows month on month from January to December
- moving annual totals (MATs), e.g. income rolling forward from Jan 1994 to Jan 1995, Feb 1994 to Feb 1995, Mar 1994 to Mar 1995 and so on.

The vertical axis of Figure 3.27 is given two scales, one for current totals and one for the moving annual total and the cumulative total.

Figure 3.26 Gantt charts schedule component tasks in a project.

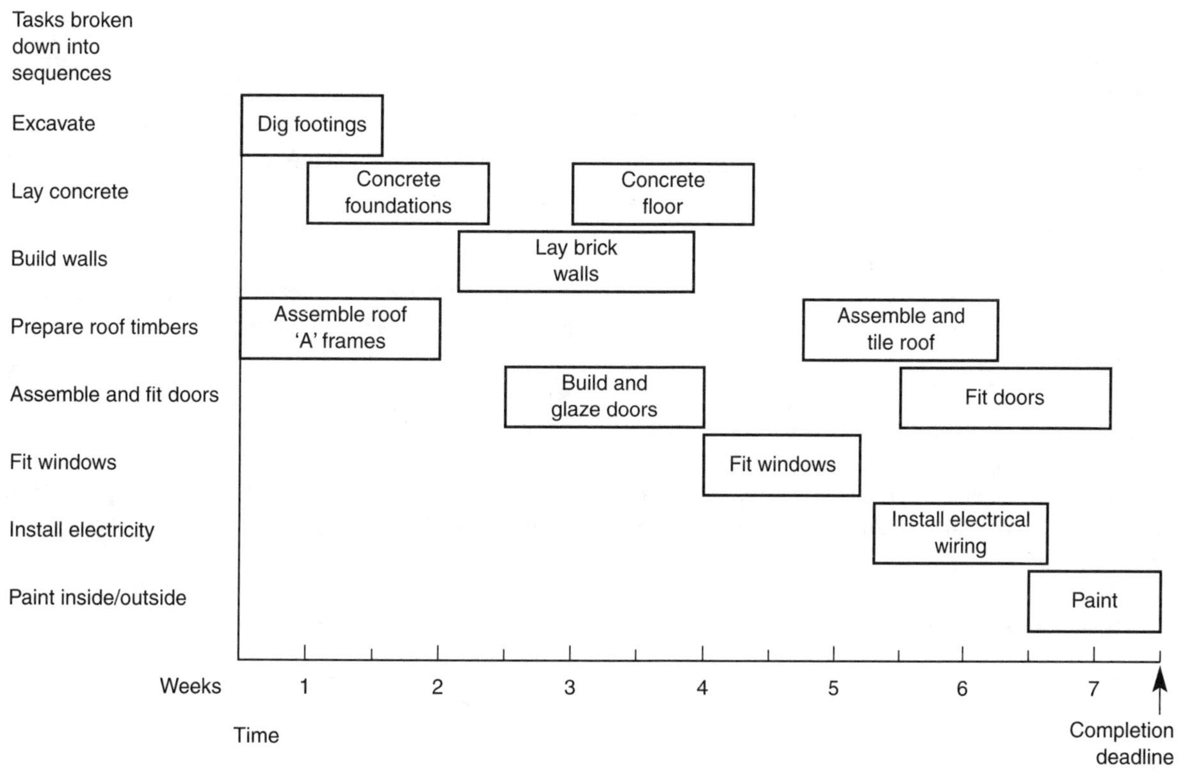

[Reproduced by kind permission of Pitman Publishing from D. W. Evans, *Advanced GNVQ Business: A Student's Guide*, 3rd edition, 1995]

Figure 3.27 Z charts: a letter Z is formed by plotting two quantities fluctuating about a mean and one cumulative quantity.

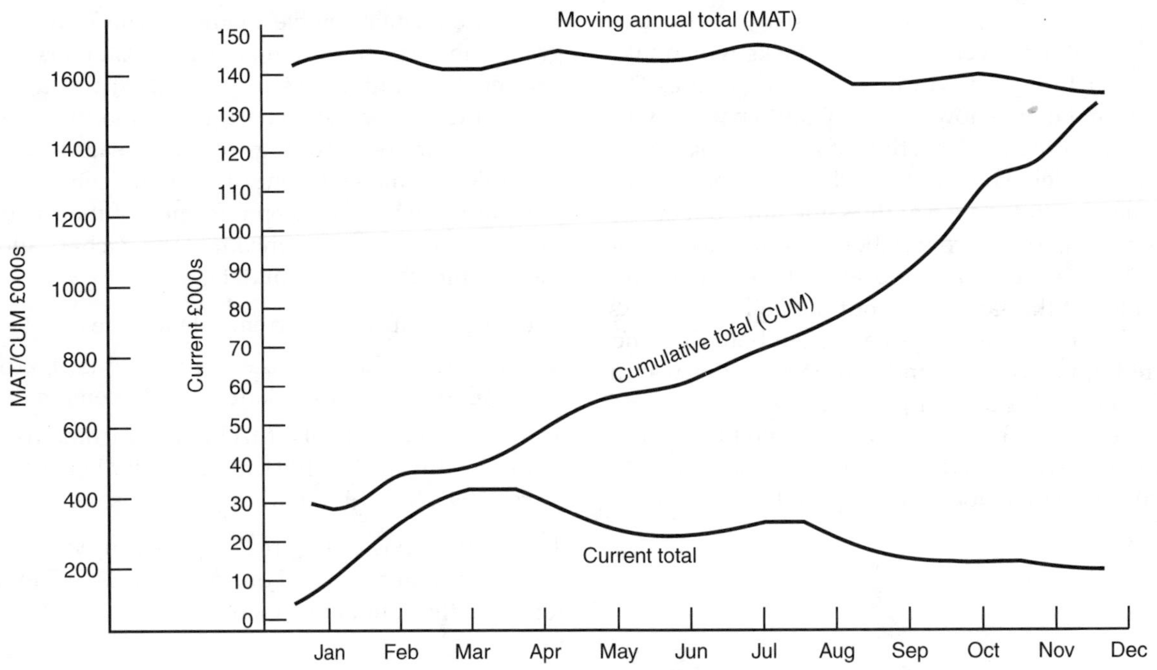

[Reproduced by kind permission of Pitman Publishing from D.W. Evans *Advanced GNVQ Business: A Student's Guide*, 3rd edition, 1995]

SUMMARY

- Select with care the chart you intend to employ for a given task; remember that each has particular strengths and weaknesses, e.g. pie charts cannot show trends but line graphs can.

- Double-check your raw data for accuracy before plotting it on to your chart.

- Remember to title and label your chart clearly and to include against your vertical and horizontal axes clear details of the scales employed, e.g. £000, units, Jan–Dec 199–, etc; also include your name and the production date.

- Choose your scales with care, so as to ensure that plotted items are sufficiently large and clearly differentiated; use the broken vertical axis technique if need be.

- Make effective use of contrasting colours or shading to differentiate plotted items.

- Include appropriate keys or legends which explain what symbols mean.

- Employ whenever possible the high-quality presentation features of computer graphics packages.

- Double-check your plotted points or bars for accuracy *before* printing.

What do you think?

1 Some people are just unable to take in number data, no matter how well it is set out.

2 By the time you've learned how to design a spreadsheet, you've done the calculations job by hand three times over.

3 According to Mark Twain, there are three kinds of lies, 'lies, damn lies and statistics!' Do you agree?

4 The main problem with computerised number-crunching packages is that people get lazy and take as gospel whatever appears on the screen, since they've lost the ability to cross-check totals using their own mental arithmetic.

5 In reality, it is numbers, not words that count in the workplace.

Self-check review test

1 List the key components of an effective map.

2 What are the major features of an expertly devised table?

3 What are the advantages of producing a table on a computer spreadsheet package?

4 On what axes are quantity and time normally plotted on a line graph?

5 Describe briefly the advantages and disadvantages of employing a table and a line graph to communicate numerical information.

6 In what circumstances would you choose to insert a break in the vertical axis of a line graph?

7 When would a pie chart prove particularly effective to communicate numerical data?

8 What is the difference between a bar chart and a stacked bar chart?

9 What is a histogram?

10 What is a Gantt chart used for?

11 Explain these terms: standard deviation from the mean, skew.

12 When would you use a flow chart to communicate information?

13 What is the difference between a flow chart and a flow process chart?

14 Explain briefly what a Z chart is used for.

15 Summarise the important ingredients of maps, tables and charts.

When you have set down your own answers, compare them with those on page 199 and consult this section again if they differ.

Diagrams

Diagrams, models, trees, pictographs and fonts mix number, text, lines, boxes and backgrounds. All are created as one-offs to meet unique requirements in an oral presentation, report, textbook or bulletin. All benefit from the earlier guidelines on harmony and balance, simplicity and clarity. And all follow the conventions of titling and labelling explained in the previous sections.

Diagrams come in an infinite variety of designs; however, there are two aspects of diagrams which are well worth keeping in mind. Either they communicate a static structure, say of staff relationships in an organisation chart, or they convey a process, where movement occurs from A to B, through to Z, like a flow chart. Static structures require clearly positioned components linked by continuous lines or by arrows. Processes also require careful thought about how the sequence of steps may best be represented from top to bottom, from left to right, or in a clockwise, circular track.

Figure 3.28 was devised to illustrate the fact that people discharge a variety of roles, both at work and at home. The context of the diagram was to explain that sometimes a single person's multiple roles may conflict when, for instance, a birthday treat at a circus for a daughter from Dad clashes with an urgent request for overtime to be worked so as to get an important export order delivered on time. The Venn diagram style provides a simple, yet effective, see-at-a-glance visual message on how Jim Simpson's four major roles overlap. For the most part (the greater areas of the circles) each role may be pursued without conflict, but occasionally father and senior clerk roles overlap, causing stress.

Figure 3.28 Jim Simpson's roles at home and at work.

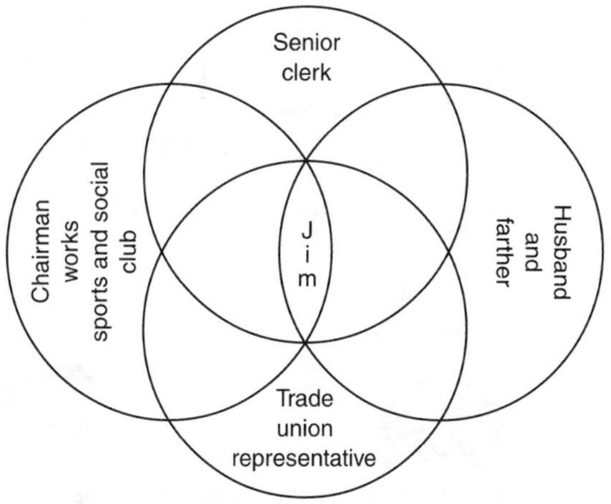

[Reproduced by kind permission of Pitman Publishing from D.W. Evans *People, Communication & Organisations*, 2nd edition, 1990]

Figure 3.29 shows how manufacturing resource planning (MRP) works. MRP represents a unified approach to the manufacturing process, and the intention of the diagram is to illustrate how MRP derives from a company's marketing and sales plans (which frame overall production policy), and then to show an MRP operations strategy which links

- the purchasing function
- the production process
- production and maintenance scheduling
- the maintenance function
- despatch and distribution

In order to make clear the relationships between each of these MRP functions, careful use is made of postioning of text in boxes, directional arrows and simple symbols. Such diagrams help to reinforce the writer's explanation of MRP by providing the reader with a visual as opposed to a textual account.

Organisational trees

Organisational trees (Fig. 3.30) owe their name to the way in which their component parts are spread out like branches, where various departments or units all spread from a single point. In a real sense, the tree is depicted upside down, since in most organisations, this single source comes in the form of the chair of the board of directors, or chief officer, who is invariably situated at the top of the tree.

Organisational trees are used to show in a visual form the structure of an organisation, and in order to grasp their meaning, it is necessary to appreciate that organisatons tend to be structured as a pyramid or hierarchy (Fig. 3.31).

Figure 3.32 illustrates the structure of a single specialist function, one of between six and eight major functions within a manufacturing company, alongside research and development, production, purchasing and so on. It shows management services functions as well as the functions of individual specialists. Note that the pyramidic hierarchy approach is followed. The department's function begins at the point of most authority, the director of group management services, then indicates the equal status of the internal audit and the projects committee, and the subordinate but co-equal status of the operations research, data processing and organisation and methods managers who head up the three sections which comprise the department. Notice also the careful use of the lines of authority and communication to indicate clearly who reports

Figure 3.29 Make careful use of text, symbols and arrows.

How manufacturing resource planning (MRP) works in manufacturing

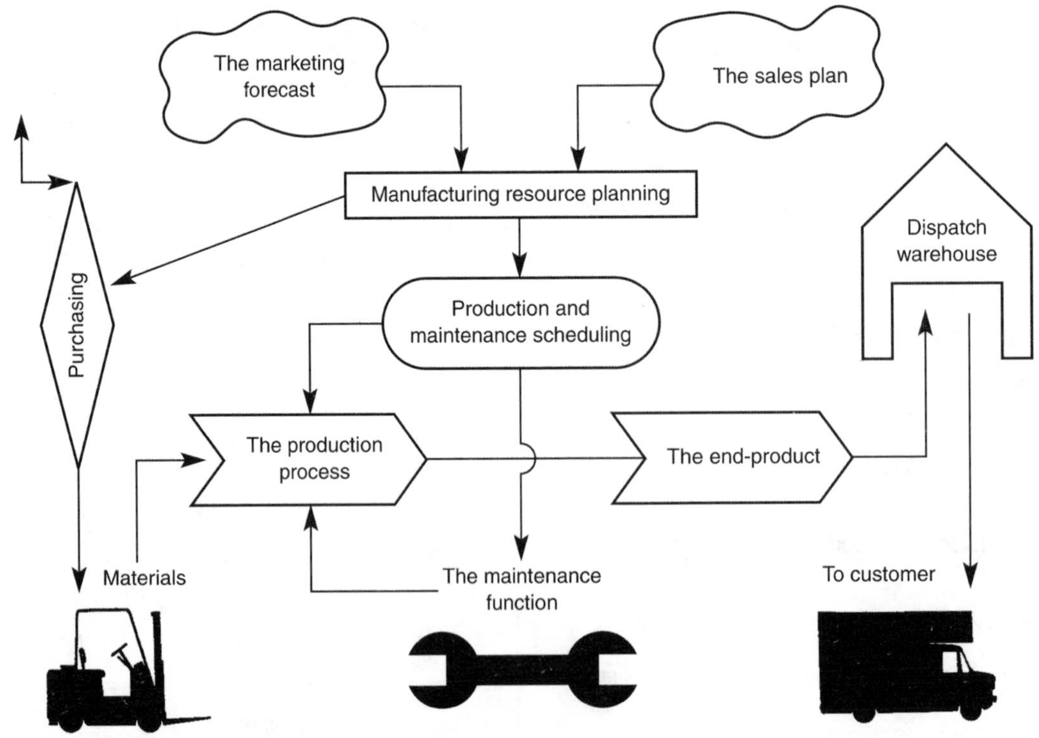

Effective manufacturing integrates: market forecasting, JIT buying, MRP planning, maintenance scheduling, storing and distributing

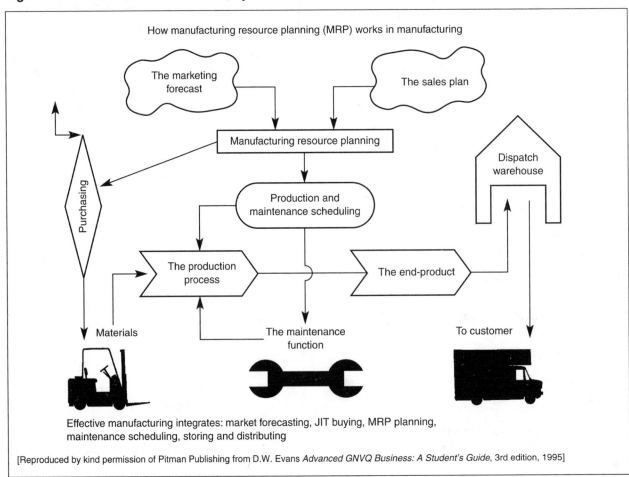

[Reproduced by kind permission of Pitman Publishing from D.W. Evans *Advanced GNVQ Business: A Student's Guide*, 3rd edition, 1995]

Figure 3.30 Organisational trees show the structure of a company.

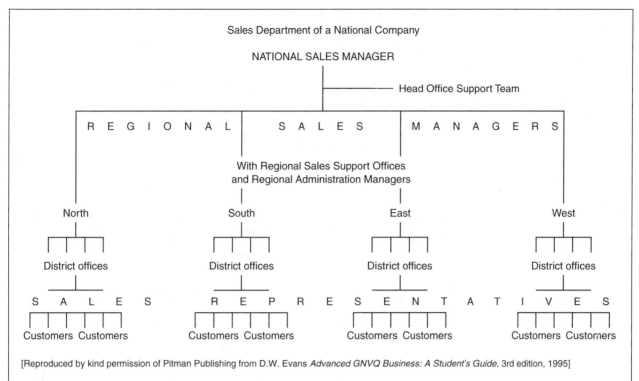

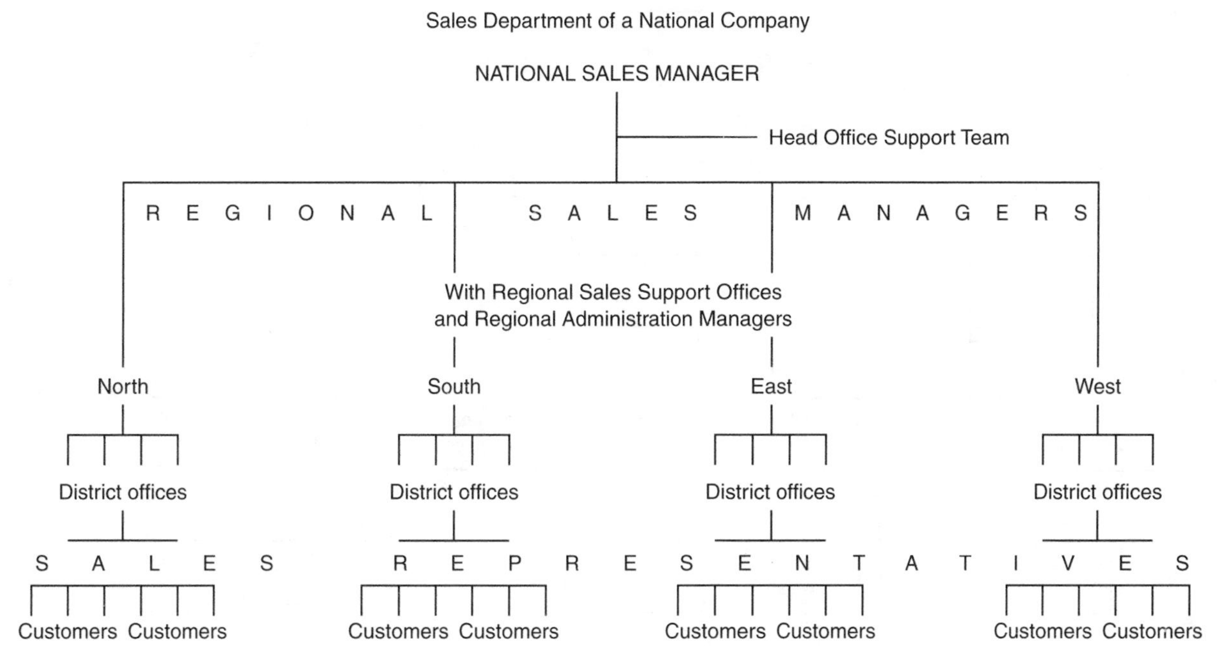

[Reproduced by kind permission of Pitman Publishing from D.W. Evans *Advanced GNVQ Business: A Student's Guide*, 3rd edition, 1995]

Figure 3.31 Organisational trees stem from a pyramidic hierarchy.

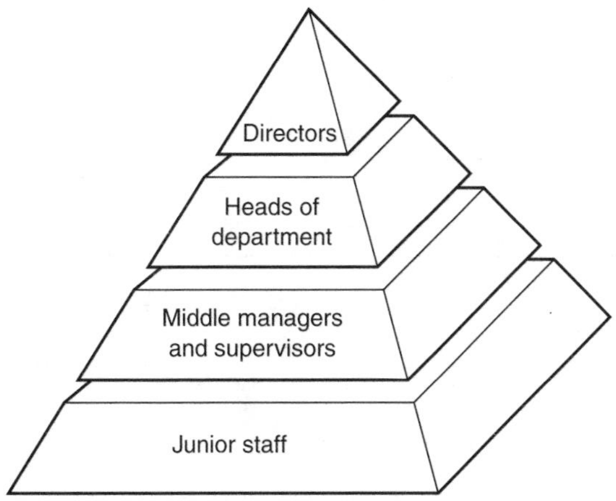

[Reproduced by kind permission of Pitman Publishing from D.W. Evans, *People, Communication & Organisations*, 2nd edition, 1990]

to whom. Lastly, imaginative positioning of boxes and arrows presents the data clearly within a relatively small space.

Pictograms and logos

If its Greek title is taken literally, *pictogram* translates as 'writing by pictures', and that is precisely what a pictogram does. It communicates information by employing a picture or graphic image to represent data. In the 1930s and 1940s, graphic designers became very fond of using pictograms to convey statistical information; perhaps 1 million tons of wheat would be represented by a stook 5mm × 5mm and 3 million tons by one three times as large. But such a statistical approach can be misleading, with the larger pictogram appearing to the human eye to be much more than twice or three times as large as its counterpart. Figure 3.33 compares two pictograms for the same information, one of them clear, the other misleading.

Almost every organisation today, whether in the private or public sector, commissions a graphic artist to design an effective logo aimed at communicating either simply or subtly the nature of its activities. As a result of intensive advertising and sales promotion over many years, some logos become instantly recognisable, whereas others appeal because they are friendly, original or impressive.

Designing an effective logo is not easy. Indeed, the best ones are effective precisely because they are simple, like the British Rail logo of rails moving in opposite directions. Yet it may have taken designers many hours to hit upon such a design.

Small group skill-building activity

In groups of 3 or 4, appraise a selection of logos and decide what makes them successful or unsuccessful.

Figure 3.32 Notice how the boxes are connected and positioned.

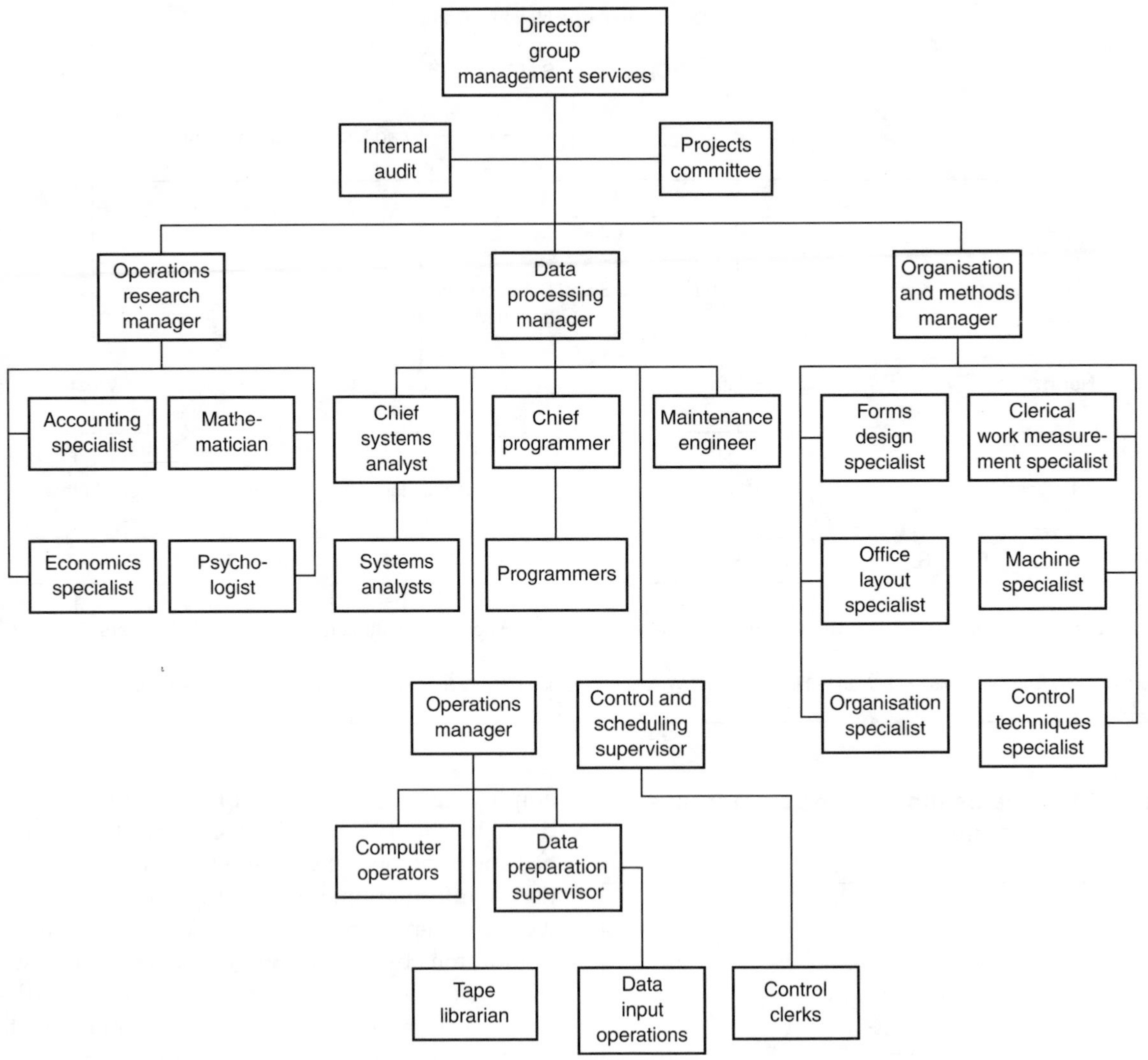

[Reproduced by kind permission of Pitman Publishing from D.W. Evans, *People, Communication & Organisations*, 2nd edition, 1990]

Figure 3.33 Pictograms enliven data but may be misleading.

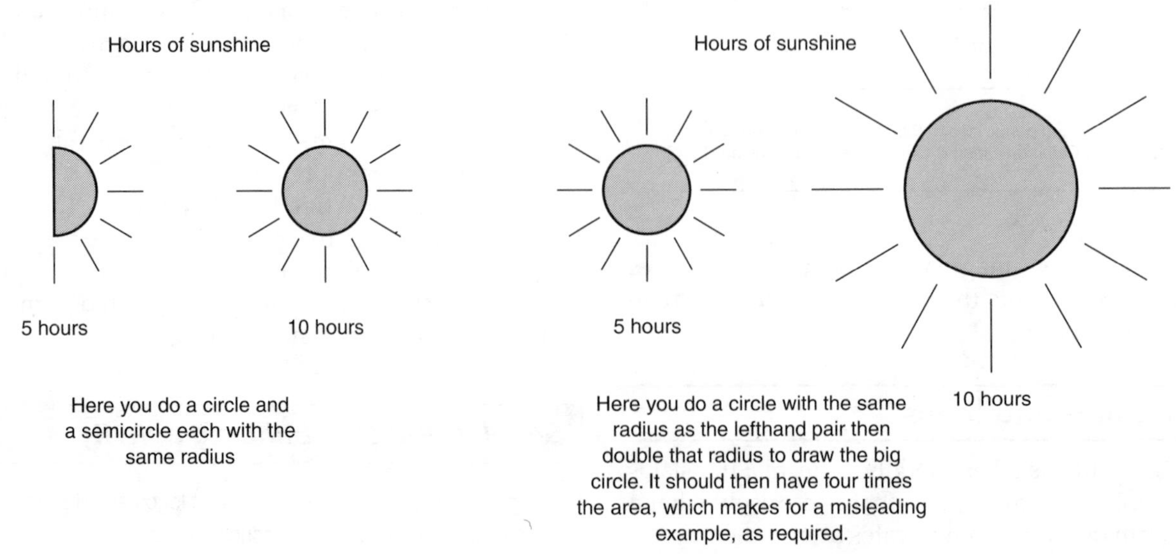

THE BODY SHOP

Riverside Waste Authority

W•R•W•A

west sussex county council

HOOVER ®

CENTURION ENGINEERING LIMITED

Newtown Business Park, Newtown, Newshire
Tel: 0294 467340 Fax: 0294 468341

[Logos reproduced by kind permission of: The Body Shop International plc, Western Riverside Waste Authority, West Sussex County Council, Longman Group UK Limited and Hoover; the Centurion logo by kind permission of Pitman Publishing.]

Icons and symbols

The introduction of the graphical user interface (GUI), such as *Microsoft Windows 95*, has led to a widespread increase in the use of icons to communicate computer software features, operations and commands (Fig. 3.34). Nowadays few users can fail to link the print command with an icon of a printer, or the delete command with an icon of a dustbin.

Icons were introduced in computer software for several reasons, to facilitate mouse operations and instant recognition, and also to enable such packages to be sold and understood internationally. Indeed, information technology appears to make the world grow smaller, and globalisation means that ever more icons are understood and accepted by almost everybody. The range extends from a mother and child for nappy-changing facilities to a black cross on a yellow background for poisons.

The essence of good logo design lies in immediate communication of meaning, absence of ambiguity, simplicity and acceptability.

communicates a student assignment activity.

Fonts and points sizes

Today literally hundreds of fonts exist in which to express the printed word. Some, like CG Times and Courier have become old friends, having been around for many years and having acquired instant recognition from their use in newspapers, books and typed documents. Others have been developed to meet the needs of poster and advertisment designers. Whatever their age and intended use, there is no doubt that we are all – consciously or unconsciously – affected by the visual appearance of a given font.

For example, these fonts inspire trust and convey a sense of reliability:

Times New Roman Universal Arial

These impart a sense of fun, drama and entertainment:

drury lane JESTER POP THUNDER

And these convey a sense of times past:

Medieval PROM ANGIE ANGIE

Figure 3.34 Computer software uses instantly recognisable icons.

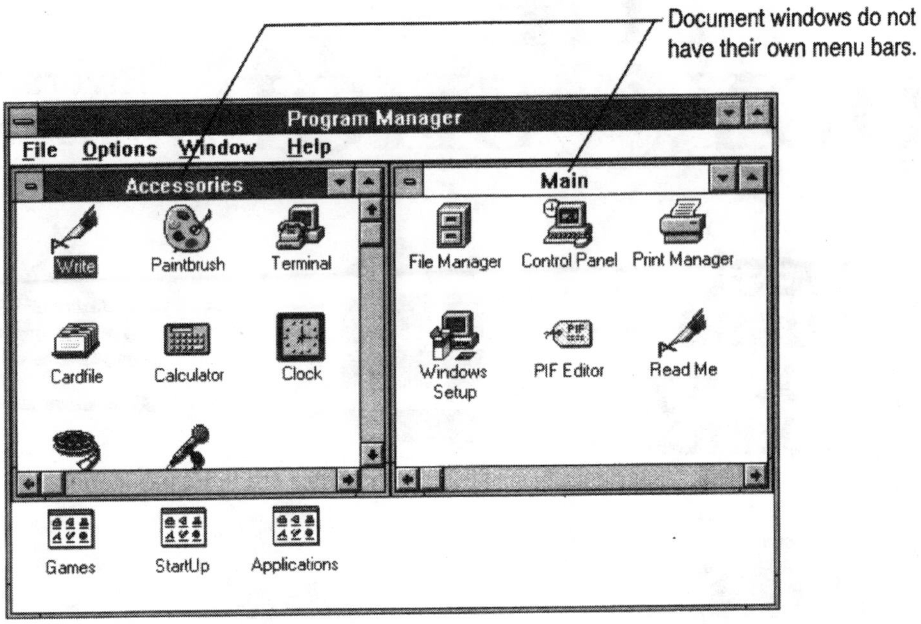

[Screen shots reproduced with permission from Microsoft Corporation]

The following sample of just a few of the hundreds of fonts readily available on either floppy disk or CD-ROM illustrate just how different an identical sentence appears when printed in differing fonts:

The Quick Brown Fox Jumped Over The Lazy Dog
– MODERN

The Quick Brown Fox Jumped Over The Lazy Dog
– ONYX

The Quick Brown Fox Jumped Over The Lazy Dog
– OZ HANDICRAFT

The Quick Brown Fox Jumped Over The Lazy Dog
– RIBBON

The Quick Brown Fox Jumped Over The Lazy Dog
– ROMAN

The Quick Brown Fox Jumped Over The Lazy Dog
–SCRIPT

The Quick Brown Fox Jumped Over The Lazy Dog
–SHELLEY VOLANTE

The Quick Brown Fox Jumped Over The Lazy Dog
– SWIS

The Quick Brown Fox Jumped Over The Lazy Dog
– TIMES NEW ROMAN

The Quick Brown Fox Jumped Over The Lazy Dog
– UNIVERS

A number of important guidelines are to be found in the above examples of various fonts and points

The term *points* when used to describe the size of a given font stems from the days when printers set type by hand. They came to use the following scale:

Approximately 6 picas = 1 inch, 12 points = 1 pica, 72 points = 1 inch

This scale may be more easily appreciated as follows:

a 72 points
a 36 points
a 24 points
a 12 points
a 8 points

Most of the print which we read in newspapers, books or magazines as ordinary prose paragraphs tends to lie within the 8–12 point range, whereas headings and subheadings tend to span the 14–72 point range. Figure 3.35 illustrates the visual impact of contrasting type.

A number of important guidelines are to be found in the above examples of various fonts and points.

1 Make sure that you select a font style appropriate to your message; consider the likely impact of the following mismatch:

Mr and Mrs Smith regret to announce the sudden death of their beloved ....

2 Ensure that you employ a point size suited to your needs; keep in mind the fact that most readers are comfortable with continous prose set in 10–12 point.

Figure 3.35 The impact of type depends on its font and its size.

INVITE ENGRAVED	36 POINT
BRUSHSCRIPT	24 POINT
TIGER	18 POINT
SHADOW	14 POINT
ultra sans	LOWER CASE 12 POINT
Ornamental	LOWER CASE 10 POINT

3 Devise a coherent style for your main heading and subheadings and stick to it:

MAIN HEADING:	16 point bold
First subheading:	14 points bold
Second subheading:	12 points bold
Running text:	10 point medium

4 Avoid the temptation to mix fonts just because they are there. Use changes of font sensibly, say to indicate an extended quotation or dialogue; by the same token, employ techniques of emboldening, italicising and underscoring sparingly to highlight phrases and titles of publications, or to emphasise subheadings. Sometimes you can go a bit further (Fig. 3.36).

5 Remember to leave double line or treble spaces around headings so they stand out. Similarly, make effective use of paragraph indenting, centring of headings and progressive indentation of line entries to mark shifts from major to minor topics.

Figure 3.36 A letter containing several changes of font.

Canon

```
MR D W Evans
Head of Management &
Business Studies
Chichester College
Westgate Fields
Chichester
West Sussex
PO19 1SB

Dear Mr Evans

While the computers in
your office might look
good, the sad fact is that
the documents they produce
tend to look boring.

This is not the fault of
the computers themselves -
the problem lies with your
printer.

Documents produced on a
normal printer look like
this half of the letter -
the same typeface printed
in the same way, on and on
and on . . .

Which, when your company
wants to present the best
image at every possible
opportunity, is of course
disappointing to say the
least.
```

MR D W Evans
Head of Management &
Business Studies
Chichester College
Westgate Fields
Chichester
West Sussex
PO19 1SB

Dear Mr Evans

Canon would like to add a little song and dance to your office routine.

We'd like to give every document you produce

- *a new image*
- *a new look*
- *a new life*

How?

By introducing you to a new kind of laser printer. A printer that will make you and your company look good on paper

[Reproduced by kind permission of Canon UK Limited]

SUMMARY

- Consider carefully the type of audience which your diagrams will have, and therefore how straightforward or technical they can be.
- Decide on whether your diagram is to be a static structure, or a process from A to Z; locate the diagram's key components carefully, and be prepared to produce a few trial drafts until you get the shape and relationships right.
- Make supportive use of arrows, lines, boxes and symbols or icons to promote easy visual take-up of the diagram.
- When designing an organisation tree, make absolutely sure that you have correctly researched function and person relationships; remember the pyramidic structure of many organisations, which shows boss/subordinate relationships and coequal functions clearly.
- Beware of using pictograms which bamboozle readers; always set comparative quantities beneath them.
- Remember that logos communicate not only *what* an organisation does, but also *how* it would like to be viewed.
- Use symbols and icons as shorthand cues and signposts for readers; remember that the best icons are simple and easy to interpret without appearing childlike.
- Select the fonts you will use with great care. As well as legibility, bear in mind their power to create responses of trust, respect, authority, fun, pizazz, gaiety, etc. Avoid the temptation to use too many fonts on a page simply because they are there.
- Employ a sensible and unchanging use of point sizes within the components of a document – headings, subheadings, text.
- Make sensitive use of white space to make the text which surrounds your images work appropriately within your whole design.

What do you think?

1. Some multinational organisations (such as British Telecom) spend millions on the design of a logo and associated livery to be used to promote their images. Money well spent, or almost a complete waste?
2. Is a picture really worth ten thousand words, or do most diagrams and models oversimplify what they pretend to describe?
3. The concepts of literacy/ illiteracy and numeracy/innumeracy have been around for a long time. Is there now a case for identifying graphicacy and agraphicacy?
4. Do we *really* think we are so daft as to be taken in by bold, punchy fonts or romantically embroidered letters?
5. Of the three – words, numbers and images – it is the image which communicates most intensively.

Self-check review test

1. List briefly the features of an effective diagram.
2. In what ways does an organisational chart reflect the pyramidic hierarchy of authority in an organisation?
3. What is a pictogram? How can they be used to *dis*inform a reader?
4. What makes for an effective logo?
5. In what circumstances do icons aid readers/viewers?
6. How is the use of different point sizes likely to impact upon a reader?
7. What good advice would you give someone about to design a communication using image and text?

When you have set down your own answers, compare them with those on page 199 and consult this section again if they differ.

Portfolio-building activities

PRODUCTION OF STRAIGHTFORWARD IMAGES

Design a map

Over the past three years or so, your study centre has been the subject of an increasing number of visits by inspectors, marketing specialists, financial advisors, overseas students and so on. For this reason, your principal/headteacher has asked for *two* new centre location maps to be produced, one to detail the immediate locality, and the other to link your locality to major communication centres such as mainline stations, ports and airports.

In liaison with your teacher, produce one of the two maps requested and provide with it a commentary of about one side of printed A4 to explain the rationale of your design concept.

Take monochrome (or colour) photographs

Your county and district councils, TEC and chamber of commerce are together sponsoring a special magazine which will feature the educational opportunities for local residents in the 16–50+ age range in a number of vocational areas, including your particular study area. Accordingly, your department has been asked to submit 2 or 3 photographs of study facilities which typify and express what your vocational area is all about, in educational terms. The photographs will appear in the magazine at about postcard size.

By arrangement with your head of department and subject teacher, research and produce about 6 photographs from which the final 2 or 3 may be selected to meet the above brief. Include a commentary of about one side of printed A4 text which details your rationale for choosing your photographic subjects.

Design (in student pairs) a coloured poster

Your study centre has agreed to take part in a national promotion aimed at attracting more people to act as blood donors. As a result, a blood-donor unit will be resident at your centre for a week in some four weeks' time to follow up an internal promotional campaign to raise consciousness and recruit donors.

You and your costudent have volunteered to design a suitable poster. One of its main briefs is to use colour imaginatively to gain attention. The size of the poster is to be A3. Produce a poster design to meet the above brief, but remember that some potential donors are nervous of the process and likely to be put off by gory scenes.

Illustrating non-verbal communication signals (a student pair activity)

You and a costudent have been selected to provide photographic illustrations of various types of NVC signals to illustrate a manual to be produced by the Institute of Human Resources. Your brief is to provide a selection (say 2 or 3 illustrations) for each of the following NVC signals: anger, opposition, nervousness, authority/power.

You may elect to find some of your material from newspapers or magazines, and some from posed photographs. In total, your NVC portfolio should comprise about 12 illustrations, with suitable printed captions.

Designing a cartoon

Design a cartoon which is to be inserted in your department's student induction pack. The aim of the cartoon is to emphasise to students the dangers of keeping all personal study notes, hand-outs and portfolio activities in a single file, carried daily between home and study centre. Your cartoon should be produced on A4 or A5 paper, but will be reduced to about 10 cm × 7 cm for the pack.

Designing a logo and letterhead

Your district is about to be supported by the creation of a local association of employers and employees in the vocational area of your GNVQ studies. The aim of this new association is to promote the activities of the vocational area, in order to attract high-calibre young entrants.

As part of its creation of an appropriate corporate image, the association has announced a local competition to design a suitable logo and headed notepaper. You decide to submit an entry. Produce a suitable design with accompaying notes to explain your approach.

Videoing of TV presenter or interview dialogue

First turn to page 19. The first activity involves the recording of a TV news or discussion programme and an interpretation of it concerning speech rhythms and intonations. Either use a video-tape you produced for this activity, or record one afresh, and give an oral presentaton to your class on why your tape meets the requirements of this speech and intonation activity. Your total presentation should not exceed 10 minutes (tape plus oral delivery).

Designing a table, bar chart, pie chart or histogram

Turn to page 33–34 and select one of the group discussion topics. Then research suitable numerical data and design either a table, line graph, bar chart, pie chart or histogram to act as an appropriate illustration for the discussion topic. Provide an explanation of the features of your illustration which you think make it effective.

Designing a flow chart

Design a flow chart to provide guidance to beginners on one of the following:

(a) how to produce an effective short, formal report

(b) how to ensure a potential source of research data (e.g. a textbook) will be useful

(c) how to prepare for and deliver an effective oral presentation

Producing an accurate and visually appealing organisational chart

Assume that you work in the public relations department or student liaison office of one of the following:

(a) your local general hospital

(b) your county council, district council or unitary authority

(c) your study centre

You have been asked to research and design one of the following organisational charts:

- For (a) or (b) produce a chart which shows simply and clearly those aspects of the organisation which a new patient or a family moving into the locality should know about.
- For (c) produce a chart which shows the key staff and student officers whom a new student should know about in terms of the support they provide.

PRODUCTION OF COMPLEX IMAGES

One-to one discussions

In liaison with your teacher, provide a suitable image to illustrate two of the following discussion topics, where one takes place with a person familiar to you and the other with someone unfamiliar to you.

1 Discuss with a partner the plus and minus aspects (in your own experience) of your Advanced GNVQ study programme. Include in your discussion an image which is appropriate to one of the main points you make. Your discussion should be about 5 minutes long.

2 Discuss with a partner what you see as potentially the most dangerous threats to the global environment. Include in your discussion an image which is appropriate to one of the main points you make. Your discussion should be about 5 minutes long.

3 First research and then discuss with a partner the financial problems which face the UK in terms of funding increased health and social welfare costs as more people live well into their eighties. Include in your discussion an image which is appropriate to one of the main points you make. Your discussion should be about 5 minutes long.

4 One of the major problems facing science today – in genetics research, bioengineering and environmental protection – is the widespread indifference of most members of the public to the arising moral and ethical issues. Include in your discussion an image which is appropriate to one of the main points you make. Your discussion should be about 5 minutes long.

5 The trouble with the UK as a long-established home-owning democracy is that, today, few young adults can afford to get on the mortgage merry-go-round, and those who can are likely to find themselves in a negative-equity situation. Meanwhile those waiting for a council house become elderly in the process. What is needed is a radical change in how people pay for somewhere to live. Include in your discussion an image which is appropriate to one of the main points you make. Your discussion should be about 5 minutes long.

6 In my Dad's day, things were made to last. Today most manufactured items – cars, fridges, washing-machines, computers, televisions – all seem to possess the proverbial built-in obsolescence factor. But the shortness of their lives is neither reflected in the prices asked for them, nor the guarantees that go with them. Your discussion should be about 5 minutes long.

GROUP DISCUSSIONS

In liaison with your teacher, form groups of 3 or 4 students and then undertake *two* of the following activities, one with a group with whom you are familiar, such as your own class, and one with a group with whom you are unfamiliar, such as a class in another department. Each member of your group should research and design an image suited to the group discussion and then present it at an appropriate moment. This image may be either self-designed, another student's, used with permission, or taken from a published source (for study purposes).

1 Despite all the consumer protection legislation on the statute book, consumers today rarely get a fair deal when they complain to the seller about a shoddy product, misleading holiday advertisement or denied insurance claim.

2 Technology this century has destroyed far more lives than it has enriched.

3 The trouble with leisure today is that too many people have too much of it and don't know how to use it.

4 The root of almost all of today's problems is easy to pinpoint – just too many people on this little planet, for the time being, I imagine.

5 The problem in Europe, and the UK, is now too much government from London and Brussels. They take about half you earn, spend most of their time telling you what you can't do and generally interfering in ordinary folks' business.

6 I'll tell you what the twentieth century will be remembered for architecturally – oblong cigar-boxes, all glass and concrete. Cheap to design and build and about as aesthetically interesting as a soap-flake packet. Prince Charles is absolutely right, most architects couldn't design a decent carbuncle.

IMAGES IN DOCUMENTS

The following activities have been constructed to enable you to design a document which combines an image with printed text.

Newspaper readership research (for student pairs)

Select with the help of your teacher a student class in your study centre. Then devise a short questionnaire which aims to obtain the following information:

(a) The newspaper actually read by each class member

(b) The newspaper each class member would read from preference

(c) The newspaper each class member considers to provide
  (i) best news value
  (ii) best sports reporting
  (iii) best fashion reporting
  (iv) best entertainment value
  (v) best political reporting
  (vi) best value for money

Having secured your raw data, design a pie chart *and* a bar chart to communicate your findings. Place your images in a commentary not exceeding one side of printed A4 which analyses your survey and seeks to explain it.

Business consultancy analysis (for individual students)

You have been called in as business adviser to Mr Jack Green, who owns a large discount electrical goods retail store in the centre of a large conurbation. For the year ended last December, the sales of his principal four products – hi-fi, home computers, televisions and washing-machines are set out in the accompanying table. Construct a line graph from the data in the table and include it in a report not exceeding 1.5 sides of printed A4.

	Hi-fi £	*Home computers* £	*Tele visions* £	*Washing machines* £
Jan	8400	6480	7890	8960
Feb	5750	5760	6760	5740
Mar	6230	4370	6430	5390
Apr	5180	4450	5590	5420
May	4400	5790	3320	6430
June	5950	4860	3160	5330
July	9840	6930	6430	7980
Aug	4790	4220	5380	4140
Sept	6860	5630	5760	5140
Oct	7940	6750	6420	6120
Nov	6880	7890	7130	5980
Dec	9530	11430	8130	4760

Your report should provide Mr Green with the following information:

- What is the nature of Mr Green's business in terms of product sales?
- Which product should Mr Green seek to sell most of, given that they each generate the same profit margin?
- What sort of product advertising approach would be most likely to succeed next year, given the sales pattern of products in this year's table?
- What areas of expansion of Mr Green's business do you consider most likely to succeed?

Graphic design article

You have been commissioned by *Graphic Artist*, a UK specialist monthly, to produce about 600 words under the heading: How to design an effective organisational news-sheet. You must accompany your article with a major illustration, indicating some of the principal elements of attractive, readable layout for the front page of such a news-sheet.

GNVQ process model

Assume you work for *Vocational Education*, a monthly journal for teachers and trainers. Currently the journal is running a series of support articles for new entrants to the profession. Your editor wants to produce a feature for the next edition on how the Advanced GNVQ programmes work. A key part of the feature is to be a diagram/model indicating visually the steps a student has to take in order to secure a grade for a submitted portfolio activity. The accompanying feature should explain the diagram/model and not exceed 1.5 sides of printed A4.

Millennium celebration idea

Your local branches of the Rotary Club, the chamber of commerce and the Federation of Retailers have grouped together to sponsor a prize for the most practical yet original idea for commemorating the millennium in AD 2000 in your locality. What is needed is a clear sketch/line-drawing or equivalent and a 500–600 word explanation.

Celebratory gala evening: news item

It is the centenary of the foundation of your study centre. The centre's corporation/board of governors has decided to celebrate with a gala evening to which local dignitaries, past and present staff and students will be invited. There will be a finger buffet with liquid refreshments, and a famous 'old girl' Dame Sophie Neilson, the internationally acclaimed opera diva, will deliver a speech. At 10:00 P.M. there will be a fireworks display followed by a torchlit display of gymnastics by the centre's sports and leisure department.

You have been asked to produce a news item/advertisement for your centre's monthly newsletter which enjoys a wide circulation among former students. The aim of the item is to broadcast details of the date and events of the gala evening and to invite former students to take part (for an entry fee of £10.00). All profits will go towards building the proposed student centre. The news item should include a suitable eye-catching illustration, aimed at helping to promote the invitation. You should also consider carefully your choice of fonts and point sizes. Your news item should not exceed one side of printed A4, including the illustration.

CHAPTER 4

READ AND RESPOND TO WRITTEN MATERIALS

I took a course in speed reading, learning to read straight down the middle of the page, and was able to read War and Peace in twenty minutes. It's about Russia.

Woody Allen

Element 3.4: Read and respond to written materials

PERFORMANCE CRITERIA

A student must:

1 select and read **materials** for a **purpose**

2 Extract the necessary information for a **purpose**

3 Use appropriate **sources of reference** to clarify understanding of the **subject**

4 **summarise** the **information** extracted

RANGE

Materials: text, text supported by images, images supported by text

Purpose: to obtain information

Sources of reference: provided for the student, sought out by the student; written, oral

Subject: straightforward, complex

Summarise information: in writing, orally

DEVELOPING READING SKILLS

Reading revisited

At this stage in your educational development, it must seem rather strange to return to a topic to which you have, in all probability, given little thought since moving on from primary school. But reading skills are well worth developing further.

As you will be aware, various approaches to the teaching of reading have been in vogue in primary schools over the past fifty years, some of which relied on children first learning a phonetic alphabet and reading phonetically spelled words, proceeding gradually to English as she is spelt. Other systems relied on breaking words down into syllables and then relinking them; still others preferred a more holistic approach, called point and say, where the teacher encouraged pupils to learn to recognise whole words at a go, moving from monosyllables to multisyllables.

Whatever the initial reading system adopted by primary schools, there comes a point in a junior reader's development when he or she is able to take on board, in a reading sense, not just individual words but word or sense groups:

> Early yesterday morning/our entire family/ set off/for the west coast of Ireland.

The above example contains four major parts which have been separated by markers, and it is in this way that we read when we are able to absorb quickly not just individual words, but phrases which form sense clusters.

Reading, grammar and syntax

Also, whether we realise it or not, in order to make sense of what we read, we look instinctively for the types of word or word groups which are the most important building bricks of sentence construction. For instance, to make sense, every sentence written in English must possess both a subject and what is called a finite verb. Incidentally, *finite* means 'doing a job'. Put another way, all sentences must include a *doer* word or phrase and an *action* word or phrase:

The silver space shuttle DOER SUBJECT PHRASE	was edging FINITE VERB
extremely slowly ·HOW EXTENSION	towards the orbiting space station. WHERE EXTENSION

The above example is typical of how we tend to construct sentences in English. We tend to start a sentence in English with its subject, unless we wish to create variety in a prose paragraph. The subject performs the action of the verb. We usually place the action statement (finite verb) immediately after the subject, followed by any extensions or descriptions to provide additional information.

You will find it extremely helpful, when seeking to develop rapid reading and scanning skills (despite the Woody Allen quotation) to acquire an understanding of how grammar and syntax work in English. Consider the following simple but extremely common structures of English sentences:

(A)	The skilled nurse SUBJECT	had bathed FINITE VERB
	the elderly patient OBJECT	very gently. EXTENSION
(B)	Successful students SUBJECT	study FINITE VERB
	with determination and patience. EXTENSION	

In the first sentence the *subject* was doing something – in this case bathing – to somebody, the patient; in grammar terms, the person or thing which receives the action of the verb is called the *object* of the sentence. In such sentences there is often an extension to communicate how, when, where or why something is done; in the above sentence the extension is *very gently*.

Thus an extremely common structure of sentences in English takes this form:

(A) SUBJECT + FINITE VERB + OBJECT
+ EXTENSION (sometimes)

An alternative sentence structure occurs when there is no object. In this case, the extension after the verb tends to add more meaning to it:

(B)	The map SUBJECT	was drawn FINITE VERB	extremely accurately. EXTENSION

Here the extension *extremely accurately* supplies additional meaning on how the map *was drawn*.

As a matter of interest, extensions which add meaning to verbs are called *adverbs* (Latin for *to the verb*) so it helps if you think of such extensions *ad*ding meaning to the *verb*. Also, you may have noticed in the above examples the words *skilled* and *successful* being used to add meaning to the subjects *nurse* and *students*. Quite simply, any word or phrase which adds meaning to a subject or object is called an *adjective*. Think of it if you like as *ad*ding meaning to a sub*ject* or ob*ject* and add on the *-ive*.

Grammar and syntax: the easy way

Already, in about half a page, you have mastered not only the key points of English sentence structure, but of English grammar, too. Study the following list carefully and commit its key terms and points to memory, for practical use in developing your reading skills.

- Doer words or phrases in sentences are called *subjects*.
- Action words in sentences are called *finite verbs*.
- Words or phrases which receive the action of the subject and finite verb are called *objects*.
- Subject and object words in sentences will be *nouns* or *pronouns* (e.g. nurse, students, map) and may well be supplied with additional meaning by describing words placed near them called *adjectives* (skilled, successful); note also that all the words in the subject cluster (e.g. the skilled nurse) are deemed to be the subject (and the same goes for object clusters)
- Word or phrase extensions which add meaning to verbs are termed *adverbs*; a *phrase* is a group of words within a sentence which contains no verb.

The above list supplies you with virtually all the grammar and syntax you need for rapid reading and scanning. However, just to complete the set of parts of speech used in English, also commit the following points to memory:

- Subjects can also be expressed in a kind of shorthand:

  Who wrote this letter? *What* is this?

  So can objects:

  You saw *whom*? She did *what*?

  Such substitutes for nouns are called *pronouns*.
- The little words we use to introduce phrases are called *prepositions:*

  down the road *on* the machine *over* the bridge *through* the pipe
- Sometimes complicated sentences are constructed by joining together two or three separate sentences because they contain closely linked information.

  In spite of the difficulty she experienced in obtaining relevant raw data, Jackie still pursued her report-writing task conscientiously because she knew how important it was to the firm's success.

  This complex sentence is made up of three main ideas: (1) she experienced difficulty in obtaining relevant raw data; (2) she still pursued the task conscientiously; (3) she knew how important it was to the firm's success.
- When complex sentences contain two or more ideas (which each contain subjects and finite verbs) these are termed *clauses*; clauses are usually separated from each other by commas or semicolons. The clause which contains the main idea of the sentence is termed the *main clause*; clauses which add meaning to the main clause are called *dependent clauses*. Dependent clauses are most often introduced by linking words or phrases (in spite of, because, etc) by *conjunctions*.

  main clause introducing conjunctions: and, next, then, yet, but

  dependent clause introducing conjunctions: because, as, since, though, although, even though, when, whenever, where, what, which, that, before, after, in order that, so that

Rapid reading: the syntax approach

By now you may be forgiven for wondering what a section on grammar and syntax has to do with developing reading skills. The answer is a very great deal, since you now possess the ability to recognise word functions in sentences, as well as the ability to identify major and minor word clusters.

> ***KEYPOINT***
>
> The key elements of meaning in a sentence tend to lie in the *subject, finite verb and,* if present, *object*

Example 1

The weary and exasperated *tourist sat down* with a huge sigh.

Key meaning words: The tourist sat down

Meaning-adding adjectives: weary, exasperated
Meaning-adding adverbial phrase: with a huge sigh

Example 1 shows that if you were reading a passage simply to gain an idea of its main sense, then all you would need to pick out from the example sentence are its subject and finite verb.

Example 2

After having *checked* the *mailsack* carefully, *the clerk ran* the last *letter* through the franking machine.

Key meaning words: checked mailsack the clerk ran letter
Meaning-adding words: After, carefully, last, through the franking machine

Here there are two clauses at work, the main clause describing the clerk running the last letter through the franking machine and a dependent clause explaining when he or she did it; notice that, because the dependent clause starts the sentence, the subject (he/she) is understood and therefore omitted; the key meaning words in terms of their grammar roles are he/she (subject), checked (finite verb), mailsack (object) the clerk (subject), ran (finite verb), letter (object).

> **KEYPOINT**
>
> When reading in rapid or scanning mode, look first for subjects, verbs and objects, and keep in mind that subjects and objects will be nouns or pronouns; look also at the verb extension when there is no object.

Example 3

A continuous prose paragraph simulating the identifying of subjects, finite verbs and objects as key meaning word clusters:

> *The crowd was waiting* expectantly *for* the band of the *Royal Marines.* Amid increasing excitement, *the band turned into the square. The* bandsmen's bright and carefully pressed *uniforms looked brand new* and their *instruments gleamed* in the morning sun. After raising his *mace*, the *drum major* dropped it dramatically. *The music stopped instantly* and the *bandsmen dropped their instruments* to the rest position, and the *crowd applauded* appreciatively. (68 words)

Note that the pronoun *it* is used to describe the mace, so it is important to take in what it was the drum major dropped. Another way of gaining an impression of how this technique appears to the scanning eye is to omit all the non-essential meaning:

> The crowd was waiting ... for ... Royal Marines ... the band turned into the square ... uniforms looked brand new ... instruments gleamed ... drum major dropped (mace) ... The music stopped instantly ... bandsmen dropped their instruments ... crowd applauded. (33 words)

As you can see, by concentrating simply on subjects, verbs, objects and key extensions, the main sense of the passage can be picked out and half the words discarded. The discarded words are the less important ones.

Rapid reading: the skimming approach

This approach makes use of an alternative strategy which relies rather on knowing where key data is likely to be found in a written document and in an amount of self-training in terms of eye movements and enlarging of sense groups taken in. This technique requires a largely analytical approach. Begin with clear reasons for wishing to skim a document.

- Is it to decide whether, say, a textbook would be worth reading in detail for making notes?
- Is it solely to gain an impression of the author's main approach to a subject with which you are familiar?
- Is it because you are hunting for data on just one specific topic?

The way in which you would skim a document would vary, depending upon your answers to the above three questions. In the first of the above cases, you would need to skim the text from cover, through contents pages, through chapter headings, through opening and closing paragraphs of each chapter, through key topics to any appendices and then to the index. For the second case, you are likely only to peruse the contents table and perhaps glance at any chapters which appear to supply original or unfamiliar material. And for the last case, you are likely to scan both contents table and index for page locations of the particular subject of your research.

Next you must bear in mind the limitations of the skimming technique. For instance, it is unlikely that a textbook on advanced calculus or existentialist philosophy could be skimmed by anyone other than a highly expert subject specialist. Nevertheless, most documents which publish material of a general interest – newspapers, magazines, introductory texts, etc – are capable of yielding the desired outcomes of skim reading.

View the document as occupying this frame or template:

- **Cover and back cover:** this yields key information about the theme of the document, the identity of the author and what its publishers believe are its key selling points.
- **Inside frontispiece:** this provides details of first and latest publication dates and the publishers; your skim may end here if you deem the book too old or the publishers to be lacking in solid reputation.
- **Table of contents:** a positively essential item to skim, since you may find all you seek in a single chapter, and you will certainly gain a clear and prompt indication of the overall structure of the text.
- **Chapter headings and summaries:** chapter titles provide short summaries of their contents and approach, and some authors provide short summaries of the topics covered in a set of points beneath the chapter title.
- **Opening and closing chapter paragraphs:** most writers summarise in opening paragraphs the key issues or topics to be handled in the chapter, and similarly summarise their major findings or views in closing paragraphs. For this reason, they are well worth visiting before skimming a whole chapter.
- **Chapter contents:** please refer to the example on page 49.
- **Appendices:** many writers add appendices to their texts in order to supply details which might have proved out of place in its main body; it could be that an appendix includes just the detail you seek.
- **Bibliographies:** authors writing on serious subjects often include a bibliography of books and other sources of information relevant to the subject; if your skim of a given text proves disappointing, you may well find an alternative to check out in the bibliography.

- **Index:** when seeking specific data at a detailed level, then the index is probably the first and best place to skim. Check out its page references not only for the probable title of your studies (e.g. skim reading) but look also under headings of synonyms for your subject (e.g. rapid reading, scanning for facts, note-taking skills). Remember that entries like **108–111** indicate where a topic is dealt with at greatest length.

As a general rule, skim reading tends to avoid and ignore examples, but in Figure 4.1 such examples would prove important to any subsequent summary, since they are central to its theme and the influence of the Romans. Notice also that the simulated skim-reading column on the right of the figure includes many subjects, objects and verbs: old *languages*, people *movements, choose,* old *words, uses,* new *technologies,* social/cultural *developments,* slang expressions, *settled, Romans arrived, viaduct, governor, place-names,* etc. But notice too that some describing words are felt to be important: *stagnant, static, imported, deep, modern,* etc.

Figure 4.1 Eye movements during skim reading.

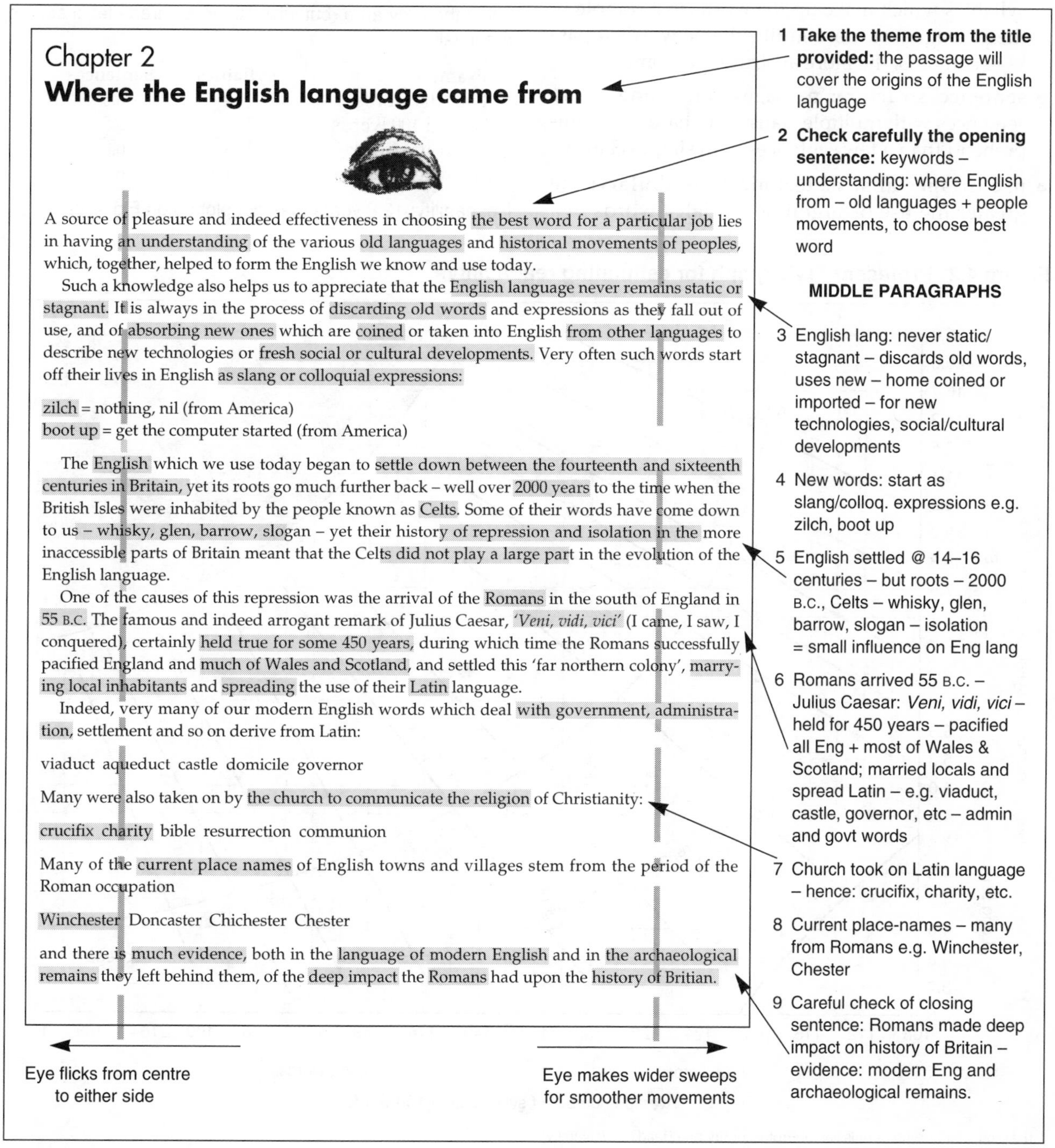

Chapter 2

Where the English language came from

A source of pleasure and indeed effectiveness in choosing the best word for a particular job lies in having an understanding of the various old languages and historical movements of peoples, which, together, helped to form the English we know and use today.

Such a knowledge also helps us to appreciate that the English language never remains static or stagnant. It is always in the process of discarding old words and expressions as they fall out of use, and of absorbing new ones which are coined or taken into English from other languages to describe new technologies or fresh social or cultural developments. Very often such words start off their lives in English as slang or colloquial expressions:

zilch = nothing, nil (from America)
boot up = get the computer started (from America)

The English which we use today began to settle down between the fourteenth and sixteenth centuries in Britain, yet its roots go much further back – well over 2000 years to the time when the British Isles were inhabited by the people known as Celts. Some of their words have come down to us – whisky, glen, barrow, slogan – yet their history of repression and isolation in the more inaccessible parts of Britain meant that the Celts did not play a large part in the evolution of the English language.

One of the causes of this repression was the arrival of the Romans in the south of England in 55 B.C. The famous and indeed arrogant remark of Julius Caesar, *'Veni, vidi, vici'* (I came, I saw, I conquered), certainly held true for some 450 years, during which time the Romans successfully pacified England and much of Wales and Scotland, and settled this 'far northern colony', marrying local inhabitants and spreading the use of their Latin language.

Indeed, very many of our modern English words which deal with government, administration, settlement and so on derive from Latin:

viaduct aqueduct castle domicile governor

Many were also taken on by the church to communicate the religion of Christianity:

crucifix charity bible resurrection communion

Many of the current place names of English towns and villages stem from the period of the Roman occupation

Winchester Doncaster Chichester Chester

and there is much evidence, both in the language of modern English and in the archaeological remains they left behind them, of the deep impact the Romans had upon the history of Britian.

1 **Take the theme from the title provided:** the passage will cover the origins of the English language
2 **Check carefully the opening sentence:** keywords – understanding: where English from – old languages + people movements, to choose best word
MIDDLE PARAGRAPHS
3 English lang: never static/stagnant – discards old words, uses new – home coined or imported – for new technologies, social/cultural developments
4 New words: start as slang/colloq. expressions e.g. zilch, boot up
5 English settled @ 14–16 centuries – but roots – 2000 B.C., Celts – whisky, glen, barrow, slogan – isolation = small influence on Eng lang
6 Romans arrived 55 B.C. – Julius Caesar: *Veni, vidi, vici* – held for 450 years – pacified all Eng + most of Wales & Scotland; married locals and spread Latin – e.g. viaduct, castle, governor, etc – admin and govt words
7 Church took on Latin language – hence: crucifix, charity, etc.
8 Current place-names – many from Romans e.g. Winchester, Chester
9 Careful check of closing sentence: Romans made deep impact on history of Britain – evidence: modern Eng and archaeological remains.
Eye flicks from centre to either side
Eye makes wider sweeps for smoother movements

How to analyse reading levels

In the context of becoming an effective reader, understander and summariser, it is useful to know how to measure the level of difficulty of a given piece of writing. A number of English and American language experts have devised systems for calculating the level of difficulty in reading a specific piece of text. These systems are generally based upon

- **sentence length:** sentence length is the average number of words in each sentence of a passage; it is widely accepted that sentences of more than 30 short words or 25 long ones become difficult for the average reader to understand readily.
- **syllable count:** syllable count is the average of syllables which make up the words in a sample of the passage; the more multisyllabic words a passage contains, the more abstruse it becomes.
- **sentence structure:** passages containing many sentences with multiple clauses are harder to comprehend than a few sentences with simple clauses.
- **use of specialist or technical vocabulary:** the greater the use of jargon or specialist words in a passage, the more difficult it will be for an average reader to understand.

Establishing the readability of a passage

The following system measures the readability of any piece of writing as a reading age; it was developed by Professor Fry at the University of Reading.

Randomly select three 100-word passages from a book or an article. Plot the average number of syllables and the average number of sentences per 100 words on a graph to determine the grade level of the material. Choose more passages per book if great variability is observed and conclude that the book has uneven readability. Few books will fall in the grey area, but when they do, grade level scores are invalid.

Example	Syllables	Sentences
First 100 words	124	6.6
Second 100 words	141	5.5
Third 100 words	158	6.8
Average	141	6.3

Readability: 12.8 years (see dot plotted on Fig. 4.2)

Figure 4.2 Professor Fry's graph for estimating readability.

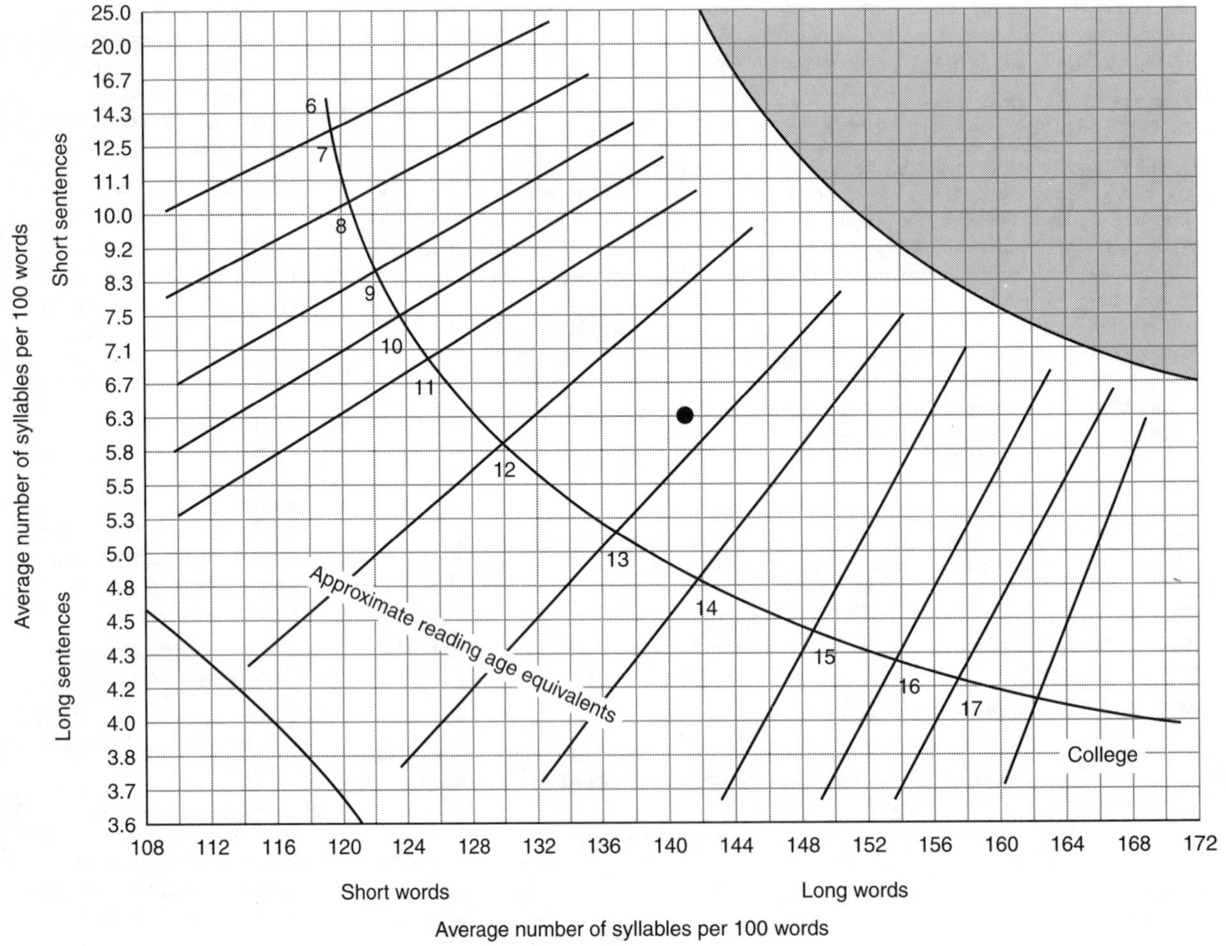

[Reproduced by kind permission of Professor Fry and Reading University]

Additional directions for working readability graph

1 Randomly select three sample passages and count out exactly 100 words starting with a beginning of a sentence. Don't count numbers. Do count proper nouns .

2 Count the number of sentences in the 100 words, estimating length of the fraction of the last sentence to the nearest tenth.

3 Count the total number of syllables in the 100-word passage. If you don't have a hand counter available, an easy way is simply to put a mark above every syllable over one in each word, then when you get to the end of the passage, count the number of marks and add 100.

4 Enter the graph with average sentence length and a number of syllables; plot a dot where the two lines intersect. The area where the dot is plotted will give you the approximate reading age.

5 If a great deal of variability is found, putting more sample counts into the average is desirable.

Individual skills-building activity

Using Professor Fry's readability graph, calculate the readability levels of the following two sample passages:

> He ripped his coat off the hook on the cabin door and tore after her into the cold of the Yukon night. Beneath his feet the ice glinted and he slipped several times without seeming to slow in his headlong pursuit. Once or twice he thought he saw her up ahead among the frozen tents on the edge of Dawson. He stumbled into town, his breath rising like clouds of steam. From *The Golden Nugget* came the sound of bawling singing as if to mock his vain efforts. He slumped against the wooden sidewalk cursing angrily at her simple escape!

> The marketing process commences with several dozen ideas which are evaluated carefully at the drawing-board stage and gradually reduced until a final embryonic product is created. The next phase is to develop in the research and development department a number of prototypes aimed at evaluating the product's capabilities and applications as well as finalizing design and appearance factors. During this process test marketing will have been undertaken to assess the acceptability of the product by the public and this may result in modifications being made to the prototype in the preproduction phase. Eventually the product will go into production to be launched in a fanfare of pre-planned advertising.

When you have set down your own answers, compare them with those on page 199 and consult this section again if they differ.

Reading for detailed understanding

So far we have examined the techniques of skim reading as a means of gaining a broad overview of the content and general approach of a piece of writing, a skill which saves valuable time and study effort. However, this skill will only take you a short way along the path of developing expert reading, comprehension and synthesising or summarising skills.

The next step is to ensure you gain a mastery of in-depth, detailed reading, for note taking and for extracting the maximum understanding from a piece of writing. The following check-list provides a set of helpful guidelines for developing the skills of reading for a detailed understanding:

Reading for detailed understanding

- At the outset, check *carefully the title* given to the piece of writing, since it should provide *an accurate summary* of the theme of the piece

- Adopt an approach which consists of reading the piece *three times* as follows:

  1 Read the piece for the first time at your normal reading pace. Do not at this stage worry about unfamiliar words or phrases, since your aim at this first reading is *simply to obtain the gist of the piece.*

  2 Next, read the piece for a second time. This time, read slowly, *making sure you understand every word and phrase you encounter*. If you come up against a word you have never met before, look it up in a good dictionary and jot down its meaning. Firstly, it could be crucial to your understanding of a main point, and secondly, by jotting it down you will help increase your own wordpower.

  3 Read the passage for a third time. This time you can adopt a sort of skim-reading approach since you are *solely seeking to understand the structure and sequence of points of the piece*. During this third reading, decide on the key topic for each paragraph, and how the author proceeds from a beginning, through a development to an end.

- Try the 3× approach before taking notes of, say, a chapter or article. You will almost certainly find you can take down your notes faster and that they are much more intelligible to you later, *simply because you took the trouble to understand the piece fully beforehand.*

- Check carefully, if appropriate, *any footnotes and/or appendices* to which reference is made in the piece, they may well throw valuable light on a difficult passage.

How to take effective notes

The above check-list of techniques on how to read for in-depth understanding is, in fact, a normal first phase for effective note taking. The following check-list provides a set of helpful guidelines on how to take notes having achieved a sound comprehension of a piece of writing:

Effective note taking

- First carry out the *comprehension reading* detailed above.
- Next, *jot down the title of the piece*, or if need be, create one of your own which accurately summarises its main theme.
- Generally, write your notes in *your own words*; avoid the scissors-and-paste approach, except for highly technical labels or phrases.
- Then work through the piece, paragraph by paragraph, or section by section as follows:

  1 *Decide on the key point of each paragraph* and jot it down in summary form, e.g.
  comprehension: essential first phase of effective note taking

  2 Then extract from the paragraph *the points which cluster around this main point*, e.g
  three readings approach:
  (1) general gist
  (2) for meaning of words and phrases
  (3) for structure

  3 Make use of the *syntax system of skim reading* which focuses upon subjects, objects and verbs; as a general rule, ignore descriptive adjectives and adverbs and also examples which only restate main points another way.

- Make use of techniques of *capital letters* for key words, *underscoring* of important words or phrases, *numbering of points* and the use of *progressive indentation* to show progression from a major to a minor point. Use *arrowed lines* to show links between points.
- *Cross-check* your notes against the original piece of writing (a) to make sure you have not omitted an important point and (b) to make sure you have not included a minor or unnecessary point.
- Routinely include in your notes the *title, author, date* of publication for an article, the *ISBN* for a book, so that you can easily locate the original in the future, if you need to.

Reading for understanding: how to use a dictionary effectively

Understanding what we read is certainly about being able to grasp sentence structures and syntax, often matters of some complexity. But it is probably most about comprehending the words an author employs to communicate thoughts and ideas.

Each of us acquires a wordbank as we progress through childhood, general education and vocational training. But it is invariably limited, and more importantly, it tends to work as shown in Figure 4.3. In our reading, we tend to encounter three kinds of vocabulary:

- words within our active vocabulary, which we recognise and understand instantly
- words within our passive vocabulary, which we more or less understand, but never use ourselves
- words we have never met before and whose meaning totally escapes us

In our private lives, say when reading a novel or hobby magazine, we all tend to gloss over the words we don't understand. And for the most part, we are still able to enjoy the general drift of a story or article. However, as a serious reader, particularly in a work environment, we cannot afford to do this. It is essential that we acquire some expertise in referring to an English language dictionary, and the following sections provide useful guidance.

Keep firmly in mind that, by acquiring the habit of looking up words you are unsure of, you will rapidly move a significant number of words out of your passive wordbank and into your active wordbank. In a comparatively short time, you will find yourself able to express your thoughts and ideas far more accurately and emphatically. In short, your communication and comprehension skills will benefit enormously. But it does take a fair amount of self-discipline to use your dictionary regularly. Nothing is for nothing these days.

What to look for when purchasing a good dictionary

Age

Check when the dictionary was last revised or a new edition published. There have been so many new words added to English recently that a dictionary which has not been revised for ten or so years will be very much out of date when it comes to current usage and popular meaning of words.

Individual skills-building activity

Practise your in-depth reading and note-taking skills by producing written notes of the following article.

IT RULES – OK?

Over the past 150 years, the lead-time – the time it takes between making a scientific discovery and marketing its applications commercially – has been growing ever shorter. And the incredible speed with which microprocessors have been introduced into equipment in use in factories, offices, shops and warehouses, not to mention private homes is ample evidence of the eagerness with which new technologies are nowadays adopted.

In this context it is well worth recalling that the first microprocessor or 'silicon chip' was introduced commercially by an American corporation, Intel, in 1971. In only 20 odd years, 'IT' technology has fundamentally changed production processes, office information systems, telecommunications, the workings of the mass media – newspapers, television, hi-fi etc, the way people shop, and even enabled the customers of one bank to organise their affairs from their own homes via their television screens and allied equipment!

Already the applications of Information Technology are abundant in the areas of the commercial office, manufacturing company, retail distribution and service industries such as banks and solicitors' practices. It is important to keep two factors, however, firmly in mind. Firstly, with the technology developing so quickly, it is impossible to predict what amazing new products and techniques will hit tomorrow's headlines – already work is underway to introduce a 'flat-screen' electronic office desk-top which will enable managers to scan different types of information appearing before them electronically as opposed to various sheets of notepaper, photographs, or paper-based diagrams. Similarly, research into voice-activated computing proceeds apace with the proverbial rainbow's end crock of gold awaiting the first company to introduce a computer system which will respond fully to voice commands. CD-ROM disks are now beginning to supplant their floppy equivalents. Here the advantage will be that information will be able to be stored far more abundantly in the same sort of space and accessed far more quickly.

In factories the introduction of robotics and computer aided design and manufacture (CADCAM) has been revolutionising manufacturing practices for the past 10 years – 'hand-made by robots' was a popular television advertising slogan of one motor-car manufacturer in the early 1980s – and now some high-tech companies are already introducing fully integrated computer-directed manufacturing operations combining the production process, the purchase and stock-control of parts, the costing and accounting functions and the despatch and distribution of the finished product!

In effect, the ordinary citizen may be forgiven for finding the extremely swift pace of technological change and innovation difficult to grasp and assimilate. Nevertheless, everyone contributing to the working life of his or her community must either meet this challenge head on and conquer it, or accept a seat on the sidelines to watch other developed countries reap the benefits which the 'post-industrial', IT led society can bring.

The second factor which must be kept firmly in mind is the need for everyone involved in IT to sustain a critical awareness of the limitations of the technology and the dangers which are implicit in it if due checks and controls are not properly maintained. Indeed, with the wonders of the technology still unfolding it almost seems presumptuous to refer to its limitations. Still, it is worth remembering that the most sophisticated computer in existence has a long way to go yet to replicate the capacities of the human brain in its reasoning, evaluating and interpretive powers. Furthermore, however capable the computer technology in operation, it remains a tool for human beings to make use of. IT is not an end in itself and we should all be careful about allowing it to reform our cultures and lifestyles in ways we may come to regret.

In sum, while becoming conversant with the major applications of IT in business and the public service, we should not allow ourselves to be overawed by the technology nor remain passive in our attitudes to the changes it is spearheading in society in general.

Pronunciation

Most dictionaries include an introduction which explains the signs and symbols which it uses to indicate how words are pronounced. Make sure you read through this carefully. For example, the sign ′ immediately after a syllable means that it is the stressed one:

con′trast   exhil′arate   psychol′ogy

The sign ˘ is used to signify a short, unstressed syllable:

arĭthmetĭc   cŏntĭnĕn′tal   ĭllŭ′strĭous

The sign ¯ is used to convey a long vowel sound of a syllable:

lĭ′lac   refri′gerāte   contribū′tion

A dot over an *ė* indicates that it is pronounced *igh*:

nak′ėd   mag′nėtize

Figure 4.3 Wordbank: an inner core and two outer regions.

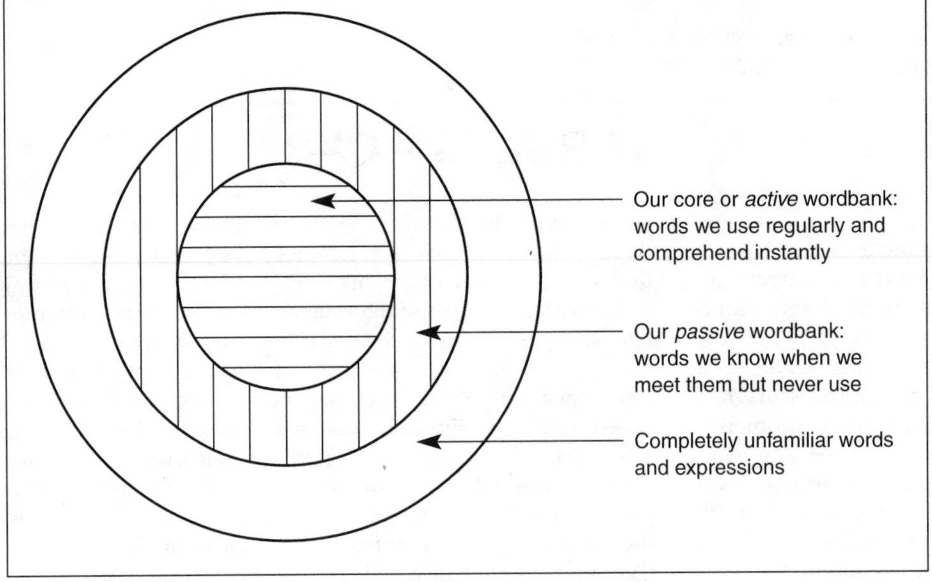

Such an introduction will also provide help on general pronunciation and the way in which a phonetic (how the word sounds) system is employed in the dictionary entries.

Plurals

The plurals of words form an essential part of a good dictionary and are often shown like this:

goose n. (pl. geese pr. gēs)

Here the plural spelling of the word is shown and its pronunciation indicated by the symbol for a long *e*.

Abbreviations

A check-list of the various abbreviations used in the dictionary will also be found as a rule in the introduction of a good dictionary. Such a list will include a range of letters to signify the part of speech of the entry – *n* for noun, *v* for verb and so on. Also, the word's origins (etymological roots) will be shown, for example, MHG would mean Middle High German.

Your efforts in learning what the abbreviations mean will be amply repaid in strengthening your word power and confidence in using words.

Many dictionaries contain commonly used abbreviations or acronyms (words formed from the first letters of a title), for example, BBC for British Broadcasting Corporation; other examples are

GP = general practitioner
RSVP = répondez s'il vous plaît
TUC = Trades Union Congress

Abbreviations and acronyms may be found in the body of the dictionary or possibly in a separate list at the back.

Conversion tables for weight, volume and distance

The good dictionary will often include conversion tables between imperial and metric measurement, for example, inches into centimetres. Other tables list the names of metric prefixes and give values for important physical constants such as the speed of light.

Words of foreign origin

Foreign words are usually listed with a detail of their pronunciation in English, and what anglicised pronunciation is commonly accepted:

Chantilly: Shan-tilly

Otherwise the pronunciation in the foreign language is mirrored:

coiffeur: kwahfer'
pièce de résistance: pēās de rāze'stahns

The addenda section

As you can imagine, the compilation of a dictionary takes a long time, and during its course, a number of words may have extended their meaning or new ones may have been coined. Others may have been omitted in error. Thus an addenda, or additions, section is often to be found at the back of dictionaries which is well worth browsing through.

Extracting the meaning of a typical entry

The following entry is taken from the seventh edition of the *Concise Oxford Dictionary* and it has been selected to show you how a typical entry is made up, and what may be learned from it.

swīne *n.* (*pl.* same). **1.** (US, formal, or Zool.) = pig 1, whence **swī'nery**[3] *n.*; PEARL[1]s *before swine.* **2.** person of greedy or bestial habits; (colloq.) unpleasant thing. **3.** **~-fever**, infectious intestinal virus disease of pigs; **~-herd**, one who tends pigs; **~-plague**, infectious bacterial lung-disease of pigs. **4.** Hence **swī'nISH**[1] *a.* (esp. of persons or their habits). [OE *swīn*, = OS, OHG *swīn*, ON *svín*, Goth. *swein* f. Gmc * *swīnam*, neut. (as n.) of a. f. IE **suw-* pig]

[Reproduced by kind permission of the Oxford University Press from *The Concise Oxford Dictionary*, 7th edition, 1983, edited by J B Sykes]

From an initial survey of this entry, the reader might be forgiven for thinking that he or she needs a dictionary to decipher the dictionary entry. Phrases like

> infectious intestinal virus disease of pigs

takes some sorting out, and words like *bacterial* and *bestial* do indeed tend to hit us between the eyes. But there's no problem, just look them up in the dictionary.

In looking at the entry for *swine*, it is worth noting that the alphabetical arrangement of the words in the dictionary follows a strict system. Clearly all the words starting with *a* come before all those starting with *b* and so on. Moreover, within each letter section – *a*, *b*, *c*, etc. – the same system applies:

> *aback* comes before *acacia*

simply because the second letter of *aback* is *b* and that of *acacia* is *c*. In the same way, the entry *abbreviate* comes before *ABC*, because the third letter of *abbreviate* is a *b* (the other two being identical) and that of *ABC* is a *C*.

The next entry against *swine* is *n.* This abbreviation, as we know, means that the word is a noun or the naming word of something.

We also learn from '(*pl.* same)' that the word swine does not change in its plural form, for example,

> Many swine browsed in the meadow.

> ***KEY POINT***
>
> No matter what type of vocational occupation they work in – business, manufacturing, science, hospitality, health and social care, leisure and tourism, art and design – managers and technical support staff are only as effective as their word-power allows. Colloquial words like *thingumajig, whatchamacallit, thingy* or *whatsit* are simply lame substitutes for not knowing an accurate, technical or apt word to match a specific context.
>
> Words are to managers in training just like a plumber's or motor-mechanic's toolset, a proper, professional job just cannot be done without them. So remember that it will pay you, personally, to make the time and effort to acquire and use a good dictionary, and in so doing, kick the *oojammaflicks* into touch forever!

The entries which follow the numbers 1, 2, 3, 4 illustrate different meanings or uses of the word and show how it may be used in conjunction with another, for example, *swine-fever*, to form a further word of different meaning.

The entry takes the trouble to inform us that the word *swine* is used formally in the United States and in zoology to mean pig and that in the United States (as opposed to elsewhere) *swinery* is used for a place where pigs are housed.

A further part of the entry refers to the proverbial expression taken from the Bible or 'casting pearls before swine'.

The smaller numbers 1, 2, 3, 4 invite us to check the entry in the dictionary, for example, for *-ish.*

Lastly, the entry concludes by showing us the origin of *swine* from the Old English *swin*, or the Old Saxon and Old High German *swin*, the Old Norse *svin* and the Gothic *swein.*

It is remarkable how much information surrounds a simple five-letter word, but then it has been around in English for a long time. Of course, you will not always wish to study a dictionary entry in such detail; you may simply wish to check on the spelling of a word, a particular meaning or a particular use. Nevertheless, it is worth knowing precisely what sort of information you may expect to obtain from the entry of a word in a reputable dictionary:

- its correct spelling (or spellings)
- its accepted pronunciation (or alternative pronunciations)
- how is it spelled in the plural, including accepted alternative spellings
- what part of speech it is, and what parts of speech are its derivative words (e.g. swine, n.; swine-fever, n.)
- the ways in which it is used and its meaning (or meanings)
- how is it linked to other words or expressions to form words (especially hyphenated ones of an extended meaning)
- the origins of the word from old (or current) languages

Bear in mind that *swine*, though it has served to show some of the major factors of a dictionary entry, by no means includes all the signs and symbols which may be employed, so do spend some time browsing through those in your dictionary's introduction. Here are some you may expect to find:

app.	apparently
Bbl.	Biblical
c.	circa, about the time of
colloq.	used colloquially or as slang
sl.	slang
sp.	spelling
P	proprietary name, e.g. Hoover
D	disputed usage

Provided that you are prepared to devote some time familiarising yourself with your dictionary's system of codes and symbols, you will find it a lifelong friend as well as a most helpful and informative tool. Correspondingly, your wordpower will increase, and with it your self-confidence and ability to capture and hold other people's attention.

Individual skills-building activities

In order to practise your reading and comprehension skills, according to your teacher's requirements, carry out one or more of the activities set out below.

READING COMPREHENSION

Read the extract on pages 156–158.

Now answer the following questions, possibly under the supervision of your teacher:

1 Explain what is meant by the term *labour turnover.*

2 What is the formula which calculates the separation or wastage rate over a given period?

3 Explain what the labour stability index is used for.

4 How is the percentage turnover of short-term workers calculated?

5 Explain the advantages to an organisation of calculating the rate of labour turnover over a period of successive quarters.

6 What conclusions do you draw from Table 17.1?

7 What is meant by the term *half-life* in the context of labour turnover within a given group of workers?

8 Supply two reasons why the use of the separation rate calculation may prove misleading.

9 At what point in an employee's employment with an organisation is he or she most likely to leave?

10 List five main costs of labour turnover.

11 What percentage would most firms be content with in terms of separation rate?

12 Explain what actions an organisation can take to reduce its separation rate, and indicate the single most important aspect which will influence such a reduction.

CHART EVALUATION

Carefully examine Figure 4.4 and then answer the questions which follow.

1 Which types of occupation are likely to grow most and least in the period up to the year 2000?

2 What reasons can you suggest for the major areas of growth and decline in jobs?

3 What sort of organisation would find the chart's data useful? Why?

EXPLAINING A DIAGRAM

Using Figure 4.5 as your guide, write an explanation in about 350 words entitled: How the European Community decision-making process works.

Figure 4.4 Figure for chart evaluation activity.

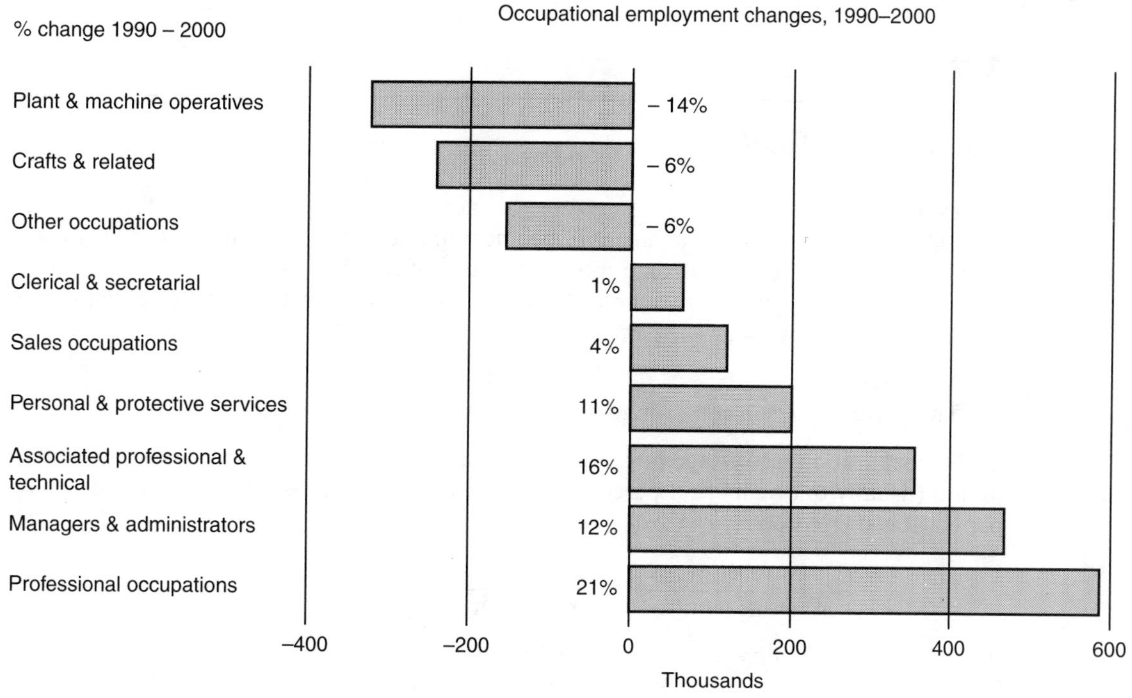

[Reproduced by kind permission of the Institute for Employment Research]

Figure 4.5 Figure for explaining a diagram activity.

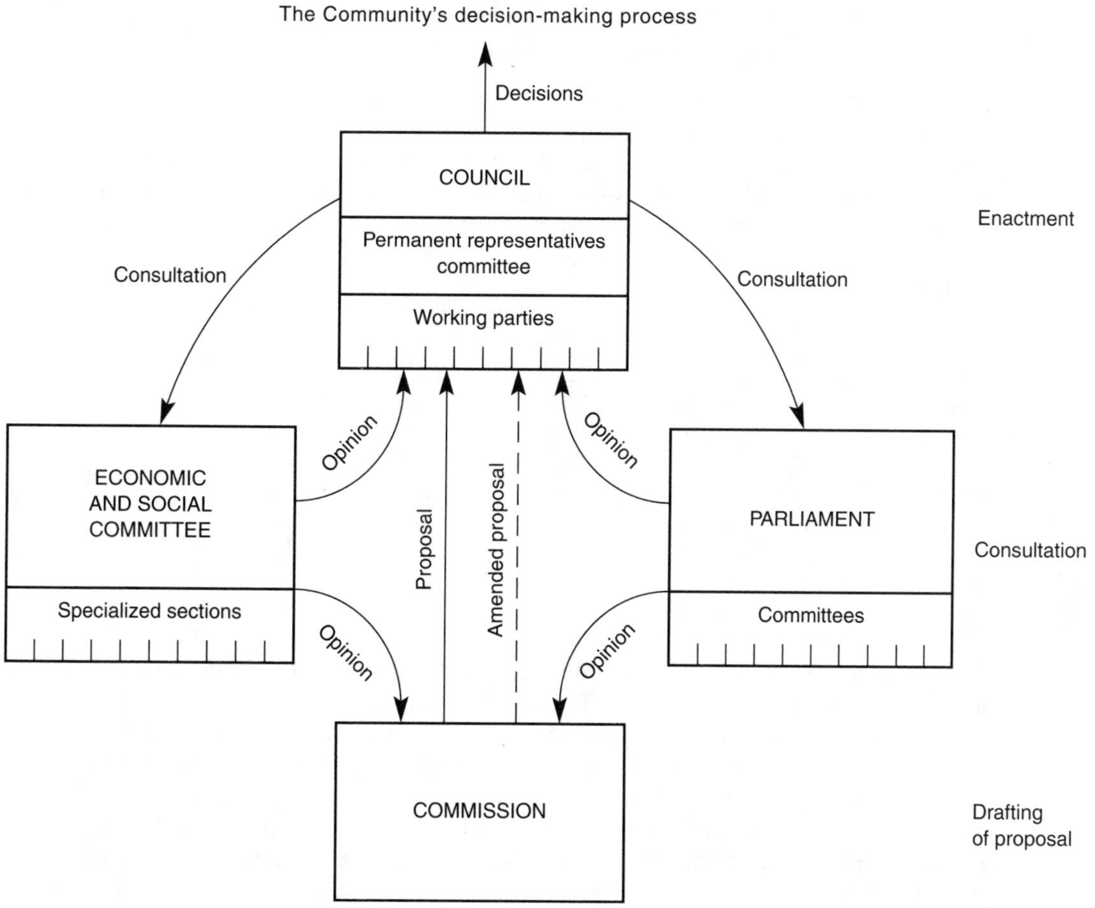

[Reproduced by kind permission of the Office for Official Publications of the European Communities from *The ABC of Community Law*]

Extract for reading comprehension activity.

17

Labour turnover

1. Definition

Labour turnover is the movement of people into and out of the firm. It is usually convenient to measure it by recording movements out of the firm on the assumption that a leaver is eventually replaced by a new employee. The term separation is used to denote an employee who leaves for any reason.

2. Measurement

Two formulae are in common use for measuring labour turnover.

(a) The separation or wastage rate, which expresses the number of separations during the period (usually one year) as a percentage of the average number employed during that period. It is therefore:

$$\frac{\text{Number of separations during period}}{\text{Average number employed during period}} \times 100$$

(b) The labour stability index, which shows the percentage of the employees who have had at least one year's service. It is usually expressed as follows:

$$\frac{\text{Employees with at least one year's service}}{\text{Number of employees employed one year ago}} \times 100$$

A variation on the labour stability index is the 'fringe turnover index':

$$\frac{\text{Number of employees who joined and left within one year}}{\text{Average number employed during the year}} \times 100$$

This shows the percentage turnover of short-term workers.

Another method of measuring labour turnover is to study a group of employees recruited during a certain period (usually three months) and record the rate at which they leave the company. An example is shown in Table 17.1 based on the assumption that the company engaged 500 new employees during the period.

Table 17.1

	Quarterly periods of service	*Number of leavers*	*% leaving*	*% remaining*
First	(1–13 weeks)	200	40	60
Second	(14–26 weeks)	100	20	40
Third	(27–39 weeks)	50	10	30
Fourth	(40–52 weeks)	25	5	25
Fifth	(53–65 weeks)	15	3	22
Sixth	(66–78 weeks)	10	2	20
Seventh	(79–91 weeks)	5	1	19
Eighth	(92–104 weeks)	5	1	18

These figures are sometimes presented graphically by plotting the percentage leaving against quarterly periods of service. The result is called a *survival curve*.

A useful application of survival curve computations is the determination of the 'half-life' survival rates of workers in various employment categories. A half-life survival rate is the time that elapses before 50 per cent of a particular cohort of workers who all began work at the same time have left the organisation. Half-life survival rates may then be compared for different departments, age groups, etc. in order to ascertain the 'staying power' of each cohort.

3. Use of turnover measurements

The separation rate is easy to calculate and is widely used. It also has the great advantage of indicating costs because separations and replacements can involve the company in considerable expense (see 4). It can be somewhat misleading, however, for two reasons.

(a) Recently engaged employees are more likely to leave than long service employees (see Table 17.1), and therefore an increase in the separation rate may simply be due to some increased recruitment a few weeks previously rather than to a sudden deterioration in worker satisfaction.

(b) Some jobs in the company may be vacated and filled several times during the year. Suppose, for example, that in a company employing 1000 workers 250 leave during the year, giving a separation rate of 25 per cent. The true position might be as follows:

	150 jobs vacated and filled once	=	150 leavers
	25 jobs vacated and filled twice	=	50 leavers
	10 jobs vacated and filled three times	=	30 leavers
	5 jobs vacated and filled four times	=	20 leavers
Total:	190 jobs vacated during year	Total:	250 leavers

In such a case the separation index can give a false impression because 100 of the 250 leavers are short-service employees (though the cost of replacing them can still be considerable).

The stability index is best used in conjunction with the separation rate, showing the extent to which the company is retaining its experienced employees. On the figures shown above, the stability index would be

$$\frac{1{,}000 - 190}{1{,}000} \times 100 = 81\%$$

Survival rates always show that the tendency for employees to leave is greatest during their early weeks with the company; they are useful in showing if the company is losing a particularly large number of employees early in their service compared with a previous period. It is often instructive to compare survival rates in different departments or different employee categories, e.g. by age groups or occupations.

4. Cost of labour turnover

Separations and their consequent replacements can be surprisingly expensive. The cost of labour turnover increases when employees are more specialised, more difficult to find and require more training. It is made up of some or all of the following components:

(a) lower production during learning period;
(b) lost production while the employee is being replaced;
(c) payment to other employees at overtime rates while waiting for a replacement;
(d) possible diversion of efforts of more highly skilled employees while waiting for a replacement;
(e) possible sub-contracting of work;
(f) cost of scrap and spoiled work while job is being learned;
(g) cost of recruitment, selection and medical examination;
(h) training cost;
(i) administrative cost of removing from and adding to payroll.

Therefore, when the separation rate is high the employer can incur considerable costs which are not always immediately obvious.

5. Reducing labour turnover

All employers expect to have a certain degree of labour turnover; without it the company would stagnate. The average age of employees would increase (meaning also that a large number of employees might retire simultaneously); and there could be insufficient new blood coming into the organisation. No doubt many companies would be content if their separation rates lay between 10 and 15 per cent, though few rates in the private sector of industry and commerce are as low as this. If an employing firm wishes to reduce its labour turnover because it considers it is excessive for the district and the industry, it may take the following action.

(a) Recalculate the separation rate for various categories of the firm's employees, e.g. departments, age groups, occupations, to see if turnover in any of these categories is particularly high; if so it can be specially investigated.
(b) Ensure that selection procedures are adequate; suitable employees are more likely to stay than unsuitable.
(c) Ensure that the immediate supervisor, by being involved in selection, feels some responsibility towards a new employee.
(d) Check that employees are being fully utilised – some may be leaving because of boredom or job dissatisfaction.
(e) Overhaul pay structure, perhaps using job evaluation (see Chapter 21).
(f) Introduce or improve an induction course.
(g) Give new employees appropriate training.
(h) Show that prospects in the company are good by promoting from within wherever possible.
(i) Ensure that physical working conditions are adequate.

In general, an increase in job satisfaction and in the cohesiveness of working groups will decrease the rate of labour turnover.

[Reproduced by kind permission of M & E Business Handbooks, Pitman Publishing from H. T. Graham and R. Bennett, *Human Resources Management*, 7th edition, 1992]

SUMMARISING AND RESTATING INFORMATION

Time is always at a premium among successful people at work, either because their ability attracts more work like a magnet, or because their nature encourages them to innovate and to take on more challenges than the average employee.

Thus it is not surprising to learn that the higher an executive advances, the more he or she is likely to depend on abstracts, résumés and summaries of information, whether produced as a set of bullet points, a pie chart or a line graph.

Probably the most valuable skill to possess, but perhaps the most demanding to acquire, is the ability to summarise key points from a piece of writing or a collection of data. Indeed, managers are frequently charged with synthesising data from a variety of textual, numerical and graphical sources.

This section provides you with a detailed set of guidelines on how to produce effective written and oral summaries of original sources of information.

What's in a name: précis, summary, abstract, résumé, abridgement, synthesis?

There exists a confusing number of synonyms for producing a shortened version of an original piece of work. These are simply explained as follows:

- **précis:** now falling out of use, it was used to describe a summarising technique which aimed to reproduce a faithful miniature of a whole original; thus its main features would be retained and examples and points of little importance omitted.
- **summary:** a term used widely today in a variety of ways; usually the person who requests a summary of a piece of writing wishes only to receive a shortened version, which may concentrate on a fraction of the original, unlike the précis.
- **résumé, synthesis:** these terms are broadly equivalent to summary; but a synthesis often refers to a form of conclusion to an argument/discussion of contrasting points.
- **abstract:** a term used to describe the shortening of a comparatively long original; a précis and a summary tend to reduce an original to a third of its size, whereas an abstract may reduce an original to a twentieth of its size.
- **abridgement:** this term is mostly employed to describe the shortening of a novel or story, such as tends to be published in the *Reader's Digest* magazine.

Five essential stages in producing a summary

There are five main stages in the summarising process, once the summarising brief has been clarified:

1. **comprehension:** reading the original for a full understanding.
2. **selection:** selection of the main points of the original.
3. **organising:** organising the selected points into a coherent order.
4. **drafting:** writing a first draft of the summary and checking it against the original for accuracy and correct selectivity
5. **final version:** polishing the draft and producing a final version.

The following check-list provides an enlarged set of guidelines for these five key stages:

Effective written summaries

- At the very outset, make quite sure that you are clear on any brief you are given about the summary: what exactly to summarise, what aspect is to be emphasised, etc. This stage performs exactly the same function as obtaining terms of reference before researching a report.
- As for reading comprehension, read the piece through three times: (a) for its general drift, (b) for the meaning of individual words and phrases, (c) for its structure.
- Either set down the author's title of the piece or devise your own. Refer frequently to this title and use it as a yardstick to measure the relevance of a given point and whether or not it is worth extracting.
- Sift steadily through the piece in the same sequence as its structure and use these tips to help you identify its main points:

  1. Is the point central to the piece's title and theme?
  2. Does the point represent a next main step in the writer's thinking, argument, explanation, etc.?
  3. Is the main point of a paragraph or section effectively restating its subtitle?
  4. Does the point make an important contribution to the paragraph's main point? ▶

- As a general rule, avoid selecting points which are repetitions of other points. Avoid examples and illustrations, except where they are crucial to the theme of the piece.
- Set down the main points you identify in your own words. Abbreviate them as much as you can without obscuring their meaning; leave space between each point in case you need to add to it or amend it later.
- Check your final list of points against the original, so as to ensure that (a) no important point has been left out by accident and (b) no trivial point has crept in. If you are subject to a word limit, bear in mind that you will double the number of words in your notes when you express them as sentences.
- Decide on the format for the final summarised version, e.g. title plus prose paragraphs or schematically laid out report.
- Compose the first draft, keeping the following in mind:

  1 Enlarge your notes into grammatical sentences and write the draft on alternate lines, so you can make amendments easily and legibly.

  2 Use the technical words or phrases of the original if they are the most suitable.

  3 Avoid the wasteful use of repetition, long-winded constructions and illustrations; stick to communicating the main points simply and clearly.

  4 Tick off each main point from your summary notes as you include it, so as to ensure you omit none; check your first draft against your points list to make doubly sure.

  5 Compare your first draft against the original as a final check for relevance, accuracy and meeting your own summarising brief.

  6 If you are working to a specific number of words, aim to produce a first draft in about 10% more words than your total, then prune back as you produce a polished final version.
- Polish and refine your draft into its final version; check carefully for any errors in spelling and punctuation, and add any titles, authors, dates and sources of original data as appropriate. Attach a copy of your summary to the original piece as a record for filing, and make copies for distribution.

Individual skills-building activity

This activity aims to produce a guide for would-be summarisers based on a summary of the article opposite, which comprises some 470 words. Assume that, because of space restrictions, the summary must not exceed 160 words. The brief requires a simple, straightforward summary to give an easy grasp of the main points.

First read the article carefully. Then choose whether to go ahead and produce your own summary, or whether you are content to look at the suggestions on the following pages. Another option would be to select the main points without writing the summary. Compare your work with the guidelines which follow.

THE TECHNIQUES OF SUMMARISING

Executives in all types of organisation rely upon the succinct presentation of ideas, information or opinion. The communications revolution of the past one hundred years has resulted in incredible advances in technology – computerised systems, fax telecommunications and image processing – which all help to meet such needs.

Such universal adoption of communications equipment has meant that managers and secretaries are deluged by a flood of documentation and oral communication. The pressure on people's time and the increase in data production and relay costs have impelled organisations to develop sophisticated summarising techniques which, by reducing communication to bare essentials, achieve an essential saving in reading, processing and assimilation time as well as a reduction in expenditure.

The plight of the senior executive amply illustrates the need for good summarising practices. If an organisation is to benefit from the years of experience and developed expertise present in such people, it must appreciate that their time is a precious asset. Such executives need not only to keep abreast of activities and developments, but must also regulate their contact with the large numbers of colleagues, associates or subordinates who make pressing demands upon their time.

In order to cope, senior managers need to avoid time-wasting minutiae and to encourage those in contact with them to discipline themselves, both orally and in writing. Ideas, factual reporting, feedback or suggestions should all be condensed to a main core which represents the main points of a complex problem, a synthesis of a discussion or meeting, or a brief analysis of an involved situation.

All those who produce information in such circumstances need to acquire summarising skills broadly identified as

comprehension
classification
analysis
evaluation
selection

Essentially, they will exercise their powers of discrimination in deciding which parts of a given piece of material need to be extracted and relayed in a particular format to meet the needs of a third party.

Indeed, one of the most valuable assets of the executive, personal assistant or secretary is the ability to relay the essence of a 'message' which will involve meeting the following objectives in whole or part:

1 Ability to comprehend a range of information, data or opinion
2 Ability to identify salient points for a particular purpose
3 Skill in analysing and evaluating material to distinguish the essential from the trivial
4 Practice in working objectively so that personal attitudes do not influence selection processes
5 Skill in using language to convey the tone or attitudes of the original
6 Familiarity with business practice to ensure that appropriate formats are used when reproducing data.

[Adapted and reproduced by kind permission of Pitman Publishing from D. W. Evans, *People, Communications and Organisations*, 2nd edition, 1990]

Worked summary example: commentary and main points list

A first reading indicates that the passage deals with the need for executives and their assistants to develop expertise in summarising in order to cope with the flood of communications and to make best use of the time available.

The second reading will, perhaps, produce a number of words and phrases which require careful scrutiny:

succinct
deluge
data production
saving in reading, processing and assimilation time
time-wasting minutiae
synthesis
exercising their powers of discrimination

Some dictionary work may be needed, or in an examination situation, intelligent guesses may be required by looking at the *context* of difficult words or phrases.

Structurally, the passage embodies five stages:

1 Introduction – communications revolution
2 The communication flood
3 The plight of senior executives and how assistants may help
4 An identification of the main areas of summarising techniques
5 A check-list of the basic skills needed by the summariser

The title required in step 3 might be *Summarising techniques: why they are needed and how they are applied in organisations.*

Following the structural plan, the main points are then listed, using the title as a yardstick of relevance.

Main points list

The main points check-list will appear, broadly as follows:

First para

1 Summarising – essential need in organisation – need for *brief* statement of info, ideas

2 Communications revolution – reliance on wide range of business equipment

Second para

3 Communications revolution – flood of documentation, inc. oral comms.

4 Consequence – pressure on person's time and increase in production and distribution costs

5 Essential reduce flow to be able to cope

Third para

6 Senior executives – their time and expertise wasted if spent on trivialities

7 Calls on their time must be rationed to core material and brief analyses

Fourth para

8 Those who summarise – need to acquire skills in comprehension, evaluation, selection

9 Must have ability to discriminate to meet a *specific* requirement

Fifth para

10 The summariser needs to develop these specific skills:

(a) Comprehension
(b) Recognition of main points
(c) Analytical skill
(d) Objective working
(e) Facility with language
(f) Sound knowledge of business practices
(g) Familiarity with document formats

In terms of the target 160 words, the notes are rather generously written, but they need to be intelligible to many readers. Personal notes may be more succinct.

The rough draft

The next stage, having established a format, would be to compose a rough draft:

The ability to summarise effectively is essential in organisations *to enable personel to cope* ~~if personnel are to cope~~ with the flood *of information* *caused* ~~brought about~~ by the communications revolution and the *consequent* widespread use of business equipment.

Organisational personnel are being flooded by oral and written communications, causing staff to waste time and ~~resulting in~~ increasing *the* costs ~~in the~~ *of* produc~~tion~~*ing* and distribut~~ion of~~*ing* information.

Senior executives cannot use their time and expertise *effectively* if forced to waste time on trivialities. Calls on their time must be rationed and communications reduced *by those servicing them* to core material or brief analyses.

To help senior ~~executives~~ *staff*, those who summarise need to acquire skills in comprehending, evaluating and selectively reproducing data~~;~~*.* *T*~~t~~hey must learn to discriminate.

Specifically, *expertise is needed in:* ~~they should develop their expertise in the following areas:~~

comprehension

selection ~~recognition of main points~~

analysis ~~analytical skills~~

objective *writing* ~~working~~

fluent expression ~~facility with language~~

sound knowledge of business pratice

and ~~familiarity with~~ document formats

(143 words before changes)

The next step is to include the title and any other helpful headings and to polish the rough draft, taking care not to exceed any prescribed word limit.

The final version

The final version will then appear like this:

SUMMARISING TECHNIQUES: WHY THEY ARE NEEDED AND HOW TO APPLY THEM IN ORGANISATIONS

Background
The ability to summarise effectively is essential in organisations to enable personnel to cope with the flood of information caused by the communications revolution and the consequent widespread use of business equipment.

The current situation
Organisation personnel are being flooded by oral and written communications causing staff to waste time and increasing the costs of producing and distributing information.

The senior executive's problem
Senior executives cannot use their time and expertise effectively if forced to waste it on trivialities. Calls on their time must be rationed and communication reduced by those servicing them to core material or brief analyses.

Skills needed by the summariser
To help senior staff, those who summarise need to acquire skills in comprehending, evaluating and selecting data. They must learn to discriminate.

Specifically, expertise is needed in

comprehension
selection
analysis
objective writing
fluent expression
sound knowledge of
business practice
document formats (160 words)

[The above worked example has been adapted from D. W. Evans, *People, Communications and Organisations*, 2nd edition, 1990 and reproduced by kind permission of Pitman Publishing.]

> ***KEY POINT***
>
> More communication fails from being too long, than from being too short!

Oral summarising techniques

Most of the techniques of producing a written summary also apply to supplying an oral summary (Fig 4.6) (overleaf). And it is important to keep in mind that in organisations, oral summarising is undertaken much more frequently – sometimes with the summariser scarcely becoming aware of the fact, as for instance when the boss asks:

> How did this morning's meeting go?
> What did you think of the software presentation yesterday? I was sorry I had to miss it.

In such situations, the boss is seldom seeking to make idle chit-chat, but to secure some useful, brief feedback in the form of an oral summary from a subordinate who attended information-giving activities.

The following check-list indicates the main techniques to follow when faced with scenarios where there is a high likelihood of having to report back by means of an oral summary, as for example in attending a meeting, going to an exhibition, observing a presentation or listening to a lecture:

Effective oral summaries

- At the outset, consider the likelihood of having to report back, so as to be aware of the need to prepare for it.
- Make sure you are equipped with suitable materials for note taking and also ensure that you sit where you can hear and see clearly.
- If possible, record the proceedings with a portable cassette recorder for subsequent reference. But remember to obtain any speaker's permission first.
- Take careful notes of the proceedings on this basis:
  - set down a clear title
  - listen carefully to the introduction
  - follow the procedures for taking notes on page 150
  - listen carefully to concluding remarks
- Make sure you collect any hand-outs or résumés of presentations issued, which may prove helpful
- Before making any oral summary, set down in capital letters a list of the main points of the speech, article or original source, just as for producing a written summary, and also make sure it follows a logical and faithful sequence:
  - Oral summarising: three stages
    1 Understanding source material
    2 Making brief notes
    3 Restating them using the spoken word

- Use your check-list (set down on cue cards) as a quick and unobtrusive means of checking where you are and to avoid missing an important point.
- When delivering your oral summary, do not forget to maintain eye contact with your listeners; do not gabble, and if you need to refer to your points list, simply remain silent for a second or two.
- Allow for questions and requests for further details as you proceed, since this approach is normal in dialogue; using your list of points, you can easily find your way back to where you were before a question was posed.
- Deliver your summary in smallish chunks so as to allow your audience to absorb the points you make; this can be demanding for listeners when no written version is available to them.
- As a general rule, let your facts speak for you and adopt an objective tone; this does not preclude you from delivering your opinion if appropriate.
- Lastly, keep a watchful eye on the length of your summary; resist the temptation to embroider, supply frequent examples or lapse into reporting trivia; listeners remember best what is short and sweet.

How to use an English language thesaurus

Most people tend to dodge any involvement with English language thesauruses, perhaps because they confuse them with tyrannosauruses and other highly dangerous inhabitants of Jurassic Park. Yet the language thesaurus is a most useful, and docile, companion, once you have learned how to use it productively.

An English language thesaurus is, quite simply, a type of dictionary that sets out collections of synonyms and expressions which are used in particular contexts. For example, a language thesaurus will collect similar words and expressions as parts of speech – nouns, verbs, adjectives etc. as follows:

Figure 4.6 The features of a brief oral summary.

Alan Spicer, giving an oral report of a departmental managers' meeting he attended in place of his boss, Mr Jones , sales manager.

Example of an oral report

As you requested, Mr Jones, I sat in on yesterday's meeting for you, which Mr Jackson (deputy managing director) chaired. Only the production manager couldn't attend.	→ **Clear beginning:** at the outset, Alan confirms those present and who chaired the meeting.
Matters were very much routine until Item 5 on the agenda, *Proposal to form a Training Department.* Mr Jackson set out the background which you know about. One important development has taken place, though, that affects us directly. It seems that the budget won't stretch to building a new training centre, so we're likely to be asked to give up our storage rooms	→ **Development of essential and relevant points in the middle:** aware of the scope of Mr Jones' interest, Alan skips over some early items of no relevance to the sales department – his report selects the particularly relevant points.
on the ground floor. However, the main point was that all the departmental heads are in favour – Miss West submitted a summary of production's views. Mr Jackson asked the personnel manager to submit a detailed scheme for discussion at the next meeting.	→ **Confirmation of action Mr Jones must take himself:** He anticipates those areas in which his boss must make a response and provides the key details, and deadlines.
Heads were asked to submit suggestions to Mr Jackson by next Wednesday.	→ **Descent to more minor points:** Alan also confirms that action may now be taken on the rota system.
There wasn't anything else particularly important, except that the introduction of the staff holiday rota arrangements were given the go-ahead. Under Any Other Business, Mrs Davidson complained about the poor response to the forthcoming Social Club Dance, so I've asked Julie to do her best to sel! some more tickets. I think that was about it. Is there anything you'd like me to follow up?	→ **Confirmation of conclusion and request for further instructions arising from the meeting:** Nearing the end of his report, which has gone through the same sequence as the meeting's business items, Alan relays details of action he has taken on his own initiative. He closes by asking if there is anything further he should do arising from the meeting.

[Reproduced by kind permission of Pitman Publishing from D.W. Evans *People, Communication & Organisations*, 2nd edition, 1990]

Verb to love	cherish, adore, worship, treasure, be partial to, value, think the world of, etc.
Noun love	tenderness, feeling, fellowship, affection, crush, pash, etc.

Possessing an English language thesaurus and knowing how to use it productively is essential to becoming an effective wordsmith and communicator. A language thesaurus is especially handy when composing summaries, since it frequently provides a suitable alternative word which can replace a lengthy phrase. It is also invaluable when the need arises to avoid repeating a word several times within two or three sentences.

Peter Mark Roget, the most famous of the thesaurus compilers, was born in 1778, and was a doctor by profession. He developed a lifelong passion for words and for classifying them into helpful categories as an aid for writers, public speakers and in fact, anyone with an interest in developing a wider vocabulary.

Roget's Thesaurus has become a faithful friend and companion for all who work with words. It collects lists of words and phrases into groups that share a similar or identical root meaning, then branches out in a logical progression to words more distant from the root word. Consider the following example taken from a contempory version of *Roget's Thesaurus;*

556. Artist – N. *artist,* craftsman *or* -woman 686 *artisan;* architect 164 *producer;* art master *or* mistress, designer, draughtsman *or* -woman; fashion artist, dress-designer, couturier, couturière; drawer, sketcher, delineator, limner; copyist; caricaturist, cartoonist; illustrator, commercial artist; painter, colourist, luminist; dauber, amateur, pavement artist, scene-painter, sign-p.; oil-painter, watercolourist, pastellist; illuminator, miniaturist; Academician, RA; old master, art historian, iconographer; aesthetician.

sculptor, sculptress, carver, statuary, monumental mason, modeller, moulder.

engraver, etcher, aquatinter, lapidary, chaser, gem-engraver; typographer 587 *printer.*

[Reproduced by kind permission of Penguin Books from *Roget's Thesaurus*]

Here we find set out in an organized form some sixty alternative words or phrases which derive from the root idea of *artist,* and almost certainly we should find an alternative word here for *artist,* whether in the field of painting, sculpture or printing.

Similar groups of words set down as nouns, verbs, adjectives or other parts of speech (see the appendix) are classified by the thesaurus according to the accompanying table. As you can see, Roget broke down his thesaurus into six classes:

1 A class given over to such abstract ideas as relationships, time and change.

2 A class for the words associated with space, form and motion.

3 A class for words to do with all forms of matter.

4 A class about the intellect, or the exercise of the mind, thought processes and the communication of ideas.

5 A class on the exercise of the will or freedom of choice.

6 And lastly, a class on emotion, religion and morality.

Class	Section	Heads
1 Abstract Relations	*1 Existence*	1–8
	2 Relation	9–25
	3 Quantity	26–59
	4 Order	60–84
	5 Number	85–107
	6 Time	108–142
	7 Change	143–155
	8 Causation	156–182
2 Space	*1 Space in general*	183–194
	2 Dimensions	195–242
	3 Form	243–264
	4 Motion	265–318
3 Matter	*1 Matter in general*	319–323
	2 Inorganic matter	324–357
	3 Organic matter	358–446
4 Intellect: the exercise of the mind *Division one: Formation of ideas*	*1 General*	447–452
	2 Precursory conditions and operations	453–465
	3 Materials for reasoning	466–474
	4 Reasoning processes	475–479
	5 Results of reasoning	480–504
	6 Extension of thought	505–511
	7 Creative thought	512–513
Division two: Communication of ideas	*1 Nature of ideas communicated*	514–521
	2 Modes of communication	522–546
	3 Means of communicating ideas	547–594
5 Volition: the exercise of the will *Division one: Individual volition*	*1 Volition in general*	595–616
	2 Prospective volition	617–675
	3 Voluntary action	676–699
	4 Antagonism	700–724
	5 Results of action	725–732
Division two: Social volition	*1 General social volition*	733–755
	2 Special social volition	756–763
	3 Conditional social volition	764–770
	4 Possessive relations	771–816
6 Emotion, religion and morality	*1 General*	817–823
	2 Personal emotion	824–879
	3 Interpersonal emotion	880–912
	4 Morality	913–964
	5 Religion	965–990

[Reproduced by kind permission of Penguin Books from *Roget's Thesaurus*]

As you will have noticed, some classes are split into divisions. Also, each class has a further subdivision entitled 'Sections' and each section is made up of a series of numbered heads. Thus, class 4 has two divisions, the second called *Communication of ideas*. This division is further subdivided into three sections, the second of which is termed *Modes of communication*, and contains twenty-four different heads. The first, numbered 522, starts with a list on *manifestation* – as of spirits appearing – and goes on to include words to do with exhibits, displays and so on. The third heading, 524, deals with the idea of *information*, and provides words and ideas such as: viewdata, computer, hearsay, broadcasting, and so on.

However, the user of the thesaurus is most unlikely to approach it in this way. He or she is much more likely to turn straight to the back of the thesaurus, to the index. Here, the root words of the 990 heads which make up the thesaurus are listed alphabetically. Suppose, for example, we wanted to find an alternative to the word *information*. We would look it up in the alphabetical list, and lo and behold, find against it the reference 524 n. This means that we should turn to head number 524 in the book and find that alternative nouns or naming words for information are set down there. The further use of this index is that it supplies under the root word different meanings or versions of the idea:

inform	**—against**
inform 524 vb.	*inform* 524 vb.
educate 534 vb.	*accuse* 928 vb.

Thus in the area of the idea *inform* we are given two places to look, either under 524 vb, where the idea is basically *to tell*, or under 534 vb, where the idea is *inform meaning to educate*. Alternatively we might be seeking the list of words where the idea is to *inform against someone*. In this instance, we are referred to head 928.

Should we turn to head 928, we would find it starts with *accusation*, and goes on with *complaint*, *charge*, *home truth* and so on. Having exhausted the nouns or naming words for *to inform against*, it proceeds to list adjectives like *accusing*, *incriminating*, *suspicious* and then provides verbs like *to accuse*, *challenge*, or *defy*.

In this way, the thesaurus can supply help, whether you are looking for another word for *accusation* as a noun, or for the verb *to accuse*.

And, as if this were not enough, the head 928 provides for certain words a cross-reference to another head in the thesaurus. For example, if the sense of the word we seek under 928 for *accusation* is to reproach someone, or cause them to think again about an action, then we are referred to head 924. A section under 924 begins with the word *reproach* and includes *hard words* and *reprimand*. In this way, the reader is able to travel backwards and forwards through the thousands of words of the thesaurus until just the right alternative word or phrase is found – and this can be a godsend to a tired brain.

Individual skills-building activites

Use an English language thesaurus to complete the following activities:

1 Consider the following sentences:

(a) One sure way out of the recession lies in a definite growth in the economy. This ...... could be achieved in a number of ways.

(b) Acquiring the business to produce this growth, however, is by no means easy. In order to ...... increased business, it is necessary to be competitive across a range of worldwide markets.

Assume that you do not wish to repeat the word *growth* in the dotted space in (a) nor the word *acquire* in the dotted space in (b). Consult your thesaurus to find two suitable alternative words which would fit the spaces.

2 Follow the same approach to find appropriate alternatives to the bracketed words in the following passage:

It is always a pleasure to be introduced by you, Mr Chairman, and indeed, it is with great (pleasure) that I stand before you all this evening to talk about improving one's English. Many experts have put forward their methods for (improving) either written or spoken English skills but there is no quick or simple route to this worthy destination. Indeed, the (route) is sometimes full of pitfalls and often goes uphill! The person who wishes to (communicate) in correct and acceptable English must possess the qualities of patience and determination. He or she must (patiently) work through a progressive programme of study which will provide plenty of opportunities for practising accuracy and style. It is certainly in the (practice) of writing that progress and development are to be won.

3 Using your thesaurus, find suitable alternatives for the words or phrases set in italics in the following sentences:

(a) The young girl looked extremely *agitated* as she waited for her driving test.

(b) The ballroom formation dancing team appeared *extremely lively* as they went through their routine in front of the judges.

(c) As he felt rather depressed, he was not *in a sociable frame of mind.*

(d) The chairman ran the meeting in a most *dictatorial* way.

(e) The bomb blast left a scene of *havoc* never before witnessed in such a quiet village.

(f) From the look on her face, it was clear that she *had resented* the remark made by the angry customer.

4 Again, with the help of your thesaurus, find a suitable alternative for the following definitions (either as a single word or as a small group of words):

youngster when taken to mean someone young, poorly dressed and presumably fending for himself

mistake meaning when something has gone wrong as a result of carelessness on someone's part

evil as if in league with the devil

to be cheeky as, for example, a child being disrespectful to adults

to voice when, for example, speaking carefully so that each syllable is clearly understood

Read and extract information on straightforward subjects

1 Read the article on page 168 and then compose a summary of it in about one-third of its original length.

2 Read the article on page 169 and then compose a summary of it in about one-third of its original length, paying particular regard to the Japanese approach.

Images change as joblessness affects all social classes

John Arlidge considers whether there are similarities between the 1930s and present day unemployment

The images have changed. Couples slumped in front of videos on modern estates have replaced cloth-capped men hanging around slum terraces. Queues to the soup kitchens have shortened. With joblessness among men at a post-war high, however, are there similarities between the 1990s and the Depression of the 1930s?

Unemployment was much worse between the wars. In August 1932, joblessness reached 23 per cent among the assured population – those eligible for the benefits of the day. This was about 16 per cent of the total workforce, compared with 10.6 per cent last month.

The jobless were more regionally concentrated. The export-dependent industries hard hit in the slump – shipbuilding, cotton textiles, coal – were located mainly in the north of England, Scotland and Wales which observers called 'outer Britian'. As sales collapsed, unemployment reached 36 per cent in Wales and 28 per cent in Scotland and the North-east.

Although unemployment rose to 13.5 per cent in London and the South-east in 1932 – today it is about 10.5 per cent – 'inner Britain' saw job growth between the wars. About 3.5 million jobs were created between 1921 and 1938 south of an imaginary line between Coventry and Ipswich.

Dudley Baines, senior lecturer in economic history at the London School of Economies, said: 'There was higher regional industrial specialisation than now. Northern industries lost markets and had nothing to fall back on. But in the South there were vacancies. Developments like the Hoover and Gillette factories in west London, all came in the 1930s.'

'Blue-collar' workers comprised the overwhelming majority of the Thirties' jobless while 'white-collar' workers, who formed a much smaller part of the workforce, were hardly affected. Today the spread is much wider. Half of the 1.5 million jobs lost since the summer of 1990 have been in manufacturing industry. The service sector – financial services, retailing, public service – accounted for about half of the remaining 750,000.

John Philpott, director of the Employment Policy Institute, an independent think-tank, said: 'Today, unemployment cannot be thought of as affecting just one sort of industry or worker. Joblessness extends across the social and occupational spectrum.'

Calculating the number of women who are unemployed is difficult. Mr Baines estimates there are 6 million more married women looking for work today than in the Thirties when about 10 per cent of married women worked. 'Single women worked between the wars but married women were by and large not part of the labour market," he said.

'It is difficult to know whether married women would have worked had there been jobs. If you accept that most of them would not, then female unemployment in the thirties was far lower than today.'

Women today form half of the 'hidden' unemployed – the estimated 1 million people who are not eligible for benefits, or do not claim them. Although changes in the methods used to measure joblessness make it difficult to make direct comparisons, it is likely that the number of hidden jobless was lower in the Thirties than now.

Using 1931 census data, Charles Feinstein, professor of economic history at All Souls College, Oxford, estimates that unemployment was 'very considerably' less among the uninsured in domestic service, farming, the post office and railways than among the insured.

With high personal indebtedness, life might seem hard now but unemployment was a more devastating experience 60 years ago.

Unemployment benefit for a single man was 17 shillings (85p), when social observers calculated the required minimum income was more than 22 shillings (£1.10), plus rent. Mr Baines estimates that the 1930s benefit for a family of four, in today's money, was £30 per week, compared with £96 now, plus housing benefit of, say, £22.

Only 4 per cent of the population had private cars. The television, now in 90 per cent of homes, was not available, and few people took holidays abroad.

Some who lived through the Depression say today's more divided communities, coupled with the higher standards of living enjoyed by those in work have created a 'crisis of expectations' among the jobless greater than that 60 years ago.

Mr Baines disagrees, 'It is extremely easy to idealise the past. The idea of chumminess of working class society in adversity is a load of rubbish. When times are hard they are hard. If you are hungry, you are hungry.

The UK car industry

The British car industry at one time was a major force in the world market. However, during the 1960s and '70s, the car industry was troubled by producing cars of poor quality, the firms tended to be product-led rather than customer-orientated, there was lack of investment, overmanning and poor industrial relations. Car firms merged to form larger businesses to take on foreign competitors. However, the mergers tended to be unsuccessful. Some British firms were taken over by foreign companies and eventually the sole remaining British car manufacturer, British Leyland, was taken into public ownership. Later this company was sold to British Aerospace and sold cars under the Rover badge. In January 1994 British Aerospace sold the Rover company to the German car manufacturer BMW.

During the 1980s and early '90s, the car industry went through radical changes. Japan invested heavily in Britain, opening car factories in Washington, Derby and Swindon. They introduced Japanese methods of production, and their British competitors soon followed these working practices. Production is leaner than previous operations – fewer people are employed, and productivity is higher. New methods included just-in-time, zero buffer stocks and quality built into the production process. There is a delegation of responsibility. For example, workers are responsible for the quality of parts produced. In other aspects of quality control, workers join quality circles to help each other to solve problems relating to quality. The attitude now is 'getting it right first time' rather than 'that will do'. Quality is not sufficient, the processes must be 'continuously improved'.

In Japanese-owned companies, people are encouraged to identify with the company. Although there is no guaranteed job for life, as in Japan, there is greater job security. Recently Nissan in Britain were suffering from a drop in world demand for cars. No worker has been threatened with compulsory redundancy and the firm is not asking for voluntary redundancy. However, the workforce has recognised that there needs to be a reduction in their numbers. The companies believe job security helps to motivate the workers.

Team spirit and single status are an important part of the Japanese working practices. Managers and workers share a common goal rather than work against each other in an 'us and them' situation. Everyone is referred to as an associate. Everyone wears the same uniform, eats in the same canteen and there are no reserved parking spaces for managers. There is no grading between workers, but each worker is a member of an identifiable team and all workers are expected to be multi-skilled and able to move between jobs. Managers and everyone else, including office workers, are expected to work on the production line if the need arises. Managers do not have offices and often have experience on the shopfloor so that they are technically competent and are available if the workers need to contact them.

To help reduce internal demarcation disputes and to help negotiations on wages and working conditions, car firms are moving to a reduction in the number of unions they will deal with. The Japanese companies tend to have single union agreements.

The production targets the British car industry are aiming for are those set by the Japanese in Japan. The time needed to produce a car in Japan is 13.2 hours while in North America it is 18.6 and Europe 22.8. Rover Cars produced 500,000 per annum in 1992, which is equal to 35 cars per man employed per year, compared with the European average of 31 cars per man employed per year.

There are potential problems with the Japanese methods of production. The type of work could be stressful because of the demand by management for constant innovation, quality improvements and the need to intensify workers' efforts. Just-in-time puts greater dependency of workers on each other. The pressure is on the workers to keep the production line moving. In Japan, workers are expected to make up lost production in their own time. Managers, for example, who are called to work on the line, are expected to do their managerial tasks later in the day. Labour is just part of the production process and their major function is to increase productivity, quality and profit.

The introduction of Japanese working practices in the British car industry is enabling it to compete with the rest of the world, especially Japan. The problem facing the car industry is that it is introducing the practices now, but by the time they have fully implemented Japanisation, the Japanese will be further down the road of increasing productivity!

[Reproduced by kind permission of Barry and Susan Curtain from *Advanced GNVQ Business: A Student's Guide,* 3rd edition, by D W Evans, Pitman, 1990]

Portfolio building activites

PRODUCTION OF WRITTEN SUMMARIES OF COMPLEX MATERIALS

Task 1

You should assume that you work as an assistant to the information manager of Sceptred Isle Holidays Limited, a company which provides package tours throughout Great Britain. Part of your department's role is to produce a monthly in-house newspaper for the company's 350 staff, which comprises resort representatives, holiday shop and administrative personnel. In the forthcoming edition of your *Sceptred Isle Holiday News,* a main feature is to concentrate on providing details on UK holiday industry background and trends, as a kind of staff development briefing delivered in a soft-sell way. Your contribution is to provide a section which covers historical background to the UK holiday industry and an overview of trends up to 1992/93. Your section will introduce the feature.

Your boss has managed to secure permission to use a part of Unit 13 of Ray Youell's *Advanced GNVQ Leisure & Tourism* as the source for your section of the feature – see pages 171–176. The extract comprises some 2,150 words (excluding tables and charts). Your boss has given you a free rein to adapt the data according to the needs of the feature (which is to supply material which is interesting and easy to digest for the firm's motivated workforce). However, you are limited in that your contribution to the feature must not exceed 750 words.

Unit 13 INVESTIGATING THE UK HOLIDAY INDUSTRY

Section 1 Overview of the UK holiday industry

Introduction

Mention the word 'holiday' to a British person and their thoughts may turn towards a 'package' holiday to a sunny Mediterranean beach resort or a winter ski trip to the Alps. What may come as quite a shock to most British people is that far more of them take holidays in the UK every year than venture abroad on holiday. Latest figures from the 1992 United Kingdom Tourism Survey (UKTS) show that 80 per cent of all tourism trips made by UK residents were taken in England, Scotland, Wales or Northern Ireland, with only 20 per cent taken abroad. What these figures do not show is that the UK domestic tourism market has remained static over the last 30 years, while trips to overseas destinations by British people have grown from around 10 million per year in the mid-1970s to just below 25 million per year at the beginning of the 1990s.

The UK has a tremendous variety of cultures, traditions, architecture, history, countryside, heritage and leisure facilities to cater for the needs of all types of tourists, both from within Britain as well as overseas visitors. Even though Britain must now compete for visitors on a global scale with countries such as France, Italy, the Far East, USA and Australia, it still has great appeal to visitors from all over the world. With a few notable exceptions, however, the British holiday 'product' has failed to keep pace with the demands of an increasingly sophisticated and discerning public that has come to expect high standards of customer service. While the steadily growing number of overseas visitors to Britain over the last 30 years is evidence of effective marketing and product development in this category, the British tourist looking for quality products and high standards of service has had little to choose from. It is ironic that the outbound package holiday market is inflicting a double blow on UK domestic tourism; first in terms of attracting holidaymakers away from UK resorts and second by exposing the tourists to the very standards of product and service they find lacking when they take holidays in Britain.

In spite of this gloomy picture of the domestic scene, tourism is still viewed by private and public sector organisations throughout the length and breadth of Britain as having major growth potential. Many local authorities see tourism as a way of creating jobs and providing income, while at the same time reviving areas of dereliction and improving the image of both town and country.

▶

The rise of UK tourism

Throughout history, people have travelled across Britain for purposes of trade, education, religion and to fight in battles. It was not until the eighteenth century, however, that the foundations of what we now regard as the British tourist industry began to be laid. Spa towns such as Leamington Spa and Buxton were frequented by the wealthy classes who came to sample the health-giving properties of the saline waters. Seaside resorts grew in popularity, helped by the introduction of the railways from 1830 onwards. The Industrial Revolution, which had been the catalyst for the development of the railways, also led to improvements in the road and canal networks in the UK. What the Industrial Revolution also began was the desire for workers to escape from their normal harsh routine and dirty environment, in favour of the relative purity of the countryside and coast.

The 1938 Holidays with Pay Act gave a stimulus to mass tourism in the UK, with 80 per cent of workers being entitled to paid holidays by 1945. Holiday camps flourished immediately before the outbreak of the Second World War, the first having been opened by Billy Butlin in 1937 at Skegness. Two years later there were around 200 camps offering self-contained 'package' holidays to 30,000 people per week.

In the early 1950s, two-thirds of all domestic holidays were taken at the seaside and the majority of holidaymakers travelled to their destinations by coach or train. The late 1950s saw the establishment of the British Travel Association, forerunner to the British Tourist Authority, which was given the role of encouraging the development of hotels and resorts.

The 1960s can be chronicled as the time when tourism came of age. Increasing car ownership, the development of jet aircraft and the growth of the overseas 'package tour' were to have far-reaching implications on the UK domestic scene. British resorts were faced with stiff competition from overseas destinations in the Mediterranean. Today the competition is even fiercer with the introduction of long-haul destinations such as Goa, the Gambia and the Dominican Republic, and European resorts which are investing heavily to 'reposition' themselves in the market-place and regain their popularity.

The facts about UK tourism

BTA figures published in November 1993 show that the total value of tourism to the UK in 1992 was £29,659 million, of which:

£10,665 million (36 per cent) was spent by UK residents staying overnight.
£9,003 million (30 per cent) was spent by UK residents on day trips.
£7,891 million (27 per cent) was spent by overseas visitors in the UK.
£2,100 million (7 per cent) was paid to UK carriers by overseas visitors to the UK.

As these figures clearly demonstrate, UK tourism can be divided into two main categories:

- Overseas visitors to Britain.
- UK residents taking holidays in Britain.

As these two elements of the domestic market have distinct characteristics, we will look at each separately in greater detail.

▶

Overseas visitors to Britian

Despite the world-wide recession and increased competition from other countries around the world, British Tourist Authority statistics show that a record 18.5 million visitors came to Britain in 1992, keeping it among the world's top five destinations (BTA Annual Report 1993). Earnings from these visitors amounted to nearly £7.9 billion, meaning that incoming tourism accounted for one-third of Britain's total income from 'invisible' items on the Balance of Payments (see Section 3 of Unit 1 for more detail on tourism and the Balance of Payments).

The importance of incoming tourism to Britain

As well as contributing vital income to Britain's Balance of Payments, overseas visitors also bring a variety of other benefits:

- An influx of tourists to an area helps create or sustain jobs, thus increasing the wage-earners' spending in the locality and leading to an improved local economy.
- The money spent on accommodation, food, transport, entertainment, attractions and leisure facilities creates profits that are used to generate more business for companies.
- The government benefits from incoming tourism since overseas visitors pay VAT and other taxes on a range of products and services including liquor, tobacco, petrol, accommodation and souvenirs.
- Overseas visitors' spending on facilities such as leisure facilities and public transport can help to keep costs down for local people, who may also benefit from a greater range of facilities provided for both tourists and residents alike.
- Income from overseas visitors can be channelled into improvements to the local environment, thus improving the quality of life for everyone.
- British theatres and the arts in general benefit from spending by tourists from overseas.
- Income from overseas visitors may help to preserve historic buildings and conserve areas of special environmental significance.
- An international reputation for cultural and sporting events can be maintained if large numbers of visitors are attracted from overseas.

The BTA, through its headquarters in London and network of offices around the world, works hard to ensure that information on the requirements of potential visitors to Britain is used to create products and services they will want. This 'market intelligence' is vital for the continued success of incoming tourism to the UK (Unit 1 has a case study giving more information about the work of the BTA).

The trend in overseas visitors to Britain

Table 13.1 shows that, despite the world recession of the early 1980s and the downturn in the economy in the late 1980s, together with the lingering effects of the Gulf War, the numbers of overseas visitors to Britain showed healthy growth between 1981 and 1992, the last year for which figures are currently available.

Statistics on spending by overseas visitors to Britain are equally impressive and are shown in Table 13.1.

The two charts show that 1992 was not only a record year in terms of number of overseas visitors to Britain, but that the expenditure was the highest ever recorded.

Table 13.2 gives a broad indication of where the majority of overseas visitors to Britain originated in 1991 and 1992.

As Table 13.2 shows, the majority of overseas visitors come from within the 12 European Community (now EU) countries, which showed a 6 per cent overall increase in visitor numbers between 1991 and 1992. In this group, Belgium and

►

Table 13.1 Expenditure of overseas visitors to Britain 1981–92

Year	*Total spending (£m)*
1981	2,970
1982	3,188
1983	4,003
1984	4,614
1985	5,442
1986	5,553
1987	6,260
1988	6,184
1989	6,945
1990	7,785
1991	7,386
1992	7,896

Source: BTA Annual Reports 1991/92 and 1993

Table 13.2 Regional origin of overseas visitors to the UK 1991/92

Region	*Number of visits*		
	1991 ('000)	*1992 ('000)*	*Change 1991/91 %*
European Community	9,381	9,977	+6
Other W. Europe	1,747	1,768	+1
North America	2,867	3,377	+18
Rest of the world	3,131	3,413	+9

Source: BTA Annual Report 1993

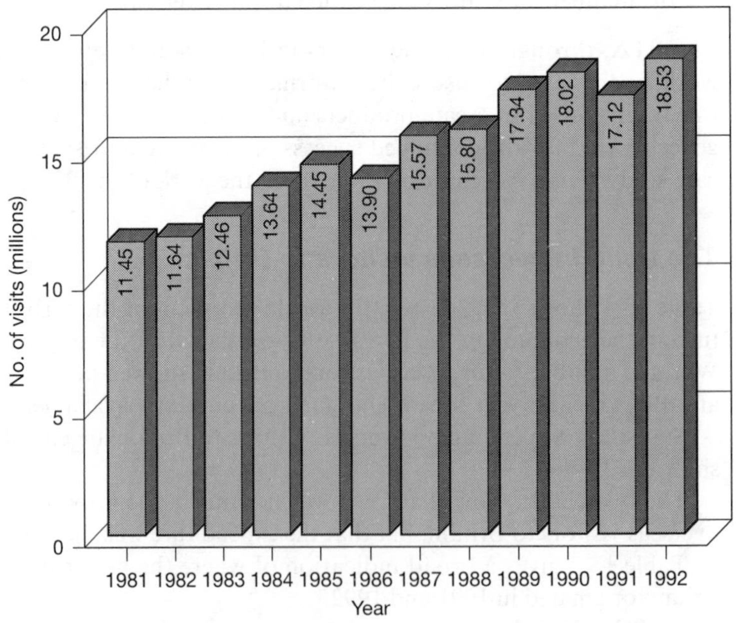

Fig 13.1 Overseas visits to Britain 1981–92 *(Source: BTA Annual Reports 1991/92 and 1993)*

▶

Luxembourg (+16 per cent), Denmark (+15 per cent) and Spain (+10 per cent) were the top three countries to show an increase in visitor numbers. Notably, visitors from Holland fell by 11 per cent over the same time period.

Of the other Western Europe countries, Austria (+14 per cent) and Norway (+5 per cent) exhibited the largest increases in numbers between 1991 and 1992.

North American visitors increased by 18 per cent overall, with the USA and Canada showing an 18 per cent and 15 per cent increase respectively.

Visitors to Britain from the rest of the world showed an overall increase of 9 per cent between 1991 and 1992. The top three countries in this region in terms of the percentage growth in number of visitors to Britain were Hong Kong, Malaysia and Singapore (+22 per cent), Japan (+21 per cent) and Latin America (+17 per cent). North Africa showed a decrease of 17 per cent over the same time period.

Visitors from the USA, the Middle East and the Far East are particularly beneficial to the UK tourism balance since they have a higher than average spend per head when compared to visitors from Europe.

Why do visitors come to Britain?

The many images of Britain, from the pageantry associated with the great cities of London, Edinburgh and Cardiff, to the quaint towns and villages of Wales, England, Scotland and Northern Ireland, all paint a picture of a wealth of experiences and adventures for the overseas visitor. Many tourists from overseas put Britain's heritage as the number one reason for their visit; famous buildings such as St. Paul's Cathedral, the castles of Stirling and Caernarvon, the Elizabethan architecture in Shakespeare's birthplace, Stratford-upon-Avon, rural and industrial heritage are all focal points for overseas visitors. The aristocracy, too, in the form of the Royal Family, their palaces and ancestral homes such as Kensington Palace and Hampton Court, is an important reason for visiting the UK.

Museums, art galleries, theatres, the ballet, and events such as the Chichester Festival and Cardiff Singer of the World, are all part of Britain's rich and varied culture and customs which attract the overseas visitor. Sporting events, such as Wimbledon, international rugby matches, Henley Royal Regatta and the Open Golf Championship, are popular with tourists from abroad. Some visitors are attracted by the excellent shopping facilities, not only in London's West End, but also in historic cities such as Chester, Cambridge, Oxford, Edinburgh, Bath and York. Many overseas visitors come to Britain to study, perhaps learning English in one of the many language schools that can be found throughout Britain. Business tourism, too, is important to Britain's tourism balance; more than 20 per cent of all trips by overseas visitors to Britain in 1992 were for business purposes.

Most first-time visitors to Britain will visit London as part of their stay, or may choose to remain in the capital for the whole of their trip. They may visit the cities and regions most frequented by overseas visitors and become part of what is known as 'the milk run'; this is a round trip that includes London – Oxford – Bath – Cardiff – Chester – the Lake District – Edinburgh – York – Cambridge – London. Increasingly, however, overseas visitors are beginning to explore the parts of Britain located far from London, in search of the 'real Britain', as it is sometimes promoted. In recent years, BTA marketing campaigns have highlighted the attractions of the whole of Britain, rather than just concentrating on the well-known images of London; the Beefeaters, Tower of London, the British 'bobby', Big Ben, etc. Such campaigns have been particularly targeted at visitors on their second and subsequent trips to Britain.

▶

UK residents taking holidays in Britain

According to figures from the 1992 United Kingdom Tourism Survey (reported in an article in *Insights*, September 1993), people in the UK took more than 118 million trips of one night or more away from home during 1992, spending more than £25 billion in the process. Eight out of ten of these trips were taken within the UK (65 per cent in England, 7 per cent in Wales, 7 per cent in Scotland and 1 per cent in Northern Ireland) and 20 per cent were taken abroad.

Where do the British go for their UK holidays?

UKTS statistics show that in 1992, the West Country, with its relatively mild climate and pleasant scenery, continued to be the most popular holiday destination with the British, accounting for 21 per cent of all holiday tourist trips. The Southern Tourist Board region was next in popularity, with 12 per cent of total holiday trips, closely followed by East Anglia accounting for 11 per cent and Yorkshire and Humberside 10 per cent.

When we look in detail at holidays rather than trips (a holiday generally refers to a stay away of four nights or more), the British National Travel Survey (BNTS) figures for 1992 show that British people took an estimated 53.75 million long holidays (4+ nights) away from home in 1992, a small increase on the 1991 statistics. The number of holidays taken in Britain was down by two million when compared with the previous year, while holidays taken abroad increased by 1.5 million (*Insights*, July 1993). In 1992, just over three-quarters of long British holidays were spent in England. Within Britain, the most popular destination for holidays was again the West Country, which accounted for nearly a quarter of all long holidays.

[Reproduced by kind permission of Ray Youell from *Leisure and Tourism: Advanced GNVQ*, 1st edition, Longman, 1994]

Task 2

You should assume the role of assistant to the personnel manager of Eurofabrix plc. Eurofabrix manufactures a wide range of light engineering equipment made to high specifications. Its workforce is primarily manufacturing oriented, but the company employs some 2,000 administrative and office staff. Your department is currently engaged in updating the firm's employee induction manual, and you have been given the responsibility for producing a section which explains to *non-expert* manufacturing staff the concepts of numerical control, NC machine tools, computer numerical control and CNC machine tools, all of which are extensively used in the company's production processes.

The following extract is to form the basis of your article for the manual, which is to be entitled: *Computer and numerical control in company manufacturing.* The article comprises some 1,970 words, and your task is to produce a summary of it in about one-third (approximately 660 words) of its original length. Remember that your readers will not be experts, but will need to possess an intelligent layperson's grasp of the concepts. You have also been tasked with devising a format for your article which will aid its uptake.

Economic considerations 1

1.1 NC and CNC explained

1.1/0 What is numerical control?

Numerical Control (NC) is the technique of giving instructions to a machine in the form of a code which consists of numbers, letters of the alphabet, punctuation marks and certain other symbols. The machine responds to this coded information in a precise and ordered manner to carry out various machining functions. These functions may range from the positioning of the machine spindle relative to the workpiece (the most important function), to controlling the speed and direction of spindle rotation, tool selection, on/off control of coolant flow, and so on.

Instructions are supplied to the machine as **blocks** of information. A block of information is a group of commands sufficient to enable the machine to carry out one individual machining operation. For example, a block of information may command the machine to move the worktable to a specific coordinate position under rapid traverse, or set speed and feed values to carry out the machining of contours. Each block is given a **sequence number** for identification. The blocks are then executed in strict numerical order.

A set of instructions forms an **NC program**. When the instructions are organised in a logical manner they direct the machine tool to carry out a specific task – usually the complete machining of a workpiece or "part". It is thus termed a **part program**. Such a part program may be utilised, at a later date to produce identical results over and over again.

1.1/1 NC machine tools

Automatic control of NC machine tools relies on the presence of the part program in a form that is external to the machine itself. The NC machine does not possess any "memory" of its own and as such is only capable of executing a single block of information, fed to it, at a time. For this reason part programs are normally produced, and stored, on punched tape.

To machine a part automatically, the **machine control unit** (MCU) will read a block of information, then execute that block, read the next block of information and execute that block, and so on. With the punched tape installed it is also possible to "single step" a part program by instructing the machine tool to pause after the execution of each block. This is semiautomatic operation. It is also possible to enter data manually, by setting dials and switches, at the machine console. After each setting the machine will carry out the instruction and wait for the next setting. Thus, it is also possible to effect control by **manual data input** (MDI).

Since a part cannot be produced automatically without the tape being run through the machine block by block, they are often referred to as *tape controlled machines*. The production of repetitive, identical parts thus relies on ▶

a) the tape being present
b) the tape being in good condition.

Any number of identical parts being produced thus imposes harsh operating conditions on the punched tape and subsequent wear, especially of the feed holes used to transport the tape through the tape reader, is likely.

The features of early NC control systems, including any required options had to be specified before purchase since, in most cases, they had to be built in as part of the hardware. They were known as *hardwired controllers*. It was difficult to add extra features at a later date and this made NC installations bulky and expensive. Since updating or upgrading was difficult, many NC machines soon became outdated and obsolete.

1.1/2 What is computer numerical control?

Computer Numerical Control (CNC) retains the fundamental concepts of NC but utilises a dedicated **stored-program computer** within the machine control unit. CNC is largely the result of technological progress in microelectronics (the miniaturisation of electronic components and circuitry), rather than any radical departure in the concept of NC.

CNC attempts to accomplish as many of the MCU functions as possible within the computer **software** which is programmed into the computerised control unit. This greatly simplifies the CNC hardware, significantly lowers purchase costs, and improves reliability and maintainability.

Updates and upgrades are relatively simple. In many cases it is only the stored **operating program** that needs to be modified. The main operating program is stored within the CNC control unit on a special memory chip. Any updates in the control system can be accomplished by replacing the chip with one containing the updated software. The memory chip removed can then be re-programmed with the current operating program. Any *circuit* modifications can be carried out with ease by simply replacing, or adding, components housed on a **printed circuit board** (PCB). Indeed, many modern electronic systems (from simple TV sets to sophisticated computer systems) are increasingly being constructed on a plug-in basis of electronic cards.

Modern CNC machines are thus tools with both current and future value. Obsolescence is, as far as possible, designed out.

CNC control units like the computers on which they are based, operate according to a *stored program* held in *computer memory*. This means that part programs are now able to become totally resident within the memory of the control unit, prior to their execution. No longer do the machines have to operate on the 'read-block/execute-block' principle. This eliminates the dependency on slow, and often unreliable, tapes and tape reading devices – probably the weakest link in the chain. Programs can, of course, still be loaded into the CNC machine via punched tape, but only one pass is necessary to read the complete part program into the memory of the control unit.

1.1/3 CNC machine tools

Many CNC machine tools still retain many of the constructional and physical design aspects of their NC counterparts. However, many new control features are made available on CNC machines, which were impossible, uneconomical or impractical to implement on early NC machines. Such new features include:

▶

a) **Stored Programs** Part programs may be stored in the memory of the machine. The CNC can then operate directly from this memory, over and over again. Use of the tape reader (and its unreliability) is virtually eliminated. For long production runs the part program may be retained in memory, even when the power is removed (say at the end of a shift or at a weekend), by the use of *battery back-up* facilities that keep only the memory supplied with power. Often, more than one program may be resident in the control unit memory at one time with the ability to switch between them.

b) **Editing Facilities** Editing can be carried out on the part program held in memory. Thus, errors, updates, and improvements can be attended to at the machine. Such edits are stored in computer memory and override the tape information as read in. A new, and corrected, tape may then be punched directly from the CNC control unit. This ensures that the most up-to-date version of the part program is retained as current.

c) **Stored Patterns** Common routines such as holes on a pitch circle, pocketing sequences, drilling and tapping cycles can be built in and retrieved many times. There is facility for user-defined sequences (such as roughing cycles, start-up routines, etc.) to be stored and retrieved in the same way. Only certain parameters have to be specified and the computer control will carry out the necessary calculations and subsequent actions.

d) **Sub-programs** For repetitive machining sequences, sub-programs may be defined once and then be repeatedly called and executed as required. This considerably shortens part programs by eliminating the need to repeat sections of identical program code. For example, it may be required to machine the same set of holes but at a different position within the workpiece.

e) **Enhanced Cutter Compensation** When a part program is written it is normally done with a particular type and size of cutter in mind. The positioning of the cutter relative to the workpiece will need to take account of the dimensions of the cutter. It may be the case that, when the part program comes to be run on the machine, the particular cutter specified is not available. CNC control units allow "compensations" and "offsets" to be made for the differences in dimensions between the actual cutter and the specified cutter. Thus, the part program is now independent of the cutter specified when writing the program. This facility can also be brought into play in the case of tool breakage during the machining cycle, where different cutters may have to be reloaded to continue the machining sequence.

f) **Optimised Machining Conditions** The extremely fast response of computer technology, coupled with sophisticated calculation ability, enables machining conditions to be constantly monitored by the control unit. Spindle speed on a CNC lathe, for example, can be perfectly matched (and adjusted automatically) as the depth of cut varies. It is common to witness the spindle speed increase when a facing cut is taken from the outside diameter of a bar to its centre. Feed rate can be optimised by monitoring power consumed.

g) **Communications Facilities** The utilisation of computer technology within the CNC control unit offers the advantage of being able to communicate with other computer-based systems. Part programs may thus be downloaded from other host computers. Such host computers may be simple databases of different part programs, or sophisticated computer aided design systems.

h) **Program Proving Facilities** Many modern control systems contain software that will process the resident part program information and indicate

▶

the component shape that will be produced before machining takes place. This is often displayed graphically on a visual display unit (VDU) on the operating console.

i) **Diagnostics** Most modern CNC machines come equipped with comprehensive diagnostic software for the self-checking of its electronic operation. For example, there might be a diagnostic routine to check the operation of the memory chips. It would write a known test pattern into memory and then read it out again, checking it for validity. Any discrepancy could indicate a memory fault.

j) **Management Information** Since the CNC system controls nearly all functions from the resident computer, much useful information on machine utilisation can be accessed, i.e., spindle-on time, part run time, downtime, etc. can be logged and output to other computer systems or peripheral devices for subsequent reading and analysis.

In addition, many modern CNC machine tools are now capable of automatic tool changing without manual intervention. A number of standard (and/or specialised) cutting tools may be loaded into a rotating turret or carousel, and called up under the control of the part program.

[Reproduced by kind permission of Longman Higher Education from *Introduction to Computer Numerical Control*, Barry Leatham Jones, 1986]

Task 3

You should assume that you work as assistant to the training materials manager for Millennium Training Limited. Your company designs and produces a wide range of training materials for personnel and training departments – large and small – across the UK. Currently you are working on a project intended for recently appointed/ trainee personnel officers. You have been tasked with producing a briefing sheet to form part of a larger pack. Your briefing sheet is to be entitled:

Key steps for the personnel manager to monitor during a job recruitment process.

Your briefing aims to provide a succinct set of guidelines for a relatively inexperienced personnel manager who has been charged with securing a new or replacement employee – from the first identification of the need to the appointment of the new member of staff. The basis of your briefing is set out on page 181. You are free to adapt it in any way, but your briefing must not exceed 450 words. It should communicate the key stages and aspects to be monitored carefully.

THE RECRUITMENT PROCESS

Lists the physical, educational, experience, aptitudes, skills and personality requirements needed in the person who could do the job successfully. Prioritises requirements as 'essential' or useful'. → 3

1 Need for new post identified.

2 Line manager details needs: reviews post for changes if it already exists, or lists fresh requirements if a new post is to be established.

Line managers and personnel department consult

Job need identified

3 Personnel specification is revised or a fresh one drawn up.

4 Job description is revised or a fresh one devised. ← *Defines: who the employee reports to and who may report to him: lists in detail the duties and responsibilities of the post-holder.*

Personnel specification produced

5 A classified or display advertisement is composed for insertion in local/national press. ← *Sells the job by briefly indicating what benefits – pay, prospects, 'perks' etc are offered in return for an applicant possessing the expertise displayed as needed in the advertisement.*

Job description updated

These may include potted history of the organisation and details of successes as well as outline of job location, duties and prospects. → 6

6 Duplicated particulars of the post and application forms are made ready for posting to applicants; the job description may be included in pack to applicants.

Advertisement placed

Applicants respond

7 Initial letters of interest are received and application packs dispatched ← *Smaller organisations sometimes ask only for 'letters of application'; large firms want the 'full application package'.*

8 Completed applications are received which include formal covering letter of application, completed application form(s) and a copy of a curriculum vitae.

Note: many organisations hire employment consultants to sift through initial applications and to propose candidates for shortlisting. ← *National and international companies receive hundreds of applications for key posts*

Applications sifted

During this period, line managers and personnel staff meet to organise interview procedures and agree who will assess what. (8 → 9)

9 Shortlisted applicants are sent letter invitation to attend for interview.

Shortlist drawn up

It is common practice in private sector companies for employees to make very confidential applications for new jobs. Their references will only be taken up with the candidate's permission, and usually after an oral job offer has been made and accepted – 'subject to satisfactory references being received'. → 11

10 Acceptance letters received from shortlisted applicants.

11 Confidential references are obtained from referees cited in application forms and copied for interview panel, along with shortlisted candidates' application forms and CVs.

References taken up

Interview panel also provided with interviewing schedule on which to record impressions and ratings. ← *This schedule gives the interviewer a means of 'marking' the candidate for aspects like: Appearance Alertness Knowledge/expertise Potential Rapport*

Usually a pro forma to detail road/rail fares, hotel and meal costs; employers usually state in application pack whether expenses for interviews attendance will be paid. → 12

12 Interviews take place. Candidates provided with expense claim forms to return after completion. Oral offer of appointment made and orally accepted (subject to acceptable references being obtained).

Interviews take place

It is good manners and good public relations to thank all applicants for their interest in the post. → 13

13 Written letter confirming job offer dispatched to successful candidate, and courtesy letters dispatched to unsuccessful applicants. ← *Some organisation advise the successful candidate by letter after the interview process as this may take place intermittently.*

14 Written job acceptance letter returned.

15 Letter of resignation sent to current employer by successful applicant.

← *While a contract of employment may be deemed to exist on the basis of witnessed oral offers and acceptance, the process is confirmed by the exchange of letters.*

Job offered and accepted

Resignation submitted

This must be received by the new employee within 8 weeks of starting in the job: it will include details of pay, holiday entitlement, hours of work, sickness pay and pension agreements, periods of notice required on either side, job description details and appropriate information about company rules and regulations. → 16

16 Written contract of employment sent to new employee and countersigned by both parties.

17 Job description also provided to new employee with company manual and prospectus etc.

Employment contract issued

Acts and statutes underpinning the recruitment process:

- Employment Protection (Consolidation) Act 1978
- Sex Discrimination Act 1975
- Equal Pay (Amendments) Regulations 1983
- Fair Wages Resolutions (House of Commons)
- Race Relations Act 1976
- Misrepresentation Act 1967
- Trade Union Reform and Employment Rights Act 1993

[Reproduced by kind permission of Pitman Publishing from D. W. Evans *Advanced GNVQ Business: A Student's Guide*, 3rd edition, 1995]

PRODUCTION OF ORAL SUMMARIES OF COMPLEX DISCUSSIONS

1 With the assistance of your teacher, arrange to tape one of the following:

(a) an edition of *Panorama* (BBC1)

(b) an interview from *Newsnight* (BBC2)

(c) a feature from *Breakaway* (Radio 4)

(d) a topic from *Woman's Hour* (Radio 4)

In accordance with your teacher's instructions, first view or listen to the tape and then summarise its principal content in a suitably delivered oral summary. Your teacher will advise you on an appropriate length of time.

2 First take part in *one* of the following class discussions, and then summarise it orally taking not more than 5 minutes to do so.

(a) Are employees entitled to job security at work?

(b) How should community care be paid for?

(c) The manufacturing industry and its political front men are ensuring the death of the planet at an alarmingly increasing pace!

(d) Joblessness is a synonym for hopelessness, yet full employment seems as far away as ever. Can *nothing* be done?

(e) Should scientists who develop nuclear or biological weapons or who carry out painful and stressful experiments on dumb animals – all in the name of research or humanitarian motives – be warmly congratulated or severely censured and ostracised?

(f) We have the Information Technology Revolution to thank for inexcusably high levels of unemployment, intrusive bureaucracy, invasive direct selling, the destruction of privacy and the increasing de-skilling of jobs! What went wrong?

Each discussion should last between 15 and 20 minutes, during which each participant should take notes to act as source data for the oral summary.

3 Adopt the approach for activity 2 for one of the discussion topics set out on pages 20 or 33–34.

4 Similarly, summarise in a suitable format one of the oral presentations detailed on pages 35–36.

APPENDIX

GUIDELINES ON USE OF ENGLISH

The ability to use English correctly and effectively is an essential skill which all those working in business or the public service must seek to master.

Many people speak or write English intuitively. They do not realise that often the most effective use of the language is the result of much conscious effort and practice.

Guesses at spellings or stabs at punctuation will not satisfy the conscientious communicator. Neither will rambling sentence structures nor the inappropriate use of slang find a place in the professional's use of English.

English is the medium through which objectives are achieved, people motivated and productive human relations strengthened. It is therefore essential for the manager, secretary or clerk to appreciate how important it is to speak or write in a way which will achieve positive results.

For example, a business letter may be the only form of contact between a retailing company and a potential customer. The manner in which a friendly and courteous receptionist takes a call may make all the difference to an important buyer. The carefully judged recommendations of a report may have far-reaching consequences. A persuasive sales letter may produce thousands of pounds' worth of orders.

For everyone, then, using English effectively is a vital skill well worth the pains taken to acquire:

- **Syntax and grammar:** understanding the rules which govern the structuring of ideas into accepted sense groups or patterns of meaning.
- **Spelling and punctuation:** reproducing words in their accepted form and linking them together clearly and unambiguously.
- **Vocabulary:** developing a reservoir of general and specialist words and expressions which permit the accurate and effective transmission of the spoken or written word .
- **Sensitivity and discrimination:** acquiring a feeling for the nuances and shades of meaning which words convey within their contexts.
- **Style:** appreciating the different effects which various combinations of words, expressions and structures will impart, and developing the ability to express ideas in informative, discursive or persuasive ways.
- **Critical faculties:** being prepared to look critically at what is to be said or written, to measure consciously its likely effect and to modify it where necessary.
- **Awareness of the recipient:** establishing a rapport with recipients so they are receptive to the message.

Like any craft, expertise in English requires a committed apprenticeship. When words are the ' tools of the trade', the good communicator must learn to build structures which are not merely purpose-built but also pleasing and elegant.

Though such skills may take time, patience and effort to secure, the rewards which they bring will be well worth while and last a lifetime.

Grammar – the parts of speech

What is a noun?

Nouns are the naming words in English which act as labels for objects, ideas, people, works of art and so on. Nouns which name real, physical things such as *letter* or *pen* are called **concrete** nouns. Nouns which express thoughts, ideas and feelings such as *efficiency* or *communication* are called **abstract.**

Sometimes nouns are subdivided into the following categories:

- **common:** everyday objects or concepts such as books, speed, garden
- **proper:** names for people, places, works of art such as John, Leonardo, London, the Mona Lisa
- **collective:** names for groupings or collections such as team, jury, class

Notice that proper nouns are given initial capital letters.

What is a pronoun?

Pronouns are also naming or identifying words which can replace nouns. They may refer to people:

I, you, him, her, mine, ours

or to things:

Where is *it*? I don't agree with *that*.

Sometimes they are used in questions:

Who is coming? *What* did you say?

or to complete meanings:

I cut *myself.*

In addition they may be used to introduce further information about a noun:

This is the gentleman *who* earlier wished to see you.
The report, *which* concerns office reorganisation, will be ready tomorrow.

What is an article?

Not to be overlooked are the hard-working definite and indefinite articles:

the job, *a* report, *an* idea.

What is an adjective?

Adjectives are essentially describing words which extend the meaning of nouns or pronouns:

The secretary typed the *important* letter.
A *good* manager looks after *his* staff.
It's only *little* me!

Sometimes adjectives are used to denote possession:

my desk, *their* pay, *your* turn

or to identify a particular object or idea:

this suggestion, *that* idea

or to introduce questions:

What price did you agree?
Which way did he go?

As a general rule, adjectives in English usually come immediately before the noun or pronoun they qualify. But not always:

The office will be *busy* tomorrow.

What is a verb?

Verbs are the words which do something, that is, convey actions, identify thought processes or denote states of being:

She *typed* the letter and *posted* it.
He *considered* his next move carefully.
The manager *was* aware of the problem.

Verbs are used actively when they directly express the actions of the doer:

The manager *dictated* the letter.

Verbs are used passively when the structure of the sentence is changed to make the doer become the agent by which something is done:

The letter *was dictated* by the manager.

Using verbs passively tends to make the message more impersonal and one trick of its use is that the agent is sometimes omitted:

Your services *are* no longer *required* (by me).

The passive is used in this way as a means of conveying unpopular news, where its communicator pretends not to have been involved.

What is an adverb?

Adverbs are used to extend the meaning of verbs or adjectives:

She can type *quickly.*
He spoke *slowly* and *carefully.*
We need an *extremely* fast photocopier.

Adverbs indicate how, when, where, to what extent, how many, etc.

Most adverbs are easily recognised by their -ly endings.

What is a conjunction?

Conjunctions are the linking words which are used to join ideas together:

The report was concise *and* had been clearly constructed.
The letter was brief *but* it included the main points.

Some conjunctions – and, but, next, then, yet – are used to link ideas together which could stand independently of one another:

The report was concise. It had been clearly constructed.

Other types of conjunction are used to link together a main and a dependent or subordinate idea:

They decided to repeat the advertisement, *although* the cost had risen sharply.
He decided to answer the letter immediately *because* it was so important.

In order to vary the way in which ideas are presented, conjunctions introducing dependent ideas sometimes begin sentences:

As you have worked so successfully, I have no hesitation in recommending you for promotion.

Conjunctions frequently used to introduce dependent ideas are:

when, where, why, what, as, since, because, although, though, even though, if, whether, so that, in order that, with the result that, after, unless, as soon as.

Some conjunctions are used as paired sets:

either ... or
neither ... nor
both ... and
not only ... but also

What is a preposition?

Prepositions are locating words and come immediately in front of nouns or pronouns:

under the blotter, *across* the road, *up* the ladder, *of* him, *to* me, *in* the computer's memory.

Sometimes they are used to form parts of verbs:

to get *down to*, to stand *up to*

What is an interjection?

The interjection is a part of speech which transmits a sense of feeling or emotion: Whew! Ouch! Oh! Ah!

Used most frequently in direct speech, the interjection may express relief:

Whew! That was close!

or delight:

Ah, that's beautiful!

What is the point?

What, then, are the practical advantages of being able to identify the various parts of speech?

Firstly, with knowledge rather than intuition comes self-confidence in recognising the different components or building-blocks of English. Constructions and sense groups appear far less intimidating as the writer begins to feel master of the medium.

In addition, such knowledge has distinct, practical value once the writer has developed the ability to recognise the function of each part of speech. If, for example, he had written or was editing this sentence:

The paint spreads quick and even.

he would recognise that *quick* and *even* both modify the verb *spreads* and so need the *-ly* ending of an adverb:

The paint spreads quickly and evenly.

Similarly by knowing that the word *principle* is always used as a noun and *principal* always as an adjective (save for principals of colleges, etc) the two spellings will never be confused.

Syntax – constructing sentences

Just as there is a practical value in being able to recognise the parts of speech, so it is also important to be able to understand the various ways in which sentences are constructed.

How, for example, does the writer come to recognise that

With reference to your letter of 21st February.

is not a sentence? Intuition may create in him a sense of unease, but there is no substitute for knowing and therefore being able to correct it by adding the essential finite verb:

I *refer* to your letter of 21st February.

What is a sentence?

A useful definition of a sentence is a group of words which conveys a complete meaning. Sentences comprise two basic components:

a subject +	**a predicate**
Mr Brown	arrived early.
I	am not going.
The last train	has already left.
You	have not signed this letter.

All sentences require a subject – a word which is a noun or a pronoun or a longer group of words which has the force of a noun – and a predicate. Here are some more definitions:

- **Phrase:** a phrase is a group of words which are related in sense and are often introduced by a preposition:

  at the moment, on his way to the office, in the ledger

  or a conjunction

  after a busy day's trading, as soon as possible

  Phrases do not include finite verbs, but may be introduced by participles:

  Turning the corner he saw the factory ahead.

- **Clause:** a clause is a group of words which forms a component of a sentence and possesses both a subject and a finite verb. Clauses are linked in sentences by conjunctions:

  He caught the train although *he arrived late at the station.*

- **Main clause:** main clauses may form complex sentences by being joined together by what are termed coordinating conjunctions:

  He stopped and *he called his secretary on the intercom,* then *he resumed drafting the report.*

- **Dependent clause:** dependent clauses cannot stand alone and are linked by subordinating conjunctions to main clauses in complex sentences:

  It is impossible to reach a decision *because* we lack sufficient information.

  As the market is so sluggish, we shall have to reduce our prices, *even though* it may mean a reduction in our gross profit.

- **Sentence:** a sentence is a group of words which conveys a meaning complete in itself. Every sentence must possess a subject and a finite verb, conventionally begin with a capital letter and conventionally end with a full stop. Phrases like

  Down in the mouth? You need Fizz, the fun drink!

  Rocky and reeling. That was the sad state of Monolithic Enterprises following rumours of a take-over bid.

are accepted conventions of advertising and journalism but such techniques are best avoided until the more conventional techniques of sentence writing have been mastered.

- **Simple sentence:** a simple sentence is one which contains a single subject and a single finite verb in its predicate.
- **Complex sentence:** a complex sentence is one which comprises two or more clauses which may be main or dependent. It must, however, contain at least one main clause.

What is a finite verb?

All sentences require a finite verb – a verb which carries out the action of the doer or subject word. Finite verbs need to meet three requirements. They must possess a

- **number:** singular or plural
- **person:** first, second or third
- **tense:** past, present, future or conditional

The verb *arrived* in the example *Mr Brown arrived early* is singular, in the third person and in a past tense.

Thus basic sentences need to contain a subject and a finite verb:

He awoke. The visitor left.

When sentences contain a single subject and a single finite verb they are called simple. When more than one subject and finite verb are used in linked sense groups they are called complex.

What is a predicate?

A predicate may include not just a finite verb, but also words which enlarge the verb's meaning:

He awoke *early*.

or which provide more information about the subject:

The manager felt *irritable*.
Mr Brown is *our chief buyer*.

Some finite verbs need an action receiver, or object, to complete their meaning:

I have bought a *new typewriter*.

Simple sentences, then, may be constructed as follows:

Subject + finite verb
Subject + finite verb + enlargers
Subject + finite verb + object

What is a subject?

Subjects are the doer words or groups of words which control or govern the actions of finite verbs. They may be common or proper nouns:

The report is on our desk.
Miss Jenkins is in Scotland.

or they may be pronouns:

They thanked him for his help.

They may take the form of a whole phrase:

Complaining about the poor service got him nowhere.

or even a clause:

That you were ignorant of company regulations is no excuse.

In English, subjects normally come immediately before the verbs they govern. Sometimes, however, additional ideas about the subject are inserted between it and its verb:

Miss Johnson, *a most efficient member of staff*, will look after you.
The sales representative, *who was experienced*, soon made the sale.

How are verbs used?

As we have seen, finite verbs in sentences are governed by subjects and need to possess a number, person and tense.

Table of verb tenses

Infinite	to write	
Present participle	writing	
Past participle	written	
	Active	*Passive*
Present	She:	The letter:
simple	writes	is written
continuous	is writing	is being written
Past		
simple	wrote	was written
continuous	was writing	was being written
Perfect		
simple	has written	has been written
continuous	has been writing	
Past perfect		
simple	had written	had been written
continuous	had been writing	
Future		
simple	will write	will be written
continuous	will be writing	
Future perfect		
simple	will have written	will have been written
continuous	will have been writing	
Conditional		
simple	would have written	would have been written
continuous	would have been writing	

When verbs literally convey ideas of action they are easy to identify:

She *cut* the paper on the guillotine.
Jack *drives* carefully.

Many verbs, however, express abstract ideas:

He *motivates* his staff well.

and some verbs consist of more than one word:

I *shall have left* for Bristol by the time you arrive.

In order to recognise verbs successfully a knowledge of their tenses is necessary, as well as an understanding of their active and passive use.

Active and passive

Verbs which take objects, when used actively, convey the action of the subject or doer on to an action receiver or object:

Miss Johnson	typed	the report.
SUBJECT	FINITE VERB	OBJECT

The same idea may, however, be expressed passively, where the object becomes the grammatical subject of the sentence and the active subject becomes an agent in the passive:

The report	was typed	by Miss Johnson.
SUBJECT	FINITE VERB	AGENT

The passive structures of verbs are formed by using the verb *to be* and, when necessary, the verb *to have* as well with the past participle of the verb:

is being typed, was typed, has been typed

Verb forms as adjectives and nouns

There are two parts of the verb which are used in sentences, not as verbs, but as nouns or adjectives. Present participle as an adjective:

The *driving* rain obscured the windscreen.

Past participle as an adjective:

The *typed* letters are ready to sign.

Present participle form as a noun (gerund):

His *going* surprised us all.

What is an object?

Objects in sentences receive the action of the verb. Certain verbs which need objects to complete their meaning are called transitive. Verbs which are capable of conveying a meaning without the need for an object are called intransitive.

It is sometimes helpful to think of objects as answering the question, What?

The manager	arranged	a meeting
SUBJECT	FINITE VERB	OBJECT

(What did the manager arrange?)
Some objects take the form of word groups:

The personnel manager wrote a *long and difficult letter.*

Objects may sometimes take the form of clauses:

The inspector detected *what appeared to be a flaw in the casing.*

Remember that when transitive verbs are used in the passive, the object of the active voice of the verb becomes the subject:

A long and difficult letter was written by the personnel manager.
What appeared to be a flaw in the casing was detected by the inspector.

As will be seen later, there are a number of uses to which the passive voice of the verb may be put.

Enlarging intransitive verbs

When verbs are used intransitively (when they do not need an object), adverbial words or expressions may be used to extend their meaning:

He awoke *with a start.*
The meeting continued *for quite some time.*

What are complex sentences?

So far we have considered sentences which are called simple – they contain a single subject and predicate. Many sentences are constructed, however, which are composed of two or more clauses with the following relationships:

main clause + main clause
She worked hard on the report
and
she did not finish until 7:30 P.M.

main clause + dependent clause
He asked her to stay late
because
he needed the report for the next day.

Main and dependent clauses may be combined by using conjunctions in a number of different ways:

Dependent	Although it was not entirely convenient,
Main	she did not mind working late
Dependent	because she realised the importance of completing the report.

Ideas are frequently linked in this way to form complex sentences which provide interest and variety for the reader and which also serve to indicate the relationships between ideas. Remember that dependent clauses cannot stand alone. They need to be accompanied by main clauses. Also, all clauses, whether main or dependent, must possess both a subject and a finite verb.

One of the problems of writing complex sentences is that it is easy to lose control of the meaning by stringing clauses together ungrammatically:

> The young typist, who wanted to make a good impression when she arrived for work on her first day, although she was feeling nervous because the surroundings were unfamiliar, despite the friendly greeting she received from the commissionaire when she entered the lofty office block.

Here we wait in vain for the main verb to follow *the young typist*. It is much better to shorten the structure of the ideas by constructing two sentences:

> The young typist wanted to make a good impression when she arrived for work on her first day. She received a friendly greeting from the commissionaire when she entered the lofty office block, but was feeling nervous because the surroundings were unfamiliar.

Practical assignments

Parts of speech

Identify the parts of speech italicised in the following sentences:

1 *I* asked *him* to read *it.*

2 The *large envelopes* are in the *top drawer.*

3 The invoices *have been checked.*

4 He read the report *slowly* and made his notes *methodically.*

5 I am pleased *to announce* that *Amalgamated Steel* has made *extremely good* progress during the past year.

6 His instructions were *clear.*

7 An *elderly* man carrying a *bulky* briefcase arrived *at* reception.

8 *Although* its price was competitive, the new product sold poorly.

9 *Either* we increase production *or* we turn down firm orders.

10 *I shall have finished* checking the draft by the time you return *and then* it will be ready for typing.

11 The meeting will require *my* staying late at the office.

12 *Oh!* I never expected such a smart retirement present!

Syntax

Identify the subject, finite verb, object or adverbial verb enlarger in the following sentences:

1 The last train leaves at ten o'clock.

2 You have designed a masterpiece!

3 An increase in output is urgently needed.

4 I followed his instructions precisely.

5 Everyone heard what he said.

6 What he said echoed loudly.

7 The speaker should have arrived last night.

8 The office party has been postponed indefinitely.

9 The performance of the energetic sales force was praised by the managing director.

10 The art of management requires achieving objectives.

11 The word processor saves time.

Clauses and conjuctions

Identify the main and dependent clauses in the following sentences and state which words are the linking conjunctions.

1 If you do not arrive more punctually, I shall be obliged to take further action.

2 Whatever the market research may forecast, the board is determined to go ahead.

3 We shall have to cancel the project as public response has been totally hostile.

4 When he had finished interviewing the last candidate, he reluctantly began to scan his notes because he knew he would not have time tomorrow.

5 As soon as you have time, Mr Jones would like you to see him in his office, which is on the fifth floor.

Sentence structures

What defects in syntax, if any, can you find in the following sentences:

1 Hoping to receive your reply without delay.

2 Unless we hear from you in the meantime.

3 However much we would like to help you.

4 Please let me know as soon as possible.

5 Despite our repeated reminders regarding non-payment of your account, which is long overdue.

6 The prices of our range of kitchen utensils, which, as you know, have not increased, despite the pressure of the increased cost in raw materials.

7 Further to your recent request for samples of our new range of fabrics.

8 Using the microcomputer, the cursor became stuck in the middle of the VDU screen.

9 Having produced a paper printout, the text was stored in the computer's memory.

Usage: helpful hints

Many writers experience problems with grammar, syntax and usage in the course of composing written documents. Such errors spring from a variety of sources – haste, a failure to read through and check a draft or from simply having missed learning a particular form of accepted usage.

Some of the most frequently encountered problems of usage are as follows:

Agreement

Remember that a plural subject requires a plural verb:

> The *sales assistant* who sold it *and the engineer* who installed it *are* responsible for the customer's complaint.

Remember also that pronouns should be used consistently and not changed because of an oversight:

> *I am* sure you will be pleased with the new model and *I* look forward to hearing from you.

Incomplete sentences

Incomplete sentences are usually written as a result of haste or a failure to check a draft.

> With regard to your recent order for 100 boxes of carbon paper.
> Further to your letter of 14 June.

Remember that all sentences require both a subject and a finite verb.

> Further to your letter of 14 June, *I am pleased* to inform you that your order has now been despatched.

Each, everyone, nobody, all

Notice that the following generally take singular verbs:

> *Each* is hand-made.
> *Everyone* is present.
> *Nobody* is willing to stand.

but that *all* usually takes a plural verb:

> *All* are agreed that the decision should be deferred.

Remember also that collective nouns may, on occasions, take either a singular or a plural verb depending upon the sense – whether the components of the collective noun are seen as a single unit or as separate subgroups:

> *Has* the working party found a solution?
> No, the working party *are* divided into two distinct camps at present.

Misrelating the participle and the noun

When beginning sentences with participle constructions, care should be taken to ensure that they are not misrelated to the noun immediately following:

> Walking along the road, the tile hit him on the head.
> Having typed half the letter, the telephone rang insistently.

Clearly, tiles cannot walk and telephones do not type. Such sentences need restructuring to provide the correct subjects of *walking* and *having typed*:

> As he was walking down the road, a tile hit him on the head.
> Having typed half the letter, the secretary heard the telephone, which rang insistently.

Mixing metaphors

Linking two quite distinct metaphors is often the result of muddled thinking and sometimes produces humorous results:

> You must put your foot down with a firm hand .
> As long as we all keep our shoulders to the wheel, we'll have a smooth flight.

Using words wrongly

Some words are frequently used wrongly as a result of confusion over their meaning:

> This faint copy is quite ~~unreadable~~ *illegible*!
>
> Placed as he was in a neutral position, he was able to voice an opinion which was quite ~~uninterested~~ *disinterested*.
>
> He was quite ~~effected~~ *affected* receiving so many letters of encouragement.

Who or whom?

Some writers find it difficult in certain sentences to decide whether *who* or *whom* is correct. Consider

> The umbrella belongs to the customer who I served.

A simple rule of thumb will solve this problem. In cases of uncertainty, substitute *who(m)* by

> he she they = who
> him her them = whom

in the relevant part of the sentence:

> I served him.

Clearly it cannot be

> I served he.

Thus the correct version in the above sentence is *whom*.

Overloading verbs

In some constructions verbs are sometimes overloaded by being required to express two tenses at once:

> Property values have and always will rise in an inflationary economy.

Here, the writer has tried to make a false economy by expecting *rise* to survive not only as a future tense, *will rise*, but as a perfect tense as well, *have risen*. The sentence needs reconstructing:

> Property values have always risen and will always rise in an inflationary economy.

Verbs in their noun forms

When verbs are used in their noun forms as gerunds, they are preceded by the possessive form of the personal pronoun used adjectivally:

> I hope you didn't mind *my* leaving before the end of your talk.

> The absence of Mr Brown will require *your* taking the chair at the meeting.

Practical assignment

The following sentences contain errors of usage. Rewrite them correctly, changing the sentence structure as little as possible:

1 So long as you don't object to me going, I would be glad of an opportunity to revisit my home town.

2 Regarding your letter of 21 March 19– concerning the delivery of a defective calculator.

3 As the consignment is already three weeks overdue, I would be grateful if you would ensure prompt delivery.

4 On entering the office late, the busy hubbub stopped and all eyes turned towards her.

5 The secretary who I recently employed is proving most conscientious.

6 Who's coat has been left on the coat-stand?

7 His consistent effort led to him winning the Salesman Of The Year award.

8 Though I have not met the buyer who you refer to, I do know the sales manager.

9 Whatever sales approach one employs, the basic requirement is to get the customer on your side.

10 Every time he opens his mouth, he puts his foot in it!

11 The deeds had laid, undiscovered, for over fifteen years in the trunk.

12 We acknowledge your letter of 28 September and are also in receipt of your order for a Summit adding machine.

Avoiding the cliché

Clichés are expressions which have suffered from overuse. As a consequence they transmit a tired, stale and sometimes irritating meaning:

> It has come to my notice
> I am writing ...
> with regard to
> with reference to
> I note that

Most people resort to the cliché occasionally but the effort to express an idea simply and freshly is always well worth while since it helps to maintain the reader's interest.

Punctuation

The system of punctuating written English is perhaps best viewed as a means of ensuring that any message is transmitted both clearly and unambiguously. The system does more than this, however, by providing occasional breathing spaces and by conveying not only what has been written, but sometimes, the feelings of a writer or speaker.

Basically, there are some eleven major punctuation marks in general use:

.	the full stop
,	the comma
;	the semicolon
:	the colon
'	the apostrophe
( )	parentheses
?	the question mark
!	the exclamation mark
-	the hyphen
–	the dash
" " or ' '	direct speech marks or inverted commas

[·] *The full stop*

The full stop has two principal uses. Firstly, it is used to signify the end of a sentence:

> He considered his next move carefully. He would call a meeting of his regional managers at the earliest opportunity.

Sometimes a succession of short sentences may be used to obtain a certain effect:

> He scanned the memorandum. It told him nothing. He dismissed it entirely.

Although too frequent a use of the above technique may prove irritating, it is generally sound advice to keep sentences short rather than to allow them to ramble. Some researchers have found that constructing sentences with more than 25–30 words leads to comprehension problems on the part of the recipient, particularly if the vocabulary used is multisyllabic. A useful motto, then, is: When in doubt, finish the sentence and start another.

The other main use of the full stop is to indicate that a word has been abbreviated:

Mr. Rev. Dr. St. i.e. e.g. etc.

It should be borne in mind, however, that some current practices in typing letters embody open punctuation in their format. This omits full stops (and commas) in those parts of the letter other than its body. Similarly, some abbreviations are currently accepted without full stops, provided that the use is consistent:

OBE Ltd HMS OHMS Mr Mrs

Sometimes abbreviations such as a.s.a.p. are used in messages to indicate 'as soon as possible', but such abbreviations should be avoided in formal documents. Lastly, remember that each sentence begins with a capital letter.

, *The comma*

The comma is used within sentences to indicate a pause between sense groups of words:

> Reaching the corner he stopped, looked both ways, then crossed.

The comma is also used to separate words (or phrases) put into a list:

> The drawer contained paper-clips, rubber bands, pencils and paper.

Another use of the comma is to show that an enlarging or modifying idea has been inserted between a subject and its verb:

> The answer, which had been quite unexpected, took them by surprise.

Note, however, that when such an inserted clause defines a preceding noun, no comma is used:

> The book which you ordered is out of print.

As a general rule, commas are not needed before conjunctions like and, or, but or then, which link main clauses:

> He spoke quietly and they listened intently.
> You must hurry or you will be late.
> The visitor was late but his host displayed no sign of irritation.

Some writers use the comma to separate a dependent clause from a main clause when a sentence begins with a dependent clause:

> Although he worked at a slow and methodical pace, John could be relied upon to keep going when others wilted.

But this usage is by no means universal:

> When he had finished he rang for his secretary.

The use of the comma in such constructions perhaps coincides with the need for a breathing space in longer sentences.
There are a number of words in frequent use which are employed with one or more commas:

> Lastly, the report indicates that ...
> It proved, however, to be of major importance.
> Nevertheless, I should be grateful if ...
> The mistake was, moreover, extremely costly.

In direct speech, the comma may be used to indicate an element of hesitancy on the part of the speaker:

> 'Oh, and another thing, don't forget to ring when you arrive.'

The comma is used to separate lists of adjectives. Sometimes writers employ several adjectives to describe a single noun:

> The report was marred by a loose, rambling, disjointed and careless structure.

Heaping such adjectives together may be a deliberate ploy to create a certain effect, but the inclusion of several adjectives before a single noun smacks of overkill rather than good style.

Some writers, though in a minority, insist, and that is not too strong a word, on using the comma, not just when occasion demands, but indiscriminately, with the effect that sentences limp, totter and stumble along, which can be very irritating, and is quite unnecessary.

As the above sentence amply illustrates, the comma should be used sparingly to assist rather than to impede the reader's understanding of what is written.

; *The semicolon*

Many writers today tend to shy away from using the semicolon and it is not used as much as it used to be. It indicates a pause which is longer than the comma but shorter than the full stop. Most frequently it separates main clauses in the following manner:

> The sales campaign had been brilliantly conceived; it caught our main competitors completely unprepared.

In such constructions the semicolon is particularly effective in securing a dramatic pause before the ensuing statement, which thus gains in impact. Notice that such a use of the semicolon requires that the two ideas expressed in the main clauses are closely related and could, if need be, stand as sentences. The semicolon in the above example could be replaced by *and* or *it caught* by *catching*. The effect, however, would be to lose the emphasis the semicolon supplies.

: *The colon*

The colon used to be employed as a stronger stop or break than the semicolon to separate clauses in a manner similar to that illustrated above. Nowadays it is primarily used to introduce an example or quotation:

> I have always found the advice of Polonius in *Hamlet* to be sound: 'Neither a borrower nor a lender be.'

or to preface a list. The list may be set out vertically, as in the notice of a bonus award:

> The following members of staff won this month's bonus award:
> Mr J Harris
> Mr T Jones

Alternatively, the list may he set out in sentence form:

> The exhibition will include pictures from several collections: the Louvre, the Gulbenkian Foundation and the National Portrait Gallery.

The inclusion of a dash with the colon:– is now obsolete.

' *The apostrophe*

The apostrophe has two major uses. The first, used in conjunction with the letter *s*, denotes possession:

> The secretary's notebook ...
> The manager's report ...

Notice that when the possessor is *singular* – the secretary, the manager – the apostrophe comes *before* the *s*, which should be separated from the rest of the word.

To show possession in the plural the apostrophe is positioned immediately *after* the *s*, which is added to most nouns to indicate their plural form:

> the representatives' calls
> the books' prices

Some nouns, however, change in their plural form:

child	children
woman	women

The apostrophe for such nouns is placed immediately after the final *n* which is followed by an *s*:

> women's coats
> children's shoes

A very useful rule of thumb is: Put an apostrophe at the end of the word and add an *s*. If the word already ends in *s*, in most cases the second *s* is omitted.

In addition, there are a large number of nouns ending in *y*, which changes to *ies* in the plural. Such nouns show possession in this way:

> ladies' fashions
> secretaries' meeting

In cases of uncertainty, a simple test may be applied to a word suspected of needing an apostrophe *s*. Try to substitute *of the* followed by the word in question in the sentence or phase:

> the fashions of the ladies
> the meeting of the secretaries
> the shoes of the children
> the report of the manager

If the wording still makes sense, then the apostrophe is needed. Remember that when *its* means *of it* the apostrophe is not used.

The other use of the apostrophe is to indicate that a letter (or letters) has been omitted from a word which has been contracted:

> do not ... don't
> it's ... it is

Such contractions are very frequently used in spoken English but should not be used in any formal documents.

( ) *Parentheses*

Parentheses are used to separate what is often a secondary or additional idea from the rest of a sentence:

> A short cut (though this is not recommended for beginners) would be to leave out the second step.
> He decided to try (although his chances of succeeding were remote) and entered his name on the list.

Sometimes the parentheses enclose a source of reference or information:

> The results obtained (see Appendix C) indicated a distinct preference for the blue colour.

? *The question mark*

The question mark is placed at the end of the sentences which are structured to form direct questions:

> How many did you sell?
> When does he leave for London?

As the above examples illustrate, the stop of the question mark serves to replace any other form of sentence-ending punctuation mark. The following practices should be avoided:

> What did he say?.
> What did she call you?!

Sometimes speakers introduce rhetorical questions into speeches. Such questions are used for effect and do not expect any answer. Nevertheless, they require a question mark:

> An entirely new approach is needed. And who among us would deny that a thorough review is long overdue? Once this need is accepted ...

Indirect questions, however, do not require a question mark:

He asked if he might be excused.
She enquired whether the train had left.

! The exclamation mark

Exclamation marks are used to indicate feelings of surprise, astonishment, sarcasm, approval or enthusiasm:

Incredible! No other word would do justice to the performance of the new Magiscribe notebook computer.

Are you going to the meeting?
You can't be serious!
So this is the new model. It's beautiful!

Some writers endeavour to increase the element of surprise or approval by placing several exclamation marks together. Such a practice is an accepted convention in comic books, but has no place in serious writing. Lastly, the exclamation mark suffers from overuse and is best used sparingly.

- The hyphen

The hyphen's function is to link together either words or parts of words. When it is employed to link words together it does so because they have become so closely connected in meaning that they are almost one word:

leap-frog
master-at-arms

Some words, however, have been used in conjunction for so long that any hyphen has been dropped: racecourse, turnover, mouthpiece. It is difficult to know for certain when to run words together and when to hyphenate them, and in cases of uncertainty the dictionary must be the arbiter.

The other use of the hyphen is to join parts of words together which must each be pronounced separately:

pre-eminent
post-modernism
sub-editor

Some current writers are tending to drop this use of the hyphen and run words together, but its use is certainly helpful. For example, *preeminent* is less clear than *pre-eminent*.

The hyphen is also used in typing and printing to indicate the continuation of a word which starts at the end of one line and finishes on the next.

– The dash

The dash is used in a way similar to that of brackets. It signifies that some utterance or additional statement has been inserted or added:

'I'll come straight to the point – oh, but forgive me, I see your glass is empty.
The sales of accessories – in fact the entire sales performance – has been extremely satisfying!

" Direct speech marks/inverted commas

The use of direct speech marks is restricted to showing exactly which words were spoken by a particular speaker:

'I don't know,' he said, 'but I'll find out.'

When a second speaker is introduced, the spoken words begin a new paragraph. The punctuation of the direct speech is all placed *within* the direct speech marks.

Double or single inverted commas are sometimes, used to indicate a quotation or a title:

'Look before you leap' is still good advice.
'Have you read "The Efficient Secretary"?'

Note that single inverted commas are increasingly replacing double ones when used to denote direct speech.

KEY POINT

Punctuation is an essential aid to understanding and interpreting the written word correctly. Similarly, the spoken word is conveyed more readily if pauses and intonation are employed to provide oral punctuation.

Practice pieces

1 Set out the following recipient's name and address as it would appear in a business letter employing closed punctuation:

j a crossman esq m sc m b i m sales manager sentinel security ltd 14 kings road maidenhead berks mb142ap

Now set it out according to open punctuation rules.

Punctuate the following:

2 he skimmed rapidly through the article he had found in his morning paper there was nothing on plant bargaining although the articles title had led him to suspect there would be

3 choosing his words carefully the chairman of the management committee who was clearly anxious to avert a head on clash expressed his desire for a calm rational and productive discussion

4 the equipment however proved more costly than the production managers estimate

5 however hard it may be keeping the customers goodwill is essential in any business

6 the first design which the advertising agency submitted was rejected by the marketing manager

7 if you dont tell him i will avowed john parker the sales manager angrily its ridiculous to set such an impossible target

8 the directors meeting will take place on wednesday 3 July at 9:30 A.M. in the boardroom

9 the sales performance for the last quarter has surpassed all expectations turnover has risen by no less than 25%

10 the following branches exceeded the January sales targets portsmouth aberdeen chester norwich and bath

11 the distribution of the companys branches map page 12 refers now provides a comprehensive nationwide coverage

12 he asked whether he could be heard at the back of the hall

13 i realise your problems and dont forget that i too began as a sales representative and i want to resolve them as quickly as possible

14 is there anyone here at this meeting tonight who seriously believes that such complex problems can be simply solved i very much doubt it

15 Using the open punctuation system, set out the following typescript section of a business letter in an appropriate format:

> your ref fj mg our ref mdf 21 october 19— mrs fiona jackson ba dms personnel manager futura fabrics ltd queens house wellington place london wc2a4tg dear madam personnel management the next decade thank you for your letter of 16 october enquiring about the publication of the above book recently publicised in our autumn catalogue i very much regret that the publication date of gordon richardsons book has been delayed it is however anticipated that it will be available by the end of next january should you experience any difficulty in obtaining a copy from your local bookshop please do not hesitate to contact me in the meantime i enclose a copy of our current personnel management publications catalogue for your consideration please let me know if i may be of any further assistance yours faithfully jean davis mrs assistant sales manager enc

Spelling: some guidelines

The ability to spell correctly is particularly important for the manager or secretary since composing and distributing a wide range of written documents form a central part of their daily work. Moreover, adverse value judgments are often made about an organisation if documents are received which are marred by spelling errors.

Though the English language is not the easiest to spell, patience, a handy dictionary and the following guidelines will certainly help in overcoming some of the more common problem areas. It is extremely helpful to keep a record of any irregular spellings or exceptions to spelling rules.

The 100% rules

- *q* is always followed by *u*
- no English word ends in *j*
- no English non-colloquial word ends in *v*

Plurals

Most English plurals are formed by adding *s* to the singular:

books posters aches

But there are exceptions:

potatoes brushes fuzzes

and foreign words with plurals which need to be learnt:

bureaux	stimuli	bases
formulae	stadia	aquaria

(though stadiums is now often seen).

Some words possess irregular plurals:

child/children ox/oxen woman/women

Words ending in *y* in the singular mostly drop the *y* and add *ies* in the plural:

secretaries ladies hobbies

If the *y* is preceded by a vowel then the usual *s* is added.

Note that words ending in: *s x z sh ch ss* in the singular add *es* to form the plural:

batches crosses mixes

Some words ending in *f* in the singular discard it for *ves* in the plural:

scarf/scarves leaf/leaves loaf/loaves

Prefixes

An especially helpful rule is that adding a prefix to a word does not alter its basic spelling:

dis/appear un/necessary ig/noble
dis/seminate pro/claim

Note that some prefixes are connected to the base word by a hyphen:

pre-emptive non-attributable

Suffixes

The adverbial *-ly* ending is added quite straightforwardly to most words:

lively freely

even those which already end in *l*:

principally critcally

The *-ing* ending is also added straight on the ends of words, except those which end in *e*, where the *e* is usually dropped:

moving scraping serving

Another very useful guideline is that when a word ends in a consonant preceded by a vowel, the final consonant is doubled:

fit/fitting tip/tipping

This rule is also true of *-er*, *-ed* and *-est* endings:

big/bigger occur/occurred omit/omitted

Note that where many verbs end in *t*, a noun is formed by dropping it for the *-sion* ending:

convert/conversion divert/diversion

The suffix *-ness* is normally straightforward, but note that when the base word ends in *y*, it is frequently replaced by an *i*:

happy/happiness lovely/loveliness

Some endings which simply have to be learnt stem from various Latin roots for which the suffixes are *-able* or *-ible*:

commendable infallible unavoidable
incomprehensible divisible

Homophones

The English language abounds with homophones – words which sound the same but which are spelled differently:

air/heir threw/through bite/bight
course/coarse what/watt

It helps to collect them, to learn their spelling by heart and then to recognise them from the context in which they are used.

Rules of thumb

The soft *g* sound in a word means that the letter *g* (or *gg*) will be followed by: *e, i, or y*:

impinge dingy intelligent

The letter *i* comes before *e*, except after *c*:

conceive ceiling deceive

If a word ends in a single *l*, preceded by a single vowel, then the *l* will double before any further suffix is added:

typical/typically crystal/crystallise
actual/actually unravel/unravelled

A word ending in t which (1) has more than one syllable and (2) has the accent on the last syllable doubles the *t* before any further letters are added:

permit/permitting

If you are not sure about a word beginning with *f* or *ph*, remember that the *ph* sound stems from Greek, so that it is likely to introduce such word components as:

phil phono phen phal phos photo phys

One further helpful rule of thumb is that a single vowel preceding a double consonant is very often short, but when the vowel sound is long, it is very often a single consonant:

fŭnnel/fūneral hămmer/lion-tāmer

scrăpping/scrāping fĭlling/fīling

spĭnning/dīning ŏtter/pōtato

Lastly, in syllables other than the first in a word, the *sh* sound is most likely to be *ti, ci* or *si*:

spacious notion confusion

Check-list of troublemakers

The problem pack

The following words have caused spelling problems for generations of writers. Study them carefully, checking especially the parts which have been underlined, since this is where most people go wrong:

accessible
accessory
accommodation
acquiesce
acquire
address
aggressive
analysis
appalling
argument
beneficial
benefited
changeable
chargeable
committed
committee
conscious
contemptible
deceive
deferment
deferred
definite
develop
disappear
disseminate
equipped
embarrass
exaggerate

existence
foreign
fulfil
gauge
government
grateful
honorary
humorous
illegible
immovable
inconsistent
insistent
intelligible
irresponsible
maintenance
manoeuvre
miscellaneous
mischievous
necessary
negligible
noticeable
occasion
occurred
omission
omitted
parallel
precede
procedure

profess	skilful
psychology	succeed
receive	supersede
recommend	technicality
referred	temporary
regrettable	tragedy
resistant	unnecessary
secede	untouchable
separate	woollen
sincerely	wreath

Assignment

Compose a sentence illustrating the use (or different uses) for each of the words displayed below as pairs.

Once you have used them correctly, you will be well on the way to eliminating fifty troublesome words from the problem pack.

Double trouble

The following pairs of words are frequently confused. Make sure you know the difference in their meaning and how they are used:

advice	advise
affect	effect
appal	appeal
canvas	canvass
complement	compliment
council	counsel
confidant	confident
continuous	continual
dependant	dependent
decent	descent
draft	draught
faint	feint
forward	foreword
farther	further
licence	license
to lie	to lay
lightening	lightning
loose	lose
past	passed
proceed	precede
principle	principal
practise	practice
stationery	stationary
strait	straight
waiver	waver

[Appendix reproduced by kind permission of Pitman Publishing from D. W. Evans, *People, Communication and Organisations*, 1st edition, 1986]

ANSWERS TO SELF-CHECK REVIEW TESTS

Page 8

1 Discussions are used frequently at work to prompt decision making, to share information, to enable consultations to take place, to motivate the workforce, to negotiate, to brainstorm innovations and ideas and to appraise staff.

2 Examples of rules which govern the conduct of meetings include company law, Acts of Parliament, written constitutions and standing orders.

3 Examples of people at work likely to chair discussions are company directors, heads of department, executive officers, overseers and supervisors, trade union representatives and officials, e.g. health and safety officer.

4 Participants in discussions tend to pursue personal agendas since they all embody job roles, e.g. senior care officer; the job role tends to direct an employee's interest and needs when taking part in a discussion.

5 People adopt different registers at work since they instinctively adopt a spoken or written word style which they believe likely to prove most suitable and effective, which the recipient(s) are likely to expect, and which they feel most comfortable with

Page 19

1 Pronunciations: orthoPEEdic, arKEYtype. montAJ, burOWS, fAYn, slEYEt, GERRilla, tourniKAY, soubriKAY.

2 Intonation and emphasis are important in the spoken word since they highlight keywords for the listener to grasp as important, and also to help the listener retain interest in what is being said.

3 Active listening is sustained by following a speaker's NVC signals, making notes, asking questions, and avoiding the temptations of doodling, chatting or becoming distracted.

4 NVC stands for non-verbal communication; its four components are facial expression, gesture, posture and paralinguistics.

5 An open question requires its answerer to enlarge upon it; a closed question can be answered either by a yes or a no.

6 A supplementary question is a follow-up question, usually asked to probe further and deeper.

7 A dominant participator may be controlled by inviting other speakers to respond first to a topic; by breaking into the dominant person's speech to invite another to contribute and by politely cutting the dominant person short.

8 Disagreement is best made by sticking to the facts rather than attacking a speaker; expressions of worry or concern may be raised; the disagreement may follow upon a concession made or an agreement; the speaker may veil a disagreement in a statement like 'I am not clear about...'

9 Positive feedback includes nodding, interjecting statements like absolutely and quite right, pleasant eye-contact; negative feedback includes remaining silent, folding arms, shaking head, muttering disagreeing statements like no or not true, switching off NVC signals

10 A popular technique is to ask for one meeting/discussion to take place at a time, or to ask the chatterer if everyone can share in what must be an absorbing topic.

Page 32

1 The most likely documents are the notice of the meeting, a general agenda, minutes of the last meeting, plus possibly details of a written motion or copies of correspondence or discussion papers.

2 See the check-list on pages 24 and 25.

3 Lobbying is a process which takes place before meetings, where individuals seek to persuade others to adopt a desired point of view or attitude to a matter

4 See the check-list on pages 24–26.

5 Arriving late, being rude, losing your temper, switching off and opting out, using crude/bad language, making personal attacks on participants, etc.

6 A discussion leader has to steer a topic through a useful debate to a clear conclusion, to encourage shy speakers to participate and to control dominant ones, to act as an umpire and diplomat, to ensure that time deadlines are not exceeded (see also page 26).

7 A chair needs to be fully conversant with procedural rules and to provide a casting vote; a chair is also responsible for the accuracy of the documentation of the meetings.

8 Cross-check your list with that on pages 27 and 28.

9 A cue card is a small hand-held card which contains a few, boldly printed key points which act as references during the delivery of an oral presentation.

10 Cross-check your list with that on page 29.

Page 43

1 Four main features of good writing at work are relevance, accuracy, correct use of English and appropriate choice of style/register.

2 Bad practices include rambling, error-filled work, failure to adopt accepted conventions of format, alienation of the reader and lapsing into irrelevance.

3 Main reasons for using the written word at work include informing, instructing, proposing, recording, persuading, disciplining and self-presentation.

4 The three main components of the writing mix are choice of vocabulary/syntax, structure and format and style/register.

5 English has so many synonyms because of the number of old languages it is derived from: Celtic, Latin, Greek, Norse, Danish, Anglo-Saxon, Old German, Norman French. It also contains more recently imported, foreign words.

6 Subjective writing involves a person allowing personal views, attitudes, and feelings to be expressed, whereas objective writing seeks to impart only facts.

7 The term register is used to describe a range of different degrees in either the spoken or written word, say a degree of formality, familiarity or objectivity.

Page 64

1 Research data should be currently valid, relevant and accurate.

2 Local information is to be found in study centre and local public libraries, university libraries, local newspaper offices, the Citizens' Advice Bureau, the county council archives department, planning departments, etc.

3 Check your answer with the explanation on pages 46 and 47.

4 An ISBN is a unique identifier allocated to certain publications by the Standard Book Numbering Agency.

5 Cross-check your answer with the checklist on pages 46–48.

6 A simple technique is to divide assembled data into three groups: essential, useful and largely irrelevant, then to classify the first group into clusters of like data which follow a logical order. The secondary points are vetted for possible additional material.

7 Such documents tend to follow a three-stage structure: background, development, action requested.

8 A short, formal report's five main stages are terms of reference, procedure, findings, conclusions and recommendations.

9 A schematic layout includes movements from major to minor points, which are signposted by the use of numerical referencing systems and the use of capitalisation, emboldening and underscoring; progressive indentation is the term for moving points downwards and towards the right margin as they become more subordinate; white space is the empty lines or area left around headings and titles to make them stand out.

10 Display techniques include using contrasting fonts and points sizes, capitalisation, emboldening, italicising, underscoring, use of boxes and shaded panels, use of borders, use of clip-art, importation of graphic illustrations.

11 A loose paragraph's main point comes first; in a mixed paragraph it is somewhere in the middle and in a periodic paragraph it comes last; loose paragraphs make opening impacts; periodic paragraphs save main points until last for dramatic emphasis; mixed paragraphs are used to supply variety.

12 A conjunction is a part of speech which acts as a linking word, e.g.

The painting was popular *because* it was unusual.

Page 109

1 Images have become popular since the 1940s particularly since, both at work and in their leisure time, people interact more extensively with visual media such as television, cinema and computers. Also, extensive use is made of icons and symbols in international contexts such as roads, airports and safety.

2 Multimedia is a title given to the material (often stored on CD-ROM) which is used in association with computers. The media include films, photographs, animated films, pictures, texts, voice overs, music, diagrams and charts.

3 Compare your answers with the list on page 105.

4 These factors include type of recipient, type of information, time available, cost, access to source material, end-use medium and purpose.

5 Unity in design embraces visual appeal, harmony of composition and clarity of message.

6 Check your answers with the listing on pages 106 and 107.

7 Black and yellow are the most highly visible colour combination known in nature, hence their use by wasps and hornets to denote danger.

8 An icon is a graphic design which conveys a specific meaning, e.g. delete, print, file. A symbol is really a synonym for an icon, which tends to be used in the context of computing software. A logo is a symbol used by organisations as a shorthand meaning for what they are and what they do; trade marks do the same for a firm's products or services.

9 A font is an alphabetic set of characters and symbols created in a particular design; a point is a unit of size employed in printing.

Page 114

1 Creating the story, constructing the set, shooting the film, editing and adding credits.

2 A storyboard is used to communicate the main steps or sequences in a film to be made.

3 *Location:* a place where filming will occur; *set:* a constructed setting for a scene, e.g. a factory bench or an office desk area; *props:* those accessories such as handbag, toolkit, brush or walking-stick which actors carry or use; *continuity:* the process of ensuring that a set and props are in exactly the same place and of the same type if a scene has to be reshot.

4 See the list on page 111.

5 Check your answers with the list on page 112.

6 *Film speed* is the classification given to a type of film in terms of its responsiveness to varying strengths of light; *shutter speed* is the time (in fractions of a second) for the camera's shutter to open and close; *exposure* is the length of time the shutter is held open; *camera-shake* refers to the blurring of a photograph due to a movement of the camera as a picture is taken; *focal length* refers to the distance between the camera lens and its object, and is used to obtain a depth of focus; *red-eye* describes the colour which people's eyes become when an indoor flash hits their retinas and bounces back onto the film in the camera.

7 Cartoons are used to create a light, humorous touch, to make a satirical point, to emphasise an underlying truth, to provide visual relief, etc.

8 Clip-art is a term used to describe ready-to-use illustrations stored on computer files.

9 A scanner is a piece of equipment used to create computer files from pictures, diagrams and photos.

10 Desktop publishing has revolutionised in-house printing by enabling trained operators to simulate and reproduce many features which hitherto could only be effected by professional printers, such as the mixing of text and graphic illustrations and the use of varying fonts and points sizes.

Page 131

1 A map needs to have an orientation, a scale and a key to any symbols used.

2 A table comprises columns and rows with subtotals and a final total of additions (or other calculations); it also needs a clear title and descriptors of quantities or units employed.

3 A computer spreadsheet, through its formula feature, is able to make instant amendments to a number of calculations once any input is changed.

4 Quantity: vertical axis; time: horizontal axis.

5 Tables are good at storing highly detailed numbers but are poor at communicating data quickly and easily; graphs are better at revealing comparative performances and trends.

6 A break in the vertical axis is used when one or more plotted items is much larger than others.

7 Pie charts are good at showing how the various parts of a whole compare with each other.

8 A bar chart compares single columns of like items; and a stacked bar chart includes several bars, in each of which several items are shown (which go to make up its height); thus the performances of four factories each making five identical products can be displayed.

9 A histogram is a collection of bars which show how a quantity is distributed.

10 A Gantt chart is used to plan a project most effectively in terms of time and effort.

11 Standard deviation from the mean is used to describe the difference between an average value and various individual values which go to make up that average; a skew is used to describe a variation from a norm in a statistical context (an outcome which would usually be expected).

12 Flow charts are used to indicate the structures and major sequences of processes.

13 A flow process chart is used mostly in a manufacturing context to record accurately the steps taken to produce an item and to move, say, from a bench to a despatch platform.

14 Z charts are used to compare current totals with cumulative and rolling totals.

15 Check your answer with the listing on page 130.

Page 138

1 Effective diagrams communicate their information clearly, simply, accurately and with visual interest.

2 Organisation charts reflect the hierarchy of authority by showing the power relationships between super and subordinates in a vertical direction and between coequals in a horizontal direction.

3 A pictogram is a symbol used to make comparisons by being shown in various sizes which correspond to various quantities; they are liable to disinform since the human eye finds it difficult to differentiate between volumes or areas that are, say, three times larger or five times larger than another.

4 Effective logos tend to be unusual but simple in design. They communicate what an organisation does and how it would like to be perceived.

5 Icons can aid readers and viewers by transmitting information instantly and by being highly recognisable.

6 A larger point size means bigger print, better at capturing a reader's eye.

7 The main need is to balance both image and text; neither must predominate. Position an image within a body of text to create a harmonious design that is visually satisfying.

Answers to the reliability activity on page 149

Given that the subject-matter of the two examples is quite different and that the second example employs a specialist vocabulary, it is nevertheless, interesting to compare their respective word and sentence structures.

	Example 1	**Example 2**
Number of words	100	109
Number of sentences	6	4
Average number of words per sentence	16.66	27.5
Number of syllables in first 100 words	131	184
Total number of syllables	131	201

As you will have worked out, the first example, set in the Yukon would require its reader to possess a reading age of about 11–12 years. The much more abstract and multisyllabic vocabulary and the longer sentences of the marketing example would require its reader to possess a reading age of 18+ and a much higher educational attainment.

INDEX

F

G

H

I

J

K

L

M

N

O

P

Q

R